for Jane
with warm
wishes
Jane Wilson-Howarth
May 2007

a glimpse of eternal snows

A FAMILY'S JOURNEY OF LOVE AND LOSS IN NEPAL

FOR ALEXANDER

अनन्त हिंउको झलक

a glimpse of eternal snows

A FAMILY'S JOURNEY OF LOVE AND LOSS IN NEPAL

jane wilson-howarth

PIER 9

contents

CHAPTER ONE

most welcome to rajapur

YOU'RE CARRYING YOUR BABY LIKE A MONKEY!' an ancient woman shouted as we ducked into the small, smoky shack. We sat down on a couple of benches; Simon ordered tea as I extracted David from the baby-carrier and suckled him. The woman wandered inside; I now saw that she was prematurely wrinkly and actually about my own age. She watched me for a few minutes, then said, 'Why were you out in the sun with one so young? Your milk will get too hot!' I was growing used to unwanted advice, but this came with a smile; it wasn't like the criticism of the doctors we'd fled from a couple of weeks before.

'The baby is beautiful, sister,' she said. Then, when David burped and regurgitated a little, 'See! He's vomiting! You've curdled your milk!' Pouting her lips towards Simon, she then turned on him. 'Is *this* the father of the children? Why haven't you bought her any gold? Aren't you embarrassed for your wife to be seen walking in the bazaar without gold?' Simon just chuckled, but I wanted to defend him. I showed her my engagement and wedding rings. 'The colour of this gold is poor, and you need earrings, *bahini!*' Then to Simon again, her eyes twinkling, 'She has been a good wife: she has made two fine sons. Why do you dishonour her so?'

Simon's eyes sparkled too. 'But my wife is Tibetan,' he lied. 'Surely you know that they never wear gold?'

'*Ah mai* — you eaters of cows, you are all the same.'

A scrawny cockerel with delusions of grandeur chased one of his harem noisily past us. Silhouetted in the low doorway, blocking out the light, was a whispering, watching huddle of young women. They didn't dare venture inside, but it was obvious who they were discussing. As I smiled at them, they started to giggle. Two fled with their hands over their mouths. We downed our glasses of thick, sweet tea and left while the young women pleaded with us to let them keep David.

At the next river, we drove down the bank and plunged in. Clear water surged onto the bonnet and over the windscreen. Three-and-a-half-year-old Alexander whooped with delight, and his excitement made little David chuckle. At eight kilometres per hour, with water churning up to the windows, the river was intimidatingly wide, but it was exciting and exquisite too: magisterial red silk-cotton trees and a range of rich greens were reflected in sparkling water. Our bow wave disturbed a pair of plump sun-orange geese and a scamper of plovers that had been picking around on the shoreline. At the far bank, we drove up onto a pristine beach, between lantana hedges, and then by a longhouse. Panicking chickens scattered between thatched huts and *peepal* trees on the edge of Rajapur village, our final destination. We passed under an arch of sprightly bougainvillaea and drooping bottlebrush trees, and pulled up in the courtyard of an imposing two-storey whitewashed house. An overwhelming smell of cow dung hit me as I tumbled out stiffly and beat the dust from my clothes.

'I don't want to do *that* journey too often!' I said.

'Tah! You softy,' Simon teased, 'it was only fifteen hours' driving.' Two tethered buffalo paused in their cud-chewing to turn and stare. I fleetingly caught the perfume of frangipani.

A striking gentleman dressed in a freshly ironed *lungi* approached; his white hair was tied into a topknot. Unusually for a Nepali, he was as tall as my six-foot husband. Smiling and with his hands held palms together in greeting, he uttered his careful English, polished for the occasion. 'You are most welcome to Rajapur.'

Mirroring the gesture, Simon replied, 'Thank you, Mr Vaidiya. We are pleased to be here.' He then switched into Nepali and they chatted awhile.

Mr Vaidiya ushered us up stone stairs and onto a large balcony. A relaxed, self-confident looking man of thirtyish sat on the parapet. He wore new jeans, Nike trainers and a carefully shaped moustache.

'You have come! Everyone from the Department of Irrigation is waiting for you, Simon-sir. Project-manager-*sahib* is here also.' He pointed into a room that was too dark to see inside, but I could hear men talking. 'There are so many farmers also who want to talk with you only.' Below, men squatted or stood around waiting, smoking.

'I wasn't expecting a meeting today,' Simon said. 'I need a drink before we start.'

'The boy is bringing filter water … here. Take.'

Simon gulped some down and said, 'We'd better start. Those must be the farmers waiting below?'

'Yes, it is so.' Still unsmiling, the man turned to me and said, 'Mrs Simon-madam, you must take shower in there.' He indicated a door while I wondered if my smell was so offensive.

I peered into what appeared to be a cupboard. 'But there's no tap.'

'The boy, Bishnu, will bring bucket for bath, Mrs Simon. And your room is downstair. Come.'

'Thank you mister, er …'

'Thapa, Himalaya Thapa. Mr Simon has spoken of me I think, *hoina*?'

'Yes, yes,' I said, not remembering.

Himalaya showed us to a dusty whitewashed room. Inside were two small beds, a pair of flip-flops, three used torch batteries and an old paint-pot containing some African marigolds. A stub of candle was stuck to the table, with some spent matches beside it. After Himalaya had left us, Alexander said, 'He was nice.' Then, 'Let's go play!'

Outside, a tall lean man was beckoning from the top of Mr Vaidiya's huge red tractor. 'Come, *babu*!' And he invited Alexander to sit on his lap while they drove round and round on piles of unthreshed rice.

The sun had set by the time Simon had finally finished his meeting. He came bounding in, saying, 'Phew, this is going to be a challenging place to work. Don't think I've ever encountered so many political agendas in one afternoon.'

Himalaya was on Simon's heels. 'These farmers will never listen to the government directives ...' He led us upstairs again to where Bishnu, squatting at two Primus stoves on the floor, was whistling cheerfully while adding the finishing touches to supper. Gratefully we devoured rice, delicately flavoured lentils, spicy vegetables and piquant chutney.

'Mmm, Bishnu-*bhai*?'

'Yes, *memsahib*? What you need?'

'Nothing. This food is delicious.' Bishnu smiled. One of Simon's engineering colleagues, Dr Josi, leaned across. 'You don't need to say these things, Mrs Simon. It is not good to be nice to this boy. Speaking like this to servants will make them grow lazy.'

Josi then fired off a random bit of flak. 'The vegetables are too salty, Bishnu!'

Simon stayed frenetically busy from that first day. As the incoming water expert, he was expected to understand everything and immediately offer wise solutions to problems that rival farmers had been squabbling over for generations. He needed to do a lot of listening and a lot of reading. Meanwhile, Alexander and I started to explore; we watched oxen being driven in circles to thresh rice or extract soya beans from their pods; we saw men scrubbing buffaloes in the river and women pulling water from wells. Rajapur was paradise. Alexander took lots more rides and the Tractor Man, whom Alexander called his special friend, taught him how to feed a new calf. While Alexander was busy, I could sit with David, soaking up the reviving winter sunshine. He was more peaceful now than I'd ever known him, and although he still didn't communicate much, I could read his pleasure or discomfort in his face. He was content and — for now, at least — he was safe, away from life-support machines and probes and drips and tubes.

Pampered as we were, staying in Mr Vaidiya's house, there was time, finally, to relax. I began to savour this first real interlude since David's birth. I started to calm down after all the anxieties and disruptions of the last seven months. I could sit basking, sifting my thoughts and reactions to everything that had happened. I often caught a puzzled Bishnu watching me. He probably heard me muttering to the pages of my diary. 'Madam is always writing!'

Writing now, though, allowed me to reason with my guilt. David's doctors had driven us into exile; they'd made us feel callous and uncaring. Yet we'd only decided to leave England once David was stable. By then we knew there was nothing that had to be done immediately; the next operation could wait a year — at least. Anyway, we'd be going back to that hospital in Cambridge in a few more months. There was no need for any more tests or tears until then.

CHAPTER TWO

new arrivals

AN UNSEASONAL SPRINKLE OF RAIN HAD GREETED US as we emerged from the Tribhuvan International Airport arrivals hall the previous spring, in 1993 — the Nepali year 2048. We were excited about the prospect of living in Nepal, but I pulled a face at the weather. Nepalis around us, though, welcomed it with smiles of pleasure. Major Chhetri, Simon's office manager, a dapper man with an air of authority, stepped from a bewildering mass of taxi-touts and unknown faces.

'Thrice welcome, Semen-sir, madam, little sir!' He marshalled us into a small, decrepit taxi with its exhaust pipe hanging off; the driver started the engine by twisting wires together under the dashboard. The men exchanged pleasantries, then Major Chhetri turned to me. 'A most timely and fortunate arrival, Dr Mrs Semen.'

I shifted to avoid a protruding spring, and to adjust my heavily pregnant belly. 'Yes, though I wondered if we'd be able to land through this cloud.'

'This is an auspicious sign. It is said that anything that starts in the rain ends well! You have arrived in rainy blessing today. You will have nice times here. There will be good rice harvest, also. Rain is a gift from heaven.' To me — a Brit accustomed to whingeing about the weather — this seemed a very foreign concept.

The driver — horn blaring — swerved to avoid a bow-legged old man in jodhpurs who was whacking a buffalo. Outside the Centre for Alternative Dispute Resolution, we swerved again to avoid a motor-cyclist on the wrong side of the road. Then a surreal image: a cow eating from a pressure cooker and a pedestrian wearing a toilet on his head.

At first the city of Kathmandu seemed a noisy, polluted muddle of grubby concrete. But that was around the burgeoning urban fringes. Our home looked over a patchwork of gloriously green rice fields that flanked the Dhobi Khola, where naked boys splashed and cavorted. From our first-floor living room I delighted in watching the scallywag mynah birds that ran around frenetically like English starlings; there were orange hoopoes poking their bills into the lawn, extrovert piebald fantails, sleek magpie robins, bulbuls with saucy scarlet bottoms, and elegant egrets. Sometimes the sounds of drums, horns and unearthly chanting wafted across from the monastery at Kopan to the north, with its maroon walls and strings of multicoloured prayer flags.

I loved exploring the medieval capital too; it was an attractive tangle of shadowy alleys, richly scented temples and mouth-watering wafts of spicy cooking. And spring was a lovely time of year there. Jacaranda and oleanders were in flower; jasmine cascaded off balconies or roof gardens so that the air was filled with heady perfume. Not far beyond the city, there were rice fields and forested ridges, then the mighty Himalayas looking benignly down from above the gathering monsoon clouds.

I had time to socialise and start to learn Nepali too. It was fun re-connecting with Simon's old Nepali friends from the days when he'd worked in East Nepal as a volunteer just after graduating as a civil engineer. Narendra described the day when Simon, who was then based in Hile at 1,850 metres, walked down to Dharan in the plains to play tennis, then back again afterwards, a journey that took most Nepalis eight hours each way. My wiry, self-effacing husband laughed it off. 'Yes, I've heard that story too.' No wonder I can never keep up with Simon.

The river pollution control project that had brought Simon back to Nepal was to run for only six months, but there were good prospects for more work that might keep us in the country long-term.

I started putting out feelers to see where I might practise. I had qualified as a doctor six years before, then more recently had done training to allow me to work as a GP. After the professional isolation of child health work in rural Sri Lanka and Indonesia, I found this stimulating and satisfying; I'd become particularly fascinated by the consultation process and worked on techniques for allowing myself to become more accessible to my patients. To my delight, the techniques I had learned in Cambridge had already proved useful in working with health volunteers and villagers in Pakistan. I was keen to develop this work in Nepal now; I met local doctors and grabbed the chance to look around the maternity hospital. Inside the Prasuti Griha, cool, airy corridors smelt of phenol disinfectant, pungently evoking memories of my own childhood immunisations and the huge treat of a single Smartie afterwards.

When I poked my head around the door of Dr Manandhar's office, I saw a grubby, ill-lit room, where two white-coated consultants were hunched over a fifteen-rupee school exercise book full of pencil-scribbled English.

Dr Kamala looked up, self-assured, beautiful and intelligent. Smiling she said, 'Ah, Dr Jane — you are most welcome to Prasuti Griha. Dr Manandhar has been telling me that you are coming from England only. I had worked in Birmingham studying for Membership of your Royal College of Obstetricians and Gynaecologists … it is spring these days there; not so cold, isn't it?

Look here, we are discussing my maternal mortality study. Dr Manandhar, he is helping me with data analysis. We can do very good maternal mortality study here; with 18,000 deliveries a year there are enough — plenty of deaths.'

She laughed, but her laugh was of the fatalistic, humourless kind — the laughter of a Nepali faced with a hopeless situation. I was to recognise that laugh more and more, yet always found it distressing. Here, one woman dies for every hundred live children born; there are babies who end up brain-damaged, and women left incontinent, to be thrown out by their husbands.

'We must do ward round now, Dr Jane,' she said, patting my six-months-pregnant belly.

More than a head shorter than me, yet fleet-footed as a spotted deer, she sped off down the dingy corridor faster than was comfortable for my long legs. The fall of her sari streamed out from under her white coat. A junior doctor stopped her with questions about patients, a husband trotted after us pleading for more attention for his wife, a brother thanked her for saving a life, a consultant colleague butted in to ask her to teach. 'I am taking too much of your time,' I said embarrassed. We dashed on, Kamala deflecting or dealing with an unending assault of queries while I marvelled at how calm she was in the face of such a workload.

We entered a ward where several women were recovering from hysterectomies. Most were in pain. Several called out, *'Dookha chha, doctor-sahib … huzoor … doo-ookha chha.'*

Pretending I had not understood the cries for help, I allowed a diplomatic interval to elapse and then asked, 'What drugs do you use for routine post-op pain relief?'

'The safe analgesics you use in UK are not available in Nepal, and patients, they would abuse these drugs. There is too much of morphine addiction here in Nepal — and heroin also.'

'So you don't even give paracetamol?' She smiled. She dealt with crises and saved lives; there was no time to think of patient comfort. I asked her, 'What is needed to improve patient care?'

'Doctors, we have enough. I tell our juniors they must help with nursing duties also. But my doctors, they do not like: it is our Asian problem with status, and pollution of our Hindu souls.'

'So who does the nursing?'

'Relatives bring food, medicines and intravenous fluids from outside, they clear up bedpans and that and this. Nurses cannot touch polluting dirty things like your British nurses; they have their technical duties only. That maintains their status nicely. If they can dilly-dally on the wards, filing blood test results and keeping away from patients, then they are happy. Then they will find nice respectable husband, isn't it?'

Dr Kamala pulled back a once-white curtain behind which delivery room doctors and nurses chatted and joked around a woman who looked grey and very, very ill. There was a puddle of blood beneath her. Kamala explained unnecessarily, 'She is having post-partum haemorrhage.'

'Yes, I can see she's losing blood.' My stomach knotted up. I wanted to help but did not yet understand how I could comment without the doctors losing face. No-one likes to be shown up, but Nepalis seem ultra-sensitive to criticism and I kept silent for fear of making the doctors even more reluctant to help this young woman. But perhaps their undemonstrativeness made them seem more disinterested than they really were. Kamala said, 'They are managing. Nurses are bringing drugs. Blood for transfusion is coming also. *Peons* will bring needles, drip stands and all necessary equipments …' By local standards, the system seemed to be working. But that woman looked dreadful; her kidneys may not have survived the disastrous fall in blood pressure. Maybe those doctors did not know what to do with someone so ill. Perhaps no-one had taught them to prioritise. I cast around and couldn't see the emergency drugs that would have been immediately to hand in hospitals that I knew.

She ushered me away down more cheerless corridors, past an odiferous lavatory, and then we burst into the gynaecology ward. Reeling in the centre of a cluster of three white-coated junior women doctors and Sister was a patient. She was emaciated, wrinkled, her flesh the colour of parchment. She was so ill that she could hardly stand. Closer, I saw that she was no more than thirty. The doctors were trying to bundle her towards X-ray, while she remonstrated, 'Doctor, *huzoor*, money I have none. No more tests, doctor *sahib*.' She wanted to go home — to die in peace — but the doctors did not want to let her go. Kamala said with a resigned laugh, 'She cannot walk and there is no wheelchair. What to do?' The doctors argued with each other while the patient's legs buckled slowly under her. Another doctor explained that a scan had shown fluid in the lower abdomen and informed us, 'This is case of mass in abdomen — abdominal swelling, but normal uterus … Not gynae case. Probably Cox's …' Calling a person 'a case' made the doctors sound heartless, but they weren't. And what was 'Cox's'? Later I worked out that they were saying 'Koch's' — their code for TB. It's called the disease of kings locally, because only a king could afford treatment. Tuberculosis, not cancer, is the disease that frightens common Nepalis most and so that name mustn't be uttered in front of patients.

'This patient is too poor,' Kamala explained. 'She wants to go home, but for her we will arrange free treatment — it is possible with special permission from hospital Director.'

'She looks so ill,' I tentatively offered, 'that maybe nothing will help her now. Perhaps she should go home to die? Maybe she's right?'

'No, no; she is ignorant. She must stay. Let us send some of this fluid to the lab to make confirmation of the diagnosis.' Sister brought a syringe. It was large. The sight of it made the patient wince. The woman was bundled back into bed and one of the doctors started trying to shove the large-bore hypodermic into the groaning patient's distended belly, but the blunt needle took a couple of hard thrusts to get — it — in. The victim groaned just a little. Other patients gasped and looked on wide-eyed. The doctor pulled back hard on the syringe and thick off-white pus appeared. All the doctors smiled and nodded with satisfaction at this prize. I felt sick. The probing continued until the syringe was full and finally after a cursory swish of cotton wool over the puncture wound, Sister triumphantly took the sample away to the laboratory.

On Kamala sped, with me riding on her bow wave. A man stepped out from nowhere. He barred her way. The talk was in fast, urgent Nepali. I couldn't make out what was going on, until the ambusher got down to touch Kamala's feet in gratitude. 'Such respect these people show to me … such respect even for me, a woman …' She giggled with embarrassment as she tried to stop the man prostrating himself. As we rushed on, she explained. 'This man's wife came here as gynae emergency a few nights before — suspected ectopic. When I opened abdomen, it was not ectopic, isn't it? There was no blood. But there was so much of pus. I got scared. I called one general surgeon but he wouldn't come.' I felt for her; in a British hospital if you called for help, someone competent came. Always. 'Finally God helped me and I found the burst appendix and so I saved this case. Now this husband is too happy!'

We passed a polished black stone bust of a woman garlanded with fresh marigolds and hibiscus. The architect had clearly intended that she should greet everyone who entered the hospital, but a grille was drawn across the grand marble entrance so that everyone had to shuffle in through a side door. 'This is Crown Princess Paropakar Indra Rajya Laxmi, present king's mummy.'

'Did she set up the hospital?'

'No. She had retained placenta after delivering her sixth child and she died of post-partum haemorrhage. After that, the royal family built the first maternity hospital in Nepal, and the Palace still contributes.'

'Unbelievable! Less than fifty years ago, the first lady died from such a simply treated obstetric problem? With all the wealth and influence of the royal family, she couldn't be saved?'

'*Achha — moriyo,* and half her children died young also.' After Princess Paropakar's death, the king required a new wife, and so a younger sister of the princess was selected. The king had enough surviving heirs, so the bride was sterilised to avoid problems of succession between the children of the two queens. In a culture and an age where women need to be mothers to be fulfilled, the operation must have been forced upon her, supposedly making her a better stepmother to her nephews and nieces.

I stepped out through the grand hospital gates dazed, reeling with the realisation that life for the average Nepali was so hard. Outside, my hormonally heightened sense of smell started to register new stimuli: the unofficial hospital urinal, drains, deceased goat, an unwashed beggar, cow dung, burning joss sticks, marigolds, spices, frying meat, jasmine. I was filled with admiration for my Nepali colleagues for going to work at all, and in awe of all they achieved each day with so few resources. Hindu fatalism must help Kamala to cope; if she were more involved she would surely go under, go mad. I wanted to tell new expatriate friends what I'd seen, yet I sensed that some of the young mothers would not want to know. For us, Kathmandu was an easy place to live, but without money, this was hell on earth. Those heart-rending cries of women in pain were still echoing in my head, '*Dooḳha chha, doctor-sahib … huzoor … doo-ooḳha chha.*'

डे डे डे

Wasn't I just a touch hypocritical to have left Nepal and elected for a high-tech, hygienic delivery in England?

Second labours rarely end in trouble, I kept telling myself. I'd had normal scans and amniocentesis, but I couldn't completely bury my premonitions of heart and other problems, which swamped rational analysis. These worries had started soon after I'd realised I was pregnant. I told myself that I was just being neurotic; but why, then, in myfirst pregnancy, hadn't it occurred to me that my baby would be anything but perfect?

Throughout David's pregnancy, my clinical self argued with my emotional self, but the doctor in me could never quite convince the mother. Now I needed to know that the baby and I would be in good hands, and I wanted all available painkillers.

Most of the time I could ignore the intuitions of trouble to come. I focussed on what I'd be doing next with my life. I had reached a stage in my career when I was being offered a range of interesting and worthwhile jobs. Life was good. I would just pop this baby out and hurry back to Nepal, and get started on some really useful health work.

My labour pains began on schedule and Simon picked up *War and Peace* on his way to the car. 'Hmm … Didn't believe me when I said this labour will be quick and easy?'

He smiled, his eyes sparkling with delight at having achieved a satisfying tease unintentionally.

The contractions built up stronger and faster this time. Pain quickly took over and I meekly submitted first to gas, then a monitor, then pethidine. The process seemed unnecessarily unnatural and I suddenly understood why non-medical friends describe a loss of control when giving birth in hospital. Soon I asked for an epidural anaesthetic too, and Simon went out of focus. Then I realised that the trace of the baby's heartbeat implied some problems. 'Better take a little blood sample from the baby's head,' said an unsmiling obstetric registrar.

'Is that really necessary?' I challenged half-heartedly.

'Better to have a scar on the head than no brain,' she mumbled from between my legs. She was rummaging somewhere inside me, struggling to get a sample, hurting me. The anaesthetist arrived and — between contractions — skilfully put the epidural needle into my back while others were fussing around other parts of me. I then experienced that strange phenomenon of time-compression, for it seemed too soon that the midwife said my cervix was fully dilated. It was time to push.

I was fit. I had started aerobics in Kathmandu and enjoyed long walks through the rice fields, often with Alexander riding 'on my soldiers'. Strong as I was, though, the baby would not budge. The stern obstetric registrar was in and out of my room a lot. Unexpectedly, she said, 'It's going to have to be a caesarean section. Sorry.'

'Why? Surely I can push a bit longer?'

'No, there are type II dips now and major late decelerations.' Someone shoved a clipboard at me, 'Sign this!' Everyone was busy, efficiently checking labels, powering syringes full of drugs via my drip into my body, gathering up notes, checking name tags.

Within minutes I was being wheeled along the clean, neon-lit corridor, feeling thoroughly bemused at being the centre of the entire controlled flap. The anaesthetist pushed more drugs into the canula in my back so that I could feel nothing below my rib cage. Simon — his lean form now attired in unfamiliar, over-large theatre greens, hat and clogs — came and sat by my head. 'You going to be all right?' I asked him. He wasn't used to blood, but he looked remarkably calm and smiled back his reply.

There was a smell of iodine and someone pulled the big operating lights around to illuminate my belly. The ceiling was a boring grey with stainless steel strips across it. Metal instruments clanked and soon the obstetrician looked engrossed. 'Feel anything? No? Good. Let me know if you do.' She was slicing into my abdomen. I felt nothing, except nausea and bewilderment, and concern that for Simon this would be a horror show. This was my environment, but I couldn't talk Simon through this and no-one was explaining things for him; as a doctor's husband perhaps he was expected to know, and he was too inscrutable to ask. All this was vaguely going around in my head, but I was feeling too ill and distracted to say or do anything.

They were taking a very long time to get the baby out. 'Suction! No here!' The strained expression on the obstetrician's face said that she was having trouble. 'Push! Oh, come on, baby!' she mumbled, through gritted teeth. 'Keep that retractor tight. Scalpel. Suction. More swabs.'

From time to time, Simon peered over at the wound in my abdomen and reported back to me. The bloody mess didn't upset him one bit. 'Fundal pressure! Oh, come on!' the obstetrician said, sounding more stressed. 'Quick! Someone call Andrew! Fast bleep him if he's not right outside!'

A baby's legs — my baby's legs — and a bottom were being pulled about and all the pushing and shoving made me feel really ill. I had no pain, but I felt unutterably awful, like death. The consultant came into theatre, ungowned, unmasked and plunged into my abdomen too without scrubbing. Why were they taking so long? Sweat poured off me and I started to retch. The anaesthetist, not for the first time, mopped my brow and said, 'You can have a general anaesthetic you know — any time.' It wouldn't be much longer. Not long now. I'd recover faster if I avoided a general anaesthetic.

I remembered a likable patient — a schoolteacher — whom I'd looked after in Swindon some years before. He'd suffered a massive heart attack. We got his pain under control, but he looked awful and whenever I asked how he felt he just said, 'Grim.' He languished for a couple of days, and then his heart stopped. I'd sprinted to his bedside on the Coronary Care Unit and in the split second it took me to take in the situation, I was astonished to see that he'd lost his haggard look. I pumped his chest. I assaulted him with syringes full of drugs designed to stimulate his heart. I shocked him. The heart-trace stayed flat and his face said he'd left us. He was peaceful despite all I'd done to him. Now I knew what he'd meant. I had no pain, but I felt grim. Really grim. Like death. Not much longer now surely.

Finally our son appeared. Immediately I felt better. I could see out again. As the paediatrician took my blood-covered baby across to the resuscitation unit, I saw the gaping black hole in the middle of his face. Strangely, I wasn't shocked and a very odd thought occurred to me: 'Only a harelip. That's all right, I can cope with that!' This wasn't the death sentence of my premonitions. The body language of the doctors and nurses who crowded around the resuscitation unit also said that there were no real problems; they were doing the routine checks, and then they called Simon across. They must be talking about the harelip. The blood hadn't bothered Simon, and nor had the harelip; during his years in Nepal he'd grown used to seeing scarred and disfigured faces, and he knew harelips could be fixed. The paediatrician kept glancing across to me, trying to conspire with

Simon. They didn't want to tell me, but Simon was quietly, forcefully disagreeing. The paediatrician seemed surprised when I asked to see the baby. He looked troubled. 'Um. There is something very distressing …' I felt so sorry for this sensitive young doctor. He didn't want to break bad news. 'Look,' I said, 'don't worry. I've seen the harelip. It's only a cosmetic thing. He'll grow a moustache when he's older. Is he okay otherwise?'

'Yes, fine. Just the harelip. No cleft palate. Everything else seems fine. Didn't need intubating. Fine.' He seemed to be trying to convince himself. That worried me.

I'd been in labour all night and the baby had finally been dragged out through the bloody slit in my belly at six minutes to eight in the morning. Simon went home to check on Alexander and maybe sleep a little. Meanwhile I was bed-bathed, powdered and given breakfast. The world came back into focus in the astonishingly bright, pristine recovery room that smelt of cleaning fluids. I put the baby to my breast and he suckled perfectly. As he took my first milk I pieced together what had happened. Our son, who was a good size at 3.78 kilograms, had an over-large head that had got wedged in my pelvis. And having unjammed it, they then struggled, pushed and shoved to deliver his head from my womb. The Prasuti Griha seemed a world away. A sobering realisation then crept up on me like a predatory animal. If I had been a Nepali villager, I would still be in labour, and the contractions and pain would have continued until I'd died. They'd saved my life — and my baby's.

A new doctor came in to check the baby over and I asked, 'What were the baby's Apgar scores?' If this doctor hadn't already realised that I was a colleague, this question should have told him. Most lay people don't know about this scoring system, which helps doctors to assess how badly damaged babies are after difficult deliveries. 'Apgars are out-dated. We now use a much more sophisticated system of assessment,' the young smart-arse doctor replied. This was the first of many lies and half-truths. In the hospital discharge letter that I saw five weeks later, my baby's Apgar score at one minute was given as four out of ten, suggesting that we should expect problems. This doctor offered nothing more. He did a cursory check and as he was leaving said, 'The consultant asked me to mention that the harelip will make it difficult to breast feed.'

Lying there drowsing, I wondered why that doctor had wanted to undermine my resolve to feed my baby and I wondered what the next few months would bring us. Where would we be living when this baby was a year old? I thought back to an evening when we'd first heard of a project that might employ Simon next. We'd been invited to dinner by engineering colleagues of Simon's from their Cambridge head office. We sat on imported sofas in a marble palace of a house in Kathmandu, small-talking as we sipped French wine from cut glass awaiting the arrival of our host. William burst in, breathlessly apologetic. 'Sorry. Plane was late.' Over supper, William talked animatedly about his trip to a part of Nepal that most Nepalis had never heard of. 'We're writing a proposal to rehabilitate an irrigation scheme on Rajapur Island.'

'An island? In Nepal? Where?'

'It's out west, in the middle of the Karnali river; 100,000 people live there apparently. The job will be fascinating technically, but the living conditions will be challenging. It's flat, very dusty, hot, remote; no electricity. There's not much there except buffaloes and *padi*-fields, and dust … dust everywhere! And it is the best part of two days travelling each way from here.'

'But Rajapur means "town of the king". Is it an important place? You don't make it sound very nice.'

'Important? No. And interesting, I'd say, rather than scenic. Simon might like it — he seems to enjoy difficult places!' I couldn't decide whether Simon's superiors were bemused by his ability to thrive in remote places or whether they disapproved of his interest in learning languages, eating local food and — as they saw it — 'going native'.

'If it's a nasty place,' I said light-heartedly, 'I expect he'll get sent there.'

William laughed, 'You two cope in remote places better than most!' Maybe he was right. Our first posting had been to a troubled new town in Sri Lanka in the middle of two wars where people disappeared or were shot by Indian 'peacekeepers'. Then Simon had a strange job supporting local engineers on three different Indonesian islands. Stones were thrown at me in the market in Sulawesi, but that was better than being groped in Pakistan. Nepal was the easiest place we'd lived so far.

Driving back that evening, I asked Simon, 'Is your name on this project proposal?'

'Probably, but it's the first I've heard of it.'

'Aren't you interested?'

'It doesn't sound appealing from any point of view, really,' he said. 'Should I push for it?'

'Why not? It'd be your first job as team leader. Haven't we been hoping for a long-term job … it is long-term, isn't it?'

'Yeah. Two years … or so.'

'Look, I've already lost count of all the places we've lived since we got married. Now the prospects are for another change in only a few more months. I'd like to stay in Nepal.'

'It'll be very remote,' he said flatly.

'Yes, but I'm not ready for yet another country. And surely even the nastiest place in Nepal will be easier than anywhere in Pakistan? I certainly don't want to go back there. You know, I've learned and forgotten how to say diarrhoea in nine Oriental languages, but I don't really feel as if I have even started to do anything useful anywhere we've lived so far. I want to help the poor; use the medical qualification that I sweated blood to get. I've done so little with it since I qualified.'

'Development work is slow. You can't cure the whole world in six months, you know.' Simon had said something like that the first time we met. We'd both been at Southampton University and I gave a talk to the Exploration Society about an expedition I'd led to Nepal. I was a mature student at the great age of twenty-five and most of my audience were young and untravelled. My tone had probably been patronising as I spoke of my studies of bat poo and parasites. Simon had asked a question and I discovered that he had just returned from working in Nepal for five years. I was wracked with embarrassment at talking down to him, but he seemed to understand my passion and my impatience. That was the moment I fell for this quiet man with the winning smile and handsome blue-green eyes. 'But our assignments have all been so short,' I continued my tirade. 'I want to help, not dabble. So far, all I've left behind are piles of survey forms, which might as well be used as toilet paper, and training manuals that will never even be that useful. The prospect of two or three years in one place — any place — sounds great.'

Uncharacteristically, Simon cut in. 'It will be a difficult place to live. You don't know how horrible the lowlands can be.'

'Surely Nepal will be wonderful — anywhere in Nepal? I want to learn Nepali; I'd love to get to know some village women. Find out what life is really like in rural Asia. Why are you so lukewarm? I thought you loved Nepal! I thought you wanted to show me your Nepal!'

'The Nepal I know is the hills.' He'd spent five years completely involved in small-scale development projects, and sometimes I felt he was more comfortable there than in England. He continued, 'The *tarai* is very different, the language is different and the job will be hard too. On my own I might have given it a go, but now …'

'I'm supposed to be an expert in child health. If I can't keep our own children healthy in a Nepali village, I might as well pack up and go home. And didn't William say that it was next to a national park? There'll be tigers, elephant, rhino?' I said.

'And blind dolphins too …'

'Freshwater dolphins! Fantastic!'

Simon interrupted my reverie with, 'But it'll be another project where we're living in two or three places. When we're in Rajapur, we'd stay in a Portakabin, then we'll have to move off the island during the monsoon.' I was puzzled; it was unusual for him to be so negative.

'It'd be an amazing place for the children to grow up,' I said, blinded by rosy images of living amongst rare wildlife. 'We'll gorge on mangoes and lychees and we could keep a pet mongoose, or another palm squirrel. You can change some of the arrangements, can't you?'

'I can't control the monsoon. Anyway, you'll get bored without a proper role, won't you?' Simon knew that remote postings are hard on unemployed wives: they crack up or pack up and go home. He asked, 'And what about your developing career as the Dung Doctor?'

'Yeah, yeah. I still want to become professor of poo, or even empress of excreta, but there's time for that! I won't get bored watching tigers, I promise. And anyway I could continue my studies of malaria mosquitoes.'

He pulled a face and said, 'It'll be awfully isolated …'

CHAPTER THREE

disease and disaster

DAVID HAD BEEN BORN JUST BEFORE THE START of the hospital working day. Night shift nurses were handing over to the day shift, and freshly shaved doctors were in evidence again. There was a lull before the wards got busy. I was suckling David when another unknown doctor came in and without introducing himself said, 'Ah, yes. It may not be impossible for your baby to breast-feed.'

'What?' I was niggled at the way this doctor used a double negative to cloud the reality that he expected me to fail. 'What do you mean? I *am* breast-feeding him.'

'The harelip … Don't be too disappointed if you have to give him bottles.' Then David choked and spluttered and the doctor gave me an I-told-you-so look.

'He's fine,' I said. 'I *will* breast feed him. There's no question about that.' Why were the Cambridge doctors so discouraging? The coughing fit was short and he fed a little more then fell asleep. I too drifted into pleasant, drowsing half-sleep, with David still snuggled against me. Then Simon reappeared with Alexander and Jill, my brother-in-law's partner. Fortuitously, she had dropped by on the very evening that my contractions began.

Alexander delightedly announced, 'Look! Drill is here — she looked after me last night. Mummy, your name sounds the same as Drill's.' And he startedto sing, 'Drill and Drane, Drill and Drane'. Then, 'The baby's nice. He's asleep.'

We told Alexander that his new brother had brought him a present, and as he solemnly unwrapped Edward the Big Engine, he asked, 'Have you got a shop in your tummy, Mummy?'

Simon had only warned Jill about the new baby's harelip as they walked into the hospital that morning. She was astonished that he hadn't mentioned the malformation sooner, but Simon has always held his own counsel — it's a family trait. His inscrutability makes him popular in Asia, but in England people often wonder what to make of him.

We chatted a while longer, until I started nodding off, and then Alexander, Simon and Jill wandered away to the playroom.

A plastic surgeon magically materialised out of the corner of a cosy dream and dragged me back to consciousness. Simon was in the room again, too. The surgeon cheerily talked at me fast, while I tried to kick-start my brain. 'We'll be repairing the harelip tomorrow morning.'

'Tomorrow morning!' I said. 'How efficient. Thank heavens we're in Cambridge, not Kathmandu! There are *adults* in Nepal still hoping to have this operation.'

I was processing the information slowly, distractedly, while he talked on. He was quite good-looking, fancied himself, undoubtedly of the Swashbuckling School of Surgery: smart suit, slick, probably drove a Porsche.

'What work were you doing in Nepal? You're both doctors?'

'Simon's more useful than a doctor. He's a civil engineer — bringing water, improving agriculture. I'm into child health and hygiene education.'

'Interesting,' he said, sounding not the least bit interested. 'I work in India, as a volunteer of course. Every year. I take a team and do hundreds of harelip repairs for people of all ages, and I train local doctors in simple plastic surgical techniques … skin grafts after burns … Conditions are primitive, the power is unreliable; everything gets infected so easily — as you know, I suppose.'

'Yes. Um. No. Not easy.' (What had happened to my brain? And why did he talk so fast?) 'How long do you spend in India?'

'Two weeks. Two weeks every year. They look forward to our visits. Your son is an interesting case. It's unusual to have a bilateral harelip and no cleft palate. I'll have a good look while he's under anaesthetic — to check for problems further back. So he'll have the primary repair tomorrow and another just before he starts school.'

'Tomorrow? Two operations?' I began to pull myself together, surface from my stupor.

'Yes, two minimum.'

'But surely it's best to do the repair later? Don't you get a better cosmetic result if you wait? We're not upset by his appearance. I'm happy to wait if the end result is better. I've seen people in Asia whose lips have been repaired in adulthood and the result is good.'

'No, we do the repairs straight away now. I've been doing some pioneering work on early repairs. My results are invariably excellent.' He talked on but, even dopey as I was, I was unconvinced.

'Surely it's much easier operating on babies when they are a few months old? The anaesthetic risk must be smaller too?'

'Yes and no. Neonatal skin is difficult to work with, but we have overcome all the problems. You're lucky he was born today. Most babies have to wait a week.'

'And what about the pits in my baby's ears, and his nose?'

'Ah … didn't notice those. I'll operate on them later.'

'Surely you don't need to?'

'They'll get infected. The pits are deep and we have to dissect out every millimetre — it's quite tricky surgery; there are one or two important structures close by. Mustn't prang the facial nerve, must we!' he said, laughing. Simon was listening carefully but saying nothing.

'So he needs *three* operations?'

'Yes, and another when he's about eight.' He was gone within five minutes, leaving us to absorb and contemplate prospects of operations and dissection. No doubt, I reasoned at the time, he knew best. A few years later, medical audit confirmed my suspicions; it is better to operate later.

The stern obstetric registrar dropped in. She didn't congratulate us on our new baby. Oozing as much feminine compassion and sincerity as Margaret Thatcher, she said, 'Is there anything you wanted to ask?' Still spaced out, I was baffled by her visit, her question. She hadn't, it seemed, come to check my wound, her handiwork. Only later did I see that she was worried I'd sue for negligence. The anaesthetist also called in. 'How are you feeling? I've never seen anyone looking so grim during a caesarean section. You know you didn't have to.'

'Yes. You told me several times, but I knew I'd recover faster if I avoided a general anaesthetic.'

'True. Even so, you were brave going through that.'

'I knew that it wouldn't be for long …'

'I could see that you dealt with it by going inside yourself.'

'I was thinking about the time I got stung by a scorpion in Madagascar. That hurt for a day and a night despite taking morphine. Then I had a morphine hangover for ages after, which was worse.'

'Any pain now?' she asked.

'No — thanks.'

I had been bewildered by my first pregnancy, unable to comprehend fully that Alexander was a product of my body, our bodies. My first thought after that delivery was, 'Thank goodness *that's* over!' I was relieved when I wasn't expected to cuddle him for long and delighted when Simon took him, looking — unexpectedly — as if he'd often handled newborns. Then suckling the new baby and keeping him clean and responding to his cries and all the sleep-deprivation left little time for sitting staring into his adorable face, listening to him cooing ... those romantic images of tranquillity, cute clothes and pink skin that I had before I became a parent.

But as Alexander had developed, my confidence, understanding and love had grown, and now he was nearly three I knew what a gift he was. I had become more maternal and my hormones were now fully tuned. Maybe that was why I found this new baby more beautiful, more immediately miraculous than our perfect first-born, Alexander. It didn't occur to me — until I saw the reaction of my mother-in-law — that others would be shocked at the baby's face. Rosemary kept saying, 'I'm sorry. I'm so sorry. It's my fault. It's from my side of the family.' I couldn't convince her that a harelip in a distant cousin was irrelevant. There was probably no genetic factor. Whatever the cause, it didn't matter. I gazed at this marvellous small person. He was wonderful and I was besotted. I looked forward to his infancy and childhood. I would observe and catalogue how he developed, understand better.

It was odd watching him feed though; his lip, cleft in two places, flapped like a miniature roller blind, and sometimes it looked prehensile, like the mouthparts of some weird sea-creature browsing on my breast. Feeding was not going well. He never fed for long and he choked a lot. An awful lot. I asked for advice, but the professional consensus said, 'We warned you. Although breast-feeding is not impossible with the harelip, there are bound to be problems. And when are you going to decide on a name for him?'

'But babies don't use their top lip to breast-feed,' I remonstrated. 'Besides, he's latching on perfectly. I've breast-fed before and know what the right position feels like. I teach women to breast-feed. I'm sure he has some other problem. Would someone check him over please?'

A wise paediatric colleague had once taught me the value of cuddling small babies, since the way a very small baby feels indicates a healthy brain — or not. Babies that are developing cerebral palsy are stiff, awkward and uncomfortable to cuddle, while floppy babies with other problems also feel odd: they don't snuggle into you. My new babe seemed not-quite-right to cuddle. 'Would someone come and check him over please?'

A different anaesthetist breezed in: a bronzed Australian. Young, attractive. I felt ancient, wrecked, wrinkled. I probably smelt of blood, sweat and stale armpits. He'd come to check the baby over before his operation. Like the other doctors, he talked to me as if I was a colleague at work, not an exhausted, stressed mother with post-op pain. 'What time was he born?'

I hardly knew my own name, let alone what day it was. When *had* he been born? Yesterday? Last week? 'Um ... I don't know, really.'

'Were the problems anticipated?'

'Problems? We didn't expect the harelip. They missed it on the scan. Um ... what was it that you wanted to know?'

डे डे डे

When David was just twelve hours old he became very ill. His blood sugar plummeted; he became cold and shocked. As the nurse wheeled him away, she said something blandly reassuring about him needing special care to get him warm for the operation the next day. Simon saw through this lie, though I had very little idea of what was happening. I slept a lot, confident that he was safely tucked up on the neonatal intensive care ward. I was called, or wheeled in in a chair, when breast milk was required, but otherwise I was content to snooze and doze. He was fine, in expert hands. He soon rallied and was transferred to Sara Ward, for newborns needing extra care. The nursery was full of babies, plugged into various tubes and monitors and tucked up in Perspex fish-tanks. All the other inmates were tiny; some were a touch yellow or blue; and with his larger-than-average head, my baby looked particularly huge and healthy.

The nurses reminded me he needed a name. 'Crikey! A name is the last thing on our minds! We took six weeks to settle on what to call his big brother, and that was after the Registrar had reminded us.' I read doubt in the nurses' faces; perhaps they thought we were not bonding with our new son. Maybe they'd seen other parents horrified by cleft lip deformities who rejected their child. They didn't know I was besotted. I looked lovingly down at him and said, 'But you're right; we need a name for his passport. What *shall* we call you, beautiful boy?'

The nurse smiled and said, 'Beautiful Boy will do fine for now.'

By the time he was twenty-five hours old, he was judged to be well enough to go for his harelip operation. He was away from the ward for a long time, but I was still too spaced out to realise how long. Towards the end of the day, when our son had been back with me for a while, the Australian anaesthetist came in. 'Your baby took a while to wake up after the surgery. His blood sugar was a bit low. When was he last fed?'

'Um; he was on the Special Care Baby Unit. I can't remember when they last wheeled me in to feed him. It's all a bit of a blur. They tube fed him with some formula milk I think.'

'When was that exactly?'

'I don't know. They even asked which milk I liked best — how the hell should I know about formula milks? I spend my life advocating breast-feeding. Do you know how many babies are killed in the developing world because they are bottle-fed?'

'No. But —'

'They get diarrhoea from the dirty bottles, and without the immunity from mother's' milk … um … what was I saying?'

'Okay, okay, I'll ask the nurses about your baby.' And he left abruptly. He didn't seem interested.

The subconscious anxieties I'd had all through pregnancy resurfaced forcefully after the anaesthetist left and whenever the baby took breast milk, but I didn't say anything to Simon. He was so busy with Alexander that I didn't see much of him: we seldom got any relaxed time. There were plenty of distractions and visitors and I simply delighted in my new baby. My parents arrived soon after the operation and my mother seemed upset by the baby's appearance too, but then she's always been squeamish about needles and surgery. To me, though, the harelip repair had made him even more beautiful. The stitching was extraordinarily fine and we told Alexander that elves had done the work. It seemed that miraculous. We settled on names. We called him after his two childless uncles: my brother David and Simon's brother Mark.

डे डे डे

Whenever I was alone with little David Mark though I wondered. Why did he take twenty-four hours to wake up properly after the operation? Why could he not coordinate the processes of sucking, breathing and swallowing? Other babies manage. Why did he choke and splutter so much? Was this evidence of some severe neurological problem? Even major problems are surprisingly difficult to diagnose in the first weeks of a baby's life, but was I worrying too much?

No-one was interested enough to discuss the subtle signs that I thought I was noticing. Some teaching from medical school surfaced: if a child is born with one abnormality, others are more likely. Did he have other problems in addition to his harelip? The ear pits were unusual and there was the deep dimple between his nostrils. Did he have internal problems too? I dared not say out loud what I was feeling; that would be admitting it was a possibility. But between waves of panic, I tentatively tried to voice my anxieties to any and every doctor or nurse I encountered. 'Can someone check my baby, please?'

'That will happen before you go home.' We health professionals are notoriously anxious — we know too much of what can go wrong. The hospital staff gave lots of bland disinterested reassurances while their eyes said wearily, 'Another neurotic medical mum.'

'Would someone check our baby over, *please*?'

'Okay, we'll ask the paediatrician to come.'

Finally — after what seemed like days, but could have been hours — a cheery paediatrician arrived, but my inner turmoil made me unassertive and incoherent. Simon wasn't there as my advocate and I couldn't say clearly why I was so scared, couldn't give a crisp, clinical condensation of my concerns. I said, 'He chokes a lot when he feeds.'

'Pity to wake him up,' the paediatrician said. 'His weight is increasing, so I doubt there's anything wrong. Babies sometimes take a while to coordinate sucking and swallowing and breathing.'

He left without really allowing me to talk or ask questions. I still wonder whether he had realised — or at least suspected — that David would have huge problems. He may have suspected, but most doctors don't give bad news until they are sure. A nurse took the stitches out of David's lip and we left hospital when he was seven days old, without any doctor having looked at him properly. When we put him into the car seat, though, he scrumpled into an uncomfortable heap in the bottom and started to cry. Strange, we thought; Alexander managed all right, and David hadn't ever cried much. He travelled in my arms.

I tried to bury my observations deep in my subconscious; after all, congenital problems are rare and we had no family history of anything worrying.

Yet David never seemed to look at me. I reasoned that he was still very young and young babies take a while to realise what their eyes are for. David's muscle tone did seem wrong, though, and he continued to choke as he breast-fed. Then the day before Simon was due to go back to Nepal, I noticed an asymmetry in his gaze and some strange eye movements. My stomach hit the floor. A squint in a small infant is most likely due to a problem within the brain, rather than in the eyes. I didn't want to articulate this and I wanted to keep it from Simon. Finally, though, I admitted my fears, but not until late on the evening before he was due to leave. We lay awake for a long time, until he rooted out a popular child health book written by a lay author for parents; it said that squints are benign and — illogically — we were reassured. Simon left for Kathmandu, hardly having met his new son, but we would all be together when we flew out to join him in Nepal in just three weeks.

David was undemanding, but I didn't sleep well. When Alexander came into my bedroom early, I'd pretend I was still asleep in a vain attempt to snatch a few more minutes' rest.

'It's breakfast time, Mummy!'

'Okay, okay; I need to wake up slowly.' We began counting off the days until we could rejoin Simon; I'd sleep better then. Life seemed under control, and yet David was vomiting a great deal, and I kept half-noticing things that should have worried me. He continued to choke a lot as he fed, he was becoming skinny, he seemed to go a touch blue around the mouth sometimes and wasn't he breathing too quickly? No, it was nothing. He was sleeping through the night — I wished I could — and this proved that he was well-fed: there were no problems. Maybe Alexander sensed the strain I felt under, because he stopped demanding breakfast early. Now he'd come in to ask, 'Are you waking up slowly, Mummy?'

My GP bustled in one lunchtime. Alexander, newly deserted by his father again and mildly put out by all the upheavals in his short life, welcomed the visitor and was confused when she ignored him. Adults were usually charmed by his blond curls and sunshine smile. The doctor started fussing over my caesarean wound and over David. Alexander tried a few tricks that usually gained him some attention — in Nepal, at least. His greeting had been ignored, so he tried to show her his favourite toys by dumping arm-loads in her lap. When this didn't work, he climbed up behind where she was sitting on the sofa and undid her bun. She was not amused, and said, 'But how will you cope all alone?' That really made me feel isolated.

'We'll be fine when the family gets back together in Nepal. And anyway, Alexander isn't usually naughty; he just likes being part of any conversation.'

Strange that she didn't seem to understand this. Alexander was a gentle, contented toddler, but he was at a loose end with just the three of us in our empty house. Time dragged for us both.

Alexander rejoined a nursery school. He seemed to enjoy it, but he puzzled the staff. 'Alexander talks of riding in buffalo carts, on elephants, seeing tigers, and going to the moon in a rocket. We're not sure how much he's making up!'

'Only the moon rocket!'

When David was a month old, my Health Visitor dropped by for a friendly chat. 'If he's sleeping through the night, there's no need to weigh him.'

'I'd like to know his weight,' I said, knowing now that I had to dig my heels in. 'He had feeding problems early on and we are going to Kathmandu on Friday.' He was below his birth weight. Blurting out, 'Scales can't be working,' my Health Visitor left abruptly.

'Aren't you going to —' But she'd fled. I sat in a daze, thinking; not wanting to think.

That evening, I phoned my GP sister and as I explained my worries, all kinds of unacknowledged clinical observations came tumbling out. 'Call out your GP,' my sister commanded.

'No, whatever it is will wait till morning. He's stable; not deteriorating. I've an appointment anyway.' Finally, reluctantly, I abandoned my fight to act like an ordinary mother and switched into medical mode. I don't think doctor-parents routinely strip their children naked and perform clinical examinations; we wouldn't stay sane if we were on full medical alert permanently, and perhaps that is why we feel bad if we fail to diagnose problems in our own. Now, though, I had a licence to act like a doctor. I took off David's clothes. I counted his breathing rate: seventy-two breaths a minute, too fast. Tracheal tug; intercostal recession. Liver edge palpable. And through my stethoscope, I heard a very loud heart murmur. Thank goodness! Here's evidence that I am not going mad, not imagining problems! *This* explains his feeding difficulties. Only a hole in the heart! Should I call Simon? I needed to talk to him but knew the news would worry him. I phoned him. Like me, though, he was relieved that there was a real fixable problem. I slept well, knowing at last that it wasn't all in my mind. What turmoil I had been in these four weeks!

The next day, Wednesday, I took David into hospital. 'Jane! Nice to see you again!' Sarah, the paediatric registrar, started checking David over. 'I hear that you passed your diplomas in Child Health. Both of them. Congratulations. And you were astute enough to make a diagnosis that everyone else missed — in your own baby.'

'Motherhood isn't like a clinical exam — thank heavens.'

'Yes, you must tell me about it sometime. You know, some parents more or less assaulted me in the lift this morning! I don't know why they were so upset with me.'

Sarah was clumsy, but very bright. She had exactly the expertise to sort David's problems, and how grateful I felt to be in the high-tech West. Soon we were gazing at the miraculous tongues-of-fire image of turbulent blood surging through two very large holes in David's heart.

'What treatment will he need?'

'He should be out of hospital by Monday, when he's stable on the diuretics,' Sarah affirmed.

'When will we be able to return to Nepal?'

'Nepal? Not for at least six or eight weeks.' The thought of more time apart from Simon finished me, and I couldn't hold back the tears. Not that anyone seemed to notice. The doctors were busy setting up a drip so that they could give David intravenous drugs to clear the fluid that was congesting his lungs. Soon he lay spread-eagled with both hands bandaged, unable even to suck his fingers for comfort. But the colour began to come back to his cheeks.

I phoned Simon again with answers to some of the questions he'd asked the previous evening, but it was hard communicating over a crackly, echoing phone line and I did not want to burden him, when he was so far away and so isolated. Instead, I began venting some of my anger on my colleagues for taking a whole month to listen to me. Why couldn't they have checked David over properly when we were in hospital during that first week?

I felt bitter. It had taken so long to get anyone to listen to my worries, and now the doctors acted as if there had never been any doubt. Simon had been at home then, but, reassured, he had gone back to work in Nepal almost as soon as we'd got out of hospital. Should I ask Simon to come back home again? He was under a lot of pressure to complete a project that was already short of time. I didn't ask. Instead, my parents came to the rescue.

On the Friday that I had planned to fly back to Kathmandu with the children and my in-laws, David became pale and very ill and over the weekend he deteriorated. I stayed in hospital with him while my parents amused Alexander. They didn't know each other well and I think Alexander found it hard. The first morning I was away, he came into my bedroom for his usual, 'Are you waking up slowly, Mummy?' and found my parents there instead of me. He didn't say a word; just looked down at the floor and went back to his room. I was so torn between the two children, but the best compromise seemed to be to let my parents take Alexander off to their home in Surrey. The change of scene would make my absence less obvious. Meanwhile in Nepal it began to rain torrentially and the phones became even more crackly and unreliable.

We were all worried for days about David while the doctors did blood tests, X-rays, a lumbar puncture, screened him for everything; they gave intravenous antibiotics and nasogastric tube feeds. It was a stormy, tense time, but slowly he stabilised. Perhaps it had been some infection or a reaction to the powerful heart medicines.

Illness and disaster were at the front of our minds, and in Nepal the rain continued to pour down. When Simon left his office in Kathmandu on Friday afternoon it was bucketing down and it went on all weekend. He was staying alone in the palatial Lotus House outside the ring road and it was not until he cycled into the office on Sunday that he learned of the extent of the floods that coincided with the stormiest week in David's life. Already-full rivers had swollen further and a three-metre-high wall of water had pulsed down through the hills; the only road into Kathmandu, the capital's supply line, was washed away in several places and most of the bridges had gone. In the lowlands, the Bagmati River burst its banks and there was devastation close to the Indian border. Thousands had been made homeless; the official death toll was 1,500 — it was probably many more. Everything was covered in silt. Bodies were found by the smell, but no-one knew whether the carcass was going to turn out to be dog, goat, cow or human. In the Rautahat District Hospital in Gaur, cobras swam between mattresses that floated along corridors knee-deep in floodwater. Much later, I asked the local health chief, 'How did you manage?' The doctor's shoulders started to shake in an Edward Heath laugh. 'So many of the people, they walked into India for treatment, and those who couldn't …' He paused, laughing again, *'Nepal ma jevan estay ho* … in Nepal, we know how to wait. What else could we do?'

Bailey bridges were flown in from Hong Kong, but it was weeks before vehicles could get through. In Kathmandu, there were shortages of everything. David began to rally as Simon pondered what supplies he'd run out of first. Our phone calls — when I could get through — became increasingly difficult and emotional. I wanted to ask him to come back, but the floods had added further delays to his project and he'd already had extra time off for David's birth. Once again, unsummoned and unwelcome echoes were going around and around my head: 'Where there is one abnormality, there are more likely to be others.' Did David have other problems as well as his harelip and holes in the heart? Simon, far from his family, was worrying too, but his senior colleague William didn't want to acknowledge the seriousness of the situation and resisted Simon's requests to come home.

Meanwhile, Simon's Nepali friends added to his anxieties. 'These are bad times.' Their eyes said what was in their hearts as a result of bitter experience. In Nepal, a one-month-old baby who is ill enough to be in hospital usually dies. Simon also recalled the reaction of a friend, a fortune-teller. Years before, he'd offered to read Simon's palm, but took one glance, looked horrified and refused to say what he had seen. That horrified look haunted Simon now. He wondered, worried, about the son whom he'd hardly met, ill in intensive care 12,000 kilometres away. Then, to add to his anxieties, William told Simon that he would be running the Rajapur Island Irrigation Rehabilitation Project: we were now committed to at least two years in that remote corner of the wild west of Nepal.

CHAPTER FOUR

david-the-interesting-case

ALONE IN CAMBRIDGE WITH MONTH-OLD DAVID, I was in shock, unable to express all the confused emotions that were churning inside me. I felt guilty about leaving Alexander with grandparents whom he hardly knew, but I was so distracted that he was probably happier with them than hanging around the hospital. David's doctors were positive and optimistic, so that some days I could ride on the euphoria of their superficial reassurances, almost believing that whatever was wrong with David was treatable. They talked of the two heart operations (two more operations!) David would need. Until these holes in his heart were patched, David would not thrive. They explained that although some holes close as the heart grows, David's were too large for this to happen: he would need surgery. They implied we'd not escape from hospital until after such an operation. I went from euphoria to depression, as prospects of rejoining Simon disappeared. At this low point in my spirits, I was at last able to voice my worries about David's brain. The paediatricians were reassuring. 'He's bound to be drowsy and unresponsive because of his heart failure. He has been very ill. When he's stabilised on his new medicines, he'll start smiling.'

I spent most of my waking hours at the hospital. Late one evening, Frances phoned. She'd heard about the new arrival. I hardly knew her, but as she was the wife of Simon's colleague, William, we had a lot in common.

'You'll be going back to Nepal soon, I suppose?'

'We'd planned to, but David has some problems and we need to stay a little longer. He has holes in his heart.' I heard a shocked intake of breath. 'It's all right. These things are all fixable.'

'May I visit you? I'm often at the hospital. You know that I do voluntary work visiting for the Chaplaincy?'

'Yes, do. It would be lovely to see you again.'

When she came, though, we ended up talking about how difficult life was as the wife of an engineer who worked in isolated places. Like us, she and William had lived in Indonesia and Pakistan, but the conversation only deepened my feeling of isolation from Simon. It underlined how much I wanted him to be here. My courage started failing me when I thought about the future and the new plan for us to go and live on remote Rajapur Island.

David's doctors, meanwhile, decided that although he was taking breast milk, he also needed food supplements to fatten him up. One of the nurses shoved a nasogastric tube up his nose and thence down into his stomach and taped it in place on his face. A dietician calculated what powders had to be given. I sat for hours at a cold, hard electric milking machine: *suck-suck-hiss, suck-suck-hiss, squirt*. Then the right mix of my milk, calorie supplements, vitamins and essential salts was poured into him by way of the tube.

He was such a placid baby, yet the tube distressed him and he often pulled it out; he objected to his calorie supplements too. Puzzled, I tasted the cocktail: it was like a mixture of scouring powder and lard, and he vomited this stuff several times a day. Each time he puked, he panicked as if he thought he was drowning. It tore me apart watching that terror in his little eyes. Now he twitched at the slightest sound; he was turning into a nervous wreck at the age of five weeks. The dietician wasn't the least bit interested that David vomited most of what she'd calculated he needed to absorb. His crying — caused by daily or twice-daily blood tests — and his struggling with the nasogastric tube made me feel so very sick. Assaults on my body didn't bother me, but I couldn't bear David's suffering.

Yet I remained optimistic, for there was a lot happening. Things could only improve. We did a day trip in a hospital car to the Great Ormond Street Hospital for Sick Children in London. They did an echocardiogram and the cardiologist checked David over. 'Is this him? Is this as active as he gets?' I saw, and didn't want to see, what the consultant had noted. Most babies are constantly on the move. David was abnormally still. I became defensive. 'We're a relaxed family. David's brother was an easy baby too. And I'm sure he'll get more frisky when the heart failure is controlled and he's put on some weight.'

The consultant said, 'As long as David is putting on weight, his heart is coping. If he becomes breathless again and starts failing to thrive, then surgery would be wise ... sooner rather than later.'

'I hope you'll let them know that back in Cambridge. David's been putting on weight beautifully since we started the heart drugs.'

'Good. We don't need to rush any decisions.'

Back in Cambridge, the ward became claustrophobic. Our shiny beige and cream room looked out onto a depressing concrete and glass courtyard. It belonged to a house sparrow whose possessive cheeps reminded me that the natural world still existed; the echo exaggerated his chirping and must have inflated his ego. I needed frequent trips along the shiny beige and cream corridors down to the coffee bar in the busy hospital concourse for time out, and to look for postcards to send to Alexander.

Breast-feeding and broken nights exhausted me. I couldn't think clearly any more, but I had realised — deep in my subconscious — that David had received a death sentence the day he was born, even if it was many weeks before I acknowledged it. Over the following ten days I careered from depression to ecstasy and back again as my fears of a neurological problem surfaced, I was temporarily reassured and then my fears resurfaced. I didn't — I couldn't — articulate my fears.

I only passed positive news on to the family. It was comfortable to repeat all the doctors' reassurances and half-truths. I had faith in the myth of medical omnipotence. I wanted to believe them, and perhaps I hoped that repeating them might make them true, though I knew in my heart that I was allowing myself to be misled. Misled and isolated.

By now David had become an Interesting Case. First his doctors had offered bland, almost patronising reassurance; now he was a medical phenomenon. Rare syndromes were discussed and exotic new treatments floated. I was furious. The doctors were chummy. We spoke the same language. I understood them, but they didn't understand me as a mother. I had been so sure that David had big problems, but no-one listened then, and no-one would talk to me properly now. They had saved my life when I was in labour; they saved David from dying in heart failure when he was a month old; but now they seemed too short of time to communicate — or were they not comfortable dealing with me?

Next time I spotted paediatrician Sarah looking at David's X-rays, I sidled over and asked her to explain what she could see. She pointed out weird y-shaped ribs and half-formed vertebra and there, at the nurses' station in public, she said almost casually, 'I think that David has some syndrome. We'll organise a cranial ultrasound and an eye opinion. And an absolute genius of a geneticist will come and see you both.' I felt sick. I felt like she'd hit me, but the shock didn't silence me. I bombarded her with questions. Only then — I think — did she realise that I was a parent, not a colleague, and she backed away mumbling that she was not an expert. I went into David's room to cry.

Each hospital day seemed to bring a new expert opinion and the next day another stranger slid into the room. He caught me staring out of the window.

'Morning! Another good one, isn't it? Not much of a view from here, though.'

'But Sidney likes it.' I pointed out my sparrow in his alcove, but the doctor didn't really look. I was acting oddly, talking of Sidney when there was no-one else in the room.

'I'm green … um, Dr Green; Clinical Genetics. Come to see, um, David. That all right?' His bumbling nervousness made me suspicious. He was going to give me bad news. As he checked David over, my stomach did somersaults. He looked up shiftily, and then enthusing like a birder who has spotted a new species he said, 'I think I know what syndrome this is! It is axial mesodermal dysplasia … also known as hemifacial microsomia.'

The word 'syndrome' made me panic again. Most are a cluster of problems including profound mental retardation or, at best, intellectual slowness. It was this that I feared most. I vaguely heard the syndrome names, but they meant nothing to me; and then from somewhere beyond a quagmire of terror-induced nausea I heard, 'David's abnormalities … heart … ventricular septal defects … bifid ribs … hemivertebra … ear pits … cleft lip … um, these, um, fit, um,' — he was getting nervous again — 'um, with a problem of mid-line fusion … um … as I said, axial mesodermal dysplasia. It is very rare, but the good news is that there is no neurological deficit associated with this syndrome.'

I was speechless as he prattled on, but he had recognised my worst fear — every parent's worst fear. David's brain was all right. I felt like dancing around the ward kissing everyone, but I must have just sat there bemused, shell-shocked. Shaking. Yet I managed to draw breath and blurt out, 'What else is likely to be wrong with him, Dr Green — if he has this … syndrome?'

'Sometimes there is a kidney missing. We'll organise a scan.'

Not long after he had left, as I sat cuddling David, watching his wandering independent eyes, I knew that the geneticist shouldn't have been so quick to reassure me. Something was terribly wrong, otherwise David would be able to coordinate his vision. I don't know how long I sat there, but a nurse whom I didn't know came to take us down for the scan. Down in the lift. Long, busy, cheerless corridors full of strangers. Neon lights. Spotless beige and cream walls. Through a set of big heavy doors. Into a dismal beige and cream waiting area containing a scrap of grubby carpet and an untidy heap of well-thumbed magazines. Finally we were ushered behind a pale yellow curtain. It was gloomy inside. A man sat with his back to us.

'Just put him there.'

'This is David.' I expected a greeting or at least a glance from this new doctor.

'Yes, yes. Just strip him off,' he said, still not looking round. Soon he was squirting oil over David's abdomen and the probe was sliding smoothly over his perfect new pink skin. The radiologist was absorbed in the screen that revealed David's organs. My mind drifted.

'Mmm, interesting …' I heard the doctor say; he seemed to be thinking out loud. He continued talking to the screen, 'Mmm, very interesting … looks like renal agenesis.' That grabbed my attention — a missing kidney. David only had one kidney. The consultant still hadn't made eye contact with me. 'Sometimes the kidney is in the pelvis but we're good here at finding them even there. I've never missed one. No, I'm certain that the right kidney is absent. Ah and look, that's air in the bladder.'

'What does that mean?'

'Fistula — connecting bladder and bowel.' He still hadn't looked at me. 'And there is some other request on the form. Can't read it. Are we supposed to be scanning something else?'

'The brain.'

'Ah. Easy. Okay … Oh, look, that's fascinating. The shape of the ventricles beneath the cerebral hemispheres here are characteristic. I'll bet that there is agenesis of the corpus callosum too. When the ventricles are rather squared off like this …'. He finally turned and looked at me. 'You're looking a bit shocked.'

'Shouldn't I be?' The callous bastard. 'You've just said that my baby has three more abnormalities.'

'Oh minor, minor abnormalities of no clinical significance.' He was backing off, realising too late that he'd said too much and was hurting me. 'They'll need to do some renal investigations.'

How much more would they find wrong with David? And did none of them have any idea how to communicate?

I started to process the day's findings and realised that the radiologist was wrong. If there was an abnormal connection between David's bowel and bladder, he would have had endless bladder infections and he would have been septicaemic by now. I did not want to be David's doctor, but it seemed that I needed to step in. Using my school rounders fielding skills, I caught a clean urine sample and persuaded Sarah to send it to the laboratory. 'Yes, okay, but there's no point if the scan showed a fistula.' The sample proved that there was nothing wrong with David's bladder.

His bladder was all right, but he had not started smiling by six weeks like normal babies should, and late smilers often turn out to have intellectual problems. Yet — I reasoned, excused — he had been ill or asleep for much of his life; it was logical for him to smile late. Wasn't it? My mind, drifting as I sat in the windowless room at the milking machine — *suck-suck-hiss* — wandered through the possibilities. What was David's future? What would we do if he had big, unfixable problems?

I emerged from the dairy still in a dream and bumped into Caroline, one of the nurses.

'You look exhausted, Jane. You don't have to carry on with the breast-feeding, you know.'

'Yes, I do!' How could she think of undermining my determination to do my best for him. 'Without breast milk, he will risk dysentery and diarrhoea when we go back to Nepal. First the doctors, then my sister suggested abandoning breast-feeding, and now you lot!'

'Will you go back? Is it still "when", not "if"?' Caroline said, looking even more concerned for me.

'Of course we're going back! That's where we live, where Simon's work is, where I shall work when David's strong. We *will* go back.'

A new nurse came on duty; an older woman, caring, generous, open; the kind of person who should have been teaching Nepali nurses what nursing is all about. She looked into David's cot, admired him. 'Tut-tut. He has no toys!' And she bustled off to find some soft colourful things to interest him. How obsessed we had become with

David's clinical state and bodily functions. How could we have lost sight of the fact that he was a baby who should be cuddled, entertained, played with? Poor David. He lay imprisoned behind the bars of his cot, tube taped into his nose, staring at blank walls. He didn't seem to have anything to enjoy; even eating scared him. And his heart medicines dehydrated him so that his lips were cracked and split close to the scars of the harelip repair; they looked terribly, terribly sore. Poor, beautiful David. The nurse came in and found me gazing sadly at him. She slung one arm around me and said, 'You are *allowed* to cry you know!' And suddenly — with her permission — I broke down and wept. She probably had no idea how much good she did. I needed to shed tears for the healthy child I would not have in David.

One day of tests and milk-pumping merged into another. The only real distraction was watching the antics of Sidney defending his stark alcove from rival cock sparrows. Or sometimes, when David was sleeping, I'd walk across the ward to stare out in the other direction, across muted greens and browns of fen-flat farmland; the only life was the occasional train coming up from London. I felt awful. Empty. Days drifted miserably by until finally Simon arrived back from Nepal.

It was so good to be together, but we were both more afraid than we wanted to admit, trying to protect each other. He looked haggard. During the birth, the obstetrician had made that careless remark, 'Better to have a scar on the head than no brain'. This had sown a worrisome seed in Simon's head. The harelip hadn't fazed him because that was only a minor problem compared to the appalling possibility of brain damage. Simon's homecoming meant that Alexander was back with us again and his innocent ebullience soon helped us to rally.

Simon was ignored by David's doctors, so I introduced him to Sarah and the other junior paediatricians. 'My husband, Simon, would appreciate an update.'

'All in good time. The consultant will speak to you both soon.' This sounded ominous.

I asked Simon, 'Don't you resent the way the doctors never talk to you? I keep wanting to tell them you are a Cambridge graduate, not a brainless nincompoop. I'm bewildered at the way you are marginalised just because you're a layman. They treat you like a deaf mute, a *lato*.'

'I don't expect anything different. Doctors don't often explain things. I'll tell you about that later.'

'Hey, you look knackered. Why don't you go home and get some sleep?'

Early the next day, Simon was summoned in from the playroom where he'd been with Alexander. They appeared with Alexander scooting himself along in a red plastic car. The consultant and his comet's tail of junior doctors, including Sarah, medical students and nurses, came into David's little side ward and sat us down. Consultants don't usually take time to sit and talk. 'How are things?'

'Awful. I've got mastitis and David is vomiting all his milk. And the vomiting panics him.'

'It never rains but it pours …' This was the only glimmer of compassion I ever saw in him, but the moment was brief. He continued, 'The tests … You know, I think, that we have identified several problems. Your baby has holes in the heart, only one kidney, low sodium, spinal abnormalities, and the fibres connecting the two hemispheres of the brain are missing. His intellectual development is not going to be normal …'

I stared at the consultant, with his neatly trimmed moustache; he must have been a lady-killer once. In other circumstances, I might have called him dashing, even handsome, but today he was neither. He seemed in a hurry to say his piece and leave. He wittered on, while I processed at triple speed. 'It is important that the baby has this open-heart surgery and a lot more investigations, tests. We need to see exactly what else is wrong.'

Alexander was finding this boring so scooted off to the playroom again. My mind played weird tricks. I was reeling, speechless; half of me was nauseated, falling backwards into an abyss of despair; yet another side of me, outside myself, was observing this cold exchange. That other me was waving a flag saying, 'Might we interrupt this consultation to teach you — the consultant — about how to discuss all this and help the parents? We could run an interactive tutorial now if you like ...?' Then another me wanted to kick him in the gonads, just to shut him up. I was ready for the news, but felt like screaming, 'Why did no-one listen to me on day one? Why have we gone through this emotional helter-skelter for the last month and a half? Why did Simon have to go through his hell alone 12,000 kilometres away from us before he rushed back home to be with us now? Why? Why? Why?'

But I didn't say any of that. Despite being a doctor, I couldn't challenge these experts who were in charge of my son's life. I said, 'Could we talk about this please? My son, David ...' (I felt I needed to introduce him.) 'Will David walk, or even talk? I am not sure about the surgery. Not sure it will really help him.'

The consultant had given us a fairly standard spiel, but I knew what he'd left unsaid. Surgery meant a scalpel cutting my baby's skin from collarbone to bellybutton; bone-cutters crunching through each rib; his rib cage being forced open, sprung back; his blood being mixed with the blood of six strangers while on the bypass machine; his heart being cut open and repaired. When people break a rib they are in pain — with every breath — for weeks. What must it be like to have twelve broken ribs? There is often pain too from the bits of wire that they cobble them back together with. Then there are the intellectual consequences of being put on cardiac bypass; the brain suffers; IQ points go; the intellectual damage is not much but it is measurable. I could articulate none of this. I could hardly even speak in monosyllables. The consultant continued, 'There is nothing threatening David's life now. These days, cardiac surgery is routine. The missing kidney should cause no undue complications ... although he may need to take prophylactic antibiotics permanently.' There was no mention of quality of life.

'Will he ever be independent?' I asked. 'If David is going to be terribly handicapped, should we put him through that?' The consultant shook his head. Maybe I misread him, but he looked slightly bored. He seemed to have dismissed us as callous, unthinking parents. Maybe he thought we were too shocked to accept the news — in denial. 'They do tens of these heart operations on babies every month; even Downs babies have their hearts fixed. This kind of surgery is routine now.'

I was so angry tears choked me. Routine? Routine for whom? Didn't he understand how healing it is to allow people to talk things through? Was he puzzled or embarrassed by my mute tears? He seemed to take my choked silence as agreement.

'When should the operation be done?' Simon blurted out, surprising me, as always, with his quick-wittedness. I was surprised to realise he too understood the implications of what was being suggested, and relieved that he seemed inclined to question the doctors' judgements. 'Can surgery wait a month, a year?'

'Probably. We'll check and let you know. But meanwhile, we'll book the DMSA scan and the other investigations.' (I wanted to scream; I wanted them to stop talking about investigations.) 'And he'll need daily blood tests until his blood sodium is back to normal.'

I managed to utter, 'We want to take him home. We need to be at home together for a while.' I didn't say any more. I could see that I was asking for something the consultant did not want to give.

'I suppose we could let you take him out for the weekend, if his sodium is up a bit.'

He didn't sympathise. He didn't invite questions. He didn't say when we'd be able to talk to him again. Yet we were not left alone to absorb this appalling news. There was work to be done; milk to collect (*suck-suck-hiss*); David's heart medicines to be ground up; salt and potassium to be forced down his tube; revolting pseudo-food to be administered; vomit to be cleared up; nappies to change; another blood test; more crying. And then at last he was asleep, and we were left alone to hold each other and cry. Then we left him for the night.

At home, with Alexander also tucked up in bed, I should have felt calmer, but I was still agitated. I asked Simon, 'What *were* you thinking during that meeting with the consultant? You hardly said a word.' I assumed that Simon thought we should do what they said.

He is often quiet when he disagrees with me. He was quiet and he wasn't making eye contact.

'Oh, I was thinking about our choices,' he said, looking at me at last.

'What choices?' I was up on my feet again, pacing about.

'Oh, I don't know. What do *you* think?'

'I don't know, either.' We were both chary to say too much, worried each would think the other callous for what was in our minds. I stood there looking for some hints in his face. 'I can't think straight. Am I overreacting? I wish that bloody man would let us talk things through … I just want to run away, really, but I'm not sure whether David's well enough yet.'

'Why don't we go back then?' He spoke with calm, quiet, unshiftable determination. 'Come sit beside me.'

'What — go back now?' I said, my heart leaping.

'Yes, why not? Is there anything urgent to keep us in Cambridge?'

'I don't think so … Do you *really* think we should go?'

'I get the feeling that what the doctors are suggesting for David are displacement activities. You certainly aren't overreacting. Most of what they said today was irrelevant. There is nothing they can do now — nothing they suggested that can't wait.'

'That's excellent. I thought you were quiet because you didn't agree with my rantings.' It was such a relief to realise we were together on this. Such a relief to know he didn't think I was mad to challenge David's doctors. Coming new on the scene after the crises, he could look at it more rationally than I could. He had no background fear of worse problems, and he saw the doctors' inconsistencies.

'No, I was just thinking. It really would be better to wait for a year. David's heart is no longer the biggest problem — is it?'

'No, he seems to be stable now. At first they thought he'd have to have the heart operation immediately, but he's beginning to put on weight and that's a sign he's getting well. It is okay to wait. And surgery will be easier when the heart is larger.'

'If fixing his heart isn't urgent, we can go back to Nepal for a while. Get the family back together.'

'I'd love to … though the prospect scares me silly, I want to take him away from all those needles, especially since I don't think that any new results will change anything.'

'I'm not so worried about all the tests.'

'You haven't seen the look in David's eyes each time they stab him,' I said, on my feet again, furious.

'I'm not so worried about all the tests,' he persisted, calmly, 'but I'm convinced that leaving would be best. I expect that they could get any that are really necessary done quite quickly — and if they are really necessary, we should allow them, shouldn't we? Trouble is, I'm not sure how crucial they are.'

'I mean to ask them about each one from now on.'

'Good idea. As well as that, I'm worried about Alexander. He needs to get back to normal. The hospital has become so much part of his life, and he so loves the hospital toys, that he doesn't see it as a horrible place: that enthusiasm isn't healthy. He prefers hospital to home. Let's get away if we can.' Then, smiling again, 'And I need some decent rice. Laxmi has perfected her sesame chutney. You must come and taste it!' We'd both felt awful since the discussion with the doctors, but suddenly our spirits lifted now we had something to plan for. Now, though, we had to convince the doctors.

Meeting the paediatric neurologist the next day confirmed our worst fears, but he allowed us to talk. He produced a large coloured diagram of the brain and explained about the corpus callosum. He encouraged questions, so I asked, 'Is it unreasonable to resist treatment for David?'

'No, not unreasonable. Neurologists know that not all medical problems can be fixed; sometimes paediatricians lose sight of that.' Like my Nepali colleagues, he recognised he had limits, wasn't omnipotent, and he heard our pleas to protect David from unnecessary pain.

'But such decisions are not always as easy as they might seem. By not treating him, he might still survive but become more handicapped or more difficult to manage. You need more information. Will his heart condition add to any disability or actually shorten his life? Would he be more comfortable with or without treatment? You must ask the cardiologist what each decision will actually mean in terms of quality of life as well as survival.' This — finally — was clear, rational advice, and he supported our idea of going back to Nepal. 'No, of course you are not being cruel. You are thinking things through, and that's fine. Try to de-medicalise David. See if he can manage without tube-feeding.'

Simon said, 'Thanks. You are the first of David's doctors to explain things in plain English, the first to talk to both of us.'

It was only at this point that we told the family about David's neurological problems. They'd been hovering on the sidelines ready to help at short notice, but we'd found it so difficult to talk to them properly. We'd isolated ourselves. My in-laws, though, had already guessed. They'd planned to help by flying back to Nepal with the new baby, but had already cancelled all that and waited, quietly supportive, in the background. My mother's response to the news was denial, 'Doctors do make mistakes ...' — but it was too painful to explain why I knew that the doctors were right. We should have shared the news with them sooner. We'd handled this badly.

The Clever Doctors preferred to forget that they were impotent to cure David, so they focussed on minutely exploring every possible abnormality. It is easy for them to lose sight of medical limitations in centres of academic excellence. They had various inspirational ideas about how David-the-Interesting-Case should be investigated and his complicated drug cocktails tweaked.

Each time I saw those looks of sheer terror of drowning, then panic, in David's eyes, my heart cried out. 'The salt supplements make him vomit; what's the point?'

'His blood sodium is still low; he needs them.'

'But he vomits most of it ... and I've been thinking about the low salt. The hyponatraemia is likely to be inappropriate ADH secretion, isn't it? Surely it will stabilise when David recovers? He *has* been really ill.'

'The consultant's got a cortical scar about sodium. You know what it's like. I expect he was involved in a case when he was a junior doctor where something went wrong; but whatever the reason, he's obsessed with sodium, so David gets salt supplements.' Sarah terminated what she knew would be a pointless discussion. 'Your husband hasn't bonded with the baby, has he?'

'Why do you say that?' I said, nonplussed.

'He doesn't spend time with David. Doesn't pick him up. Doesn't seem interested.'

'Simon is jet-lagged and worried. He's also got his hands full entertaining our older son. And he's an undemonstrative person. He's fine. When we get out of hospital and back to acting like a normal family again, everything will be fine.' I trailed off, realising how bizarre this conversation was, wondering what was going on in her head. I had thought that we were friends, but here we were discussing my husband as a clinical object. Because I was a doctor, she seemed to assume I wasn't like other parents.

She'd been so very chummy, but even doctors — or perhaps especially doctors — need to be touched by something personally to understand the suffering of others. At medical school we were taught about the enormous power over life and death that is invested in us; we can be deluded into thinking we are almighty. Almost instinctively we view death, incurable disease and disability as challenging our power. We forget that this is all part of life. The neurologist knew this, and Nepalis know it, but David's other doctors were too busy or too threatened by failure to stop and think. I guess that we doctors all have to defend ourselves against the human suffering that confronts us every day, otherwise we'd quickly go under. Medical jargon helps keep us remote, yet seeing colleagues suffer is hard. If we think too much, we realise that we — and our loved ones — are just as vulnerable as the rest of humanity.

My turmoil continued, but no-one seemed to notice. Those terrified looks in poor David's eyes and the prospect of two open-heart operations were sheer torture for me. It would be torture for him too, and I wanted to protect him. When I asked which of his abnormalities could be fixed, doctors mumbled and changed the subject or talked of more investigations. Yet they weren't experimenting; they were meticulously documenting everything in the vain hope that they might either find something treatable or otherwise uncover information that would help them give David a prognosis.

'We'd like to go home for the weekend. All of us,' I told the doctors.

'You can go if David's sodium is normal on the next blood test,' Sarah said.

'We *need* to go home — we need time together. Alexander has forgotten what home is.'

'We'll wait for the sodium result.'

When it came and it was still low on Friday, they must have realised we'd go whatever they said. I scooped David up, his nasogastric tube dangling from his face, and almost ran out in case they changed their minds. I dared not even look over my shoulder in case they tried to stop us. It was so good to break free.

Slightly to my surprise, the neighbours soon noticed we'd escaped and were wonderfully supportive despite hardly knowing us. They invited us to supper, invited Alexander to play … and listened. That was most important: they listened. Caroline said, 'Oh, Jane, you've been to the edge of hell and back!' Why didn't doctors say empathetic things like this?

Mary from a few doors down stopped in the street to ask how things were going and I poured out my story in a long, bitter monologue. She was attentive, sympathetic, but I suddenly stopped my verbal outpouring. 'Oh, I'm sorry. We hardly know each other and I'm burdening you …'

'Oh, Jane, I *do* understand. Addenbrooke's is such a miserable excuse for a hospital. Your story sounds so much like when Charlie was diagnosed. They didn't talk to us or explain anything. I don't know why we put up with it, but you do, don't you? Or maybe because you're a doctor you can challenge them?'

'No, not really. It's been the same for us. We're just as in awe of medical authority — when they are in charge of your loved ones, anyway.'

'I know you're brutalised now, but having Charlie with his learning difficulties has introduced me to some really wonderful people. I've made some terrific friendships … met some really super women. You'll value all this once you've got away from Addenbrooke's!'

What strength their sympathy and understanding gave me! I began planning steps that would make us independent. One step was the feeding. Children become lazy about eating if they get what they need effortlessly down a tube, but if a baby takes a breast-feed while being tube-fed, they associate the effort of suckling with the pleasant sensation of a full stomach and try harder. In hospital, I fed David while a nurse poured feed into the half syringe attached to the tube and then held this miniature reservoir while it trickled into David's stomach under gravity. At home, this took a bit of inventiveness. I'd fill the syringe and hold it in my mouth while suckling David and hoped no-one would phone or ring the doorbell. One Saturday afternoon during a feeding session, a GP friend called by. He was forced to listen to a diatribe, my wrath overflowing against David's disinterested paediatricians. The phone interrupted my tirade.

'It was the ward … with the result of yesterday's bloodletting; his sodium is down again and they told me to pour more salt into him. It's bonkers. The more salt we give him, the more he pukes!'

My calm, logical doctor-friend was surprisingly put out on my behalf and said, 'I think I'd find all these phone calls very stressful; you can't even relax when you're at home!'

'No, it's better at home — much better. You can't imagine how much better!'

When David pulled out his nasogastric tube and breast-fed contentedly, I convinced myself that this was his rebellion against tube-feeding, so that he was without his tube almost all weekend. By the time we turned ourselves in on Monday morning, David was less twitchy, had not vomited for two days, and he was content and peaceful. Seeing him relaxed increased my resolve to protect him. I was very angry — a tigress ready to fight for her cub. The next time a doctor breezed cheerily into David's side ward to take blood, I got up, putting myself in her way. 'I'm sorry, but I'd like to know what this sample is for.' The doctor continued her preparations to take the blood. 'Look, I know that you're busy … but I am asking what this is for … before I give consent for this.'

She wasn't really listening.

'If David is to be hurt, it must be for a good reason. I've decided that now.' Silence. '*Could you tell me what this test is for, please!*' I wanted to swear at her, slap her; do something to make her listen.

'Just routine. Sodium, and repeating the chromosome analysis.'

'Look. I forbid any more invasive tests unless you can explain the immediate value to David's wellbeing!' I spoke loud and slow, like I was addressing a drunkard.

'Okay,' she said, 'no problem. But first we'll do blood tests for DiGeorge syndrome and killer T-cell function. Remember we talked about this yesterday?'

'No, no, no!' I shouted, and burst into tears. Uncomprehending, she wandered out of the room mumbling, 'Okay, the tests will wait till tomorrow.'

David was part of the hospital system now. I had seen others sucked in like this while disempowered relatives looked on helpless, knowing their child had never had a chance to live. These patients could so easily spend most of their lives in hospital or going endlessly from clinic to clinic, test to test. This was not going to be David's life.

The next time the consultant paediatrician came, he asked pleasantly, 'How's the baby?'

'David is all right.' I screwed up my courage and took a deep breath. 'But he seems so much more at ease away from here. We don't want any more invasive investigations. No more needles or tests unless you can prove they will be of direct benefit to David — improve his quality of life.'

The consultant eyed me up. He seemed cold and distant. Why couldn't we communicate?

'All right; we'll arrange the DMSA scan and renal investigations as an out-patient then.'

'No,' I said, 'No ... more ... tests.'

He started to try to explain, but I interrupted. 'No. We fly to Nepal on Sunday.'

The consultant said nothing. I had won this first skirmish in what promised to be a long, bloody war. But were we condemning David to death or giving him a chance of life?

CHAPTER FIVE

escape to sanity

I OSCILLATED, ONE MINUTE FEELING THE EUPHORIA of liberation and the next agonising about my failure to convince David's doctors that we were doing the best for him. I even wondered whether I was growing paranoid; imagining their disapproval. Whatever they thought, though, I needed to focus on practicalities: what medical care could we expect for David once we got back to Nepal? How would we get nasogastric tubes, medicines and calorie supplements? Might I find a physiotherapist, dietician, or someone to advise on special educational tips and tricks or on games that would get David mobile? I didn't yet know enough to select any specialist equipment, though I knew there would be none available in Nepal.

Simon said, 'You know what I think about the health services. But are you happy to take that on — with no back-up?' He was confident in me, but knew I might be further burdened with guilt.

'I think so. My clinical guesses have all been more astute than theirs. And that's all they seem to be doing — guessing. Maybe I haven't been listening enough to my instincts. But that reminds me — you promised to tell me about why you don't expect doctors to communicate.'

'They just don't. Even when I was admitted to the old Shanta Bhawan hospital with meningitis.'

'I'd forgotten. That must have been really scary.'

'I was too ill to take much in at first, but then when I left hospital all they said was that my headache would get better, and they gave me half a kilo of aspirin.'

'Half a kilo!'

'Yes — a three-month supply, presumably to discourage me from going back and complaining about the headache.'

'That doesn't sound quite right. How long did it last?'

'A few months, so they were right. The doctor who was looking after me was a missionary — well-meaning, but underqualified. I think he was a bit overwhelmed.'

'I think he might have been. Going by the scars on your back, he attempted the lumbar puncture at least four times. But, anyway, are you okay about the Shanta Bhawan being David's next hospital?'

'No, because it won't be. You'll be looking after him,' he said, with a smile.

'Glad you've got confidence in me,' I said, ambivalent.

'Well, you seem to have always been a step ahead of David's doctors.'

'Mmm, I never talked about my premonitions of David's problems before he was born, did I? I expected the heart defect. And do you remember when I miscarried? I knew that baby would never be born as soon as I realised I was pregnant. Isn't that weird? If a patient had claimed that, I wouldn't have believed her!'

The weight of the responsibility I'd brought upon myself suddenly seemed enormous. I started making a list of all the medical textbooks that I wanted to take with me, and I pondered on what else I would need to keep David well. We'd intended to rent our house out, but cancelled this plan, so that I could return to England if it all got too much — or if David became too ill.

We saw the neurologist again and he encouraged me to talk through my confusion about what was best for David. 'We are still thinking that if David's heart should start failing again or if he got some infection, we won't treat him, except to keep him comfortable.'

He said, 'I can understand your view. Sometimes it seems right to let a child go — if the future looks bleak.'

GP friends also understood. 'Countless patients are over-investigated and over-treated. There's a momentum in the system and it's easy to get carried along by it and not question doctors' omnipotent right to interfere with people's bodies. The human costs can be huge. But then, GPs are almost the only doctors these days who understand all problems, can see the whole person … spend time with the dying … see things through to the end.' They understood, yet none of us realised how completely medically unsupported I would be in Nepal. The letters of introduction that the Cambridge paediatricians wrote for the 'medical team' in Nepal who would take over David's care were never opened. I was the team.

We'd left the hospital in Cambridge feeling drained and guilty, struggling to exorcise the doctors' unspoken accusations. We didn't care about our baby, otherwise why would we want to take him away? We also felt bad about how little we'd involved our families in all of this and how we'd be leaving before they'd had a chance to get to know David.

We'd bought so much new clutter — board books, music, toys — that we opted to go to the airport in a taxi. And rather than enduring long, sad goodbyes at the airport, we encouraged everyone to come and visit us soon in Kathmandu. The first to come would be Simon's brother Mark and his partner, Jill.

On the day of departure — our flight back to Kathmandu, the Flight out of England — we dressed carelessly in unironed clothes. All the recent emotional surges made me feel as if I'd aged ten years. We must have looked haggard, battered, scruffy. Despite the psycho-logical hammering we'd taken, the lack of sleep and physical exhaustion, my spirits began to soar. I chatted to the Royal Nepal cabin crew as they smiled indulgently at David. Simon, too, was happy and I could see his mood lift as we got further from Cambridge. He leant across to me smiling and whispered, 'You know what those two air hostesses were saying to each other? "How is it that such ugly parents have managed to have such beautiful children!"'

'I dare you to say something to them in Nepali so they realise you understand them!'

Simon just smiled and said nothing, and we giggled at their unintended insult. David was beautiful despite the nasogastric tube dangling out of his nose, his harelip and his 'defects'. They saw his soft unblemished complexion, his blue eyes. We'd already re-entered sane, baby-loving Asia.

By the time I'd been flying for ten hours my blouse was stiff with milk that David couldn't drink. It had been a long flight but Alexander was happy and relaxed, looking forward to returning to his beloved Nepal, and being with his father again. And Simon was in high spirits by the time he could see the Kathmandu Valley. He became positively garrulous. 'Look … dear old Kathmandu. How lovely the rice fields look; and see how that luscious green contrasts with the red brick gabled houses … and the *stupa* at Bauddha — its great dome standing out so white amongst the chaos all around.'

Laxmi, our cook, welcomed us home. She fussed and cooed over David and made us feel like long-lost relatives. Alexander was pleased to be reunited with night-watchman Purna Bahaadur, whom he idolised.

'You know, Mummy, Purna Bahaadur has brave trousers! That's why he's not scared of the dark.'

'Mmm,' came my puzzled response. '*Bahaadur* means brave.'

'I know that! But you can't say *bahaadur* nicely, Mummy.' Three-year-old Alexander was already correcting my clumsy pronunciation.

Soon if felt as if we'd never been away. Our Lotus House seemed like heaven on earth now. After the claustrophobia of the hospital ward in Cambridge, it was truly wonderful to be able to look out from our living room and watch squabblesome mynah birds, flamboyant picky hoopoes and shy tailorbirds, or tune into the other-worldly sounds of drums, horns and chanting from the monastery at Kopan. I never tired of looking out at the ever-changing colours and shadows of the ripening, undulating rice, the terraces, the forested ridges and the mighty Himalayas looking benignly down from between the thinning monsoon clouds.

Simon's work, planning how to clean up Kathmandu's rivers, took him all over the Valley. We often took weekend riverside walks. Even the holy Bagmati was an open sewer, but the temples and bathing *ghats* were still attractive and busy. Kathmandu's rivers are used to wash carrots before they are taken to market, to cool buffaloes, to dump rubbish and to absorb abattoir waste. So the river is busy, and attracts scavenging dogs and screaming pariah kites. David would burble happily, responding to the sounds and the changing light and shadow. We passed intricate Newar wood-carving and magnificent medieval temples along the Bishnumati River beneath the glistening golden *stupa* of Swayambhu.

One stroll took us under a new bridge and into a squatter settlement where friendly young mothers surrounded us, giggling and wanting to compare babies. 'How did you make such a beautiful baby?' 'How old?' 'Son or daughter?' 'Can he speak Nepali?' 'Won't he suffocate in that?' Other mothers came to look at this strange way I was carrying David — in a papoose on my front. Local babies are wrapped onto mum's back with a cloth. I took him out to show him off and they said, 'He is so beautiful, so clean!' Their admiration was a forgotten delight of having a new baby. No-one in England dared talk about him, ask about him. One of the women offered to swap her son for David. I was stunned until Simon said, 'She *is* joking.'

Another said, 'Look at those dimples in his ears; these are a gift from heaven.' Doctors in England included these ear pits amongst the list of David's abnormalities. Here in Nepal, they made him special. How healthy. How constructive! 'Come! Sit with us.' And they brought a thick comfortable rice straw mat so that I could sit, chat and suckle David. An older woman joined us, studied me for a while then pulled out and tweaked a wrinkled breast. She said, 'Look! I've got milk too, sister!'

'Oh! Er ... very good! Um. How old is your baby, *didi*?'

'Fifteen.'

'Ah, fifteen months?' I looked to Simon to translate.

She replied, 'No, my daughter is fifteen years old. The milk is for my granddaughter. I feed the baby while her mother works by day, and my daughter feeds her at night.' Grandmother thought us narrow-minded in the West because only one woman in the family lactates for each baby.

In Cambridge, David's paediatricians had said it was crucial to continue giving him salt supplements and essential to take blood samples every week until his sodium levels were normal. I just didn't believe that his low sodium was a real problem, and since the salt made him vomit, I'd given him less and less. After we had been in Nepal about a week, though, David became pale. Guilt and fear seized me. I needed to arrange a blood test, if only so that I could sleep easier. But the American clinic doctor said, 'We're not real good at drawing blood from kids. Go to the Kanti hospital.'

For that trip I borrowed Basant, one of the office drivers. He was a small man, forty-something, wearing a big grin, tight jeans, a tank top and high-heeled cowboy boots. I overheard him explaining to Nepali friends, 'This new son of the *sahib,* he so sick he need oxygen through that pipe.' Basant's English was fluent and wonderfully quirky. He prattled good-naturedly as he drove. 'I am so happy you come back, Alexander. I will show you everything about Kathmandu. Look — dog playing guitar!' A scabby mutt was strumming at its belly. Then, 'Look at that buffalo!'

'I can't see a buffalo,' said Alexander. 'There's a cow. He's stolen some radishes.'

'She not stealing; she giving blessing. But look at that buffalo traffic policeman — he making traffic jam. And here! Chicken riding bicycle!' Ten chickens were dangling upside-down from handlebars, passively blinking, going off to have their throats cut. 'Weather is very sticky, *memsahib* — very human.'

'Basant, please will you teach me the names of all the *himals* that we can see?'

'Sure, *memsahib*; no problem. This one upside is Annapurna. This one backside Manaslu.'

'And is that Langtang *himal,* Basant-*dai*?' I said, pointing due north.

'No, no, *memsahib*. You see Langtang from Pokhara-side and Everest also.'

Basant didn't know his local mountains; he prided himself on being entertaining rather than informative and we often giggled at how his stories evolved, each time getting better in the telling. We hit a large pothole, which prompted Basant to remark, 'This is properly dancing road, *memsahib*.' Then as we passed a splendid old *peepal* tree, he performed a private prayer, touching his forehead, his heart and his head again.

Inside the children's hospital, a matronly woman with permed hair introduced herself as Dr (Mrs) Dickshit. When she heard I was also a doctor, she became very chummy. 'Look. You do one thing. Don't bother to go to main hospital for blood test; that takes too much of time. Go to stall outside hospital. Buy one five-rupee syringe then take it and this *chitthi* to blood sample technician. Then you can get analysis done in Special Care Baby Unit upstair.'

Clutching my syringe, I entered the little blood-letting room. It was noisy and packed with anxious, pushing people. I was thankful that Alexander was outside with Basant. I couldn't tell who amongst the throng were patients, relatives or staff, but a man dressed in jeans, T-shirt and a baseball cap beckoned. He gave David's arm a cursory swab, unwrapped our hypodermic and started ineptly digging into the flesh at the front of his elbow. Oh, shit; the technician didn't know what he was doing. This was not a good place to take blood from an infant. Sweat poured off me. The needle slid in and out of different puncture wounds. I felt sick. Should I flee? Take over? I shut my eyes. David howled. I tried to hold him still. I couldn't cope with this.

Logically, taking blood is a trivial procedure. I, myself, submit to blood tests; it doesn't hurt much. I'm a blood donor. Needles don't upset me, but motherhood does strange things to logic. On our first assignment to Pakistan when Alexander had been three months old I packed the vaccines he'd need and on the appointed day laid him down and unthinkingly shoved a syringeful into his thigh. Then my stomach contracted and I nearly vomited in the realisation of the pain I'd inflicted on my own child. My reaction surprised me, but thereafter I got others to immunise my kids.

David was still howling. I really didn't want to take over but I knew that I was more expert in taking blood from babies than this technician was. I was holding back my tears; this was even worse than David's experiences in Cambridge. Finally, through sheer determination rather than skill, the technician had sucked out enough blood. I grabbed the syringe and, sobbing slightly, fled upstairs for the analysis. David's sodium was normal. Normal! He'd sorted out his sodium himself. He would have no more blood samples, no more salt, and no more lard-and-scouring-powder-flavoured food supplements. I positively skipped back to the car, with David cooing contentedly as he bounced along in my arms.

डे डे डे

'How is poor David today?' This was always Basant's first question. Other babies are in paradise at this age, burbling to themselves, perpetually eating, surrounded by love and admiration. David did not smile, though, and even eating was a trial. He had not seemed strong enough to stimulate my breast milk properly, and without the electrical breast pump that I'd been using in Cambridge I had expected that my milk would dry up, so I found someone with a buffalo to supply milk for both children. David took the rich creamy milk and also started suckling really effectively. Without salt and other supplements, his appetite improved dramatically and he put on weight. Children with heart problems often manage solid food better than milk and when I offered him baby rice he hoovered it up. He seemed to enjoy it.

Soon he started to burble and for the first time seemed content. He'd stopped twitching at sudden noises; he'd lost that panic-stricken look. Yet sometimes when I gazed into his wandering eyes and tried to attract his attention with songs, my stomach knotted up in fear. He had gone through a lot — been ill for most of his life. *This* was probably why he was so slow to connect with me. I had to convince myself that although it was difficult making contact with him now, he'd find us in his own time. There was no rush.

Years before, I'd cared for a ten-year-old girl who was admitted to hospital from time to time to give her mother a break. The child had been born badly damaged. She could not feed herself or even chew; she couldn't scratch her nose. The nearest she got to communication was to open her eyes a little wider when she saw her mother. I thought then that if this had been my child, I would have found some route to euthanasia; but I wasn't a mother then.

'Why has this pathetic creature been allowed to survive?' I'd asked my colleagues.

'Her mother loves her,' my consultant said, firmly ending a difficult discussion. Was it right to keep someone like this alive? I felt sure that David would not be as badly disabled as that ten-year-old girl, but what sort of life would he have? Would he enjoy life? I pondered these questions, but finally realised that nearly all my colleagues agreed that a doctor's first priority is to preserve life. My mother also often said, 'Where there's life there's hope.' Her philosophy on this was at odds with ours, yet it was a subject that she would not discuss. I guess that had made it difficult to talk to her properly around the time of David's diagnosis.

The dilemma is that it is often hard to know how handicapped a child might be at the moment of birth. When a paediatrician is called to resuscitate a newborn baby, she has to react immediately. There's no time to assess the situation; no time to think; no time to ask the parents, even if they are in a frame of mind to be able to make a decision. And anyway, if they could be involved and could contribute to a decision to withdraw treatment, could they live with the smouldering guilt that would accompany that choice? The doctor's moral and professional duty is not to play God and decide who should live and who should die. Yet by the time the child is old enough for the damage to be obvious, putting an end to a life would be murder. Legally it would be murder, and it would *feel* like murder.

Another patient of mine was a lad in his early teens; he was stiff, immobile and totally dependent because of cerebral palsy. He was in hospital having some tendons released to render his unyielding joints less seized. His mischievous eyes sparkled every time I sped past his bed and I wondered just how bright his mind was, locked into his disobedient body. He couldn't speak, he could hardly move, but he started to nag me to remove the drip from his arm. He'd make eye contact, then stare down accusingly at the drip that I'd stuck into him before the operation. And he did it every time our eyes met, many times a day. How impressively he could nag without even a sound, but how frustrating life must be for such a child. I was thankful that David's body — so far — wasn't stiff and disobedient.

The peace and pace of Nepal made me patient, less ambitious for David. I could cope with the present, but as the weeks of our exile panned out, I grew increasingly scared about the future. I tried to avoid thinking about it. What would happen when we were old? No need to think about that now. The only way to cope with David's problems was to take a day or two at a time.

Things were getting better for him, though. The nasogastric tube stayed in less and less. Sometimes I'd slip it in when David's appetite was poor, but he would pull it out within twenty-four hours and then I'd not put it back for at least a week. I just wasn't convinced that it was necessary anymore, and it was clear that he didn't like it. He was quite good at communicating what he *didn't* want, and he certainly didn't want the tube. I offered him buffalo yoghurt and he took a great liking to that too, though some of the other expatriate mothers were horrified. The locally produced yoghurt is sold in large, rough, flattish fired clay pots, which are so crudely made that if you scoop a spoon too close to the pot side, you harvest the gritty clay that it is made of. And the surface of the yoghurt usually has collected a sprinkling of dust, buffalo hair and sometimes even sawdust. It was safe enough, though, and we all enjoyed it.

By the time David was three months old, I had donated his nasogastric tubes and calorie supplements to Kanti hospital, where they could be used to feed tiny newborn babies who really were in need. He became chubby and Basant stopped calling him 'poor David'. He was no longer the nervous baby of his awful early hospital days.

At ten weeks of age, he started smiling at me. I couldn't believe it at first, then suddenly it was as if he'd always smiled. This was a milestone that severely brain damaged children never achieve and although I was sure in my heart he'd develop, it was such a relief to see him responding to me like this. It made my soul leap for joy when I'd pick him up to cuddle him, feed him or take him out and he'd look admiringly into my eyes and smile and burble at me. He was calm and placid. He became more responsive and more vocal, cooing and chatting away, 'Glaa, glaaa …' He'd smile, too, if I blew raspberries on his cheek.

David was most animated when there was lots of children's noise around him, so I was especially enthusiastic about socialising with other mothers. We talked of how our children needed contact with other children, although they had no problem making local friends because they didn't need a common language to be able to play together. I could see David responding to sound, but he did not look much. He seemed preoccupied with analysing patterns in brickwork, or ceiling designs. I began to wonder whether he could see properly. Children and Nepalis took him for what he was, tube or not, vision or not. I noticed four-year-old Matthew studying David, and finally he approached me and asked, 'Are you going to give your nice baby some milk to drink from your … um,' and he pointed at my breasts, '… bottles?'

Elegant, fashionable Joanna seemed horrified by the tube that dangled out of David's nose the first few times she met him; I could see her wondering, and finally she said, 'Shouldn't he be in hospital?'

'No, he likes being at home with his family; all they do in hospital is blood tests. He's really thrived since we came here. Life no longer scares him.'

Debbie was troubled in a different way when she heard David's story. 'Where did you deliver?'

'Cambridge.'

'Then you can sue. They failed to diagnose all his problems when they did your scan. You must sue.'

'We don't really have a culture of suing like you do in the States.'

'But you said he was born in Cambridge.'

'Cambridgeshire, not Massachusetts. But on both sides of the Atlantic, there is a culture of perfection, isn't there? When I went for a scan in Pakistan, I was roundly reprimanded for even implying I might consider a termination if the baby had Down syndrome. The gynaecologist said, "Here we are happy for any baby God gives us!" At the time, I was bit unsettled by her attitude, but maybe she was right.' Debbie knitted her brows to say that she didn't agree.

'Anyway, suing won't help us,' I said. 'Now that David is a person, I can't go back in time and imagine him as a collection of cells in my womb, and I certainly couldn't discuss in a court of law whether or not I would have aborted him. That would not be healing or helpful. Suing takes a huge amount of emotional energy. Now we're away from the hospital I don't feel bitter. I don't want to wallow in all that anguish again, particularly since it won't do anything to correct his problems.'

With Laxmi to help me, I could afford to spend time exploring. And when the scenery enticed us out, we could just go. The snow-covered *himals* were stunning. We often walked miles amongst the rice fields and villages. Women approached shyly to feel Alexander's blond curls and see a foreign baby.

'Kasto ramro! Kati sano!' ('How beautiful! How small!') 'Son or daughter? He is how old?'

'Only six weeks! How young — but big and healthy!' How I loved being able to show him off to the world; the normal, baby-loving world! They were quick to admire him, but they were critical of me taking a tiny baby out of the house so soon: they hadn't guessed we'd just travelled more than 12,000 kilometres. We often went out — on long walks most weekends. Even within the Kathmandu Valley, there was lots of scope.

डे डे डे

'Come, drink tea!' The grandmother who had shouted across at us sat straight-backed, cross-legged, in the shade of a crude, mud-plastered verandah; she was selling cigarettes and Glucose biscuits outside the village tea shop. I wandered over to ask her, 'Is the tea good here?'

'Of course good. So you speak Nepali!'

'A little.'

'The baby has no hat! Why? It is dangerous for him to be out in the sun with no hat.'

I extracted infant David from the papoose while she watched, looking at once amused and concerned. Local kids gathered round to see. 'The baby is drinking his mother's milk,' they whispered.

Nearby, two vast, black, hairy pigs grunted luxuriously in the mud at the bottom of a storm ditch. The enticing smell of wood smoke and warm buffalo milk filled my nostrils. Grandmother spoke again. 'Drink tea and I will hold the baby.' She looked admiringly at David. Her face said that even though I was an incompetent mother, I had managed to produce a beautiful baby nevertheless. Our dignified new friend jiggled David on her lap while we sipped glasses of thick, sweet, reviving tea laced with cardamom. Alexander dunked Glucose biscuits into hot buffalo milk.

Simon's GP brother Mark and his partner Jill came to stay. We'd set out on a walk early, but the countryside was already busy. Where the metalled road stopped, a throng of people queued in the shade of a *peepal* tree to pour milk into a tanker. Schoolgirls in navy skirts and sky-blue shirts shouted a few halting phrases in English. 'What is your country name?' 'Cute babies!'

A man fell in with us; he was dressed in traditional black jacket and jodhpurs. He carried a portable radio, dressed in floral cloth. Nepalis say that chit-chat and listening to Hindi film music shortens the journey.

Simon asked him, 'Where are you going?'

'Down,' he replied. When he realised that he could talk to Simon, he wanted to ask the questions, and later I extracted a translation.

The man asked, 'Where do you go?'

'To Namobuddha. Is it far?'

'It is the distance to dry a handkerchief. Why go there?

'We are pilgrims.' (He appeared to believe Simon's answer.)

'What is your native place?'

'England — *Blighty.*'

'What is your work?'

'Irrigation.'

'You must be rich. How much do you earn?'

'Enough.'

'Where do you work?'

'The *tarai.*'

'It is too hot there and the plains people are too dark. You should work here — we need irrigation. Your government will pay.'

'Look at all the rice growing here. You don't need any help,' Simon countered.

'But I have just ten *ropani* of land and three daughters to marry off. Take one. She could live with you in England and look after your children.'

'She wouldn't like it there. We have no rice and no chillies.'

'How can anyone live without rice and without chillies?' Then abruptly and without a goodbye he skipped off the road and disappeared along a tiny path through the rice fields.

The path started to climb through fine, scented pine forest and then, up ahead, the trees were strewn with line upon line of colourful handkerchief-sized prayer flags; from a distance it looked like a giant spider had been at work — hanging out the laundry. As we achieved the top of the ridge, the white archway of the holy village of Namobuddha came into view; behind it, houses huddled around a cluster of domed *stupas* reminiscent of the snowy Himalayas.

A woman sat in the courtyard plaiting rope out of aloe. A child played with a discarded cigarette packet. The wind tugged at tens of multicoloured prayer flags on tall flagpoles. Cicadas sang. Three goat kids chased each other between the *stupas*. Buddhists have a talent for creating these wonderful oases of calm in beautiful places. When a Buddhist offers a prayer or puts up devotional flags, he doesn't know if it is getting him or his worst enemy closer to *nirvana*. This is an antidote to the self-obsession and striving for physical perfection that is the Western disease. Here in Nepal, people seem satisfied with being ordinary, and even the gods have flaws and failings.

A man approached and addressed us in halting English. 'You have come to most holy Buddhist place. I wish you have a nice day.'

Simon acknowledged the welcome and switched easily into Nepali again. 'How are things?'

'Good.'

'Tell us why this place is so holy, brother.' The man smiled, for Nepalis love telling stories, and he entertained us for half an hour with the tale of how the Buddha on encountering a starving tigress with cubs cut strips off himself to feed her.

We wandered on with lots of stops to feed David and play 'hiding-seek' with Alexander. Finally, after a thigh-deep wade across a river, we arrived at another cluster of shrines and *stupas*, and the road at Panauti. The sun was setting and the buses had all stopped for the night.

Simon walked purposefully away, issuing instructions that we should have a glass of tea. Ten minutes later, he reappeared with a grin and news that for the princely sum of 400 Nepali rupees (about $12.50) he'd chartered an entire bus to get us home to Kathmandu.

डे डे डे

David was nearly three months old and Nepal was at its best. The monsoon petered out — on schedule — by mid-September leaving everything fresh, green and particularly beautiful. Afternoon light, filtering between remnants of monsoon clouds, picked out gullies and spot-lit patches of forest and scrub on the convoluted ridges of the rim of the Kathmandu Valley. Or, after a rainstorm, wisps of clouds clung to the forest as if scared to let go. Behind, *himals* peeked out shyly between the clouds. I could stand forever gazing dreamily at the changing shadows and colours, the butterflies and birds and the trees and swaying rice.

Mark brought information about David's syndrome and about what a lack of a corpus callosum implied. Like most medical information it was totally depressing and dwelt on the very worst aspects: there were lots of references to severe mental retardation.

'But all these syndromes are a continuum, and no-one can prognosticate,' I said switching into medical jargon to protect myself, but not believing what I was saying. Part of me wanted to talk this through, but part of me wasn't ready. Jill had been through two late miscarriages recently and I wasn't sure that I should burden her, anyway. I didn't feel I could talk, but we had lots of enjoyable trips out together and how I enjoyed just wandering through villages in the Valley, especially in such good company.

CHAPTER SIX

david's first trek

'WHY *DO* YOU FOREIGNERS LIKE TREKKING SO MUCH?' Rajesh, like most status-conscious Kathmanduites, couldn't see the point. Nepalis only trek for a purpose — a pilgrimage, visiting relatives or for work. 'And who's looking after the children while you are away?'

'We're all going.'

'So you're all going on a strenuous journey to nowhere for no reason? This is typical of Simon but you, Jane, are still recovering from your caesarean section. And surely you won't take the baby high into the mountains? What about his heart?'

'He'll be fine. There's no medical reason why we shouldn't all go. We love the mountains. It'll be fun — I think.' Three-month-old David, after all, needed even more stimulation, interest and amusement than other children. Now that his weight was steadily increasing, I knew that he was well: the medicines that I meticulously ground up and squirted into his mouth three times a day controlled his heart failure.

While I felt reasonably sure David would be fine, I wondered whether I was fit enough, so soon after his birth, even if our day-walks in the Kathmandu Valley had been enjoyable.

Simon picked a route. 'We'll keep low and mainly follow the river.'

'We *are* going to avoid that 3,000-metre climb to Ghorapaani this time, aren't we?' I pleaded, recalling the tears of sheer exhaustion I'd shed years before when we'd first walked up the Kali Gandaki.

'We could take the route towards Annapurna base camp; it starts gently, and you'd be fitter by the time we begin the real climbing. And there are plenty of lodges so that we can walk as much or as little as we like each day.'

'Sounds good,' I said, not admitting that I was intimidated by anything that Simon might call 'real climbing.'

In the following days I vacillated, one moment full of enthusiasm, the next knowing that it was definitely a crazy idea. My midwife in Cambridge had given me a chart of suitable activities for rehabilitation after a caesarean; the final goal was hoovering the house *including the stairs*. Was this as strenuous as a three-week trek to an altitude of 3,800 metres? And might the exertion reduce my milk supply? I packed some milk powder in case.

We first flew west to Pokhara. The uniformed woman in the domestic terminal did a cursory security check and asked in English, 'This is baby?' David burbled, 'glaa, glaaa' in response, while my sarcastic inner self wanted to reply, 'No, it's an archaeopteryx that I found in the garden today.'

'He's so cute!' she said.

In Pokhara, I developed a high fever and mastitis again. Although David seemed to be feeding well, it seemed that there was something wrong with his technique, my technique, which allowed infection to set in. I felt dreadful, but the antibiotics soon worked, and by the time Simon had found some porters, I was raring to go again. But I also added more antibiotics to the medical supplies we'd take. Just in case.

Simon introduced me to Chhetra Bahaadur and Kesab, two hard-up students who would work as our porters. They were an unlikely partnership; Kesab was a slight Brahmin with a face that was gravelly from acne. His high caste should have made him shun Chhetra, an untouchable blacksmith, but worldly wise Chhetra looked after his naïve young friend.

Six of us piled into a small, clapped-out Toyota Corolla taxi; the boot and one door were held closed with string. The suspension had also collapsed, but the car contained the two items that local drivers deemed indispensable: a multicoloured feather duster and tissues in a filigree box. We tumbled out with bruised bums at the tea shop at Phedi. Phedi means foot of the hill, a common name in Nepal. Kesab, who was unloading our heavy luggage, gasped at the steps that snaked up from the road at an angle of forty-five degrees. I said, 'Good grief, Simon! You said that this is the gentle route! It's vertical for a couple of hundred metres — at least!'

'I've never actually *walked* this bit of the path. It'll only be steep for the first few minutes. You'll do fine … and it will be more fun than hoovering the stairs.'

'Are you telling me *now* that you don't know this path?'

'Well …'

'You misled me, you stoat!'

He knew that there is no such thing as a gentle walk in Nepal. The first few hours are always horrendously steep.

Chhetra took charge and elected to carry David, while slender, spotty, tentative Kesab would struggle with most of the luggage. A Tibetan grandmother watched as we ineptly tried to organise the conical woven bamboo basket for David to ride in. She was selling thunderbolts crafted from silver, black ammonites sparkling with fool's gold, topaz bracelets and other trinkets. She was explaining to a tourist couple that the ammonite was Ganesh's curled trunk and therefore very holy. They were unimpressed, so she walked over to us.

'Are you really taking this small, small baby up into the mountains? He's beautiful. What happened? Did he have a harelip? And it's been repaired already, so young? He will suffocate in this basket. And how will you keep the sun off him? This umbrella is no good. He's so beautiful … such blue eyes.' I loved her cheery bossiness. She showed us how to make a sunshade, commanding Chhetra to use his freshly sharpened *khukuri* to fashion two hoops of bamboo to support some cloth. She supervised closely and only once she was satisfied did she allow us to start walking.

David rode in his basket, comfortable on his supply of Pampers, burbling happily while Chhetra chatted to him or sang songs. I envied him, mumbling bitterly as I struggled upwards. I didn't even have the energy to look for birds in the forest that clung on here. It was steep for what seemed like several hours … or days. Finally I caught up with Simon.

'You conned me, you devious dung beetle,' I glared. He grinned.

'But just think about all the housework you're avoiding!'

'Bog off!' Then, 'This is bloody silly! How do you expect me to walk in this kind of terrain!' My abuse was unfair, though. Simon was absorbed in preventing three-year-old Alexander running over some precipice or, using games of hide-and-seek, enticing him to walk. When Alexander was tired of games or the path was too dangerous, Simon carried him. How I admired and envied Simon's strength. He was happy to be in his beloved mountains. And how he patiently absorbed my childish complaints. 'Remind me what the Effingham Junction we're doing this for?'

'C'mon. You're doing well. We're already ahead of those tourists who started before us.'

I felt as if I'd been progressing at quarter speed, but this fact cheered me enormously and encouraged me on.

When the vertiginous path allowed a pause, I stopped — shaky-legged — at a rocky ledge where I could have spat onto our taxi still parked 200 metres below. Vertigo made my head spin. I felt sick; my hands grew clammy.

I looked around to make sure Alexander was safe. He and Simon were skipping up the next series of huge uneven stone steps. Slowly, feeling elderly, I followed, but at last the way was less steep and I began to be able to pace myself. And as I breathed easier, I started to see the beautiful forest, tune into bird-calls, see wall creepers and woodpeckers. I could enjoy the contrasts of coming out into cultivated land, walking amongst little terraces where maize and beans were growing, through villages, across grazing grounds dotted with tiny blue flowers and back into forest again.

Children called to us, and colourfully dressed adults stared approvingly at Alexander. '*Kasto ramro bachha!* Look how this beautiful *bideshi* child can walk!' (And, they must be thinking, look how the mother struggles!) 'And a small, small baby too!' Delighted villagers came to peek under David's sunshade-cloth and giggle and admire him. '*Such* white skin! Two fine sons! Leave one with us!' Plenty of tourists came this way, but they didn't bring children, and how Nepalis love comparing babies! Even the checkpost policemen seemed delighted to meet the children and chat. They complained that Israelis keep getting lost and give them a lot of work. Trekkers consistently ignored the boys, though, and while Alexander socialised happily with Nepalis, he soon decided that European adults were not worth even a hello.

It took more than Simon's predicted few minutes to climb the 1,500 metres to the first village of Dhampas. And only when we came out onto the top of this first grassy ridge could I look up. I scanned across the fallow fields to the cloudy horizon. 'Nice view, eh?' Simon remarked. I looked and must have frowned because he said, 'No, look up!' Emerging above the cloud layer was the towering amphitheatre of the mighty Annapurna horseshoe and nestling inside was the stately pyramidal peak of Machhapuchharé. The summit of the mountain fans out like the upturned tail of a fish and that gives it its name.

'Wow! What's my favourite mountain doing up there?' I said. 'It seems so close. Look how the snow glistens and the ice sparkles. And how blue the sky is up here!'

'Do you still wish you were back in the Fens?' Simon teased.

We gradually climbed up along the ridge, and then down into a steep, densely forested valley. I was pacing myself better now, but only when I stopped (to feed David or catch my breath) did the world really come back into focus. I'd lose track of whether Alexander and Simon were ahead, or behind me. They'd often branch off on a game of chase, then I'd hear the sound of a small boy making motorbike noises and Alexander would come running past me — such enviable energy levels. They were having such fun that I could set my own pace, rest when I wanted. I didn't admit it to Simon, but I was loving this trek. I'd half forgotten how awe-inspiring it is to be in amongst these mountains and the majestic forest.

Feeding David took some inventiveness. His conical basket looked precarious when 'parked', so while I prepared his food I propped him in a triangle made by resting my right ankle on my left knee. I could bounce him here to entertain him while I ground up his medicines or mixed baby rice with hot water from the thermos flask. I'd often find myself gazing at him, wondering about his future, wondering what really was wrong with him, with his weak muscles, failing heart and sensitive stomach.

Whatever the future, he was happy and peaceful now that he was no longer a clinical object; now that he was surrounded by love and admiration, and by the tranquillity of the forest. He developed a kind of silent laugh when he heard interesting noises or I sang to him. He cooed and chatted to me here amongst tree ferns, huge hemlock trees festooned with orchids, staghorn ferns and mosses. There were patches of intoxicatingly perfumed daphne, twittering scarlet minivets, sunbirds and whistling thrushes. Purple primroses and delicate violets poked out of damp rocky crevices.

Suddenly Simon was beside me. 'Beware of those flowers!' he said.

'Why? They're only aconites, not triffids.'

'They're called *beek*: it means poison. Gorgeous blue, though.'

'Do you know of anyone who has been poisoned with it then?' I asked.

'No. I heard it from Limbu friends; but they'll say anything to make a good story.'

'But I've read that it really is toxic. Medea used it to poison Theseus.'

As we climbed higher, the path became precipitous again; the river, way below now, sounded like a distant raging beast. Simon worried about Alexander going over the edge but I was so obsessed with just getting myself along the path that I was hardly aware of them up ahead. All I could focus on was the path. I reached the top of a ridge only to descend, then up and up again.

As I panted in to the hamlet of Jhinu, Chhetra asked, 'You like hot bath, *memsahib*?'

'Ha, ha, very funny. Don't you start teasing me too!'

'I am not teasing. We coming to hot water place.' I wasn't keen to make any detours, but a hot spring was irresistible. Boiling sulphurous water had been cleverly diverted to mix with the right amount of cold water, creating a pool that was at perfect bath temperature. I longed to go in, but locals would think it unseemly if I took off my clothes. I dipped David in and he smiled as he kicked his seldom-used legs. Then — and he must have been watching me all along — I saw the langur lookout sitting on a large rock in the middle of the river; his troop-mates were browsing, furry bell-pull tails dangling in trees that overhung the river. When I smiled at him, he looked away and examined his fingernails. He was handsome, lanky, mostly cream-coloured but with a spiky shock of white hair, whiskers and beard surrounding an intelligent, jet-black primate face.

It was a long, hot, dry struggle further on up. Sometimes I'd walk right behind Chhetra, listening to David chatting softly — 'glaa, glaa, glaa' — while I gasped for every breath. Sometimes I'd collapse onto some rock to rest while Chhetra chugged steadily, strongly upwards ahead. From time to time, he would stop and wait until I'd arrive gasping, 'How is he?'

'My Dabid is fast-asleeping,' Chhetra would smile, proud-parent-like.

Then again I'd follow for a while, concentrating on watching Chhetra place each footstep, concentrating on keeping my breathing even, needing to stop frequently. Once I caught them up to hear David burbling contentedly, while Chhetra chatted amiably back, 'Be happy, Dabid!'

Then Chhetra said, '*Sahib* is feeling very weak today.' Simon seldom complained, even if he was ill. Maybe he had gastroenteritis. Had Chhetra seen signs of illness in Simon that I was too exhausted to notice?

'Let's wait for them here,' I said, crumpling onto a narrow, grassy patch of flattish ground. From here, I could look down almost vertically on Jhinu. Nepali voices floated up from there. The valley was covered in terraces for thousands of vertical feet, down to the river, way, way below — and up the other side. These rural people work hard just to survive. Simon was taking a very long time; I began to worry. I'd had plenty of time to catch my breath and by now some of my fatigue had seeped away. Just as I was beginning to wonder if I'd ever see them again, Alexander wandered up the steps, grinning happily. 'Want to play hiding-seek too, Mummy?'

'Not today — sorry. You are a hero, Simon!'

'So am I!' said Alexander. Simon's pace was either very slow when he encouraged Alexander to walk or, if Simon carried Alexander, they walked faster than most Nepalis and twice as fast as any tourist. This puzzled Chhetra. If the *sahib* could walk fast, why did he loiter?

I started to get up, but my muscles had seized solid. I felt as if I was audibly creaking as I struggled painfully to my feet. This was only my third trek ever; the last had been four years before and I was very, very unfit. I switched my brain to automatic as we continued up and up lots and lots of steps. I'd been overtaking and overtaken by a wizened old porter carrying a pile of tables for a party of trekkers who were camping. He — like me — stopped often to catch his breath. My halting Nepali allowed a bit of a conversation.

He asked the usual questions. 'Where have you come from?'

'Where will you sleep tonight?'

'What is your husband's work? How much does he earn?'

'What is your native place?'

'Are your other children in your native country?'

Then, 'Only two children? *Memsahib* is unfortunate.'

'How many wives does *memsahib*'s husband have?' My responses to these routine questions sounded fluent, but once we got beyond those phrases, I gave up trying to communicate and sat grinning inanely at him; it was easier than talking or thinking. I overtook him for the last time just as I reached the top outside Chomrong village. Finally, he asked, 'Are you suffering, *didi*?'

Trying to disguise my breathlessness, I strode out strongly, but my knees were wobbling and it was obvious I was exhausted. Spotting Alexander running in the garden of the Annapurna View Lodge encouraged me on, and finally I arrived at some tables. I stood with my legs trembling, wondering for a moment whether I could sit, but soon slumped onto a bench hoping I'd never need to get up again.

A notice caught my attention:

> *IN THIS HOTEL — Freeze for cold drink — Rooms are decorated floor mat*

And before I got my breath back, Simon (with David in his arms and Alexander at his heels) planted a kiss on my steaming forehead and thrust a hot lemon drink into my hand. 'You made it!' he said.

'Careful! Haven't you seen the notices? Look —'

> *THERE MUST BE NO OUTWARD SIGNS OF AFFECTION IN THE ANNAPURNA CONSERVATION REGION*

'Perhaps you should respond to this, then?' He pointed to another sign that asked, 'Is your guid handling you in right places?'

'No — high-altitude trekking inhibits the libido.'

'Hmm. Yours, maybe,' he said, nudging me.

Alexander chipped in. 'Look, I've got this shiny streering wheel.' And he put his imaginary car into gear and drove off using a metal plate to steer. By now, he'd perfected asking politely in Nepali for an empty plate at any lodge we stopped at, and brrmm-brrmmed happily around until the rice was cooked.

Once I had rehydrated, I began to look around. Chhetra and Kesab were having an animated conversation — but I couldn't get Simon to translate.

'It's just inconsequential, time-filling chit-chat.'

I looked out at the spectacular mountain scenery. Seemingly only a stone's throw away stood Annapurna South and its Siamese twin Hiunchuli. The Patal Ganga Glacier, wedged between the two giants, slid, cracked and jerked painfully downwards like an old arthritic beast. I watched an avalanche — like a cloud pouring off the mountain. I sat in awe, feeling absolutely no desire whatsoever to conquer even a minor trekking peak.

'How close Machhapuchharé looks now! Look how it's dwarfed against the Annapurnas,' I said, gazing at the superb angular pinnacle that peeked out shyly from the clouds; the jet stream blew snowy spindrift off the knife-edge ridges. 'You don't want to climb it then?' I added, thinking he might be feeling frustrated not to be up there.

'Not today,' he said. 'Looks completely impossible. Hard to imagine that a team almost summitted it thirty years ago. Once they'd got safely back down, they persuaded the king to declare it sacred, so no-one could better their attempt. No-one's been given permission to climb it since.'

'Now why will you pontificate about mountaineering and refuse to eavesdrop for me. I wish you were more interested in gossip!' I said, feeling frustrated at being an outsider. I had only been half-listening really; perusing the menu was more interesting. 'Can you order me some food? I can't move … legs have seized. I'll skip the Vegetable Craps. Mixed Tonic Soup sounds just what I need.'

'I'll order some and find out what it is. Give me David. You grab a shower before you cool down too much. There's a solar water heater.'

'Sounds delicious.' And it was. The floor was cold but the feeling of hot water washing the sweat and stickiness away was unimaginably luxurious.

Next day, Simon and Alexander were soon way on ahead of me again. The thin air at 3,000 metres really took away what little spare breath I had. It wasn't until much later, and breathing hard, that I caught up with them. 'I thought you said that we'd contour around to Ghorapaani today. This is a mountain-assault, not a contour walk!' I said testily.

'Everything's relative! Is it more strenuous than hoovering the stairs?'

'Shut up!' I spat. '*You* can have the next baby, you elephant dropping.'

'Thanks. But it seemed an easy route last time … though I walked in the opposite direction. I forgot that there was so much climbing. C'mon, it is worth the effort getting up here, isn't it?' he said, putting an arm around me.

'Yes, I suppose so. The rhododendron forest is glorious. I love the sinuous red trunks, and look how the sun reflects off the waxy leaves.'

'And the Annapurnas in the background,' he said, gazing across to the snow.

'I still reckon that you conned me, though.' I still felt miffed with him.

'Never mind. Look, there are gentians everywhere. Aquilegia, too.'

'Huh. They're only animal food really,' I said, determined not to seem impressed. 'Have you noticed how dark the butterflies are up here? The higher you climb, the darker insects become — the sun warms dark insects quicker and so they can fly in cold mountain air. Clever, eh?'

'I suppose several people have done PhDs on the subject,' Simon said.

'Probably. And one Dr Mani has written a huge tome on high altitude insects.'

'Sounds irresistible. But I can do one better. Someone — a British vet — has written a book about the leeches found inside the noses of Nepali goats!'

'Great — how useful,' I said witheringly. 'Look, Chhetra is way on ahead with David. Let's go on.'

Even standing for a moment made me feel as if I would creak as I started walking again, but the path took us gently downhill towards a village straddling a saddle in the ridge. 'This is Ghorapaani next, isn't it?' I asked Simon. 'I thought *ghora* meant fair-skinned?'

'No that's *gora*, with normal unaspirated consonants. *Ghorapaani* means horsewater — the *g* is aspirated and the *r* is retroflex.'

'Say both of them, then, cleverclogs.' He did, and I couldn't really hear the difference. 'I'm never going to learn to speak this language, am I?' I said, feeling defeated — by the terrain too.

'You will. Be patient,' he said.

The next time I caught up, Simon had the binoculars trained on something. I clumsily stomped up to him and asked, 'Bird?'

'No, some nineteen-year-old alders.'

'You're bullshitting again. How do you know they're nineteen years old?'

'They're growing on a landslide. Can you see it?' he said, pointing across to the other side of the steep-walled valley. 'There, where all the trees look the same size.'

'Is it a very special landslide, then?' I said sarcastically, thinking this must be another of Simon's wind-ups.

'No, but twenty years ago, when I was a VSO, I was asked to stop that particular landslide taking that village down the mountain,' he said, pointing again.

'What did you suggest?' I asked, impressed he was that useful even as a new graduate.

'Oh, to plant some trees and dig a few drains.'

'Is that enough to stop a landslide?'

'No, but it probably helped a bit. It is good to see that the village is still there!' Then, never being one to dwell on his successes, he said, 'Hey, would you like a sardine?' Simon handed the tin to Chhetra, who skilfully opened it with his *khukuri,* and the five of us shared this unexpected treat.

While I nibbled and David suckled, I watched a dung beetle laboriously rolling her treasure across a patch of bare ground. I was sitting on a *chautara*, a stone resting place built around the tangled roots of two imposing figs trees: a *peepal* and a *banyan*. Simon explained that they were often planted together and when they reached maturity there was a formal marriage ceremony. These tree-couples are planted all over the middle hills of Nepal to provide resting places in the shade for countless travellers, and the stepped stones make it easy for porters to put down their loads.

The path took us on down to the Kali Gandaki, but within minutes of reaching the river, the glaring, hot path started to climb again; we scaled increasingly vertiginous drops, only to descend a few metres further on. This valley walk had us climbing up to cross a spur, then down to the river, and up and down and up for a couple of days. Alexander motored on, giving us some anxious moments when he practised three-point turns close to precipitous edges. David, happy as ever, babbled, cooed and chuckled, or just slept. Chhetra never hesitated as he plodded sure-footedly onwards, and I appreciated why he, not frail Kesab, was carrying David.

Around eleven each day, we'd walk past huddles of porters cooking rice on wood collected from the forest, or shovelling rice down their throats. In order to eat enough to work as a porter it is necessary to beat the appetite by eating very fast. There were lots of ripped-up playing cards scattered on the path: a memorial to fiery gamblers' emotions.

As we walked into the village of Ghasa, I caught the cosy smell of wood smoke. A woman sat out in the sun in the doorway of her house, a few-month-old baby in her lap. She was massaging it with thick, yellow cooking oil; she looked like she was preparing a joint for the oven. Two giggling young women shouted out something to Simon about oranges.

'What was that about?'

'They were complimenting me on the size of my woman's breasts! Teasing — being lewd.'

'You'd have been embarrassed if an English woman said something like that!'

'No, I wouldn't!'

I was amused at his split personality; he seemed so much more comfortable with himself and others when speaking Nepali. Some things were just easier to express, perhaps.

Children stampeded out of their flat-roofed houses and along echoing, cobbled paths. They came to stare and scrounge sweets. I asked, 'Where is your school, brothers and sisters?'

They conferred in whispers. 'These foreigners can speak Nepali!' An older boy replied, standing to attention, 'There is a school in Ghasa, *didi*. Close by.' They then battered us with questions, delighted to be able to communicate. I'd become quite fluent in answering the usual queries about the children, but I still needed some help from Simon with translations.

'What class is madam's first-born son in?'

'How old do you think he is?' I responded, surprised by the question.

'Seven.'

'He's three!' I told them. They were incredulous. They asked, 'Why do you have only two children, madam?'

'Two is enough.'

'But who will look after your goats?' A small surrogate mother joined in. 'And auntie, it is dangerous for the baby to have no hat. He must wear a hat!'

'How old are you, little sister?'

'Eight.'

'Do you go to school?'

'No, auntie. School is not possible. My brothers go, but I look after the younger children and the goats, and I bring water, firewood.' Then I noticed we were entertaining a child with cerebral palsy. He was about ten and had been left out to bask in the sun and watch the world go by while his siblings and cousins and neighbours played around him. He was part of the community, well cared for, involved; he wasn't hidden away like our handicapped children are. Here, each and every child could have normal friendships, and thus teach those without a handicap what life is like for the disabled.

Each box-like house in Ghasa had a ladder or tree trunk with notches cut out so that people could climb onto the flat roof to sun themselves, do household chores or lay out maize or apricots or apples to dry. A drunk staggered up and lunged at Alexander, intending to tweak his cheek, but Alexander, well used to what he considered a wholly bad Nepali habit, skilfully dodged, wandered off to find more civilised company and was soon talking with another group of kids. We walked on up through the steep, cobbled main street as Alexander ran to catch up.

'What were you talking about?' I asked him, intrigued at his ability to communicate.

'It's a seclet.'

'Were you speaking Nepali?'

'I was teaching them English!' he explained, as his new-found friends shouted, 'Seven socks!'

Then Alexander spotted an avenue of long, thin, vertical prayer flags leading to the temple. 'Ooh, can I bang the gongs?'

'No, I don't think that would be respectful.' But the *lama* who ushered us into the scented gloom showed Alexander how to hit them to make the most noise. The painted roof was supported by two huge, magnificently carved timbers arranged as a T: a design that withstands earthquakes. It took a while before we made out statues of the Buddha and saints, and lines of huge drums made of goat skins. In an anteroom, Alexander was also delighted to find a gaudy, three-metre-high prayer wheel that rang a bell every time he turned it. Outside, covered courtyard walls were painted with ferocious protector deities.

Innumerable landslides scarred this stretch of the valley. One slip and you'd tumble into the boiling river 300 metres below. Small Nepali feet had made narrow tracks across the slips that allowed only one-way traffic. I watched a team of porters carefully adjust their loads and edge down. Their bodies were shaped by a lifetime as beasts of burden: their calves, latticed with varicose veins, were almost as thick as my thighs; their skulls were permanently furrowed from the weight borne on headbands; faces were lined by harsh, Himalayan sun and cheap cigarettes; feet, crevassed as any glacier, were shovel-like, with toes splayed. Several carried well-worn bamboo hoops to scrape off sweat. The average Nepali porter weighs fifty-four kilograms and carries seventy. The last in the line looked overloaded even by local standards.

'How much are you carrying, brother?'

'A hundred kilos!' the porter replied, with a huge, proud grin.

When it was our turn to cross, I said, 'Chhetra, please be careful!' He smiled at my nervousness, radiating calm competence. This was his country. Yet it was a country that did not treat him well; when we looked for lodgings, he concealed his pariah status by giving a false name. Low-caste people like Chhetra are called *paani nachunne*: literally, 'must not touch water' — someone who is forbidden from taking water from the same well as high-caste Hindus; those who transgress are beaten sometimes to death. An untouchable might not be allowed to lodge even amongst outcaste foreigners. His caste was with him for life — unless he converted to Islam or Christianity, but even then people would know. He was in his late twenties but still struggling to save money and pass his Intermediate Certificate for eighteen-year-olds. Job prospects in Nepal are bad enough; they are worse for untouchables, and without exams he would have no hope of steady work. He showed me his English grammar book; it contained useful vocabulary like 'man-of-war', 'chain mail' and 'seductress'.

There were now lines of pine trees growing wherever the slope would allow. We were getting high again. The valley was so very sheer now that our necks ached from trying to see the sky, and the sun hardly reached us. The silver-grey cliff walls we walked between rose sheer for at least 1,000 metres and then on up to the real 8,000-metre mountains. Like the boy with cerebral palsy, we basked like lizards whenever we could find a patch of sun, although when I breast-fed David, I tried to sit with my back to the rays so that it warmed me without dazzling him.

We stopped for lunch at Hotel Deep of Worldtop. The owner came over and asked, 'You need how many plate *daal bhat*?'

'Five. Please put in lots of ginger and garlic and chillies; we like spicy food.'

'But you foreigners cannot eat spicy food.'

'We can; we do. And tell us, brother, about the name of your hotel.'

'This deepest valley in world. One side Annapurna; otherside Dhaulagiri: highest and deepest of worldtop.'

The food came and Chhetra mumbled a now-familiar complaint: 'Food in tourist lodges has no taste. They never put any spices.' And he asked for dried chillies to nibble between mouthfuls. Simon said, 'I'll have some, too.'

'There's something wrong with your palate, Simon!' I said. David ate well. He was more vocal and was clearly enjoying the trip. His one occasional concern was the wind on his face. It provoked a primitive diving reflex that made him hold his breath for a second or two, but it was easy to protect him in his snug basket. And if he seemed unsettled, Chhetra would say, 'Be happy, Dabid!' and sing him a song. In hospital in Cambridge, where all the vomiting and fluid-wasting medicines dehydrated him, David's lips had become horribly cracked and sore, but strangely that wasn't a problem in this harsh, desiccating mountain air.

We'd crossed the Himalayan watershed and had reached the edge of the desert of the Tibetan Plateau. Terrific winds funnelled through the sheer, stark valley and obviously made landing a light aircraft hazardous: there was one nose-down in the river at the end of the runway. Jomsom, the capital and administrative centre for the Mustang District, was an army camp surrounded by concrete houses and shops, lodges and new hotels. The main street was smelly with deposits left by children, yaks, dzos, mules, goats and chickens. We didn't linger. Beyond, the going was flat: a wasteland of cobbles in the wide, wide flood plain of the river. A biting, dust-laden wind sandblasted us. David was the only one who was comfortable, warm and not choking, cosily tucked up as he was in the top of his big bamboo basket under a large bath towel. He kept up long burbling conversions with himself.

Om mani padme hum (the mantra 'Hail, jewel in the lotus') was carved four-metres-high in Tibetan script on a huge boulder. Ahead at 2,807 metres, Kag Beni — the fortress town controlling trade north to south — looked remote, exciting. It was set amidst a patchwork of fallow fields and apricot orchards surrounded by crags covered with a thin sprinkling of snow. We entered the town through a low gateway topped by a huge breast-shaped *stupa*, and then plunged into a labyrinth of alleys and tunnels between cram-packed houses. It smelt medieval, with whiffs of unwashed humanity whenever anyone passed.

We unloaded at a lodge, ordered food, and — while the rice was cooking — wandered out, me carrying David in the papoose. At the edge of the village, a group of women sat in the sun, spinning and removing lice from each other's hair. They called us over when they saw Alexander; then they noticed David and giggled with delight. They were even more pleased when they realised I could speak a little Nepali. 'Take him out! Let us see him! We must hold him!' Then, 'What beauty he has! What happened to his face, *didi*? And he has had an operation? How neatly the harelip has been repaired! There is one boy in Kag Beni; he must go to your country for this operation.'

'It is possible in Kathmandu too.'

'Yes? Kathmandu is also very far.'

David made a sound, so they immediately thrust him back into my arms. 'He needs your milk!'

The final climb up a side valley to Muktinath got us out of the wind at last. The air was thin. So little oxygen. I couldn't. Fill up. My tiny, shrunken lungs. No bigger than a dog's scrotum. However deeply. I inhaled. Had to stop. Often. To suck. Air in.

As I paused to get my breath back, I saw out beyond my feet again. The mountain air was hugely invigorating and the scenery sublime. Looking back down the river, the water sparkled like cut glass. The sun spotlit lines of deep-green pine trees on the interlocking spurs that had forced the river into meanders. The valley and mountains above were spectacularly folded and coloured by metal ores; subtle red, purple, orange, green, bluish and heron-grey strata were stacked like playing cards. The landscape of scree and crags had a stark grandeur that moved me, but … I needed to catch up again.

Alexander either ran on ahead or swept the path with bits of dried bush. We walked with wealthy townies dressed in brand-new peach or pink tracksuits bought especially for their 'pilgrimage'. Hindu pilgrims and ascetics had been walking up this way from India since 300 BC. Now people fly to Jomsom, and thence flabby parents stagger under their fat children; grandmothers in saris totter behind. Chhetra said disdainfully 'Look! Nepali tourists!'

Finally, we reached Muktinath at 3,800 metres, where amongst the poplars each chilly morning at dawn fasting pilgrims bathe in ice-cold water that pours from 108 carved-stone cow's-head spouts and pray at the holy, natural gas flame.

We joined other trekkers huddling around the fire in the lodge that evening. A woman of twenty-something who spoke with a Home Counties accent said, 'Gosh — children! My, you're brave bringing kids up here!'

Then, to Simon, 'What *are* you drinking? It's steaming.'

'*Rakshi*.' Then, in response to her puzzled frown, Simon added, 'Distilled fermented anything. I think that this was made from maize, which has the worst hangover potential. The connoisseurs say that the best is made from millet.

'You sound like a connoisseur yourself. Do you work here?'

'Yes. I'm a civil engineer. What do you do?'

'I'm a secretary — in London. It must be wonderful living amongst these happy, carefree people. They're always smiling. They have a wonderful life, away from all the stresses we have.'

'They have stresses, too. Illness, no doctors, no food. Their smiles cover a lot of grief.'

'Nepalis live for each day,' I said, 'like people with a cancer or alcoholism.'

'That's what I mean. They're so spontaneous.' She wanted to keep her mirage. 'Are you going to cross the Thorong La?' she asked me.

'Of course,' Simon chipped in to tease me. 'We'll get a horse for you!'

The secretary said, 'The guidebook says that crossing from this side is harder — it's a long, hard, 1,300-metre climb.' Kesab looked worried that we really might want to try the pass.

'It's a hell of a climb,' said one guy. 'I sucked up *all* the air that's up there!' The chat was all about high-altitude illness, avalanches and deaths, yet it looked a deceptively gentle climb. I was tantalised, but crossing would put the children at risk. I left the trekkers — to wash some undies in painfully cold water, while Simon told Alexander the story of Goldilocks and the three yetis.

It was a long, cold, cold night. Delicate David was fine, but Alexander was off-colour and, as he slept, there were long gaps between breaths: the gasping Cheyne-Stokes breathing pattern of the dying that healthy people adopt at altitude. I lay awake for most of the night, worrying. As soon as Simon woke, I blurted out, 'I don't think we should go up.' My breath hung in clouds in front of my face. 'We don't have enough warm clothes. I'm really not up to this climb, horse or not. I don't want to go higher. You know David puked? It's strange for him to be sick at night.'

'Relax, I was only teasing you about the horse!'

As I put on my painfully cold, clammy clothes, I was relieved we'd decided to head back — south. The skies cleared and the air began to feel less icy. Sharp, silver sunlight reflected in the river and picked out the colours of the rocks and the sturdy pines. Above, spectacular minor peaks beckoned Alexander and Simon. Soon they were scrambling up amongst grey boulders and scree, towards the closest glacier. I was content nibbling tangy dried apricots.

We meandered pleasantly on down over three days. Local kids welcomed Alexander back in Ghasa with cries of 'Seven socks!' Then, on the nineteenth day, we reached the road and caught a Super Sonic night express home to Kathmandu. A woman asked, 'Your baby is how old, *didi*?' Then, 'Four-month-old Nepali babies can stand on their legs,' she said.

'He's not so strong; he's been ill.' I was too tired to struggle to explain in broken Nepali and I let the conversation fade so that I could muse and catnap. It had been a superb trek. I was proud of Alexander: he had walked half the distance — one hundred miles — and he'd enjoyed it. We all had. Even David, with his delicate stomach, light-sensitive eyes and weak heart, had been animated by the trip. I had been scared many times. I thought about the risks we'd taken, how David or Alexander might have perished on the trek. It wasn't until much later I saw that my inexperience and fatigue had exaggerated the dangers. Towards the end of our five plus years in the country, we covered some of the same ground again and Simon and I were amazed how easy the route seemed that second time around. By then, though, we were mentally stronger; less vulnerable.

I celebrated our return to Kathmandu by buying *Tintin in Tibet*. Alexander was delighted, for it contained all the elements of our trek: rocky paths, snowy mountains, *lamas*, gongs, drunks, yaks and a plane crash, as well as a kindly yeti.

CHAPTER SEVEN

the clever doctors

BY NOVEMBER — WHEN HE WAS FOUR MONTHS OLD — David seemed so amazingly well that I finally summoned up my courage to reduce his heart medicines. This was the only way to discover whether he needed them. I was, though, still intimidated by the Cambridge doctors, despite being a doctor myself and their being 12,000 kilometres away. My logical, clinical self argued with my emotional, maternal self. I anxiously, guiltily cut the doses by a quarter; no difference. To a half; no difference. Down to a quarter of the original doses. No difference. I stopped the medicines one at a time. No difference.

I waited, on edge for weeks, wondering when David's heart would start failing again, making him breathless. But it never did. He remained resilient, rosy-cheeked and thriving, if a touch skinny. His murmur was growing louder, too: a sure sign that something was happening to the holes in his heart. What was going on inside his little body? The Clever Doctors had said that the holes in David's heart were too big to close on their own; that he would definitely need at least one operation. But David *was* getting better. Could the experts be wrong?

Basant, talking as effusively as ever, noticed it too. 'David is looking little bit fatty these days. I think he is getting well, no? It is good now he not needing pipe in nose, *memsahib*.'

'Yes, Nepal suits him.'

'He need new suit, *memsahib*?'

'Maybe, but not today.' I kept forgetting that I needed to edit idiomatic expressions from my chit-chat with Basant. He continued indefatigably, 'You must get hat for him. He got no hair so he needing hat or he get cold inside!'

David was improving and feeding well; he smiled, burbled and seemed content. He was happiest and most comfortable when he was left lying flat on his back on a cotton-stuffed quilt on the floor, where he regarded the ceiling with rapt absorption. He seemed easily tired when we picked him up or cuddled him, so we kept him in the room we were in, or in the kitchen while I cooked. I'd put him in a bouncy chair where he could see us better. Or I'd take him out in the garden while Alexander played, always trying to keep him involved in whatever was going on.

I played lots of music. I also frequently made conscious efforts to pick him up, get close, talk, touch, play games and sing daft songs — not that I'm very musical. I made one up to a tune that started like that nauseating ditty 'If You're Happy and You Know It' and degenerated into something like 'On Ilkley Moor Baht 'at'; it went *David, David, how are you? David, David, how are you? David, David, how — are — you? David, David; David, David, how are you?* And, holding his wrists, I tried to get him doing a kind of hand-jive. He seemed to listen but he never made eye contact and hardly responded however hard I tried. I was besotted, but he remained so still — like a rag doll — that I sometimes got scared thinking that I might never really reach him. The mother–baby bond is a two way thing: most babies find innumerable ways of getting themselves picked up, ensuring that they are always the centre of attention. Was it that he did not want to make contact, or was he almost blind?

Thinking about how life would be for him as he grew threw me into a spin. Babies usually smile before their sixth week; he hadn't smiled until he was ten weeks old. I tried to reason that he would just take longer to achieve each of his developmental 'milestones'. So far he seemed to be developing at about half speed. I took great comfort in any signs of progress, though, and as life was easy for us in such a child-friendly place, managed mostly to avoid pondering on his future.

One evening Alexander and I squeezed aboard the crowded Kathmandu-bound trolley-bus in medieval Bhaktapur. We'd been out exploring all day, and David in the front-carrier was tired, hot and unimpressed.

Everyone stared as he howled, but I was jammed in so that I could hardly have even picked my nose. Women pointed at my breasts: 'Give him milk!' 'Feed him!' A seat was freed for me; everyone beamed as, slightly embarrassed, I sat down to suckle him while Alexander was given sweets and plonked on someone's lap close beside me. Then everyone in the bus touched a hand to their forehead, then their chest and their forehead again: a prayer on crossing the holy Bagmati River.

The polyglot playgroups continued, and we continued to enjoy getting to know the city and the Kathmandu Valley. We ate out a great deal and often met Simon for lunch. To pass the time waiting for the order, we would pick out all the spelling mistakes in the menu. Then we compiled a composite menu of the best ones, thus:

MENU

LIGHT FOOD

Scrumpled Egg or Anykind

Muligatwany Soup — an Old Indo-Anglican Dish

Boiled Green Salad

Cold Slow Salad

Egg Wege Fried Chowmein

Chicken Snowballs

Spigot with Garlic or Meat Sauce

Finger Cheeps

HEAVY FOOD

Seasonal Veg All Gratin — Freshgarden vegetables with cream sauce under salamander

Tender Lion Steak

Coq Breasts Boiled in Wine Sauce

Vegatable Jhal Fridge

Giardinella Pizza

Sordid Vegetables

Mass Potato

PUDDING ITEMS

Crepsuzer

Banana Flambeau

Apple Pi

Apple or Banana Filtre

Mixed Fried Custard

Leeches with Ice Cream

DRINKS

Hard Drinks by Peg

Bears: Carlsberg, Ice Berg, Tuberg, San Miguel

डे डे डे

By December, Simon's work on the Bagmati Basin Management Plan in Kathmandu was coming to an end. He and the team had produced a vast report of detailed suggestions for how to clean up the polluted rivers of the Kathmandu Valley, and how water resources could be improved. That task completed, there was time to return to Britain for a Christmas holiday before he started work on the Rajapur project.

It was great to reconnect with our family — let them get to know David a little more — but it was with trepidation that we took him back to see all the specialists who felt they should have some control over David's life. Simon came to these appointments too, but the doctors rarely talked to him. He wouldn't understand, being a lay parent. And he rarely said anything — except later to me.

I was especially nervous as we entered the cardiologist's office in Great Ormond Street. It felt like turning David in for sentencing. I was knotted up inside, anxious to perform well as David's advocate. I not only had to admit that I had stopped David's medicines, but we would be making plans for those risky, painful operations to close the holes in his heart.

'How is he?' The consultant asked.

'Very well — I think. I hope,' I said, forcing a nervous grin.

'What dose of captopril is he taking now?'

'I, um … stopped his heart drugs,' I sheepishly admitted. 'He didn't seem to need them.'

The consultant smiled and said, 'Actually, Addenbrooke's still had him on the tiny test dose anyway; you are right, he clearly does not need them! He's fine, well-perfused; no cyanosis. The holes in his heart seem to be closing spontaneously, too.'

'Closing? Are you sure?'

'Yes. They're much smaller now. I never would've guessed he would do so well. He may never need those operations.'

Encouraged by this near-admission of fallibility, I confessed, 'Um, we took David up into the mountains. To 4,000 metres. I suppose we shouldn't have, but it was great, and he stayed well.'

'To 4,000 metres? That's significantly high. Interesting. Mmm … David's polycythaemia makes him better at coping with the low oxygen at altitude. Fascinating. Will you be doing more treks?'

'We hadn't planned anything — for a while anyway … but, um … will you be frank with us? Do you think it would be all right to take David to somewhere remote, long-term? It's not in the mountains. It's an island with no electricity. We want to go. The climate will be healthy: warm and dry. I'll have plenty of home help, but no medical back-up. Is it a crazy idea?'

'No, you've managed to look after him fine so far. Just don't delay treating him if he gets any chest infections. He'll be more susceptible than other children.'

I liked the way he carefully avoided using the word 'normal'. There was David, and there were 'other children'; it sounded wonderfully Nepali. 'Just come and see me next time you are in England.'

Outside, Simon asked, 'What's polycythaemia?'

'Too many red blood cells. David's producing more to compensate for his heart failure, so he's pre-adapted to altitude! And "well-perfused" translates as rosy cheeked. You know, that's the first doctor we've seen who has implied that I'm competent to look after my own child. It's such a relief not to be treated like a naughty schoolkid.'

'Yes, he was good, apart from the usual surfeit of medical jargon. He explained things and let us talk — answered questions.'

'Does that mean we can go home then, Mummy?' said Alexander.

'Yes, we're going back.'

'Goodie! Back to nice old Kathmandu!'

'So … if we'd listened to David's doctors, he would by now have had his ribcage sawn open twice and, assuming he survived, there would have been more tests, and those calories to build him up and make him vomit. They quoted a one in ten chance of dying from the operations. Do you remember my cousin Kevin's son — with Down syndrome? He died suddenly at thirteen months, just ten days after his big open-heart operation. So finally we know we were right to take David away.' I was dizzy with euphoria. 'We've been vindicated at last!'

‘Maybe it’s time for some champagne!’ said Simon.

The large, bumbling genetics consultant wanted to see us too. This time he was jovial and informative, and took time to introduce himself even to Alexander.

‘Hello, young man. What’s your name? I’m Dr Green; you might guess that, because of my green jacket!’ Alexander regarded the nurse, who was dressed in scarlet. ‘Is she Dr Red?’

Dr Green made us feel safe enough to ask questions that we’d dared not ask other specialists.

‘I did everything wrong in my first pregnancy: drank alcohol, ate dangerous foods, conceived immediately after stopping the pill, no vitamins … and Alexander was perfect, still is!’

‘Are you never naughty, Alexander?’ Dr Green asked.

‘Sometimes,’ he said, pouting slightly.

‘I was careful during my pregnancy with David. I was teetotal, took the vitamins, folic acid, had amniocentesis. Perhaps something I did during my pregnancy caused David’s problems?’

‘As you know, we’ve already done the tests and as far as we can tell there is no faulty gene, so it is difficult to say.’

‘Might the immunisations and malaria pills have been to blame?’

‘Immunisation ten days before conception may have given you a slight fever, which would theoretically increase the risks of abnormalities. There was some research even suggesting that taking very hot baths in early pregnancy increased rates of foetal malformations, but the evidence was a bit thin. Chloroquine, now … that can occasionally cause problems; but, again, we cannot lay the blame there. I’ll send you the review paper so that you can make up your own mind.’

‘How about inadvertently eating pesticides on food while we lived in Pakistan? There’s no control and they spray them about everywhere. Fruit sellers even squirt pesticides onto fruit and tomatoes to make them look nice and shiny!’

‘Hmm … not recommended practice, but pesticides in the environment — an unlikely culprit. I think the answer is that we do not know.' He fielded our questions expertly and with each answer he was reassuring. 'There are probably no reasons. You are not to blame in any way.' But he did little to alleviate my nagging guilt about somehow causing David's problems: logic and medical reason just didn't help. If I'd not had that vaccine, if I had not taken malaria pills, if I'd refused to live in Pakistan and so avoided eating pesticides, might David have been born whole? I'd never feel completely easy in my mind.

Then out of the blue, and to my great surprise, Simon asked, 'And what is the chance of another child being affected, if we decided to have another baby?' He was one step ahead of me again.

'The risk is low, but slightly increased: two to three per cent,' he said confidently. 'And — of course — the screening can be more meticulous, with special scans for heart and neurological defects.'

As we walked out of the hospital, I said, 'Those numbers he quoted, they seemed good odds: safe enough to try for another baby.'

Simon pulled a face and said, 'Sounds risky to me.'

'It's not risky compared to the one in five chance each Nepali has of dying before its fifth birthday.'

'Possibly.' Simon disagreed.

We saw an ophthalmologist and orthoptists who said, 'You should probably patch David's good eye, to make his squinting eye do some work.'

'Probably? Will it help him?'

'It might, but we are not sure what he can see,' the orthoptist said. 'You can patch David's good eye closed for half an hour each day and then you must play games to make him look with his weak eye.' They seemed so unconvinced that it would help him that, although I took the patches, I didn't know whether I'd use them.

We saw the neurologist who had been so supportive before we'd fled to Nepal with David. I had tried to corner him into giving us a prognosis when David was six weeks old, but when he'd sidestepped direct questions we didn't pursue the discussion, for our minds strayed to more immediate issues. I think at that time we also blocked his gentle hints of news that we didn't want to hear. Now that David was doing more, I pressed him again to predict David's future, expecting a more optimistic bulletin.

When he said, 'We continue to have concerns,' I started to dislike him.

'What are the chances that David will ever be capable of living independently?'

'I don't know.'

'Do you think he will ever walk … or talk?'

'I don't know.'

'Look, I know that you can't be sure, but could you just give us some idea of the possibilities?'

'I don't know.' He looked straight at me, unblinking. Lizard-like. I hated him now.

'We are not going to hold you to anything if you are wrong. Please won't you, as one doctor to another, let us have some idea? Your best educated guesses will help us; we need to know.'

'All I can say is that if this was my child I would have grave concerns. There are three scenarios. The worst is that he'll be immobile, unable to communicate and doubly incontinent.' The best scenario seemed little better. He gave no more away. Or that's how I saw it at the time. Now I understand that he felt very pessimistic. He was wise in not confronting us. He was telling us in a way we'd absorb when we were ready. If I'd wanted to hear, the message he was giving was loud and clear, although the way he spoke to us made us incredulous. We had seen David progress; the neurologist was mistaken. We needed unrealistic hopes. If we'd known everything then, it would have been hard to cope. Right from the start we'd had our fears, clutched at straws of hope and gradually realised they were only straws; and then the next bombshell dropped and devastated us. But the straws kept us afloat.

'What is David's likely life span then?'

'Again, I do not know, but these children do not live as long as others.' I didn't want to analyse what he meant by 'these children'.

'No-one is sure why; maybe it is because they are unable to communicate that they are ill and so they are sicker by the time they get treatment; sometimes there are other medical problems that also make them more susceptible to infections, as would be true for David.'

Simon and I did not talk much about what the neurologist had said. Each was trying to protect the other from hurt. We were shocked and confused. Neither of us wanted to hear what he'd said, but he'd reinforced our subconscious fears. I didn't know how to ask Simon what he was thinking. I didn't even know what was going on in my own mind. I thought about what the neurologist had said about the time, early in his career, when euthanasia had been common but unofficial practice, when children were allowed to die if their lives had become too dominated by illness and suffering. It was harrowing for parents and doctors, he'd said, for the death was lingering. It was easier if pneumonia or some other illness took them.

Then I thought about when I worked as a paediatrician and helped look after a child whom we didn't allow to die. I guess that, without thinking about it properly, I'd decided that euthanasia was occasionally a reasonable option. Our consultant bosses told us very firmly that it was illegal, but it was a touchy issue and they halted any discussion. The rest of the juniors and I mostly accepted that dictat: it was easiest for us to do nothing and then send these children home. We avoided thinking too deeply about it but I felt more than a little guilt at having been part of this system, a system that anyway was inconsistent. I no longer thought of euthanasia as an option, but knew that sometimes there are decisions that might lengthen or shorten life. I wondered whether Simon had thought about euthanasia, but I dared not ask. My own feelings were so confused that I could not even articulate the right questions, and Simon did not encourage me to talk. He liked to mull things over quietly; we were both coming to terms with the situation in our different ways. Were we still thinking along the same lines — the right lines?

My feelings lurched from despair to imagining a normal family life, through adoption (immediately dismissed), and back to the fear of seeing David suffer again. How were we going to cope? What was David's fate? Would he suffer more or less if we took him away from First World medical care again? How ill might he become? What I was sure of was that I wanted David to be happy, and if life was going to be unremittingly miserable, I would not want it to continue. I also knew that I couldn't stop him living. Nor would anyone else.

Thus the muddle meandered around my consciousness. Eventually, though, I realised that we were agreed on two things. First, we'd be happier — much happier — back in Nepal. Secondly, that if David got ill, we would keep him comfortable but wouldn't automatically treat him. If an illness threatened to take his life gently, we would let fate decide. Or at least that's what we thought we'd planned to do.

The more we considered it, the more we were convinced that David would suffer less if he was kept away from British doctors. We didn't trust them to do what was best for David; they'd be concerned with disease, not his wellbeing.

It wasn't a comfortable decision, and it wasn't one that we felt easy discussing even with close family. I knew that my mother's philosophy was 'where there's life, there's hope' and that she'd be appalled at the idea of challenging David's doctors. Yet, although I knew they might not agree with our ideas, it seemed wrong to exclude them, too, especially since we'd failed to communicate with them around the time of his birth and diagnosis.

I now felt ready to introduce David to the wider family. We arranged David's christening in my parents' church. We're agnostics, but Simon in particular likes to hedge his bets; it was a lovely excuse for a party and David looked splendid in the silk robe that my father-in-law's great-grandfather had been christened in.

We spent as much time with the family as we could, mindful that by living in Nepal we were keeping David away from them. We also caught up with lots of old friends and some had babies to compare. David's babble was encouragingly similar to normal children of his age. If his language development was on schedule might the doctors have misjudged his intelligence too? He *was* developing. Maybe he'd catch up. Perhaps he was intellectually normal. Time would tell. Or were we clutching at straws again?

Whatever turned out to be true, I could leave Britain again with an easy conscience — relatively.

Check-in at Gatwick Airport was chaos. At the front of the queue were twenty surprisingly short Gurkha soldiers, all called Mr Limbu and all dressed alike in navy blazers. The Royal Nepal ground staff were trying to work out who was whom, but when they spotted us they beckoned us forward and welcomed us back like old friends. I was already feeling good about leaving Britain, but our reception turned my good mood into euphoria. We'd not only protected David from the traumas of open-heart surgery, but now we were off on a great adventure. This was to be a ground-breaking new project in an unspoilt corner of Nepal. I was excited and confident — in pioneering mode. I was buoyant throughout the long flight. Simon, too, visibly relaxed when we set foot on Nepali soil again. A big, new sign in English in the arrivals hall made us giggle:

> *Please be in queue in front of proper*
> *counter and help to have clear the*
> *immigration process before you Pass Out.*

Simon had a few days' work in Kathmandu, so I had time to shop before we went down to Rajapur. Going out with the children wasn't always easy, though; Alexander grew rapidly bored and indulged in diversion tactics. Six-month-old David was becoming more awkward to carry and quickly tired of trying to control his heavy head as it lolled about. But finally we had a huge quantity of supplies packed into aluminium trunks. I'd bought tinned food, corned beef, pasta, sweets that wouldn't melt, milk powder, torches, batteries, candles, matches, a bicycle for Alexander, mosquito nets, repellents and insecticide, boxes of Nestum baby rice for David and sieves to process food for him. Now we'd earned a treat. Joanna and some of the others from the mother and toddlers group drove out to the King's Forest at Gokarna. It was nominally a royal hunting park. Clumsily we climbed aboard three elephants. I perched on top clinging nervously to the boys, wondering whether Alexander or David was most at risk of falling off. I was at pains to protect David from jarring his neck, but he seemed amused by the weird motion. He was listening, and tracking the changes in light and dark. He was certainly taking an interest in his surroundings, and clearly enjoying his outing. Blackbuck and muntjac wandered close and fearless. Alexander said, 'I like the deer.'

'Yes. And we'll see even better jungle and wildlife when we go to Rajapur. It'll be fantastic.'

Back in the hotel and doing a final pack, I slid some tin trunks noisily across the concrete floor, then became aware of a dirty belly-laugh coming from the bed where David was lying. I moved the trunk again, and he laughed even louder. 'Alexander — David is laughing!' It was an infectious laugh; Alexander and I chuckled too. How wonderful: this was his first real laugh. Finally David was showing the pleasure he was getting from new sensations. He was reacting to his environment. He was sharing our world, our enjoyments.

I moved the case again and there was more laughter from David. When Alexander and I laughed too, it made David laugh all the more. We laughed till we cried. After that, any unusual or happy noise would make him guffaw: children playing, cows mooing, cockerels squabbling, dogs barking, the gull-like screams of kites, parakeet squawks, scrapping cats, doors slamming, cars backfiring, tyres screeching, motorbikes hooting, spluttering auto-rickshaws, trailer-loads rattling, arguments erupting, new music thumping. Kathmandu was alive with sound.

Then, to his delight, Alexander discovered that if he did gymnastics, fell over or clowned about, this was guaranteed to make David laugh.

He suddenly became a hugely cheering influence. It was right for us to be together in a country we loved — where wee David did not have to be perfect to be admired. Where he was no longer an Interesting Case. We were right to have challenged David's doctors in England. He'd achieved one 'milestone' that showed he was developing and learning. At last my doubts faded to nothing: moving down to Rajapur Island would suit us — all four of us.

CHAPTER EIGHT

worse by candlelight

IT WAS EFFORTLESS STAYING IN MR VAIDIYA'S BIG house on the edge of Rajapur bazaar. Here, fifteen hours' drive from Kathmandu, there was neither running water nor electricity. Instead of mod cons, a squad of silent Tharu women crept about like ghosts. They cleaned, swept, washed clothes, filled the bucket to flush the toilet and cleaned and refilled hurricane lamps. They were too shy to respond to my greetings or even look at me. I couldn't make contact — not yet. But I enjoyed trying to chat in Nepali with the ever-patient and always smiling Bishnu. At lunchtimes and in the evenings, too, there were chances to catch up with Simon and his team.

'Mr Vaidiya must be rich,' I remarked, through another delicious mouthful of Bishnu's curries. Vaidiya's house, the biggest on the island, was large enough to accommodate several of Simon's colleagues and the project office. 'Where does his money come from?'

'From growing rice,' Simon replied, 'like everyone else on Rajapur. He's also the Ayurvedic doctor. But I don't imagine he makes much from that. He used to sell Ayurvedic medicines in Kathmandu, but the city got too busy and polluted for him, so he stays here all the time now. He says that life — and servants — are much cheaper.'

'When I can speak Nepali better, I'll be able to pick his brains. I'd love to learn about traditional medicine — we'd be able to talk shop! Did I tell you that Bishnu is teaching me Nepali now?'

'He doesn't speak nice Nepali, Mrs Simon,' Dr Josi butted in as he wandered into the room, hands in pockets. Clean-shaven, bat-eared, he wore his stomach over his jeans.

'Will you teach me, then, Dr Josi?' I smiled hopefully at him.

'No, Mrs Simon, that will take too much of time, and I am very busy on the engineering works.'

'It'll have to be Bishnu, then. I like him and I find his Nepali easy to understand.'

'He cannot teach you, Mrs Simon. He is uneducated,' Josi sighed, having lost interest in the conversation and me. He turned to see how the food preparation was going. It wasn't anywhere near ready. Another sigh from Josi.

'My name is Jane — why don't you call me Jane?'

'I had heard of this English name, Mrs Simon.'

Then it was Alexander's turn to chip in and, pointing to a framed print on the wall, he said, 'Why is that lady in that picture blue?'

'That's Lord Krishna,' I said. 'He is always painted blue — maybe it's a reminder that he's a god.'

Most days I would wander into the bazaar with Alexander, and David in his baby-carrier. I wanted to see what we could buy locally, and what we'd need to bring from Nepalgunj, a four-hour drive away. Rajapur market was busy, full of life, full of colourful people, bicycles, cycle-rickshaws and horse-drawn *tangas*, but it was a tiny, unattractive shanty town of galvanised iron shacks, centred around a dusty dirt road strewn with rubbish, cowpats and children's turds. Emaciated pariah dogs, missing half their fur, searched listlessly between stalls; there wasn't much for them to scrounge. There wasn't much for sale either. Rajapur was no longer a town of kings. Maybe it had been more important once.

My life may have been easy but I began to pine for my own space, so we found a house to rent — in a quiet spot on the edge of the bazaar, set in a lush garden of mangoes, mulberries, jasmine and flame of the forest. Finally, the day came when we could move in. Alexander excitedly ran up the three steps and I followed, pushing aside a piece of filthy pink cloth. It felt greasy. Inside, a narrow, dark corridor led straight through to the garden; there was no back door, either. Four warped wooden doors led off the dingy corridor into four small, gloomy rooms, each about four metres square, where unseen creatures scurried. Thick dust covered everything. My dreams of living in traditional style were shattered. This, the second biggest house in Rajapur, was a nasty, cramped concrete box. 'We're going to live *here* for the next two years?' I said to Simon.

'It's the best house on offer! It will look fine when we've got some furniture and something to cover the floors,' he said confidently. He didn't — as other men might have — remind me that I'd encouraged him to take this job.

The house was squalid and completely bare except for two small, unstable *charpoy* string beds and a paint-spattered, wobbly wooden chair. Even the geckoes had left. 'The Gautams have left us this pink object ...' Simon said, indicating a vile crocheted wall-hanging.

'So, you think this is fine, then?' I wondered whether he cared where we lived, although he later admitted that he too was struggling to see something good about our new home. 'It'll do,' he said.

'I don't like this house!' Alexander echoed my gloom.

We went outside to inspect the bathroom. Alexander wasn't impressed. 'Where's the toilet?'

'That hole there,' I said. 'But I've no idea how we flush it. There's no cistern or tap, not even a bucket — anywhere.' Bewildered and disheartened, I wandered inside again mumbling, 'There isn't even a front door! I didn't notice when we looked around the house before.'

'I'll get Himalaya to find a carpenter tomorrow.'

I worked the hand pump in the garden and splashed water on my face. It was good. My crushed feeling began to fade. Squawking fruit bats and the *pea-ow* of a peacock coming from beyond a dense bamboo thicket reminded me that we really were somewhere special. We could make it homely here. It *would* be a great adventure. It certainly would be more exciting than anything we'd have been doing in Cambridge. The chill brought by the gathering dusk, though, sapped that transient remnant of pioneering spirit. 'Let's go back to Kathmandu,' said Alexander. 'I want to play with Rahoul ... and where's the light?'

'We have candles,' I said, rummaging for matches. 'I'll light mosquito coils, too. We'll get it looking nice; and it will be fun, you'll see.'

The house looked worse by candlelight. With nightfall, diesel generators started and the twangy disharmonies produced from warped cassette-tapes competed with the two cinemas that blasted out distorted Hindi film music over bad loudspeakers; the background of *pop-popping* rice mills, by contrast, was pleasantly rhythmic. I tried to get the hurricane lamp going and got covered in kerosene. I could not find the soap. I was close to tears. What if I had to abandon Simon and take the children home to Cambridge?

He lit the hurricane lamp effortlessly. 'What do you think of the real Nepal, then!' I just looked at him, irritated by his breeziness. 'C'mon, cheer up. This is going to be far more interesting than our decadent expatriate lifestyle in Kathmandu last year. Or we might still be in Cambridge endlessly visiting medical experts who do nothing for David and just wind us up.'

Alexander chipped in, 'Yes! Let's go back to David's hospital and play on that big red car again!'

'No, you're right; this is an improvement on the hospital — just!'

A glorious descending *boobooboobooboobooboo* call broke in. 'How wonderfully exotic the coucal sounds!'

The paediatricians in Cambridge would have been horrified at David's new living conditions, but he was content now. He revelled in all the attention lavished on him and he enjoyed all the new sounds. For the first few nights, Alexander slept rolled up in one quilt on the smaller *charpoy* and David snuggled cosily in his carrycot on the floor. He chatted to himself — 'dad-dad-dad, gardengardengarden' — before falling into blissful sleep.

Both children settled easily despite the night chill, but Simon and I were restless, sleeping fitfully, uncomfortably huddled on the larger — but still minuscule — *charpoy*. The string bed was astonishingly lumpy and the sag made us roll together. Simon had worries about his new job so I tried not to burden him, but in the small hours, trying not to fidget and wake him, I agonised pointlessly over whether I should ever have come to Rajapur, whether I should have encouraged him to take this difficult job. Right or wrong, though, here we were, a few weeks into a contract that would keep Simon on Rajapur Island for two years — at least.

डे डे डे

'Moti will drive us back to Nepalgunj,' Simon told us.

Moti was a gruff-voiced, balding fifty-year-old with a stubbly beard and a potbelly. He was straightforward and seemed self-confident, a bit of a Local Hero. I bade him a formal '*Namasté*' as, cradling David, I struggled clumsily up into the Land Cruiser. Already inside was Josi, still uncomfortably dressed in jeans and a checked shirt whose buttons were under tension. He was coming with us to buy himself a quilt. Nepalgunj is only seventy kilometres east of Rajapur as the crow flies, but we had to take a huge detour because of the wild, unpredictable, forever-changing river that Simon's team was here to tame, and which fed the intricate irrigation channels of Rajapur Island.

Moti drove west, down to the nearest point on the river, plunged in and powered through the first watery obstacle. Pairs of ruddy shelduck, perfectly reflected in the water, uttered surprised *ooh ooh oohs*. Then we were into lush, uninhabited jungle on a long, thin alluvial island; it was alive with twittering birds.

The next ford was deeper and the water more turbid; a pothole in the wrong place would have water flooding the engine, but we reached a broad stony beach safely; then on through the fly-ridden dustbowl that was Suttee bazaar; how much nastier Suttee was than our Rajapur. Suttee means 'virtuous wife' and I thought about the 'virtuous wives' who were burned alive on the funeral pyres of their husbands. This practice had given the place its name. It was prohibited in British India in 1829 but continued as late as 1877 in Nepal.

A hopelessly bogged-down truck languished in the middle of the next major ford; it lay impotent in the swirling water while the driver revved and horn-honked, going nowhere. Other traffic was floundering up- and downstream, while the stuck truck-driver, still honking hopefully, delayed the moment when he'd have to unload and dig it out. Knowing there would be a long wait, we went for tea.

As we approached the familiar adobe shack, there was a shriek of '*Queerie ayo*!' A gabble of Nepali followed and I asked an uninterested Simon to translate.

'Oh, they're just saying something about us having come back again — with the baby. And they're calling everyone to come and see. I expect there will be a stampede now,' he said, wearily.

'How I wish you were more of a gossip,' I said, expressing my continuing frustration at always being left out of conversations.

'You don't, really,' he said, looking pleased with himself.

'No, you're right. But isn't calling us *queerie* rather rude?' I asked him.

'Not very rude, and not very polite either — it's just unsophisticated, village Nepali for white-skinned foreigners. *Queero* means cloud: our complexion is the colour of clouds; or maybe we're so tall or naïve that our heads are in the clouds.'

As I bobbed low to enter, the scent of wood smoke and warm milk welcomed me. This time, the young women jostled for positions in the doorway, blocking out what little light there was.

They were talking about us again, and Simon translated. 'They wonder whether, if they could speak English, we'd tell them our recipe.'

'What recipe?'

'The recipe for making beautiful children!'

'What? Not the facts of life?'

'No, no, they think we must have taken some special whitening medicine!'

I knew enough Nepali to ask them if they wanted to hold the baby. One of the young women ran away shrieking, but the two bravest came over to take David in their arms. He smiled up at them and they seemed so delighted you'd think they'd never held a baby before. 'A boy? He's beautiful. So white.' They made chuck-chuck noises to make him smile. 'His face was cut, *didi*?'

'He had a harelip, but it was repaired in England,' Simon replied for me.

'An operation. Very good. Now he looks beautiful. You come from England in America, *dai*?'

'England — *Blighty*. England and America are different, like Nepal and India are different.'

They weren't interested in that kind of information.

'Baby is how old? Seven months and he does not sit? Is he very ill, *dai*?'

'His heart is weak.'

'You must take him back to *Blighty* — your doctors can cure him?'

'No, he can't be cured — not even in England.'

'*Ah mai*! Not even in England.'

David responded courteously to his admirers and bade them a friendly 'Dad-dad-dad!' They misinterpreted the sound as unhappiness and thrust him back at me. 'Give him milk, *didi*!'

'Can I have some milk too, Mummy?'

I smiled, realising that little Alexander already understood a lot of Nepali. I asked him, 'A glass of buffalo milk, and your favourite biscuits too?'

The women turned their attention to Alexander. 'Hey, come, *babu!*'

'I'm *not* a baby!' Alexander was indignant, but was soon pacified with a gift of sweets.

The women asked us about our home in *Blighty,* about our family, about the school Alexander (aged three) must be attending, and the two hours it took to clear the ford passed quickly. We left the tea shop promising we'd see Binu and Laxmi again. *'Pheri betau la*!'

A few kilometres beyond the concrete and corrugated iron mess that was Lumki, the dirt road degenerated into a maze of deeply rutted tracks carved out by a succession of lorries.

'The East–West Highway!' Simon announced.

'Where?'

'We're on it. The smooth tarmacked road that one day will run the entire length of the country — maybe.' Each time a truck passed, we wound up the windows, but dust still made us sneeze and grit got between our teeth. I held David close to stop his head lolling against the window when we hit yet another rut. Whatever would happen if we needed to get back to Kathmandu in a hurry? Would I be able to look after David if he got one of the nasty chest infections predicted by the Great Ormond Street cardiologist? I'd buy more antibiotics, emergency drugs and painkillers in Nepalgunj. At least that might help absolve some of my lingering guilt about taking David away from high-tech care.

In less than thirty kilometres as the cormorant flies, but two bone-shaking hours from Rajapur village, we reached the new bridge over the Karnali at the Chisapaani gorge. We raced over and along the new *pukka* road that cut through the Royal Bardiya National Park. A stone-faced soldier stopped the car. He ordered Moti to get out and write in a book. Then he saw David, grinned broadly at him, and waved us into the Park. Here David became absorbed by the ever-changing patterns of green. In a dry riverbed, wiry, grey-bearded, pot-bellied langurs peered disconsolately at their genitals, like bored old men. Spotted deer flowed in an elegant stream out of the forest and across the road. Tigers, rhino and many rare species watched us driving by, no doubt.

'This jungle is most dangerous place, Mrs Simon,' Dr Josi suddenly announced, having taken no interest in the wildlife that I'd been enthusing about. 'It is most dangerous and we cannot even take deer or wild boar from the interior. And there is one local problem about blue bull: this *nilgai* is sacred and we shouldn't eat it but it tastes very good. Now, spotted deer, this is also good meat, and *mahseer,* this is big river fish (he spread his arms to indicate a metre-long beast) — fried, it is too tasty.' He smiled, savouring the prospect of further cultivating his ample girth. He seldom smiled except when talking about food.

As we sighted the newly built Babai weir, he began to talk incomprehensibly with Simon about siphons, sediment transport and energy dissipation. Josi, now with brows knitted, seemed surprised by my lack of interest. 'After all, Mr Simon's company designed all this.' And he waved his arm grandly at an expanse of sterile bleached concrete. I tried to appear interested, but I was looking at a huge rosy pelican that stood on the weir, scanning the river below; she looked as if she'd just eaten too much and needed to burp. 'But the canal doesn't seem to go anywhere,' I said, as I distractedly fiddled with David's attractive new blond hair.

'Ah, this is all fault of India.' Josi became angry. 'Their politicians are so corrupt. This weir was completed ten years ago and now India does not let us use our water. Our water!' Moti, bored by the conversation in unintelligible English, casually pointed out a thin-beaked gharial sunning itself on the riverbank downstream. 'Hey! Look, Alexander, look! A fish-eating crocodile! That's an endangered species!'

'Where are the fish? Fish don't eat crocodiles!' Alexander said.

Too soon we were outside the park again, and I could see David's attention caught now by the colours in hoardings and people's clothes. On the outskirts of Nepalgunj, we passed a crude, brightly-painted, plaster statue of Shiva, and Moti put his hand to his forehead, down to his chest and up to his forehead again in a discreet prayer.

Josi was bored before we'd even tumbled out of the Land Cruiser; he found mundane the scenes that delighted me. To him, Nepalgunj was as dull and unattractive as Milton Keynes is to a Londoner. He trailed around looking increasingly depressed. 'What is the purpose of going there and here? Good *sirak* are not available.' He'd failed to find his quilt. 'Everything is such poor quality, and costly, also. And where shall we take our *tiffin*? There is nowhere to eat. What to do?' Josi looked like a downcast Pooh Bear separated from his honey. He was a Newar from the Kathmandu Valley, but he had spent most of his life working away from his family, grumbling about conditions in the plains. Conversation usually seemed to cheer him, so I asked, 'What does the *gunj* in *Nepalgunj* mean?'

'These are new *tarai* towns: Beergunj, Maharajgunj, Bahaadurgunj, Nepalgunj ... like that. There are even some Indian towns named after Britishers: Forbesgunj and Macleodgunj.'

'Beergunj sounds like brewery leftovers.' Suddenly he smiled, but not at my weak joke. He'd spotted an unattractive shop offering Bengali sweets. A rich, fudgy smell enticed us in, and he had soon settled himself at a grimy Formica table. We joined him, perching on hard, greasy Formica chairs. David lay on my lap, delighted to be flat at last. The only other customer in the sweet shop stared blankly ahead of him; he wore Band-Aid sticking plasters symmetrically on each temple where he'd have been unlikely to have sustained grazes. The hugely fat, lank-haired sweetshop owner was dressed in a limp, faecal-brown *kurta-pyjama* and wore a moustache that looked as if it had crawled onto his face and died there. He grunted orders at an unwashed child who came to spread more grease-streaks across the table with a damp grey rag. 'How old are you, *bhai*?' I asked him in Nepali. He kept his eyes averted and didn't answer. 'Madam asked how old you were, child,' Josi repeated.

'Don't know, *huzoor*.' He was cowed in an apology for being alive, or — perhaps — in anticipation of the next kick or slap. He was thin, and the size of an English six-year-old, but I suppose he was at least ten. 'Bring tea and sweets,' Josi ordered and the boy brought a heap of amorphous globs of sickly boiled milk, crawling with flies. 'These Indians are so mean; they don't put enough sugar. Hey, shopkeeper-*ji!* Bring more sugar!' Josi shouted. I forced down two sweets, but then to my horror more food arrived: sweet white buns filled with tasteless, chilli-laced lentil sludge that scoured away the lining of my tongue and throat and made my eyes stream. David laughed at my paroxysms. 'Surely eating shouldn't be a physically distressing experience?' I said as I dissected out some non-toxic bun for Alexander. 'Mmm, this is nice, sweet bread,' he said.

'You'll get used to the spices.' Simon answered. 'Peace Corps volunteers say that if you are forced to eat bad food, you should chew lots of chillies and then, at least, the air tastes good afterwards!'

'Well (hiccup) clearly,' I spat, 'unlike you, I was not (hiccup) Nepali in my last (hiccup) incarnation!'

'Mr Simon has enjoyed his *tiffin*,' Josi added. Then, 'There are too much of chillies. It is not possible to get good food in Nepalgunj, but ... what to do? You need water, Mrs Simon?'

Alexander leant across and whispered, 'I need a wee.' Not confident I could even attract the attention of the sweetshop owner, I asked Josi where the toilet might be.

'Hey, shopkeeper-*ji!* Bathroom *chha?*' he shouted across the restaurant. (I could have managed to say that!) The shopkeeper came over. '*Chha!*' The heavily aspirated, garlic-laden affirmative reply made me reel backwards. 'Bathroom is backside,' the owner explained, waggling his head and pointing over his shoulder. We parted a lank, once-green cloth and outside the owner proudly showed us a pile of bricks where, he said, a bathroom would be built. Alexander christened the bricks exuberantly.

'You speak English?' I asked him, hopefully.

'Of course!'

'That boy — your helper — he's a good worker,' I said conversationally. The shopkeeper looked blankly at me. I tried in

Nepali. The look was still blank. Simon wandered over, hands in pockets. 'Need an interpreter?'

The man replied at last, 'The boy has to work hard, otherwise I'd send him back.'

'Back where?' I tried to ask, then, turning back to Simon, 'Could you translate then — since you offered?' Again, I felt exasperated by my inability to communicate.

'The shopkeeper said he'd send the child back to his uncle in the village. His parents are dead and his uncle doesn't want him, so that's quite a threat, I guess.'

'Nice of him to look after the child, then,' I said.

'Not nice at all. The child is a slave; there's no pay, just some food and a corner to sleep in somewhere. Come on, let's eat.'

Back at the table, I asked the garrulous Josi, 'Would a child like that go to school?'

'No. These ignorant people can't afford the school.'

'Isn't it supposed to be free?'

'There are exam fees, books, uniform, like that, and the child must eat.'

Josi shoved a toothpick into his mouth, stood, stretched and belched as I loaded David back into the baby-carrier. 'I think now, Mrs Simon, you must buy your household items. I must go to take rice in a proper hotel. And you must put a hat on the baby, or he will get sunstroke!'

Nepalgunj seemed pleasant enough. The chaos of the plains seemed friendlier and easier than the chaos of Kathmandu. Bazaar brats stared, but politely greeted me, 'Good morning, sir.' 'This baby, how old is, madam?' They clamoured to admire David, breaking off to taunt or kick each other. One boy, the same age as Alexander but two-thirds his size, carried a younger sibling around by the head, but the victim seemed happy enough. A cycle-rickshaw passed by; the back of it was shaped like a horse box and it was stuffed with uniformed children, *tiffin* tins on laps, on their way home from Little Rosebuds EM School. Another followed from the Divine Cosmopolitan English Boarding School. Nimble, five-striped palm squirrels chased each other along walls and up huge tamarind trees. Alexander chuckled at a water buffalo that sat in the middle of the road chewing contentedly on a cardboard box — buses, auto-rickshaws and people on bicycles just drove around her. A man led a dishevelled sloth bear by a chain through its nose.

There were tooth-*docters* squatting next to an array of false teeth and successfully pulled molars, ear-*docters* fishing for wax, Ayurvedic practitioners, bicycle mechanics, rhythmically treadling tailors, and a woman sitting out in the sun kneading her well-oiled baby like she was a lump of dough. The sweet smell of frying jelabis reached our nostrils. It was all so wonderfully exotic — so much to stare at — and we weren't the only gawping outsiders. Sun-wrinkled mountain men wearing felt jerkins and knee-length boots walked wide-eyed through the bazaar, wondering what to buy on their winter shopping trip to the Big City. Shaven-headed *lamas* in thick orange and maroon robes fingered rosaries as they ambled by; other visitors wore nothing but dangly loincloths.

Goods from open shop-fronts spilled out onto the roadside. Simon remarked, 'Funny to think that this is one of Nepal's biggest towns now. When I first came to Nepal in the seventies, it was even smaller than Rajapur is now.' Yet despite its size it was hard to find the furniture and kitchen equipment that we needed. There were no proper grocery shops; no refined cooking oil, no butter and few tinned foods. One promising shack seemed deserted. Then there was a noise from behind the counter. A snore. 'Hello? Shopkeeper-*jï?*' Snores turned to mumbled complaints and a bleary walrus-face slowly surfaced from behind the counter: bald head, rheumy eyes, splendid bushy moustache and bristly, stubble-studded chin. He belched extravagantly.

'Any baby food?' I asked.

'Ke?'

'Baby food? Have you got any?'

'No — I have this only.' He grunted again as he struggled to his feet. The walrus-shopkeeper found, by rummaging at the back of his hut, a battered pack; he blew the dust off to reveal Cerelac, sugary baby food. In other stalls, we bought rice straw mats, buckets, bowls, gas bottles and a two-ring burner, handleless saucepans and other kitchen utensils, orange bed sheets with huge ugly roses, more quilts, some vile green metal cupboards and a set of tacky off-pink easy chairs with legs of different lengths. We also placed orders for other basics, including the bed.

A Westerner pedalling a hefty, black sit-up-and-beg bicycle wobbled to a halt, as surprised to see us as we were him. 'Y'all new in town?' He spoke with the drawl of the southern United States. 'Mmm, Rajapur, that's a ways further west. What's your work? Are you with a mission?'

'No, an Asian Development Bank funded irrigation project,' said Simon.

'Y'all'll need to come to Nepalgunj for supplies a lot.'

'Yes, I'm sure we will ... but what are *you* doing here?' I asked him.

'Not enough. We — the Catholic Mission — have a home for retarded kids. We teach 'em a little, counting and such, but none of 'em will ever be independent.' Funny that at the time I did not think of David as retarded. Disability and handicap then were medical problems, part of my work; they were nothing to do with my personal life. 'You need a paediatrician?' I offered.

'Sure do. And so do lots of other folk. Y'all'll have no problem finding useful work. There's quite a li'l expat community here, 'bout thirty souls. I'll introduce ya next time y'all come to town.'

'Excellent, Father Jack!' I felt a surge of elation with this realisation that it mightn't be so hard to find something worthwhile to absorb me. 'But now we must get back through the National Park before the anti-poaching curfew at dusk.' And we drove west again, back to Rajapur.

CHAPTER NINE

a proper toilet

BACK AT OUR HOUSE IN RAJAPUR, ALEXANDER ASKED, 'Where are we going tomorrow?' Life had felt nomadic lately.

'This is home, Alexander,' I said, trying to hide the monumental feeling of anticlimax that had hit me since arriving back here to stay. Neighbours gathered to see what was in our very full pick-up; what we'd brought from Nepalgunj. 'What a lot of things!' they said, cataloguing our huge material wealth. This also made me feel uneasy: I was no materialist.

When Simon went to work next morning, I wondered what to do with myself. I was always slow to settle and establish a reassuring routine in a new place. That day the loneliness descended heavily. I had no-one to talk to because my Nepali was limited to a handful of words and a few stock phrases. I wandered around the house and garden knowing that there was a lot to do, yet not feeling like doing anything. We'd cleaned up a corner for David's carrycot, trying to unpack the minimum for fear of getting everything filthy. It was going to take weeks to shift the thick layer of dust.

Seven-month-old David's huge smile cheered me a little; he had nothing to worry him and he was pleased with his new surroundings and the ever-changing cacophony of new sounds to make him laugh. Alexander accepted almost everything as either normal or interesting and lost no time in making friends. He had just one complaint. 'Can't we stay in a house with a proper toilet — a proper, sit-down toilet?' The brown-stained, pour-flush, ceramic hole-in-the-ground intimidated him, but if this was his only problem, we'd be fine. I envied his three-year-old's vision. I felt isolated and worried about the children: what if they became ill, or Alexander fell and fractured something? Simon was preoccupied and his family needed to be a comfort, not an additional burden. He was uncharacteristically uncertain about this new project. It was his first time as a team leader and the responsibilities he faced, in almost absolute professional (and social) isolation, were huge. He knew that the work was going to be tough technically as well as politically.

Still subdued, I picked David up and climbed the outside stairs. These were a death-trap; rusty bits of the steel used to reinforce the concrete stuck up ready to impale anyone who tripped. And the flat roof had no rail, nothing to stop anyone tottering over the edge. I looked out on an alien scene. Someone blew on a conch. I took in the big sky of the plains. Beyond our house there was a lovely patchwork of a bright yellow crop and lush winter wheat. The colours were sharp and astonishingly crisp. I could have been at home in England hemmed in with grey drizzle, or brushing by people cocooned by stress and self-absorption. I thought of the life I'd led, commuting with my brain switched off, ignoring the world; cars and personal stereos keep reality out.

A cock crowed and received several answers. I started to see again: people herded cattle out to graze or took flowers to the temple; there were soft groans of buffalo- or ox-cart wheels as men moved rice, brought timber or thatch. Tharu women wearing bright blues and orange walked elegantly erect with water in pots or piles of firewood on their heads. Tinselly Badi women dressed in pink and purple swept out their shacks after the night's lucrative work. Months before, I'd asked Nepali friends in Kathmandu about Rajapur. Surprisingly few knew anything, except that they'd heard of the Badi, an infamous community with a long tradition of prostitution.

West Nepal was unspoilt, I'd read. People still lived in harmony with nature, needing nothing from outside, using only local natural resources. The indigenous Tharu people were even said to be especially resistant to malaria so there would be scope for me to do groundbreaking research on what keeps them healthy, as well as offering a medical service. I'd already fantasised about living amongst these untouched people, helping them to improve their lives, contributing to the local conservation effort. And now I was here. There would be plenty to do.

Someone invited their chickens to eat breakfast: *'Ah-ah-ah-ah.'* Small boys chased each other in and out of storm ditches. Seeing Alexander was amongst them made me smile. Another conch-call and I looked towards the central temple, its light-green, squared-off dome towering over the low shacks of the bazaar that seemed to huddle against it as if for comfort. The telephone rang, jolting me back into busy doctor mode. But the nearest of Rajapur Island's seven phones was a kilometre away at Mr Vaidiya's house, Simon's office. The sound was not a phone, but a bird: even the bird calls were wonderfully exotic. I scanned around and made eye-contact — an owlet blinked and turned his head away. Behind him, up to the north I could see the gash in the Himalayan foothills that is the Chisapaani Gorge, with ridge after mountain ridge behind, until far away, dimly visible, were the seductive eternal snows. I longed to walk up into the mountains along the old trade route that tacked through the Siwaliks and the Mahabharats and beyond: the route that had made Rajapur prosperous. For now, though, there was lots to do here — it was time to set to and make our new home comfortable.

डे डे डे

We still often ate with Simon's colleagues. Josi was usually first to sit and we were soon also joined by Mr Adhikari the project manager: the government man Simon was here to work with. He had studied irrigation at Cornell, was urbane, distinguished, good-looking and coloured his greying hair with henna. I asked him, 'Where is Mrs Adhikari these days?'

'In Kathmandu, with the children.'

'Does she visit sometimes?'

'She will never come here. The conditions would not suit her, and she has her work.'

'I'm lucky. I can work here and … um, I like spending time with my husband.' Many of our Asian contemporaries had had marriages arranged for them — in their teens, to complete strangers — so that I was shy to suggest such a romantic attachment. 'I'd like to set up a health education project. I have an academic link with the Institute of Child Health in London and they are keen to work here on a research project.'

'You could make much more money by practising in Kathmandu,' said Mr Adhikari, 'and where will you send Alexander to school?'

'He'll go to school when he's older, or I will teach him myself. Maybe he will go to the English-medium school here. That way, he'll easily make local friends.'

'These local schools are not good. It is better he studies in Kathmandu. There are many *firstclass* boarding schools there.'

'He's only three!'

'That's no problem; good schools take boarders from three years of age, and the baby can go to nursery.'

Some Kathmandu schools didn't have a good reputation; I'd heard a rumour about a five-year-old boarding school pupil who was locked in a lavatory as punishment. She was reportedly found starved to death some weeks later.

'The schools here in the *tarai* are no good,' Mr Adhikari continued, 'and the climate is terrible. When it gets hot you must use so much foot powder!'

'Yes,' Dr Josi agreed, 'too much of foot powder, and it is not available in Rajapur. Nothing is available in Rajapur — only so much of dust, and snakes, like that.'

'And watermelons,' Mr Adhikari added.

After supper, we wandered out into the market and saw that Josi was right. The shop-shacks had seemed well-stocked at first, but they all sold the same things: mainly cloth, plastic buckets, bangles and flip-flops. Then there were three shops in a row selling poor-quality stainless steel, from which men wearing crocheted white skullcaps scowled out. There was another Muslim-owned hardware shop, which sold ploughshares, parts for hand pumps (for which we were often to be grateful) and second-hand sandpaper.

The most pretentious, Agrawal's, offered telephones, Chinese umbrellas with dragons on the handles, Japanese personal stereos, Italian olive oil, All Function Shampoo from Shanghai and Lovely Curves Cream to increase the bust. Not even Agrawal's stocked much of what we considered essential or even enticing. I foresaw — without relish — many more shopping trips to Nepalgunj, and Kathmandu, too.

We met Josi. 'It's a lovely evening for a stroll!'

'Maybe, but there is nothing to do in this place except walk in the market. Aren't you going to put a hat on the baby? He'll get condensation on his head!'

Rajapur village was a vista of islands of buffalo shit in a sea of dust; rubbish blew against our legs. A rat lay beside the dirt track, its brains pecked out. '*Rattus norvegicus* — sounds exotic here.'

'*Rattus defunctus,* more like.' said Simon. Soon a ragged crocodile of grubby, excited bazaar waifs fell in behind us. They shouted '*Am-ri-can*' and chanted at us in unintelligible Hindi, tugging at our clothes, delighting in annoying us. Adults looked on dispassionately. Simon was quiet — even for him. 'Was it a mistake coming here?' I asked.

'I don't know. Why does no-one scold the kids for pestering us? I hate the apathy here. Hills people seem more dynamic, less accepting. It was easy to make friends, too.'

I felt much more of a target if I went out without Simon. I'd run a gauntlet of urchins who had no respect for anyone. One particular lout loved to show off his ten words of English by dancing around me chanting, 'What is this? What is your name? What your country?' Ignoring him was no discouragement, and I didn't want to follow the local custom of whacking him with a big stick.

'Badmas! Naraamro bachha!' I tried calling him naughty, no-good.

'Ooh — baadamass! Aah … Nerumrauw!' He jeered at my pronunciation. I hated him. I hated them all. That evening I asked Simon, 'What can I call the bazaar brats, to make them leave me alone?'

'How about *bandar*?'

'Monkey? Far too mild! Can you teach me how to swear in Nepali?'

'*Salah* seems to be the swearword I hear most often.'

'What does it mean?'

'Brother-in-law, or rather wife's younger brother.'

'That doesn't sound very rude or insulting. Don't you know anything stronger?'

'I suppose *jatta* would be most appropriate for those miscreants.'

'Which means?'

'Pubic hair.'

'And I can say that in public?' I queried, wondering whether he was winding me up.

'Why not?

'That'll do nicely, then.'

The taunting soon stopped, and I relished my daily outings. I kept myself busy as well, too busy to get disheartened. So we could eat an English breakfast, I made marmalade out of pomeloes and limes; each day I baked bread, in two handleless saucepans one inside the other and separated with a layer of sand. It tasted surprisingly good, especially when I coated it in sesame seeds. I began to enjoy the challenge of producing good food from minimal ingredients.

The bed had finally come — a crude wood and plywood object with T-pieces hammered onto the head- and tailboards to support a mosquito net. We slept on pieces of foam rubber until the mattress arrived.

The tap in our tiny outside 'bathroom' cubicle didn't often have water in it, and when there was, it was bitingly cold, so I heated buckets of washing-water on the kerosene stove. I fantasised about installing a bath. I am not enthusiastic about domestic details at home, but here I dreamed about having a kitchen. Ours lacked cupboards, work surfaces, tap, sink; there wasn't even a drain-hole.

Everything was more complicated than I was used to. Even drinking water had to be boiled and poured into the big kitchen filter. The simplest tasks took time, like taking Alexander to the outside toilet. He was reluctant to enter and perfected the technique of peeing into it from outside the door. We'd brought a child toilet training seat but it was no use here. At first he would only hunker down over the intimidating hole with me squatting behind him to help him balance.

When Simon came home each evening, I tried to amuse him with silly tales of domesticity. 'Something struck me when I was squatting with Alexander in the loo today ...'

'Not literally, I hope.'

'No, Alexander is a good shot. When we were last in England, my folks talked about my cousin's marital problems, and as an illustration of just how incompatible she and her husband are, my mother said, "They can't even agree about which way round the toilet roll goes in the holder." So, see what you've saved me from by bringing me here? We can't argue about loo rolls.'

'We could get a carpenter to make some kind of holder if you feel deprived.'

'Absolutely not.'

Before we'd even started to get ourselves settled, Mr Gauchan and two other engineers arrived to sleep on camp beds in our new home. Gauchan's mellifluous Nepali and smooth manners seemed at odds with my memory of his home in Jomsom: a mess of concrete and steaming piles of yak, dzo and mule dung.

'Do you like working in the *tarai,* Mr Gauchan?'

'Yes. This is little bit like my native place: both Rajapur and Jomsom suffer most terrible dust storms. These will be new interesting experience for you, Mrs Semen,' he said with an enchanting smile.

'Do you need anything? Towels? Soap?'

'Your house is quite perfect, most comfortable,' he said, not telling me that I'd made one vital omission. Nepali plumbing is easily blocked and I did not know to provide a bin in the loo for the paper. Over the three nights that the otherwise genteel engineers stayed, they littered the garden with soiled pink Chinese toilet paper. After they'd left, I made a little bonfire of it.

By the time we had got a front and back door in place, the subdued *shee-shit-shat-shats* from friendly geckoes made the house feel less stark. A truckload of hardware arrived from Kathmandu, but the excitement of unpacking was short-lived. The long-awaited mattress didn't fit the creaky new bed and it was so thin that we'd need several more to make it halfway comfortable.

Then Keith arrived; he wore an anorak and clutched his protective bottle of whisky to his paunch.

'Welcome!' I said, delighted to have an English speaker in the house. 'You timed your arrival perfectly; your bed and desk came a few hours ago!' Keith looked unimpressed. Until then, I'd been feeling quite pleased with my efforts to make his room less stark. It was clean. There were flowers, a mattress and bed linen. 'We're only just getting settled ourselves.'

'Where do you wash?' He asked, putting down on the Formica table his whisky, an open packet of biscuits and a photo of an unattractive, bat-eared child. I pointed into the garden.

'Oh, the hand pump … I've never actually *used* one before, although of course I can install them. Isn't there a tap in your bathroom?' he said, accusingly.

'Ye-es, but there is only water in it for an hour some days; the pump water is much warmer. It steams these winter mornings! Simon's planning to install a shower heated by solar energy.' I could see he was growing restless with my small talk, so I asked, 'What is your area of expertise?'

'Small dams,' he said, deadpan. I had to leave the room before a fit of giggles overtook me.

Keith emerged from his room next morning looking seedy: the combination of jet lag, howling dogs and a wedding party hadn't allowed much sleep. 'They really know how to party here,' I offered, unsympathetically. 'That row is our local mutation of karaoke, broadcast from hired, two-metre-high loudspeakers. Little David appreciates it; it makes him laugh.' I pointed out the baby, whom Keith hadn't seemed to notice, perhaps because David was quieter than most; he never made any attempt to move from his quilt, but he played contentedly with small toys, and his hands. His head had always been big but I realised that his brow was becoming more prominent so that his whole head looked heavier, even with the new hair that he'd recently sprouted. I wondered how abnormal he looked to outsiders.

Keith burst in on my thoughts. 'You like it here, then?' he said, with an expression suggesting that only the insane would be comfortable here. He continued to completely ignore David and took little notice of Alexander despite his attempts to explain all about the interesting things that there were to see and do in Rajapur. Keith spent his evenings with his nose in an anthropology book, and in drinking his whisky.

He had come to look at the provisional designs to rehabilitate the irrigation scheme and quickly decided that the first weir was in the wrong place. He suggested moving it, but that meant redesigning or moving other structures. The more he and Simon looked into the irrigation scheme, the more changes they saw were necessary. He stayed three weeks, long enough to develop a nervous tic, break the hand pump handle twice and finish his whisky. As we watched Moti drive him away and the dust slowly settle again behind the disappearing vehicle, I said to Simon, 'I'd forgotten already just how awkward the average British bloke is with kids. You know, I never saw him even looking at David. Seems so odd here.' It felt good to be so far from Cambridge. 'And anyway, why is it that so many British engineers are such complete drongos, and scruffy too, when all your Nepali colleagues are so suave and cultured?'

'Thanks for that touchingly affectionate admonition,' Simon replied with a chuckle. 'But aren't you being a bit hard on drongos? I thought they were sleek, intelligent birds.'

'Josi says that they are low-caste — like crows,' I said, trying to squeeze some information out of my uncommunicative husband.

'Josi's not necessarily the oracle on such things … unless it's edible,' Simon said.

'You mean he talks complete piffle?'

'Sometimes … no, often. And his attention span isn't any better than Alexander's.'

I was disappointed that Keith had been so horrified by Rajapur, because I was beginning to enjoy our tranquil backwater.

One evening, though, Simon arrived home in such a distracted state that he didn't even notice David's welcoming, 'Dad-dad-dad, dugaduga.'

'You're cheerful. What have you been up to?' I asked.

'I've just come from another big meeting with the farmers.'

'It didn't go well then?'

'Not really. I asked them for their views on some of Keith's suggestions. One thing led to another and they grew angry. They said that we weren't doing anything — just talking.'

'What do they expect — don't they want to be involved?'

'No, they're sick of waiting. They just want water. Want me to build something.' Simon looked overwhelmed.

'What do you mean, "sick of waiting"? We've only just arrived!'

'Planning started five years ago, and they don't want to wait for another couple of years while I decide what to do. The problem is that I can't even talk to them to find out what they want.'

'But with you being able to speak Nepali …'

'No, it's not a linguistic problem. There are so many fiercely opposing factions on the island that as soon as one person says something, someone else will argue with them. They don't care about the details.

They think that's my job. They said that we should know. I should do a major redesign, but I'm not sure whether I dare suggest that. I so wish we could have a rational discussion and develop a consensus. These people know their island and I'm sure they'll have useful suggestions.'

'Yes, surely they've been irrigating here for hundreds of years? They must be used to co-operating.'

'Or fighting. The local politics are so complex that it's going to be difficult to get everyone working together, and there's no time. They've already been waiting too long for development they've certainly none of your romantic illusions of a natural unspoilt Rajapur. They want concrete. The Asian Development Bank in Manila is saying that they need results too; that we are two years behind already. They want us to build something and spend money — fast. The Minister of Water Resources, too, is already asking why there has been no progress.' Simon was up on his feet and pacing about. Suddenly he looked under enormous strain. He'd been worried about becoming team leader of this project and I was beginning to understand why now.

'You make it sound like no-one cares how well it works when it's built?' I empathised, concerned.

'Well,' he said wearily, 'they think it's all been planned properly and is ready to build.'

'How much redesign do you need to do then?'

'We could do it in six months but then we have to get the farmers to agree to the changes and the government to approve it. And the problem is that there are so many hidden agendas. For some here, political points are more important than growing rice.' He stared distractedly out of the window.

'Even here — in a country where people still starve?' I said, incredulous.

''Fraid so. Clearly Rajesh wasn't joking when he said that Rajapur was a difficult place to work! I wondered at the time whether his was sheer townie prejudice.' Simon was smiling again.

'Yes, he did seem negative about the region. Do you remember him saying that the West is famous for *dacoits*?' I said.

'When I suggested that *dacoits*, thugs and armed robbers were a thing of the past, he told that story about that member of his staff who was robbed at gunpoint while taking money to a contractor who was building a health post. He thought that the police were involved.'

'He also said that the heat would kill us: that we couldn't live here, not with the children. That was nonsense. We managed through the hot weather in Pakistan,' I said, remembering how miffed I'd felt at his implication that I wouldn't survive.

'The humidity here makes the pre-monsoon heat feel fierce and we don't have the electric room-coolers that we used in Sindh. Then there's the dust. *And* the drains stink — really stink.' He was playing to my oversensitive nose and my preoccupation with smells.

'It isn't only Rajesh who is negative about the region then. You're not keen on the *tarai,* are you!'

'When I stayed in Biratnagar at the other end of the country, I used to climb into bed under a wet sheet; it was the only way to get cool enough to sleep in May in the lowlands.'

डे डे डे

The Rajapur landscape was a strange mixture of familiar and exotic. Cabbage whites and admirals flirted with spectacular swallow-tailed butterflies; bulbuls and house sparrows had chirping contests; crows cawed; pariah kites whined and wheeled overhead. At ground level, ladybirds and dung beetles stomped silently about while pied mynahs squabbled and squawked just like English garden starlings. Wagtails were familiar friends, too. The winter sun always brightened my mood. This was where I wanted to be, yet I still hadn't quite managed to exorcise the lingering doubts and pangs of guilt about David. Had living abroad during my pregnancy caused his problems? Was living far from 'civilisation' now going to harm him further?

The 'telephone bird' called, rousing me from my musings. I peered towards the call but I could not see the bird. My mind drifted again, transported by unfamiliar sounds. Some bird called *renal agenesis … corpus calloSUM*. The names of David's abnormalities echoed inside my skull, and worries came crowding back: *tik tik tik, David's sick-sick-sick,* a tailorbird taunted. Was I right in bringing him here? I'd read about the mysterious agenesis of the corpus callosum before we'd left Cambridge. The bald facts were that the two halves of David's brain were unable to communicate with each other. Some very clever people manage without this connection, so how would it affect David? How good it would have been to be able to cycle to the library and learn more about the corpus callosum.

That sent me off into a daydream. I was pedalling out from our Cambridge-white-brick Victorian terrace. A thrush was singing his wondrous twice-repeated melody. I wobbled along narrow Silver Street, over the Cam, stopping to laugh at some incompetent punters on the river, past Queens', turning right along the Backs, glancing to admire the chapel at Kings, framed by autumn gold and russet chestnut trees. But the warm mood of my reverie changed as I thought about the amount of money that had been spent on this decadent building when the common people of fifteenth-century England didn't have enough to eat. When I'd started my virtual cycle journey, I'd thought the idea of being able to browse in a medical library attractive; but then I recalled that Mark, my GP brother-in-law, had done an Internet search for me, and I'd found it too depressing to read: too many references to mental retardation. I couldn't think of David as a clinical object, described coldly in medical terms. I just wanted to see how things would turn out for him. I needed hope and I needed to be optimistic.

One Saturday morning, we celebrated Simon's one-day weekend by taking a stroll down to the river. By the time we reached the first beach, David was tired and uncomfortable and Alexander *had* to stop to build a castle. I laid David down on a soft patch of fine, white sand and sat and looked around. Red-wattled lapwings picked about at the water's edge or flew low, with long yellow legs trailing and wingtips touching the surface like oversensitive debutantes dipping fingertips into very cold water. Some scolded us for disturbing their breakfast: *Did ye d-do it? Did ye d-do it? D-do-do-do-it?'*

We wandered upstream to where several families were camping. 'Who are they?'

'Kumale. They trade all over the hills,' Simon said. 'They find a place with good clay to make their pots, stay until they've satisfied local demand and then move on.'

'How excellent to be able to set up a factory with so little!'

'They don't have much.' Men turned potter's wheels by hand outside their homes — a dozen rough, thatched shacks. Giant molehill kilns smouldered like volcanoes. They'd made cattle troughs from turf plastered with mud. Their ingenuity and their natural lifestyle delighted me.

'They certainly don't have much,' Simon repeated. 'Look at their flimsy clothes.' The men were in tattered shirts and loincloths and the women in thin, ragged saris; no blouses covered their wrinkled breasts. The children were mostly naked; they all shivered with the morning chill. Only then did I see their poverty. They were so gaunt; even their cows were skin and bone. Several adults coughed: painful, racking tuberculous coughing. They were poor and they were ill. I wandered back bewildered, wondering what it is like having nothing, with no prospect of escape to anything better. After a long time, Simon said, 'You're quiet.'

'Yes. I've been in Nepal months now, and this is the first time that I've really seen the poverty. It has been all around me, yet I wasn't seeing it.'

These desperately poor people made our worries about David's future seem trivial. Life hadn't been easy for us, but we were living comfortably, and we had so many choices. How easily I'd become totally absorbed in my own dramas and how self-centred I'd become because of them. Seeing these people now, I couldn't feel bitter about what had happened to us.

CHAPTER TEN

exploring our island

'... AND MRS SIMON IS COMING TOO? WITH THE children?' Josi couldn't believe a mother would be so reckless. He turned to involve me in the discussion. 'The roads on the island are very bad; it is too dangerous. If the vehicle falls in some ditch, then what to do?'

'You need not worry, Dr Josi.'

'I must worry. And the baby still has no hat; aren't you scared that he will get sunstroke?'

'Sunstroke — in the car?' I was charmed by Josi's protective cautiousness, but wondered whether I should give him my credentials: tell him about intrepid scientific expeditions I'd led, my work as a cave rescue warden, the white water canoeing. But he'd never have listened. Rajapur Island was small. If the Land Cruiser got bogged down, we could walk back, or hire a bullock cart. Josi instructed Bishnu-the-cook in what we needed to sustain us. 'Make proper English toast for Simon-*sahib*. Dip bread in oil and warm it up a bit.' He sent a *peon* ahead on a bicycle to organise lunch.

Simon had conferred with the resident engineer, Basistha, and decided to head for the point where the river enters the island and feeds the irrigation system that Simon's team was here to rehabilitate. The trip would help Simon get a picture of the scheme; for me, it was a tourist jaunt.

Moti drove us out through the blaring bazaar and north, along the silty bank. Morning mists skulked over the river. Sitting on my lap, eight-month-old David was absorbed in watching images flash past. He smiled as we chattered enthusiastically about all we could see.

We tacked inland beneath the shade of eucalyptus trees, the track bordered by fleshy euphorbia hedges or stone walls topped with crimson Madagascar crown of thorns. Patterns of light and patches of green made David chuckle. The narrow, sandy lane that is the main road from Rajapur village to the northern tip of the island was busy with queues of buffalo carts, stacked high with thatch grass, slowly plodding northwards, vying for space with equally huge convoys of carts pulled by long-legged, doe-eyed oxen, bringing rice south to the mills. Reduced to their pace, we settled down to watch buffalo drivers struggling to marshal the chaos, ineffectually tapping on massive shoulders as cartloads plunged into steep-sided storm ditches; then they'd go nowhere as the two buffaloes pulled in opposite directions, or, if they could be persuaded to pull together, carts were often dragged out on their sides. Alexander watched, wide-eyed. 'Buffaloes aren't very clever!' Then he giggled. 'It's fun here.' His giggles made David laugh, which made us all smile.

A rufous mongoose darted across the road. Alexander asked, 'Can mongooses fly?' Livid, blue-bearded bee-eaters and sleek black drongos dive-bombed unsuspecting flies. Smells of dust, dung and burning rice husk floated in through the window. We looked out on clear, golden winter sunshine gently illuminating a neat patchwork of luscious green winter wheat and startling expanses of yellow; there were huge, solitary red silk-cotton trees, an occasional white-flowered frangipani, carpets of forget-me-not blue flowers at the roadside. 'What's the yellow crop?' I asked.

'Mustard — the oil is used for cooking, but it's a bit pungent for me,' Simon explained.

Josi added, 'Rajapur mustard oil is pure, thick and most tasty. In Kathmandu, the oil is always adulterated, so every time I go home, I take it back for my wife. Look, they are trying to grow linseed also. It is a good cash crop: everyone needs oil. Buffalo carts need *too* much of oil for the wheels.'

'In England, we only use linseed oil to condition cricket bats.'

'Ah, of course you British would need to; you like cricket, don't you. Does Mr Simon play?'

'Yes, but not very well,' said Simon.

'This is because you are so thin and weak; you have no meat on your body!' said Josi with endearing directness. Simon, who runs marathons, just laughed.

'My Daddy is good at cricket! He can really whack the ball!' Alexander rose to Simon's defence.

Josi laughed, too. 'He's very clever, your boy! I saw him fighting off eight bigger children outside your house yesterday. Very strong and very clever! I can see how the British held India for so long! I hear that he is already fluent in the Tharu language, and Nepali and Hindi also.'

We paused to ask the way. The grey backs of two people were visible as they worked, stooping, amongst the winter wheat. The workers raised their heads, transformed into sarus cranes and flew away.

The first proper settlement was Tharu. Dogs sped out, snarling furiously. A brigade of children followed. The oldest boys led the charge, girls carrying younger children hurried as best they could, while toddlers struggled way behind wailing because they feared they'd miss the spectacle of a car. Adults came out to gawp, too. We stared back. How much more civilised this village seemed than Rajapur bazaar. Here everything, except the hand pump for their drinking water, was built with local materials. It was immaculately clean, freshly swept and tidy except for the litter of old, broken buffalo carts. Women washed clothes in a canal shaded by citrus trees and clumps of giant bamboo. Men were busy hammering and planing, or plaiting grass to make rope. The smells were of rice straw and jasmine blossom, wood ash and cooking. 'Dr Josi, this village is so clean. Where do people, um … go?'

'Go?'

'Do they have latrines?'

'Latrines? Of course not. These people are backward and dirty. They go to field only.' David hiccupped and laughed at his hiccup. 'See! The baby is unhappy. It is not good to bring children to these primitive places.'

'But he's laughing, Dr Josi!' I said.

We tumbled out and, while Alexander was engrossed in chasing chickens, we strolled around. Everyone lived inside three, thatched longhouses, arranged in a half-square around a packed-mud courtyard. The simple, attractive, light-grey, mud-plastered buildings looked beautifully cool. African marigolds grew against one longhouse wall; there was a line of orange and red canna lilies; banana plants. Madagascar rosy periwinkles. Pigeons cooed in their cotes. Cowpats and vivid red chillies were drying on one roof, stone-like pumpkins grew over another and, on a third, a tiny girl in a frilly puce dress pottered confidently on the thatch. The biggest longhouse was decorated with ochre handprints, charcoal-grey blobs, and stylised reliefs of stags, peacocks, elephants and trees: the Tharu people must be keen observers of their wildlife. I longed to be invited inside, but we weren't. Women in full, bright red and blue skirts, infants on hips, stared expressionless from low, open doorways.

An odd rasping sound made me turn to see a large, black, hairy pig scratching a flank luxuriously against the solid wooden wheel of a buffalo cart. Inside her own little thatched wooden house, a huge pie-bald sow grunted contentedly as her litter suckled. 'Those stripy piglets look like wild boar youngsters. Strange. And look at that dug-out. Odd having a boat here …' Villagers, and even the undernourished dogs, regarded us suspiciously from a safe distance. 'I'd like to help these people.'

'It is no use, Mrs Simon. You cannot work here. They will never pay you.'

'Do you think they speak Nepali, Dr Josi?'

'Of course they must speak their national language!'

'But I don't suppose there are many functioning schools here?'

'There are schools in every village, but these villagers are too ignorant and don't go to school. They're busy with their field works and their cattles.'

'Are there enough teachers?'

'No. But it is also attitude problem of these people.'

The car had been surrounded by dozens of giggling children making faces at their distorted reflections in the shiny blue paintwork. At our approach, they fled to a safe distance, regrouping as we drove away. They ran after us for as long as they could. Dogs kept up with us even if Moti accelerated to forty kilometres per hour, then, breathing heavily, they snarled a final 'good riddance'.

Turning to Simon again, I said, 'I thought this was Tharu country, but there are lots of non-Tharus too, aren't there?'

'Ah, now Basistha is the real expert on Rajapur; he says that the Tharus *were* in the majority until recently, but things are never stable for long in Nepal. Originally there may have been a few Tharu people farming there, but there were also Kurmi and Abhir hunters and fishermen, and some Sonaha — gold-panners. Most people came only a couple of generations ago when part of the island was cleared of its virgin forest. Thousands of Tharus who'd been displaced from the Dang Valley came to cultivate land on behalf of rich absentee landlords. Malaria was a big killer then, and most of the landowners were scared to visit for long, but people say that the Tharu are immune to malaria. No-one knows where the Tharu people came from originally, either, where they were before Dang. Some think they came from Rajasthan; some say they are from the hills. Now that malaria has gone, though, they are being forced out again, as they were in Dang.'

'So can you tell what language people speak from their dress?' I asked.

'Sometimes. I expect that there are a dozen different languages spoken on this island alone. High-caste, Nepali-speaking Brahmins and Chhetris wear saris, even in villages. And the women who wear *lungis* — like a sarong — they're settlers from the hills.' I felt a slight pang of envy of Simon's intimacy with Nepal and his fluency in the Nepali language. He understood so much, but his quietness meant that I was slow to learn from him. He could eavesdrop, although he seldom did. I longed to gossip with my neighbours. 'I never feel very secure in a sari — I once dropped most of one into a loo.'

'You should learn to pee standing up, like Nepali women: they just stand with their legs apart and a puddle appears,' said Simon.

'Hmm. If Nepali women can wee without squatting and without getting their skirts wet, I should take some lessons! But first tell me about this place. Does this canal feed a big area?' I asked, as we drove past another big watercourse.

'This one's a drain,' Simon corrected me. Then, 'This irrigation system is incredibly intricate; it's going to take me months just to map out what flows where. It is impressive that such a complicated system has worked so well for so long. Seems incredible that the farmers dug it all out by hand over a hundred years ago and have been managing it ever since.'

'So why do they need you here, then?'

'Floods do a lot of damage — every year. After one bad monsoon, it took six years to get it working again. So they asked the Department of Irrigation for help and DoI have asked the Asian Development Bank. But I'm not sure I like the idea of dabbling with an irrigation system that works quite well. Ours is not to reason why, though. The Bank wants us to spend twenty million dollars on improving the island's rice irrigation. The idea is to transform this hundred-year-old scheme that works into a system that still works but doesn't need rebuilding every summer.'

Our island was beautiful, alive; a lush forty-kilometre-long silt teardrop emerging from the Himalayan foothills. Meandering through this maze of dirt tracks, we only knew we were weaving roughly north because we could see the grey outline of the Siwaliks ahead.

'Can we see the *himals* from here?' I asked.

'Maybe, on a clear day,' Josi replied, with an expression that said that he had no interest whatever in the mountains.

Winding, dusty buffalo cart tracks took us past attractive villages. We tacked between the water courses, as Moti gingerly edged the Land Cruiser over insubstantial makeshift bridges that creaked and groaned ominously, or plunged us down and through small irrigation canals or drains, disturbing men scrubbing buffalo backs. Single-log footbridges — some carved from the beautiful, red acacia wood — allowed villagers to cross easily, even with their bicycles. Men carried baskets of leaves, dangling like weighing scales from a pole balanced across one shoulder. They stopped to stare open-mouthed, eating airborne silt.

'What's that?' I asked, pointing to a large, rusting, squarish thing.

'The ferry; it was washed down here in the last big flood.'

'How did it get such a long way from the river?'

'Surfing on a big flood-wave: they come powering down from the hills from time to time. A landslide sometimes dams a river and then the water bursts through with terrific force. The Koreans built a massive bridge over the Seti at Dipayal. Days after the work was completed, a storm moved the bridge 400 metres downstream. The engineer responsible was in tears.'

'Poor man … but there are watercourses everywhere.'

'It is the largest farmer-managed irrigation system in the world: 12,000 hectares of rice fields.'

'Blimey — these units don't mean a thing to me.'

'A hectare is a hundred metres square, and there are approximately 2.47 acres in a hectare …'

'Approximately?'

'It's about two-and-a-half acres, but you can work it out precisely knowing that there are 3.28 feet in a metre and 4,840 square yards in an acre … Why are you laughing?'

'I'm amazed you can carry those numbers in your head, when I still haven't mastered my eight times table. I suppose you know the conversion factors for all the Nepali units, too?'

'Some of them … but some are non-standard, like the *hal,* which is the area you can plough in one day, or the *ropani,* the area that you can transplant in a day. Strictly though, the *hal* and the *ropani* vary according to terrain, soil type and the strength of your oxen.'

We crossed and recrossed a network of irrigation canals and ditches. Water was being diverted with little mud dams, rough brushwood weirs, dug-out aqueducts and untidy wire baskets full of river-worn cobbles. Simon followed my gaze. 'Gabions!'

'Pardon?'

'Gabions, they're called. Those boulder-cages.'

'Are these the dams you've been talking about? I was expecting something more substantial.'

'The farmers used to use bamboo and grass-rope to hold cobbles and boulders together, but these gabions survive the monsoon better.'

'They're not very scenic! Don't they have protector deities like we've seen in Sri Lanka?'

'Yes, but the environment is so fluid that there are no statues; people just go in for *pujaas*. These gabions and *bundhs* aren't decorative, but they reduce the amount of hard labour needed to survive.'

'This seems so like an Eden that it is hard to accept that people starve here,' I said.

'But they do.'

It was a slow journey to nowhere. Josi and the suave Adhikari were sitting together in the big front seat; they were gambling partners and chatted in fast Nepali. It is a beautiful language and Alexander was already beginning to pick up on its poetry; he played clever cross-language syntax games and made up puns, too.

Bored with eavesdropping, Simon challenged me to come up with some Nepali words that have been adopted into English. 'There's *mish-mash* for a mixture of things, *guru, jungle, pukka, chit, randy, thug, lorry*… But what I find irritating is the way that the subordinate place of women has been institutionalised into the language!' Simon was supposed to address me in the familiar form — like *tu* in French — whereas I was often scolded for failing to address him in the honorific form — like the French *vous.* One of the words for husband, *pati,* also translates as lord. Gallingly, then, I was expected to re-establish my inferior status compared to my husband every time I talked of him or to him in Nepali.

Josi and Adhikari nattered on but I recognised *cancer, radiotherapy, CT scan, asthma* and even *seasonal affective disorder* in amongst the Nepali. Knowing there was a doctor in the car, I expected them to ask me the latest. I wanted them to ask — I wanted to be involved — but they never did. I made a whispered comment to Simon and he said, 'In Nepal, the quality of the conversation is much more important than the accuracy of the content. The Nepali word *guph* means this kind of chit-chat and this must be the origin of the English word "guff", so there's another word for your collection. Maybe we get overexcited about information in England?'

Smiling, I gazed down at David on my lap, but the medical chit-chat unexpectedly jolted me back and I recalled two families whom I'd helped look after when I'd worked as a paediatrician in a teaching hospital in England. One baby had suffered devastating viral encephalitis that had destroyed much of her brain. She was so badly damaged that her skull shape became abnormal, and she changed from a pretty baby into a disfigured, disabled, unresponsive creature who had fit after epileptic fit. Her parents were articulate, rational, calm mostly, but very angry. They had asked for treatment to be withdrawn so that she could be allowed to die. 'We have already lost our baby …' We were put out by the way these parents challenged us. We were critical of this well-dressed handsome couple, who found their daughter unattractive and inconvenient. David's doctors in Cambridge had made similar judgements about us as parents.

Then there was another family. A skeletal little boy with a hole in the heart had gone for a test. But the routine investigation had gone terribly wrong and a clot blocked the blood supply to his brain; then all that seemed to remain was an awful, penetrating, high-pitched cry. It was a haunting, tortured sound that never let up: a screaming, dying brain. The parents wanted us to stop the suffering. 'His brain is finished, he should be made comfortable, even if that means putting him to sleep for ever.'

The consultant said, 'We can't do that.'

'I have already lost my son. Now let him go; he needs to.' That's what his mother said.

The consultant didn't hear the mother's plea for mercy. Even when the child developed pneumonia, he wasn't allowed to slip peacefully away. He was treated and sent home, still continuing with his unremitting, tortured cry.

I don't know how long he lived. At the time, my heart went out to those parents, but those family crises did not affect us junior doctors much. We mumbled about the callous consultant and about what we as doctors were trying to do, but the victims left hospital and were no longer our problem. We could forget them and move on to the next, more interesting case. How different it was now, from the other side. And how thankful I was that David was so easy and so happy. Yet we were lucky to have been able to leave England. David *was* in the right place here ... I was nearly sure of that. He was happy. I was really sure of that, now.

Rajapur came back into focus as Moti put his hand to his forehead, down to his chest and up to his forehead again in a modest silent prayer; we were passing a tiny temple. There were six-foot-high mud-plastered grain bins nestling under the thatch, like modern sculptures. There were clumps of sugar cane for domestic use, and yellow-flowered lentil bushes growing on canal sides. Trailing *loka* — marrow-like, edible gourds — or passion vines grew on roofs. 'It's a big island!' I said, 'How many people did Basistha say lived here?'

'There are about 150 villages. More cattle than people. The official count is around 67,000, but the census ignores the *kamaiya* — maybe another 40,000: more than 100,000 people live on the island.'

'What are *kamaiya*?'

'Bonded labourers — slaves, more or less. There is a sort of annual renewal every January. Some are forced from their tithe land, others choose to go; hence all these buffalo carts full of furniture.'

At each village, a brigade of angry mutts with ribs showing tried to outflank the car; they were incensed at our intrusion, baring their teeth in rabid fury. I looked back and saw three grinning children's faces through the back window, riding for a few ecstatic moments. The faces laughed at us, then abruptly disappeared into the pall of dust. When the children were far behind, the pack of demented dogs were with us still, snarling, indignant outriders. 'I don't like dogs!' said Alexander, but then, realising that he was safe inside the Land Cruiser, he taunted them from the window.

Adhikari was now telling a story about Chinese contractors who had been working near Beergunj and were out hunting snakes after dark.

'What did they want the snakes for?' I asked.

'For eating! The Chinese eat anything! So … these people were scrambling around with torches. The locals got alarmed and, mistaking them for *dacoits*, mounted an attack. The Chinese spoke no Nepali, so couldn't explain why they were acting so suspiciously. They got beaten up and complained to the police!' Josi and Adhikari laughed until Josi continued, 'Mrs Simon, you are always worrying about our rabies problem in Nepal. The solution is to get more Chinese contractors working in Nepal; they will eat all the dogs and we will have no more rabies.'

'You could call me Jane, Dr Josi.' After a pause, I said, 'Look — that Tharu family are demolishing their house. I wonder why?'

Josi replied, 'When the man dies, everything is divided between all the sons, and even the timbers holding up the roof of the house are shared. It is not a good system. It make so much of work to build new houses, but these Tharus are not clever.'

We stopped in a village where Josi asked a man for some water; the villager shouted something unintelligible in Tharu over his shoulder at women who gawped at us from the shade of the longhouse. This too was decorated with stylised reliefs of wildlife.

'Every doorway seems much too low,' I commented. 'Doesn't it make it difficult for people?'

'Not difficult,' said Josi. 'This is for protection.'

'From wild animals?

'No. Ghosts cannot get inside, like that,' he said, in a matter-of-fact tone. 'Ghosts cannot bend down,' he explained, wearily, as if I should know, 'so these doors keep them out. Only the *murkatta*, the headless ghosts, can enter here, but this kind of ghost is rare.'

The woman who brought Josi the water was graceful. Her back was dead straight, right up to the little bun of hair on the crown of her head. She wore the traditional short, bright-red bodice and a full, gathered, below-the-knee skirt — scarlet, with a broad, royal-blue border. She dared not look at any of us adults, but was mesmerised by the children.

Josi peered into the steel cup and, seeing black flotsam on the water, chucked it into the mud, put the cup on the ground and said, 'Come; let's go!'

'The way you threw away that water seemed a bit rude?' Simon said.

'They do not care if we are polite or insult them. All they ever do is stare — like cattles.'

Further north, the engineers got out to examine sediments and discuss flow-rates. I wanted to get to know our likable driver. Alexander had come to hero-worship him, and whenever Alexander offered him his serious '*Namasté*', his face would break out into a disarming smile. While Alexander was busy roly-polying down a sandbank, I asked, 'Where's home, Moti?'

'Nepalgunj.'

'And your caste?' I now dared ask a question that seemed racist, but was acceptable small talk.

'I'm Bhujuwa.' This is a little-known caste, indigenous to this part of the *tarai*. Then I asked him about the beautiful, rusty-orange wildfowl that were bobbing on the river: they were strikingly marked with black tail, wingtips and bill, and glossy green feathers at the armpits of the wings; always in devoted pairs. '*Raja-haans*,' Moti said.

'King-ducks. Keep some close to your house and snakes will never trouble you.' They were ruddy shelduck or brahminy ducks. These portly birds fly up through the Chisapaani gorge and actually manage to cross the Himalayas to their summer breeding grounds in Central Asia each year.

My eyes then lit upon some strips of red and white material tied around the shaft of the steering wheel. When Simon returned to the car, I asked him, 'What are those nasty-looking scraps of cloth for? They look bloody.'

'They're from the Desai *pujaa* last October; each driver sacrifices a chicken to Durga to keep the car and its occupants safe. It even guards against breakdowns!'

In Shanti bazaar there were three tea shops. 'The tea here is not good, *sahib, memsahib*!'

'Come on, Moti-*dai,* it's not so bad.' We entered while he mumbled, 'Filthy place ... We won't get good tea here.' The unwashed proprietress, wearing a grubby, nightie-like garment, served her strong, sweet, thick, milky brew in small, dirt-smeared glasses with outriders of several dozen houseflies. It was steaming hot and tasted wonderful. I drank standing outside, grateful to have been able to wash down the dust, and enjoying watching people peering into the car at David and making him laugh. He so loved being a celebrity.

The single story building next door bore a sign:

SHITALL
GANGA ME
DICAL HALL

A low Tharu curse? It was written in English, and the red cross implied it was a pharmacy. *Shital* means shady and cool (it's also locally a brand name for lavatories), and Ganga is the holy Ganges River, but it took me a long time to read the rest as 'Medical Hall'. A bored dispenser stood outside, advertising his skills with his stethoscope hung around his neck.

Shanti is roughly in the centre of the island, and the only place other than Rajapur where there are any permanent shops; even these had only existed for a couple of years. It was like a wild west town: a row of tatty, one-storey buildings flanking the main street, surrounded by flat open country as far as the eye could see. We left the shantytown and soon were driving through Patabhar, an attractive village of several longhouses where naked children played in the canal. Rice straw was stacked ready for repairing roofs, and men slept under mango trees. Another litter of stripy piglets suckled a sow that didn't seem to be their mother. 'Are those wild boar piglets, Dr Josi?'

'Yes, maybe. Villagers kill wild boar mothers and keep the babies. It is illegal, but never mind; they are very tasty. Let's see if we can buy some,' said Josi. During the negotiations, a thick, waxy, crimson blossom fell from a silk-cotton tree with a surprising thud; it looked more like a red cabbage than a flower.

On we drove to Guptipur, a Brahmin village, where a man of about thirty-five made a beeline for our vehicle. He offered none of the usual polite preliminaries, but launched straight in with, 'Elephants have been giving us a lot of grief again this year.'

'Elephants? Many?' Simon replied.

'Last year there were only two; now there are seven. They come most nights at this time of the year. They crush the wheat, and two nights ago they broke down our lookout shelter.'

'Can you frighten them away?' Simon asked, thinking this all seemed a bit farfetched.

'We light fires and the elephants wander away to our neighbours' land, but while the wheat is young, they keep coming back night after night. Last year those two *badmas* elephants destroyed our rice crop — after all that work. We had stacked it up ready for threshing and they came, ate some and scattered the rest all over the place. Wild boar and porcupines also steal our food, and jackals and wild dog steal our chickens. What can we do?' I realised that the thatched huts raised on seven-metre legs were lookouts for elephants and other thieving wildlife. 'And if it's not the elephants, it's rhino and deer. It is so hard living here. No government compensation. We've planted linseed rather than wheat this year; the elephants don't like linseed, but maybe the porcupines will!' He sounded so angry, and so different to the Tharus we'd first tried to talk to. Simon explained that he was working with the Department of Irrigation and could not help with their problems with the wild animals. Josi added, 'I like porcupine. It tastes like chicken.'

We continued meandering north. There are no houses at the northern tip of Rajapur Island, but wherever we stopped people appeared from nowhere and gathered around to stare. We tried to converse, but none uttered a syllable; we were back amongst Tharus. Most had not seen Europeans before, but they seemed amazed by Western-dressed Nepalis too.

डे डे डे

Where closely cropped grass grew beneath widely spaced trees, we stopped for Alexander to have a pee, and heard a sound like a billiard ball dropping onto marble. The grazed woodland merged into shrubby rosewood forest, and then into ferociously thorny scrub, dominated by small, flat-topped acacia trees; patches of elephant grass struggled out of sand and silt.

Further on, we stopped for the engineers to examine the intake — where irrigation water enters the island. 'Is this it?' I had expected lush, tree-lined riverbanks hopping with wildlife, but the river had ripped away root systems and scoured away soil, saplings and even full-sized trees, leaving small, naked, glaring white dunes. We were surrounded by water, but the dry atmosphere and dust had sucked all the moisture from my skin.

Alexander rushed out to paddle in the river, so I slid out from under slumbering David. As I stepped out onto an expanse of silt-muted coloured cobbles, stone-grey grasshoppers flew off in an explosion of sky-blue underwings. Little thrived here except a few stunted shrubs with dull mauve flowers and thick leathery leaves. I was disappointed, but Mr Adhikari appeared beside me. I'd taken him for a townie with no interest in the countryside, but he was obviously enjoying the trip. 'My wife used to have trouble sleeping, but now she has a pillow made from this *aak* plant; now she sleeps nicely,' he said.

Eventually we reached the river twenty-five kilometres and three hours' drive from Rajapur bazaar; we tumbled out of the car to look out from the wild northern tip of the island. Here the clear blue waters of this, the largest tributary of the Ganges, splits to embrace Rajapur Island. This river is an unpredictable, wilful creature that we were to grow to respect: it could rip away trees, scrub, beaches and good agricultural land, and was to maroon us on the island many times. A devoted pair of plump brahminy ducks bobbed about in an eddy, still digesting huge breakfasts, getting fat in readiness for their long, hard migration north. A podgy black ibis stomped about as elegantly as someone wearing wellingtons that were five sizes too big; its tiny head was covered in lepromatous red warts. Then it took to the air and was transformed into a sacred spirit. 'Wow. Look!' I said.

'Yes. Look at that magnificent structure!' Josi agreed, pointing upstream to the bilious-green bridge at Chisapaani. Here, just five kilometres from the foot of the first ridge, I could pick out the scrumpled sandstone beds, some rusty orange, some yellow, some cream-coloured, with occasional strata of grey-blue slate. The mountains were superb, but the bridge stood out like a sore. 'The guidebook says that this is the longest bridge of its kind in the world,' I said, trying to seem interested.

'It's Asia's longest single-span, unbalanced, cable-stayed, cantilever bridge,' Josi corrected me.

'What does that mean?'

'The whole structure is balanced on one rock in the middle of the river — on one leg! And the weight at each end of the bridge is borne by that central pillar, standing on that rock, through those big cables. It is *most* impressive, built by Japanese.'

'Look! On that silt island over there — a troop of rhesus monkeys!'

The monkeys cantered down to the river edge for a drink. Beyond, to the east, the opposite bank was a horizon of unbroken forest: the National Park. 'Look at all that pristine jungle over there!' I said.

'Jungle? Are there tigers?' Alexander asked.

'Yes, more tigers than anywhere else in Nepal, they say, and rhino too.'

I was standing within an inland delta of one of the huge rivers that emerge from the Himalayan foothills and spread out into a network of braided channels and silt and cobble islands; those that wore untidy topknots of rosewood and acacia trees must have survived the process of creation, destruction and recreation for several monsoons. The scene had seemed desolate at first, but the longer I looked the more I saw. There was the motionless form of a white-necked stork. There were crimson dragonflies, greenshanks, redshanks, sheepshanks. At my feet, honey-coloured ground-nesting bees came and went from their burrow. A butterfly the size of my hand doggedly flapped across the river. Upstream, I could see where the river cut through the first, thinly forested 1,000-metre ridge. Behind this were other higher and higher ridges and mountains until, above it all, was a glimpse of the cool, white, inviting Himalayas, far, far away.

Shadows were lengthening again. The river had turned golden, and the soft light made red silk-cotton trees look even more majestic; it picked out sun-orange geese perfectly reflected in a patch of glistening water; a stately V of snowy egrets flew home to roost; a coucal called a descending *booboobooboobooboo*. The white-necked stork took to the air.

The beauty and tranquillity made me feel romantic, and I moved towards Simon, but then felt constrained by local sensibilities, so I just stood close, feeling affectionate. This was the adventure I had hoped for: living in an untouched corner of Nepal. Rajapur was not going to be an easy place, but how exciting it was going to be living amongst natural people and rare wildlife. This was a childhood dream come true. David, too, responded to our enthusiastic chatter, for he burbled and chuckled contentedly on my lap all the long, bumpy way back to Rajapur bazaar.

CHAPTER ELEVEN

vultures

WITH NO FRIDGE AND NO CONVENIENCE FOODS, I had to shop in Rajapur bazaar most days. David also needed to be in a lively, busy environment where there were lots of sights and sounds to make him look and draw him into our world; this was the way to stimulate him to develop.

But whenever we went out he quickly tired of the effort of controlling his head, so we'd often take a break at the 'hotel'; I'd sit outside on a string bed, and he could lie flat on my lap while I drank a glass of thick, sweet, cardamom-laced tea and Alexander drank thicker, sweeter, lurid Frooti mango juice. Locals quickly began to recognise us and, as I started to relax, the bazaar felt more familiar and welcoming.

Everyone soon knew who we were, but I could still hardly communicate. A few men would try out a bit of broken English, but it was never more than a few stilted stock phrases. I could chat to Simon, yet he worked long hours, six days a week. 'Do you think there are *any* women on Rajapur Island who can speak English, and might teach me Nepali?' I asked him one evening.

'Not unless one of the high school teachers can. I doubt you'll find an English-speaking friend. But you'll pick up Nepali, when you have no choice. That's how I learned. It's surprisingly easy to get by in the basics, especially in villages where it's a second language for most people, and they don't use flowery constructions and fancy Sanskrit words.'

It was daunting — I'm no linguist — but soon I knew enough Nepali to respond to questions about my children. People coming to admire them would say, 'What a beautiful baby!'

'He is son or daughter, *memsahib*?'

'He is how old, *didi*?'

'Eight months, and he can't sit up? Nepali babies sit at five or six months.' It did not occur to them that David might have problems; we looked, acted and talked so differently that they assumed our children develop differently.

Next, I learned the names of the common foods, then gained the confidence to ask prices, rather than just pointing and waving one hundred rupee notes at the stallholders. Quite quickly, I found that I understood the answers. I was rapidly starting to communicate.

The bazaar was interesting, but I was itching to get into the jungle. The western boundary of the Royal Bardiya National Park is the Karnali River, which flows along Rajapur's eastern shores, but getting into the best forest safely and legally meant a three-hour drive. By leaving Rajapur on Friday evening, we could spend Simon's precious twenty-four-hour weekend in a tourist lodge that became our retreat.

Our first Saturday there, we rose before dawn, when everyone with any sense was still asleep; it was cold and still. Dew dripped from the vegetation. Mist oozed out of the *sal* forest, disguising the she-elephants that stood rocking gently as they waited for us. Alexander skipped ahead enthusiastically and shouted, 'Wow! Look! Look at that motorbike!'

We scrambled aboard the precarious *howdah*, and as the elephant moved off, we all swayed to different rhythms, crashing into each other. It was a most awkward motion, but soon we were seduced by the tranquillity of the forest. At first glance, it seemed dry and unexotic, not at all like my image of steamy *jungle*. Yet ironwood trees were in flower and filled the air with an intoxicating perfume reminiscent of jasmine tea, and these smooth-trunked *sal* were strangely patterned, like giraffe necks. Huge knotted vines, some thrown into half-hitches, were carelessly strewn like streamers tossed by partying giants. Strangler figs had grabbed healthy trees, embraced them and slowly squeezed the life out of them, leaving a wooden filigree tube that the sun shone through. Cobwebs tickled my face. A long, white ribbon rippled by, paused and turned into a paradise flycatcher. Vast leaves fell, crashing into rattly leaf litter. 'Barking deer!' I whispered to Alexander, pointing to the half-metre-high muntjac; it looked tiny from our perch on top of the elephant, four metres off the ground. It stood sleek and taut, half hidden in the scrubby undergrowth, then shot away like a bullet. 'Do barking deer say "woof", Mummy?'

'They bark when they're frightened, but they are very brave and will fight a leopard if one attacks.'

'I think the leopard would win.'

Close to the river, the three-metre-high elephant grass felt subtropical. Herds of elegant spotted deer darted away as we ploughed through it, while lurid insects flitted and the feathers of tiny, brightly coloured birds caught flashes of sunlight. Lal Bahaadur, the elephant driver, between turning around to grin at Alexander, pointed out several four-toed pug marks. 'This morning's!' He leaned over the elephant's ear scanning for further signs. As we approached a dense patch of elephant grass, our mount became jumpy. 'She smelling tiger, *memsahib*!'

But David howled. Out of the shade of the forest now, the bright morning sun hurt his eyes because his pupils were slow to respond to changing light intensity. Lal Bahaadur remonstrated with me to silence the babe. I offered breast milk, I changed his nappy, lifted him up, cuddled him, jiggled him, laid him flat beside us in the *howdah*, but he howled all the louder. David was tired of elephant-riding and the stabbing sunlight. The tiger laid low. We headed back.

डे डे डे

As soon as the Land Cruiser pulled up outside our house in Rajapur, the landlord's wife shambled up and asked unsmilingly in her priestly, high-caste Nepali, 'Where have you been?' Maybe I was getting a bit over-obsessed with birds, but she reminded me of a vulture. Her sari was vulture brown and her dowager hump and posture and beaky nose all recalled those skulking scavengers.

'We went into the National Park — into the *jungle* — on elephant back. It was wonderful!' I said.

She shuffled off while I was still trying to enthuse in broken Nepali. As I watched her walk away, the jarring noises of distorted radios, the cinema and the hubbub of small town *tarai* life assaulted me; the tranquillity of the forest was already a long way away.

Early the next morning, Vulture reappeared. She wanted something. I offered her tea. She pulled a face, as if I had suggested she drink stale horse piss.

'Surely Nepalis are like the British — we all drink tea!'

She gave me a withering look. 'I am Nepali.'

Oh, blimey. My weak attempt at a harmless tease — to get her to loosen up a bit — had offended.

'*Aunus, busnus* ... come sit, then.' How I wished I could chat easily in Nepali. I had little in common with this woman and was worried about making some cultural blunder. I tried, '*Ke ḳanuhunchha?* What foods do you like, *didi*? What can I offer you?'

'I have already eaten *daal bhat.* I do not need anything. But I do not enjoy my food also.' Clunk. What can I ask next? 'What things are of interest in Rajapur?'

'There is nothing interesting in Rajapur.' Both she and her husband taught at the high school. If she was a high school teacher, her English should be considerably better than my Nepali, though she never, ever tried to speak English. Having to struggle in Nepali was good for me, yet I hated it and wondered when she'd go. I hoped David would start crying, but he was too content to rescue me. The conversation lurched on. They had three children, all away at school in Kathmandu.

'You must be lonely without your children?' I suggested.

'Yes, I am lonely. And Rajapur is a difficult place to live; too much dust; too many flies; the Tharus are not good people.'

I tried a different tack. 'I need a Nepali language teacher. Know anyone?' I thought I'd try appealing to her sense of superiority. 'Some people who live in Rajapur do not speak good Nepali, do they?' The muscles maintaining my sickly grin grew weary.

'True; few in Rajapur are educated — they cannot speak correct Nepali. But I have no time to teach you.' I found little to like about this woman but — to her credit — she was fulfilling her teaching commitments, in a country where students fail because teachers and lecturers seldom come to work. 'When my daughters come back on holiday from school in Kathmandu, they may help you. They can practise their English too.' She changed the subject. 'Why can't the baby sit if he is eight months old?' She, at least, recognised that David was behind in his developmental 'milestones' but she seemed strangely uninterested, unsympathetic.

'He has a few problems, but he will grow stronger. I think he likes Rajapur.'

She looked at me as if I was more than a touch mad. 'There is no hospital here, you know!' I did not say that Rajapur's lack of clever doctors was one of its big attractions. Talk of hospitals jolted me back to Cambridge and sapped what little enthusiasm I had for this stilted preamble to the real reason for her visit. The next silence finally encouraged her to say what was on her mind. She wanted a consultation. She had stomach problems. She produced her medical records, an X-ray, endoscopy reports, ultrasound reports, and prescriptions for tablets, tonics, capsules, syrups, creams and injections. She had already spent a fortune on doctors' fees, medicines and investigations. As I asked her about her symptoms, I became more sympathetic. She probably had a stomach ulcer. No wonder she was so unsmiling.

'If you avoid highly spiced food, no chillies, no *paan*, take small frequent meals, eat soothing yoghurt, your symptoms should improve. There is also a good medicine that you can try if the gentler diet does not help, although you'll have to go to Nepalgunj to buy it. I'll write it down.'

She listened attentively, querying, 'One medicine only is necessary?' And, for the first time, I saw a hint of a smile. 'It is very good that we have a real MBBS doctor as a neighbour.' She straightened, gave me an extravagant '*Namasté*', hands placed together as if in prayer, held up to her forehead, her ingratiating smile forced wider. She got up to go, but just as she was leaving, I asked her, 'Do you know anyone who wants work? I need someone to help me in the house.'

There were no labour-saving machines, so my chores took a great deal of time. Just getting the laundry done consumed most of the day. David vomited often, so there were soiled sheets and towels to wash, plus all the nappies. If I was going to do even some voluntary work, I'd need help.

'Of course.' She shambled away through the garden, the fall of her washed-out beige-brown chiffon sari blowing in the breeze, while a garrulous red-whiskered bulbul, his ridiculous, erect crest of black feathers mocking her, chattered, *Off ya go. What a twit. Off ya go! What-what-what a twit!*

A woman arrived within hours. She walked into the house without a word, squatted down and began sweeping out the dust with a grass broom, and then mopped the floors. 'Good. You have come to work for me! What is your name, *didi*?' She smiled, but didn't look at me, and continued mopping as she tittered softly to herself.

A little later she came outside and spoke. 'Where are the clothes to be washed?'

'*Hera,* I am happy you have come to help me, *didi*. What is your name?' She smiled a sunshine smile that lit up her whole being, but she didn't reply. The smile and her stately bearing made her attractive, yet she was dressed in faded, tattered clothes and her hair — drawn back into an uncomfortably tight bun — was grey and thinning. By local standards, she was old. 'Where are the clothes, *bahini*, or shall I clean inside a bit more?' Nepalis sometimes mistook my blonde hair for grey and she may have found it hard to judge my age, but if I addressed her as *didi* (older sister), she could — she judged — call me *bahini*, little sister. This straightforwardness was refreshing after the obsequiousness of Vulture and my other Brahmin neighbours. Excellent. I looked forward to some frank and revealing briefings about life in Rajapur. 'Here are the clothes and *sabon* too, *didi*. Won't you tell me your name?' It was inconceivable to have an employee whose name I didn't know. And I had no idea how much I should pay her either. She smiled and walked away without saying anything more.

डे डे डे

My new maid delighted in her children, and mine too. She had seven of her own; seven survivors, that is. Whenever she cleaned my boys' bedroom, I'd hear her giggling to herself as she experimented with the battery-operated fire engine. She'd often tickle David to make him laugh, or take him on tours of the house. Then, as if to justify picking him up, she'd say, 'He was crying.'

'I don't think he was unhappy; he was just talking.'

'He can't talk,' she said, her eyes twinkling.

'Baby talk … David's language; he talks to himself!' Knowing that lots of Nepali babies are half-starved, inert and silent, I tried to explain baby babble.

'He can't talk.' We were in danger of entering a can-can't-can-can't argument, her eyes sparkling with amusement whenever she looked at me. 'He was lonely,' she said. 'I picked him up because he was lonely.' She reprimanded me gently for neglecting my baby.

'That's okay. I like you playing with him. Please do. Whenever you want.' Nepalis were universally appalled at the way I left David alone as he happily burbled to himself, absorbed in thoughts about who-knows-what. Suddenly, though, there was a distinctly unhappy grunt from David, saying it was time to put him down. 'There!' my maid said, vindicated. 'He is hungry, give him milk!' She thrust him at me and beamed with delight as I suckled him.

My maid wouldn't admit to a name, but I discovered that her youngest daughter was called Atti, and she stayed while her mother worked. From time to time, she would open her mother's blouse to help herself to some breast milk. The child must have been about four, but she was doll-like, tiny, a head shorter than three-year-old Alexander. She must have been terribly ill and malnourished — and silent — in infancy. My maid's second-youngest child, Siru, became good friends with Alexander. They were a similar size and did not need to be able to talk to each other to play chase, ski down ditch-sides or shoot each other in mock battles. Siru soon became fluent in the necessary English phrases — 'Me first!', 'Catch me!' and 'Come on!' — while Alexander developed a useful vocabulary of the local names for wild fruits and trees.

Vulture told all her friends about me, so while Siru entertained Alexander, I felt as if I was meeting all the high-caste women of the locality. People began to come with handfuls of pills and ampoules.

'Is this good medicine, madam?' they most often asked. They were baffled when I haltingly tried to explain that perfectly 'good medicines' for somebody might not be the best medicines for all their friends and relations, or for all diseases. 'But is it a good medicine?' they'd repeat, without explaining what symptoms they wanted treated. I began to realise that only some of my problems in communication were linguistic. I'd come to Nepal feeling smug, thinking that I was now experienced enough to be useful, but I knew that it would be a very long time before I'd be able to provide good health care for these people. Nepalis worry about themselves even more than we do in Britain, because disease and death surround them, and the gods are unreliable. Yet they do not recognise or seem interested in the causes of illnesses, nor do they know of psycho-somatic symptoms; they merely wanted pills for a quick cure. It came as a shock to me that these people — just like many of my patients in England — found the idea of a magical, medicinal fix more appealing than altering unhealthy habits.

I said, 'I don't want to run a clinic. It will make the local practitioners angry and, anyway, I don't have a work permit.' Vulture brushed aside my objections. 'You are not being paid' — clearly she and her friends did not intend to offer — 'so there will be no problems.' Nepali doctors make money by selling at least five drugs per consultation. I owned no dispensary, so I could not be practising. Thus they reasoned that I was not a threat to local practitioners. 'My friends and relations are only asking your opinion, that's all.' Anyway, they thought, I was lonely and needed company.

However many questions I asked during these consultations, I never seemed to get the whole story of any illness, and could never work out what previous practitioners had done, and why. Yet my visitors clearly expected me to pronounce knowledgeably on the latest development of a long, long illness distorted by drug side-effects. None of them understood that most often doctors make a diagnosis from listening to the full story of the unfolding symptoms; because I was an outsider, they somehow seemed to expect me to divine the information I needed. Also, I was puzzled about what they wanted from me. Was I supposed to be supportive and sympathetic? (That was something that few local doctors had the time or inclination for.) Should I take over their cases? (They didn't seem to want my advice.) Or were pills and medical files a passport to come and interview the new celebrity in town — cheap entertainment? (Surely I wasn't that interesting? And, anyway, as an outsider with no caste, I could pollute my high-caste visitors. They couldn't eat with me, and strictly they should not be with me.) Did they feel sorry for me in my isolation? (In Nepal, it is abnormal to want to be alone). Why ever they came, they all seemed unimpressed. (Was I misreading Nepali undemonstrativeness?) Several asked if I was a doctor at all.

Our house was just around the corner from the Badi, whose breadwinners are women who are a caste of hereditary prostitutes. These potential patients *did* interest me. Each evening they'd set alight piles of rice straw and stand seductively silhouetted against the flames. Their ancestors had been court entertainers performing religious dances, but now that the princelings are no more, the women have turned to prostitution. I asked Simon, 'Do you know anything about the Badi?'

'Mmm, of course!' he said, licking his lips. 'They're a big topic of conversation at the office!'

'Go on then. You're obviously dying to tell me!'

'There are twenty families. They charge fifty rupees a bonk and, judging by the number of used condoms littered around that part of the village, they know all about safe sex. Prakesh seems to be involved in his own special study of the caste. Apparently they are doing really well from the project staff!'

In most cultures, prostitutes are deprived of health care, and I wondered if I might help them. Before I could approach these women myself, I would need to find a translator; yet there were no English-speaking women on Rajapur and my translator must not only be an English-speaking woman, but ideally free from prejudice, too. Local women were reluctant even to talk about them, though; they uttered *randi*, the word for prostitute, under their breath: an obscenity. I'd have to wait until my Nepali was more fluent before I'd be able to approach them, offer to help them.

My domestic work rate was slow and I was often — enjoyably — distracted by the children; daily shopping trips took time, too, especially when I needed to hunt out scarce items. If I wanted eggs, I'd have to buy from three or four different sellers. 'Madam likes chicken eggs or *buttock* egg?' It took me a while to realise that the stallholders used a mixture of Hindi and Nepali: *buttuk* is Hindi for duck. We didn't eat chicken; I could have plucked and gutted one, but couldn't face the killing. And anyway, Nepali chicken is so tough that when Alexander had his first taste of chewing gum, he remarked, 'I like *this* kind of chicken.' We bought old goat from the Muslim butcher, who squatted under a magnificent flame of the forest tree amongst the piles of horse dung near the post office. Street dirt had to be cleaned away and the hairs individually picked off the meat before I pressure-cooked it for hours. Then it tasted good.

Returning home from one shopping trip, I spotted a grotesque huddle of grey-brown vultures as they pulled their heads out of a buffalo carcass to fend off some dogs. Greenish stuff dripped from their beaks; there's something macabre and fascinating about seeing them pull stretchy scraps of half-rotten meat from a ribcage. Dogs hung around just out of range, waiting for an opportunity to snatch a morsel.

'What are those birds *doing*, Mummy?' Alexander asked, pulling a disgusted face.

'Just eating; being dustmen.'

'Yuck!' Another vulture flew close over us, undercarriage down, ready to land on the carcass. It ruffled its feathers as if trying to shake off filth before its next banquet: no wonder they are considered low-caste birds. The great ugly creature rustled like it was wearing a new silk sari, and the strange sound caught David's attention too: he looked up, smiled and gave a chuckle. The contrast of these outings to a shopping trip to Tescos only emphasised the tremendous distance we'd put between David and that hospital in Cambridge.

I needed more help if I was to spend time working with David on exercises, games and songs. He was so content that I realised he would need lots of stimulation to motivate him to develop. Although he played with his hands, most of the time he ignored his legs and lay with them flopped sideways. I had to encourage him to use his legs; I needed to stretch and massage him and teach him to roll over, take some weight on his arms and, above all, to look. Noises attracted him, and music and tickling games. With interruptions from Alexander ('Can we make a suit of armour out of paper now, Mummy?') or David saying 'ergh … ergh … ergh' ('give me a drink'), my days were full.

The routine kept me sane, but I also wanted to contribute a little to the poor of Rajapur while we were here. I hoped to do some community health education work. I wanted more time. Yet everything needed careful, labour-intensive sorting and cleaning. Stones had to be picked out of lentils, weevils and beetles sieved from the flour, ants picked out of the sugar. Milk had to be boiled before it was safe to drink and bread had to be made for breakfast each day. To save our teeth and our fillings, I needed to learn to sift rice using the local gold-panning technique — or employ someone to remove the stones, and maybe kill an occasional chicken. My maid's eldest daughter, Sita, came to work for us next. She was in her early twenties and had her mother's joyful eyes.

'What can you do to help me, *bahini*?'

'It is not known, *memsahib*.'

'Would you like to work for me?'

'It is as *memsahib* likes.'

'Please call me *didi*. What can you do?'

'Whatever *memsahib* wants.'

'Can you cook?'

'I cannot, *memsahib*.'

'What can you do?'

'Nothing.'

'I think you can cook tasty Nepali food.'

'It is not tasty, *memsahib*, not good food.' She was excruciatingly shy and this was going to make communication really difficult. I'd never be sure whether she'd understood my broken Nepali.

I asked Vulture's advice. 'Tharu people cannot cook and they are dirty. You must find a Brahmin cook.'

We tried one cocky bulbul of a boy, but he irritated me from the start. He addressed Sita (who was probably a couple of years older than he) as *babu* (child), and spent most of his time listening to a badly tuned radio or looking for opportunities to grope her.

I asked Sita, 'Do you like this Brahmin boy? I think he is being disrespectful.'

'I do not like him,' she said dispassionately.

I was angry for her. 'I am going to sack him!'

'No please, *memsahib*. He will give my family grief.'

I asked Simon's office manager, Himalaya Thapa, what to do. 'Sita is correct. It is not necessary to speak about her. The food that this boy cooks — is it tasty?'

'No, it's awful.'

'Then tell him his food is not good.'

'I can't do that! It's rude.'

'No? Then I will tell him! That is no problem. These Tharu women, they like to tease the high-caste mens, *hoina*? It doesn't matter; they are used to it. But if his dishes are not tasty, I will tell him he must go. I think he is a useless boy!' said Himalaya. 'But finding cook is big problem. Tharus are not good cooks. They are too poor; they eat rice and chillies only. This is not suitable food for you. They are good at the manual labours — they will work in hot sun all day — but they say that cooking is menial work.'

'What, then, do you suggest, Mr Thapa?'

'I know one Brahmin cook who worked on our project in Mahendranagar. I will send for him.'

A week or so later, a stranger loomed up on me while I was sitting writing in the garden. He was flabby and looked unwashed. 'I am cook,' he announced, standing to attention. Gosh. An English-speaker.

'Ah, good … Are you looking for work?'

'Yes, *memsahib*.'

'Can you cook?' (No harm in establishing some basics first.)

'Oh, yes, most certainly, *memsahib*. Full English menu. All dishes. Potato. Boil carrot. Boil spinach. Egg any style. Every thing.'

'Any meat dishes?'

'Yes, *memsahib*. Boil meat. Anykind.'

'All right. You come and work here for one week, so that we can taste your food. Then, after some days, we can decide if you should have the job. When can you start work?'

He looked thoughtful and with the thumb of his right hand counted down the three joints of his right index finger, then three of his middle and stopped at the tip of his ring finger. 'I will come on Wednesday. I must go to home, bring clothes and spices and special cooking things. Tell wife.'

Now, here was a glimmer of hope. The average Nepali is no more a gastronome than the average Englishman — filling up is more important than taste — but there was a fair chance that this guy was a good cook. I'd met Frenchmen who travelled the world with a little culinary survival kit: a garlic press and essential cooking herbs. But the flabby, unwashed Nepali didn't come back until a full year later — although on a Wednesday, as promised. He seemed mildly put out that the job was not still available.

Another hopeful pitched up. 'You need cook, *memsahib!*' It was a statement rather than a question. 'Er ... maybe.'

'I have been tourisss cook in Kathmandu, Thamel-side. You like finger-cheeps, yes?'

'Yes, sometimes. When can you start work?'

'Now,' he said, and immediately made himself busy while I cooked and sieved David's food. This new cook produced a rather sparse pizza, boiled rice, mashed potato and macaroni. I explained our taste for less starch, and the next day he suggested cooking *mahseer*. We looked forward to tasty steaks of large river fish, but when he served the dish, I had to ask what it was.

'Boil fish with ee-special English brown sauce.'

'How did you make the sauce?'

'Flour and water mix with little bit warm Mazola oil.' It had the appearance of the effluvia that runs out from pigsties, but less flavour.

'And the vegetables? What are they?'

'This is *mish-mash* — boil cauliflower and banana mix.'

'Boiled banana?'

'Yes, madam. Any problem?'

'Perhaps tomorrow you can cook Nepali food for us.'

'You cannot eat Nepali food.'

'We like it.'

'That is not possible. Foreigners do not like.' After a week this cook presented himself unusually early and said, 'I need go Kathmandu.'

'You have a problem?'

'Wife sick.'

'When will you go?'

'Now. I will take two o'clock bus from Kothiyaghat. You must give money also.'

'I will pay you for the time you have worked. When will you come back?'

'Maybe after three days.' He didn't come back.

After that, and rather to Vulture's disgust, Sita and I cooked. Her *daal bhat* was tasty and I taught her some Western dishes. Having an all-female domestic team felt comfortable for me and — like secluded women behind the *purdah* — we could get on with our work without male interference. Women responded better to the children, I could breast-feed unabashed, and I wasn't treated as a *lato* (a deaf mute) because of my inferior sex.

CHAPTER TWELVE

a real doctor

SITA BEGAN TO TALK TO ME A LITTLE. ENCOURAGED, I asked, 'What is your mother's name?'

'*Memsahib* must ask her,' Sita said.

'Your mother won't tell me.'

'That is her will. It is only for my mother to tell.'

'How many years of age have you completed?' I asked.

'It is not known,' she replied.

'Really? You are teasing me!'

'Teasing I am not, *memsahib*. My mother might know my age. Ask her.'

When I asked my maid, she replied, 'It is not known. She is *jeti* — my eldest daughter; my second child.'

Sita and her mother were bemused by my questions and by the tasks I gave them too. 'Please bring me a bowl of warm water to bathe the baby,' I requested. They looked wide-eyed at me and then at each other and started to titter. 'Warm water? Water to bathe the baby?' They conferred in Tharu. 'We should buy oil for the baby?' they queried, as they tried to stifle laughter. Nepalis oil their infants and never do anything as dangerous as immerse them in water. 'No, warm water. That is what we do in *Blighty*.' They brought the water, then squatted down to watch and giggle some more.

I had to improve my Nepali and needed ways of motivating myself with little projects. I started to label various jars and tins in the kitchen, thinking this would also help Sita find things easily. 'What do you call this? … Is this how it is written?' I asked, as I laboriously formed the Devanagri letters.

'Read I cannot,' Sita replied.

'Didn't you go to school?'

'For a few weeks only. Then my father said that I must work. Girls do not need to go to school.'

Then one morning I asked Sita to go shopping. 'I need …' Curses: what is the Nepali for tomatoes? Damn — she'll understand the Hindi. So I asked her to bring half a kilo of *tamatar*. Then, 'I remember — the Nepali is *golbera*; that's it.'

'*Golbera* is not a Nepali word, *memsahib*. *Tamatar* is correct.'

'No, *golbera* is Nepali and *tamatar* is Hindi. Look, it's written here in my dictionary.'

Books didn't impress them, and there was no point in trying to argue. Here, so close to the Indian border, the two languages mingle, and get mixed with Tharu and other local languages. Hindi is more useful in the plains. The Nepali language wins out in the hills because it is good for shouting across valleys. But with such linguistic cocktails, no wonder I was struggling.

I needed tomatoes and I also told her (I thought) to buy six chicken eggs (*kukhura ko phul*).

She started to snigger. 'Buy what, *memsahib*?' She'd heard 'dogs' eggs' (*kukur ko phul*) and exploded with merriment. When she told her mother, she too joined in uncontrolled hysterics: dogs' eggs could only be testicles. Even when I pronounced chicken eggs correctly, Sita's face would crease up, she'd start to quake and she'd often run off with her hand over her mouth as she failed to stifle her guffaws. Any mention of bananas caused hilarity too — this was slang for penis; oranges were a euphemism for breasts and anyone called a radish was stupid. I was delighted that my idiocy made the women more relaxed with me, but began to feel insecure when talking about food, even if I was beginning to accumulate a useful vocabulary of insults. Pronunciation was also still a struggle, and I couldn't make clear the difference between *char*, four, and *chha*, six. Often I'd approach a vendor and try to say, 'Please give me six eggs.' They'd pick out four. 'No, I'd like six.'

'But I *have* given you four, *memsahib*.'

'I need two more.'

'Why did you ask for four then?' I started asking for five instead.

There were very few vegetables on sale in the bazaar: people were either too poor to afford them, or had plenty of land and grew what they needed. So Sita's father, Arjun, was the next to join our household — as gardener and watchman. His nails were black and broken, his hands reptile-rough; on his head was a colourful cloth pillbox hat and his ears were adorned with two large, piratical earrings. He wore a white, long-sleeved shirt, a maroon waistcoat and a Gandhi-style loincloth that left his legs bare. He worked barefoot, using his toes to twist grass into lengths of garden twine or to hold bamboo that he was cutting to length. It was fascinating watching him work, improvising, crafting, nurturing.

Arjun spoke better Nepali than many Tharus, but he used tenses randomly so that I would have trouble untangling whether something he was reporting had happened or was about to happen or was an idea of what he thought should happen. Arjun became the one who organised me. Like Josi, he felt touchingly protective towards us, but he wore his responsibilities heavily. I soon got mischievous urges to pull faces at him, but my attempts to make him relax and laugh only puzzled him, and I never could stop him from standing to attention and addressing me as 'sir'. He was puzzled, too, about my status. As the *sahib*'s wife, I had influence and money, but I understood so little about life. I was clearly very ignorant, I was only a woman and I asked some really silly questions. 'What plant is that?' 'Why are you doing this?' 'When will the rains come.' 'How long will it be before we will eat the first spinach from our garden?' I asked.

'Maybe as much as six weeks!' Soon the heat would stimulate everything into luxuriant growth in our lovely, tree-shaded garden, with its already voluptuous bougainvillaea, mango, papaya and banana plants, mulberry and jasmine hedges, mesembryanthemums, carnations, and African marigolds.

Sometimes Arjun would share some of our secrets with neighbours. I often saw him leaning over the garden gate earnestly discussing our habits with passers-by. 'They *can* eat rice … but they eat lots of bread and *kilos* of potatoes!' He'd allow a favoured few to peer into the 'bathroom', where the visitors discussed the toilet paper.

No-one understood our need for some privacy; for a while, Sita's mother even started giving her Tharu friends conducted tours of the house — and us. None of her friends could speak Nepali; I smiled at my visitors while they gaped at me, a zoo exhibit in my own home. I haltingly explained that I found it embarrassing to have strangers wandering around my home. 'Why?' she queried.

'Life's like that,' I said, which was apparently enough to stop the Tharu women walking in whenever they liked. Higher castes still came sightseeing, though fortunately they always waited to be invited inside. I had so little in common with these women and my Nepali was still so halting that we never had much of a conversation. I also found the endless succession of visitors a strain. Yet it was forcing me to improve my Nepali, and what excuse could I find to avoid them?

Meanwhile I kept pestering my maid. 'Please, *didi*, won't you tell me your name?'

'It is not a good name.'

'But for my caste, it shows respect to use a person's name,' I explained.

It was several weeks before she finally admitted that her name was Guliya, meaning sugar-sweet.

Often I'd sit out on our front steps, rocking David on my lap, watching. A pair of huge pied hornbills might flap clumsily overhead.

A flock of parakeets would do a fighter squadron fly-past, a tight formation of exclamation marks with wings. A man dragging a goat. An intrepid chicken. A posse of dogs. Alexander cavorting with his friends. Our house was raised on four big steps above the surrounding land and, as seemed to be standard locally, a ramp had been constructed in the centre of the steps that made a perfect slide for small bottoms. Siru, Atti, Alexander and one or other of the neighbours often played sliding down the ramp, each shouting, 'Me first!' or, more often, 'Me fost!' before the launch. The Nepali children had no idea of the meaning of these magic words. I marvelled at how Alexander managed such carefree play with children with whom he had little or no language in common, and it amused me to see playground games familiar from my school days played here too. There was something that I would have called British bulldog; there was the ladders game, in which pairs of children sit straight-legged with their soles pressed together to form the rungs of a ladder while other children race along it without treading on the 'rungs'; and there were endless games of tag or wars with pretend guns and flying kicks. Then there was *chungi*, a Nepali special that was ideal for play where ball games were impractical. A blob of sliced, folded and tied bicycle inner-tubing was the 'ball', and kids had to kick the *chungi* to keep it in the air. It took a lot of practice and skill.

I loved watching the games; the merriment made David laugh, too. When they moved off to play elsewhere, I wrote long letters to my parents, my sister and to several friends I'd been on expeditions with: friends who understood how important links with home were. I spent a lot of time just musing, too, or reading or chatting to David and doing his exercises. I tried to engage him by singing to him while I moved his limbs in a kind of dance. He seemed to enjoy it, and he continued to laugh at interesting sounds; otherwise, he showed no interest in making contact. But why? If I knew more, might I help him develop and become more sociable?

Sometimes his lack of response and total self-absorption was demoralising; sometimes it made me even more determined to learn to communicate with him, connect with his carefree happiness and fight to keep him involved. He seemed most content when he was completely ignored, left lying alone on a bed. He began to object if I took him out. It was just not possible to plough a pushchair through Rajapur's silt-dune tracks and he was uncomfortable now after more than a few minutes in a carrier. Yet frequent changes of scenery pleased him, even if cuddles didn't. How could I stimulate him and keep him happy?

Whenever I was visible from the front gate, people gathered to stare. They opened the gate, walked in and squatted down to get a really good view, from close up. These intrusions embarrassed me because I longed to chat but couldn't. Some days, being permanently on show was really wearing and I expect I was moody and distracted. But whenever the line-up of starers in my garden got too well-established I'd simply go inside to do some exercises with David. I'd leave Alexander happily absorbed in teaching passers-by how to say 'aardvark', 'baked beans', 'Gatwick Airport' (he had a thing about Gatwick Airport), and other useful English vocabulary.

Then one afternoon Alexander ran inside shouting, 'There's a lady up a tree! Come Mummy, look!' He pointed to a corner of our garden, to a Brahmin neighbour in a red sari five metres up one of our tallest trees. Her flip-flops waited for her at the bottom. I greeted her. She stood to attention on her branch and gave me a '*Namasté*' in return. The ridiculousness of her solemn greeting from up there made me chortle.

I asked Guliya, 'Will she feed these leaves to her buffaloes?'

'This is not buffalo food,' she said, with an expression that said, what kind of imbecile would think that buffaloes could eat these leaves? 'It is for a house *pujaa,* a ceremony with the priest — tomorrow.'

'Why does the house need special prayers?' I persisted.

'That's life.' She didn't care about Brahmin goings-on.

Sita announced, 'People have come,' and I found two strangers wandering in the garden.

'Come inside,' I said. 'My small son is in here. Come, drink tea.'

'Tea is not necessary, *didi*; we have just eaten rice.'

They perched uncomfortably on chair-edges, wide-eyed. My visitors had dressed carefully for this audience. The spokeswoman wore a rich, royal-blue sari; she was rounded, attractive and vivacious. Her sister-in-law was dressed in beige; she was taller, but gaunt, hollow-eyed and slow of speech. She looked as if she hadn't smiled for a very long time. Her great beak of a nose, with her gawky colourlessness, made her seem like a caricature of a stork.

Vivacity said in Nepali, 'What a lot of things you have, *didi*!' We thought we were living simply, but they could see our wealth and were impressed. I didn't like being labelled as materialistic.

'Why do you have Tharus in the house?'

'Why not? Sita and Guliya are good workers.'

'Tharus are honest, and you don't need to pay them much, but they are dirty, and they can't cook.'

David, who was lying on the floor on a quilt, then vomited copiously. As I fussed about clearing up they said, 'See … your Tharus should do that. But you can't teach them domestic chores!'

They smiled sympathetically while I struggled to articulate a defence, then gave up.

'Do you work, sisters?' I asked them.

'We are *gurus* in the English-medium boarding school.'

I soon tired of this excruciating conversation in halting Nepali. Knowing, though, that they must teach in English, I tried some slow, carefully enunciated questions. They understood very little. After several more long, awkward silences, they asked about the consultation that they had come for. Stork had a stomach ulcer, belly aches, breast tenderness, infertility, headaches, dizziness, insomnia, poor appetite, fatigue, there were freckles that she wanted gone, and she was too thin. My heart sank. I was reminded of a woman with 'an incurable skin disease' whom I was called to see when I worked in Quetta. As I walked to her compound my mind raced through the possibilities: leishmania, leprosy and cancer were top of my list. She was a pale-skinned Hazari who turned out to have freckles. I smiled with relief when I realised, but she wasn't at all impressed when I told her that many English men find them attractive and there was nothing I could do about them. I was surprised at the time that in such a war-torn region anyone would complain of such trivia, but they are no different from anyone else. Everyone wants to look beautiful.

I asked Stork lots of medical questions to allow me to untangle and identify the problems, prioritise them and decide which might be treatable. The women rapidly lost interest, not realising that I was more likely to make a diagnosis through cross-examination than from CT scans, blood tests and X-rays. I suggested eating fewer chillies and recommended medicines to heal her ulcer.

My guests looked around the room once more. 'What a lot of *things* you have,' they said again. 'And so many books too! What was the cost of this chair? … You paid too much! Which shop? Ah, it is so, they often cheat people.' They were as obsessed with bargain-hunting as any English housewife. They disapproved of the rice straw mats and colourful *durries* that covered the floors and said, 'You need *carpet*; why don't you buy some proper *carpet*?' They used the English noun.

'*Carpet* would not be good in Rajapur, with so much dust,' I ventured.

'Not true. *Carpet* is best.'

Later, I visited Stork's home. She was, by local standards, wealthy, but her only room — which doubled as bedroom and sitting room — was bare. There was a double bed, a sofa, a small coffee table and a cupboard on which sat a cheap trinket box and a stained jam jar of dusty, battered plastic flowers. That is all she seemed to own. There were no books. Her floor was covered with shiny, colourful lino; their *carpet*. To reach the room, we had climbed several flights of stairs and walked through a tiny dark annex that was packed with three-tiered, sixty-centimetre-wide bunk-beds, where the school's boarders slept. There was no space at all between each bunk — children scrambled in over the bed heads.

We couldn't converse freely: I knew what I wanted to say, but could not find the words. Witty throwaway remarks were misunderstood or stale by the time I'd articulated them. This, I thought, must be what the start of dementia feels like. My hostess and her sister-in-law were kind, patient and pressed their hospitality nevertheless. They brought tea.

'Don't like tea,' Alexander said, sulkily.

'Will he take milk then, *didi*?'

'He loves milk. Thank you.' They brought huge, globular fudge sweets from the bazaar, boiled eggs and freshly boiled milk.

'The milk is too hot!' he whinged. And, 'Can't we go home now?' Alexander kept whispering, as I tried to communicate that it would be impolite to leave too soon. I hoped that David would cry to give us an excuse to leave. But he was content lying on the bed, fascinated by the new environment, enjoying being with new people; listening.

Then, just as I was feeling I might have stayed long enough, some chicken curry arrived. It was delicious, though the chillies gave me paroxysms of hiccups. I struggled inelegantly to eat with my fingers, dribbling sauce down my arms, and resorted to using one of David's nappies as a napkin. Then a round, curly haired, jolly man wandered in. 'My missus has told me all about you and your kindnesses. It is an honour and a privilege to meet you. And in my own modest establishment itself only! Welcome, welcome! I am headmaster here and owner also of this humble school.' He gave a small bow, giggling like a schoolgirl.

'The pleasure is all mine. And where did you learn such excellent English!'

'St John's — one convent in India. Ah, those were the days of very fine education ...' He prattled on pleasantly, implying a camaraderie between us — of the educated marooned amidst plebs. 'If you need anything, just tip me the wink and I will do the needful! I am at your service!' he said bowing again.

At first, I felt exploited by these sickly Brahmin women who seemed so dour and self-obsessed. It took me a while to accept that Nepalis don't say 'thank you'. Instead of thanks, gifts arrived: a bowl of steaming mutton curry, tasty home-made pickles, fresh yoghurt.

Their expressions of gratitude came in Nepali time, and were delicious. Then, as more patients consulted me, I began to enjoy the unfamiliar luxury of being able to spend as much time with a patient as they and I wanted.

डे डे डे

By early March, I was already avoiding going into the bazaar when the sun was at its highest. I carried David in the papoose whenever we went out, but the heat and his muscle weakness made it very wearing. Men came up to me and announced, 'Madam. Your baby, it cry. He no happy.' As if I hadn't noticed.

We'd been in Rajapur just a month, but already everyone seemed to know us and I'd taken to wandering around the market with a benign grin on my face, ready to greet anyone who greeted me. Then a small, lean man approached me in the bazaar and offered an extravagant '*Namaskar, memsahib*', his palms held together high above his head. 'I came to know, madam, that you would settle for some time in Rajapur,' he began in loud, halting English, 'and today only it is my privilege to be meeting you here at last! Welcome! It is known that you are real MBBS doctor … no?'

'Yes, er, thank you, mister, er …?'

'I am Gopal' — and he bowed —'general secretary of Geruwa Rural Awareness Association and we are most looking forward for you, madam, to do some clinics for the poor. May I ask your good name, madam?'

'Jane.'

'Ah, thank you, madam; Dr Mrs Jane is lady-doctor, no?'

'I'm a doctor, but not a gynaecologist; my field is preventative medicine.'

He looked interested as I talked about the value of health education: its effectiveness in reducing grief and suffering, that it is cheap, that it encourages poor villagers to be independent of unscrupulous practitioners and that the benefits continue after outsiders are long gone. As I went on, and on, his brows knitted and his puzzle-ment grew. I was talking too fast — relieved to be speaking English.

'Yes, yes. Why not? And after this um … health education, we must make clinics for the poor, yes?'

'Clinics cure a few people, who quickly get ill again. Health education helps everyone — long-term.'

'Madam is not doctor, then?' He was crestfallen. I hadn't convinced him, but I did suggest meeting his committee to talk about the work we could do together. He brightened again. 'All right. A meeting. Very good. Why not? We will discuss our Jointed International Health Program and clinic!'

A couple of days later, I was at the Geruwa Rural Awareness Association headquarters; the huge GRAA sign led me to a dark, steep staircase and into a tiny, two-roomed office. It smelt of damp sacking.

While we waited for the latecomers and tea, Gopal asked, 'What I can do? My gastric problem is terrible these day?' I gave my now routine spiel about taking less *paan,* fewer chillies and stopping smoking. 'But what medicines must I take, Dr Jane?' asked Gopal insistently. 'I must go for endoscopy examination also — yes?'

'No. Try to stop smoking!'

By the time that Gopal started the introductions, there were not enough chairs for the fifteen men who had come to meet me. I produced the all-essential visiting card. 'Ah! Dr Jane has many qualifications! This is very nice for us!' And he chatted amiably about the Association's income-generation programs. My mind wandered, and I gazed around the poky little room. There were the standard portraits of the king and queen. The windowsill was adorned with a handful of dusty pink and orange plastic flowers, stuffed into a baby-milk tin. Minute flour weevils wandered over Mr Gopal's desk, the chairs, all over the walls. Their antennae looked as if they had slipped down to the end of their elephantine snouts and were perched there like pince-nez spectacles. They were struggling to gain the summit of an untidy heap of files on Mr Gopal's desk. The weevils climbed, fell back and lay upside-down for a while, waving their legs. Then they managed to turn over, and made another mountaineering attempt on the monstrous pile of papers. Mr Gopal talked on. He showed me children's clothing that village women had made and would sell; a few weevils strolled around in the folds. 'And our adult literacy work, that is going very nicely. We teach the village ladies to read and a little bit counting.'

'Do you think that the literacy program is helping the women?'

'Helping, I don't know, but they are empowered — most certainly — and causing some trouble in villages. Some ladies have stopped *rakshi* production because they were tired of drunken husbands always beating them. And now these men, they are complaining to this office!'

The GRAA seemed to be an organisation that could do huge good locally. 'Do you work with the Badi?'

Gopal looked embarrassed. 'We cannot work with these womens. These are bad womens.'

'I'm sure it is best to start with people you know. Your work sounds impressive, and now by adding in health education you can save lives too; health work will dovetail beautifully with your other projects. We'll need to think how we can train your community volunteers and then support them.'

'Ah, yes, yes, Dr Jane — awareness and empowerment …'

'You know all the jargon!'

'Why not! Jargons are important also and so … you, your goodself Dr Jane will organise a trainings.'

'No, I will help *you* to organise any training sessions. I'll *empower* you to become health experts!'

Nepal is a country that has the reputation for being a difficult place to work in — difficult, that is, to make any useful and sustainable contribution to the destiny of the poor. And Rajesh had warned us that Rajapur was difficult even by Nepali standards. I decided at the outset, then, that the energy and drive for any health work must come from the locals and not from me. This was the only way that this project would succeed. I could rush around and make myself feel virtuous by Healing the Sick, but what would I leave behind afterwards except unfulfilled expectations? I would not push the GRAA too hard. I had plenty to keep me busy, plus David's daily physiotherapy to do, and the children to enjoy. I could afford the luxury denied to most hectic development workers: time. I could wait long enough for them to come around to owning this work, because surely they would eventually appreciate the great advantages of a health-promoting project over a curative one.

I issued a challenge. 'I suggest that the GRAA committee might think about the key health issues locally. What are the priorities? Talk with the communities in which you work. Then in a few weeks we'll meet again to discuss your findings and produce an outline of how we should proceed.'

'Yes, yes. Why not? We will meet after two weeks.'

This meeting had gone well and I left full of ideas about the good work that we would achieve.

Over the following months, whenever I bumped into Gopal he talked through *betel*-stained teeth, belched copiously, and usually had a cigarette in his hand. 'How's your stomach?'

'Bad. Terrible, Dr Jane. Too awful.' Burp. 'I need endoscopy, no?'

'You need to treat your body more kindly! You are still smoking and you're still chewing *paan!*' I wondered why I ever posed as a health education expert, when no-one ever seemed to take my advice. Gopal deftly changed the subject. 'The committee is still *thinking* about your program ...'

'No, no, *your* program.'

'And when *will* Dr Jane start clinics for the poor?'

I had dismally failed to motivate Gopal to look after his body and I'd failed to convince them about the value of prevention of disease. 'I'm sorry. There's no point in me running a clinic when I'll be leaving soon after it's established. The people of Rajapur deserve better!'

'These are poor people — it doesn't matter,' he said, flooring me completely. But I would continue to wait for the committee to come around to the idea that prevention is better and cheaper than cure. I could wait — for a year or so.

CHAPTER THIRTEEN

arranged marriage

'TEA, MR THAPA?' HE WAGGLED HIS HEAD SIDE TO SIDE to accept. Himalaya Thapa, a high-caste Chhetri, placed his expensive sunglasses on the cane table and sat on a rough chair under a mango tree. He often dropped by, and I enjoyed his chit-chat. I asked, 'How's the office — busy?'

'Of course, all ways busy!' He was rather underemployed. His English was fluent, but sometimes his intonation made me pause to think. I put some flapjacks on the table, with a small flourish. I felt rather pleased with myself for managing to produce an English titbit from the contents of a rusting tin of Indian porridge oats that I'd unearthed in a shack-shop in Nepalgunj. The plate rocked on the uneven table surface. He peered at my offering suspiciously. 'It is not necessary for me to take these. I have just eaten rice, *hoina?* Are these um ... flak-jackets a traditional English cooking?' He nibbled tentatively at an edge.

'I suppose they're English, or maybe Scottish. These are a bit hard …'

'Yes, too hard. English dishes are too sweet, also. Actually this dish, I think, is for children only. Dick, from my last project, always cooked custard-food. This, also, is too sweet and I do not like.' Awkward pause. 'So … how's the baby?' he asked.

'He's been vomiting a lot again, but he seems happy in between times. I think he's okay.'

'You're the doctor, *hoina?*' he laughed humourlessly, while I wondered what he was thinking. I dearly wanted to talk about my worries to someone, but he was not to be my confidant. Nor did I ever manage to get him to talk about the spirituality that is so clearly such an inseparable part of Nepali life; it just went without saying, didn't need explanation or analysis. Himalaya was smooth, efficient, likable, spoke good English and had worked for British engineers for more than a decade. Dredging for a topic to interest us both, I said, 'There's a rambling, blue-flowered plant that we call morning glory. Does it have a Nepali name?'

'It is *besharma*. That means "shameless".'

'Why shameless?'

'Shameless like those Badi women. Shameless because it grows anywhere, and it blocks canals, *hoina?* It is problem!' said Himalaya. Then, another lurch in the conversation. 'You have a good chance to start work!' he announced. 'There is no clinic for ladies here. Every spring, one family planning camp comes to Rajapur, but it's been cancelled again. The people are angry. Government clinics always let them down. What to do? You could make a lot of money if you opened private clinic in Rajapur.'

'But I don't want to make money.' He looked at me as if I was mad.

'You know *docter* Bhandari is very busy. People come looking for him in middle of night and they wake us up too many times.' Then he added casually, 'Two men died of rabies last week.'

'Aggh. How awful. I think that is the worst way to die!' I said.

'I have heard the AIDS is much worse; most horrible.'

'If I had a choice, I'd choose AIDS rather than rabies!'

His expression said that I was deranged. Then, without a hint of shyness, he announced, 'I'm getting married!'

'Gosh. How lovely. Congratulations. When?'

'After two months. My father has fixed the date,' he said.

'Where does your wife-to-be live?' I enquired.

'They haven't decided who yet; my parents know one Nepali girl who lives in Bombay. I may marry her, but we have to see her horoscope before we can decide.'

'Have you met her?'

'No.'

'Will you meet her before the wedding?'

'I think so,' he said, sounding not a bit interested in the woman who would share his bed.

'Will she come to live in Rajapur?'

'Of course!'

'That might be difficult, for a middle class Nepali brought up in Bombay.' I thought of the elegant, beautiful women I'd met in India's cities and knew that none of them would find Rajapur attractive.

'You live here; why shouldn't she?' Himalaya said.

'Living in a remote part of Nepal is exotic and exciting for someone from the West, but I also like it here because I am interested in wildlife. Won't your fiancée become bored?'

'She will live here!'

Clearly, once married, she would have no choice and I wondered how much she would be told before the ceremony. Time to change the subject again.

'I'd like to ask for your help to get the house improvements done. A *mysteri* has been here, but he didn't understand my Nepali.'

'No, they speak Hindi only. They are Indians.' Delighted to be given some work to do, Himalaya abandoned the flapjack, leapt to his feet and said, 'I will go and come, *hoina*?'

We had taken over the high school maths master's house, which was, by local standards, very decadent. Each of the four small, bare rooms had unglazed, barred windows with clumsy wooden shutters inside, which didn't shut. The kitchen had been added as an afterthought; it partially blocked a dining room window.

Himalaya soon reappeared, having conjured up the foreman of the *mysteri* team. 'Please, Mr Thapa, explain that we need front and back doors made and hung. We also need mosquito screens.' He used his expensive sunglasses to direct them. The foreman seemed so languid that I couldn't believe he'd motivate anyone to do anything, but over the next few days, things started to happen. Nine-month-old David loved all the activity and laughed at the banging, but he was often covered in wood-shavings and constantly in danger of having hammers dropped on him. The *mysteri* team worked in every room at once and were not used to encountering babies left lying around on the floor: Nepali mothers carry their infants everywhere. It was safest for us to move onto our flat roof.

I came to enjoy the major national pastime, *guph garnu*: conversation and story-telling. Josi and Basistha often tried to outdo each other with frightening *guph*. 'Have you heard of the *loo* — the hot, hot wind that suffocates people?' Basistha said. He was an intense, troubled-looking man.

Josi continued, 'These storms start in March and they are most dangerous when they come between midday and 2 pm. They suck out all air, so it is not possible to breathe, and people get like fried meat. Most people die from *loo* when there are no onions in the market — onions give protection.' I looked at Josi's face to see if he was teasing me, but this overseas-educated engineer believed what he was saying. 'You have nothing like these winds in England. Even Mr Simon does not know about *loo,* after so many years in East Nepal … And the storms are dangerous also — trees and houses fall on people and cause terrible injuries. The season is coming. You must make sure that the shutters in your house shut tight.'

Himalaya, being a *tarai* man, was less alarmist. 'The *loo* does not come often. It will not come this year.' Even so, he ordered the carpenters to attend to our shutters, which had been warped by several monsoons and strong sun, and only then start work on the doors. They responded by going off to assault the window bolts with a small sledgehammer, a tool that I hadn't regarded as a carpenter's before.

One afternoon, the dust and dreariness of our concrete box home drove me out and, once in the bazaar, I decided to go in search of tinned food, tinned anything.

We bumped into Basistha. He was serious even by Brahmin standards, but the worry-lines on his brow looked even more furrowed than usual. Poor Basistha worked so hard and was a good engineer, but had the wrong political affiliations, so he wasn't progressing in his career. He was pushing hard for a transfer, but this manoeuvring was to result in him ending up worse off in a remote outpost in the hills with no work at all.

I offered him a weak joke to cheer him up, but it fell flat. Alexander felt the need to explain, witheringly, 'That was one of Mummy's drokes.'

I asked him, 'How are things? Have you had news of your family?'

'Yes, bad news. My daughter has just failed the entrance exam for St Mary's School. I don't know what she will do now. This is the best girls' school in the country. She should have got in … she studied hard.' He wore a hard-done-by expression.

Basistha's biggest preoccupation was badgering the Department of Irrigation to transfer him from Rajapur to somewhere closer to his family. His room was bare as bare: no books, nothing to distract him from his loneliness. Like Josi, he was missing seeing his family growing up. 'Your daughter is only five. She'll get a chance when she is older.'

'That is not possible. This was her only chance.' He looked so sad; he always looked so sad.

'How is your house, these days?' he asked. 'You must make sure cobras cannot get inside. Tell the *mysteri* to nail strips of bicycle tyre onto the door bottoms; otherwise cobras will kill the children.' Basistha had grown up in the *tarai,* so he knew.

'Do snakes often get into *pukka* houses?'

'At monsoon time, the baby cobras come. They have no fear. They strike and strike, and you cannot chase them out. I have found the most deadly snakes in top floor of my very house itself,' Basistha said. 'Kraits climb vertical walls and live in the roof, eating lizards and mice.'

'But snakes are scarce and shy; surely it is only agricultural workers who get bitten, after they disturb a snake?'

'They kill many, many people in the *tarai,* in rice fields, and inside houses also. I have seen. One fine day, I saw a Tharu farm labourer, who was bitten by one cobra. There was no health post; and, anyway, no-one has serum. The labourer was very, very ill and nearly died before they got him to the holy man in the village. The *guruwa* cut into the place where the snake had bitten; he then cut the head off a chicken and put its bottom to the wound. There is some suction which draws poison into the chicken,' Basistha explained. 'They cut twelve chickens to clean the bite before he recovered. It sounds crazy, doesn't it? I didn't believe it either, but the man was cured. I saw it! And without this treatment he would have died surely — one hundred per cent sure!'

I thought that I knew about snakes, and I didn't really believe that any would get into our house, but if locals said that they did, perhaps my information was wrong. Smaller beasts certainly managed to get in. One stormy night, a horrible silhouette startled me. Dancing in the candlelight, projected on the hallway wall, was the image of a huge scorpion. My nightmare creature had been resurrected after 300 million years; metre-long *Brontoscorpio* lived! Then I realised that the creature responsible for the shadow was small. I seized Simon's shoe and flattened it. It was time to follow Basistha's advice and fix bicycle inner-tubing along the screen door bottoms to keep scorpions and giant centipedes out. I was not becoming paranoid again. It was crazy not to take precautions, especially since David spent all his days lying on quilts on the floor.

Later, out in the garden, a small movement caught my eye. It was flowing like quicksilver. When it stopped, I made out a plump, stumpy-tailed, pinstriped skink. I squatted down to see. People wandered over to watch what I was watching and were horrified. Arjun arrived and confirmed that the skink was deadly. I'd expected people who lived close to the land to be more knowledgeable: the skink has no teeth, no venom. Were they conspiring to unnerve me?

Nightmare images are ingrained in Nepalis because naughty children are controlled by scary tales. They are told that twenty-centimetre-long, hairy moth caterpillars stick by their sucker-feet to naughty children's eyes and suck out their eyeballs. Such misinformation, and the rumours of malign winds that cook people, made it easier to understand why Nepalis worry so much. It began to freak me out, too, and I started to mistrust what the zoologist in me knew. Then Alexander appeared from the undergrowth in the garden, crying. 'It stung my hand!' He held it out to show me the redness. I was alarmed, though all the while thinking that the worst whatever-it-was was likely to be was a field wasp. 'What was it?' I asked him.

'A little teddy-thing — it was alive. It looked nice, but it hurt me!'

The 'fur' of the hairy caterpillar consists of thousands of minute, venom-packed hypodermics, and these had stuck into his skin. I had to pick each hair out individually with pointed tweezers. Soon after that, lots came into the house, but having realised they were unpleasant we scooped them up on pieces of paper and fired them into the garden. Alexander delighted in lobbing them high into the air, saying that he was teaching them to fly — so that they'd know how when they became moths.

I'd already started trying to put names to all the local birds, including the tantalising one I called the 'telephone bird', which I heard everywhere but never saw. And there were huge, unsteady flap-flap-glide birds that flew around, always in pairs. The first couple only offered a rear-view silhouette, and I asked Arjun, 'What were they?'

'Birds, sir,' he solemnly assured me.

'Yes, but what kind of birds?'

'Large birds, sir,' he told me, in all seriousness.

'You know, "sir" is really for men; you shouldn't call me "sir". Call me *didi*.'

'Sir?'

'Oh, never mind.' A while later, the ungainly flap-flap-glide birds came back. 'Brilliant. See those, Alexander? They're hornbills, pied hornbills.'

डे डे डे

A stranger walked into the garden. She clutched another great heap of laboratory reports and doctors' notes from hospitals in India and Nepal. This patient was in her mid-twenties, but thin and haggard: old before her years. Even from a distance, I could see that she was suffering, and I asked her to sit and tell me of her symptoms. She was on the waiting list to have part of her stomach removed, an operation that is considered obsolete in the West, now that powerful ulcer-healing medicines have been developed. I rifled through her medical files and was mystified, for she didn't even seem to have an ulcer. 'These sleeping pills that you are taking, though, are a bit too strong for your stomach. You should stop taking them. Then your stomach will get better, and you will not need the operation. Why are you taking sleeping pills?'

'To help me sleep,' she said, without a hint of sarcasm.

'Do you have any special problems or worries?'

'No' (puzzled look).

I looked at her and she looked at me. So much for psychotherapy. My Nepali was still very basic, and I also was chary of criticising local doctors who are so overwhelmed with patients that they have no time to keep up to date. I could easily undermine them, but then, when I left town, who would they turn to? And when it came time for us to leave Nepal after more than five years, I would realise how out of touch I had become. By then, too, I had discovered how stultifying the local approach to disease was. It was good business to keep patients ignorant and dependent. Patients were discouraged from taking responsibility for their disease or learning how to avoid the next attack.

'If you don't start to feel better after stopping the sleeping pills, you should come back and I will see if you need another medicine.' Suddenly she got up to leave. I couldn't get used to the abrupt way that Nepalis end conversations: no thanks; no good-byes. People just wander off at the end of a sentence. She never came back; either I'd deeply offended her (I didn't think so) or she was cured by taking my advice (perhaps) or she thought I was a complete idiot (probably).

Over supper that evening, I asked Simon, 'Is Himalaya a popular name locally?'

'I've never heard it before I met Thapa, although I know plenty of people called after individual *himals*. I know several Annapurnas, and a Manaslu, but commandeering the whole range seems a bit greedy.'

'Did you know Himalaya is getting married? He says it is all arranged, the date fixed, but they are not sure whom he'll marry yet! Can you believe it!'

'Oh, it's normal. I expect his family has picked an auspicious day, then started to look for a woman of the right caste. Maybe they are in a rush, since he's already in his late twenties!'

'He seems nice enough, but I feel sorry for the woman. Can you imagine a fashion-conscious Bombayite teetering around Rajapur, picking between the cowpats, her high heels sinking into the silt? Will she have any choice?'

'Depends on the family. Some are strict, others listen to the girl. And there are women who elope.'

'That sounds more exciting …'

'Yes, and elopements can even be "arranged". They're cheaper than proper weddings. Remember Tara? A very poor Brahmin who fell for a middle-class Newar. Neither family would have agreed to the marriage, so they eloped, and soon the match was accepted. Now they have a twelve-year-old son; they're still content.'

'Ah, a rare Nepali story with a happy ending!'

'Not so rare. I helped arrange Narendra's elopement, and he's happy with Laxmi and their two children, despite theirs being another cross-caste match that no-one approved of — at first anyway.'

डे डे डे

At home in Rajapur, we were constantly watched: when we emerged from the toilet or shower, as we walked between one room and another, as we sat in the garden or up on the roof, and when we were out anywhere. It was not until we returned to Tigertops and the National Park again that I recognised the strain I was under, being constantly observed, and with my struggles to understand and communicate without unknowingly offending. It was a release to indulge in normal, relaxed English conversation again with Westernised Nepalis. It was great to escape, but what most impressed Alexander was the 'proper sit-down toilet'; he loved sitting, enthroned, singing 'Tom, Tom the Python's Son'.

The first morning there, we were confronted by the sight of a very large American woman being helped aboard her elephant by nimble, good-looking Ramdin, the naturalist, who suggested that she sit behind and astride her elephant driver. As she struggled to get her huge thighs into position, she looked as if she was mounting him, not the elephant. 'There,' said Ramdin, grinning cheekily. 'This is the *maharani* position!' He made it sound like something from the *Kama Sutra*. The American's knuckles showed white as she clung onto the *howdah*; she could not believe that Alexander and David were going into the jungle too. Simon and Alexander rode on one elephant, and David and I would follow on another, on this, the first of half a dozen dawn and dusk rides into the forest. Their elephants shambled off into the forest, their vast backsides recalling the fat American's, except that the elephants looked as if they'd dieted successfully and were still wearing trousers that were four sizes too large.

We progressed through the dry, sleeping, *sal* forest in an ungainly, ponderous but surprisingly silent convoy. I was getting the knack of this weird motion, needing to concentrate less on keeping David comfortable, so that I was better able to look for wildlife. I loved the spotted deer: wide-eyed, anxious and always ready to run for their lives.

Then I had an eerie feeling of being watched, and noticed a small face was looking back at me. The jungle cat peeked out from a fork in the low branches of a tree, but as soon as we made eye contact it disappeared, and in the half-light beneath the canopy, I could have believed that it had melted away like the Cheshire Cat in *Alice*. The elephant driver steered a meandering path, and then, unexpectedly, he stopped to point at a smooth grey boulder, quite close. The boulder lifted her head to peer short-sightedly at us: a great Indian rhinoceros! Her one-year-old calf shuffled around behind his mother. They stared for a few seconds and bolted for safety. The calf was amazingly solid and bewilderingly nimble; yet with their thick folded skin, they look strangely prehistoric.

Onward, and we paused for the *mahout* to point out a circle of crushed grass where a tiger had slept. There was another abrupt change of direction, and our elephant driver kicked our mount to go deeper into the elephant grass. I then realised that what I had mistaken for smoke on the horizon was a wild elephant having a dust bath. 'Let's go close!' The *mahout* was nervous about approaching, but even from one hundred metres I could see that this individual had a strange profile, with a weird domed skull and fine tusks. He was one of the seven belligerent bull elephants then in the park — frustrated, perhaps, without feminine company. We did not imagine then that much worse elephant trouble was to come.

We pushed through scrubby jungle, passing a tree that had been snapped off one-and-a-half metres from the ground, with its stump peeled like a banana — by elephant. David burbled, happily entertained by the dappled patterns of green that moved over his face. But when we moved out from under the trees, he screwed up his eyes as if stabbed by the sunlight. His pupils were still terribly slow to accommodate to changes in light intensity, and he was easily dazzled, especially when he lay on his back in the *howdah*. There were peacocks everywhere: idiotic, ungainly birds. Closer to the river, we heard hysterical snorty-grunt alarm calls; the elephant driver became very animated, and by kicking our elephant behind her ears encouraged her to speed over towards the sound. The motion was even more uncomfortable, and I had to concentrate hard on protecting David, so that his head did not hit the restraining rail of the *howdah*. I could not really see where we were heading, or why.

The author of the grunt alarm call was a large, ivory-white langur sitting at the top of a tree over another big patch of undergrowth. He alternately grunt-called and looked down anxiously between his legs, the frill of light-coloured fur that haloed his jet-black face making him look as if his hair was standing on end in fright. As we approached the patch of tangled thorny scrub, a tiger roared: *aw-oom,* a lonely sad sound. The elephant stopped abruptly. We lunged forward; I grabbed David. The elephant's ears went out and the elephant driver pointed. I hardly dared breathe. I stared and stared, feeling foolish, repeatedly asking, 'Where, where …?' After several long minutes, I made out a stripy bottom. How did he see that tigress? She was less than ten metres away, but so, so difficult to see; her stripes broke up her profile so that she merged into the dappled scrub. The tigress yawned, wearily got up and wandered into the undergrowth.

The *mahout* drove our elephant around the patch of scrub and then into the tangle again. Suddenly, we came face to face with the tigress; she was just a few metres away — close enough to be frightening, even though we sat four metres above her. She sat sphinx-like, facing me so that I could see her beautiful white throat and chest. The end of her tail twitched like a domestic cat's. She opened her mouth in a silent snarl and left. She slunk away, and we didn't see her again.

David slept. A cockerel crowed, surprisingly, *cock-a do* … Were there still villages within the reserve, or do villagers encroach? It called again. It was a strange, stammering, tinny, truncated *cock-a do* … and a magnificent male red jungle fowl, head thrust forward, sprinted across a clearing ahead of us; he looked like he was running for his life. His metallic, emerald-green tail flashed in the dawn light, contrasting with his fine red comb. Then, a minute or two later, he went sprinting across in front of us in the other direction: a bird of small brain.

The motion of the elephant was soporific, and the sounds of the forest lulled me. Tennis racquet sized leaves of *tatri* trees crashed when they fell in this pre-monsoon 'autumn' at springtime. Crickets sounded like someone winding up a watch. A jolly Indian tree-pie sang *I've-got-four-toes*. There was a *tyou-tyou* from an oriole and *see-see-you* — the mating call of the great tit. My poorly slept mind started to garble birdcalls again. *See-see-you*; CCU; Coronary Care Unit … Intensive Care … Special Care Baby Unit; VSD; ventricular septal defect. In came a hawk cuckoo with an ascending call of *renal ageneSIS*. Anatomical and illness words — borborygmi, febrile-febrile-febrile, corpus callosum — echoed around and around my head and worries about David came flooding back: *bobili* — he's *really ill*. Then a manic tailorbird's *tik tik tik* nagged: *David's-sick-sick-sick. Take him home! Take him home!* Words and worries whirled inside my head until suddenly a black-headed oriole asked *Glass-of-beer?*, bringing me back to consciousness. Mmm, beer … and I tuned back into bird-watching and butterflies again; but the knot in my stomach took a while to fade away.

Later that day, Manager Karan Rana joined us for supper. 'What did you see today?' he asked.

'A rhino and calf; she was wearing a collar. Why the collar?'

He told us that rhinos had became extinct in Bardiya because of poaching, but in 1986 a male and three females were tranquillised in Chitwan — the park in the *tarai* to the east — and zoologists put collars on them and dragged them into a truck. By the time these animals had been driven half the length of Nepal, they were awake and very angry: releasing eight tonnes of furious rhino was exciting! Those four did well, more were brought and now there is a healthy population.

'I was impressed with our *mahout*,' I offered. 'He was wonderfully observant, and knowledgeable!'

'Yes, they know the jungle. But you must not call them *mahouts*. They are *phanits*; the *mahout* is the lowly boy who cleans up after the elephant!'

There were urgent yelps from close by. Sensing fear in the call, I asked, 'What was that?'

'The alarm of spotted deer,' Karan told us. Then, 'There's a leopard about!'

Here we were, comfortably tucking into our dinner while life-and-death struggles were going on within a few hundred metres of us. There was a large contented sigh from Alexander. 'I like it here,' he said. We'd hardly noticed that the attentive waiters had brought him portion after portion of lemon pudding, until finally he'd had enough. 'Pop goes the Alexander,' Simon chuckled.

Walking out after settling David for the night at the tented camp, I startled a dhole — an endangered, long-legged Indian wild dog with a bushy, black, foxy tail. I rushed into the restaurant to tell Simon, and then he and I spent a relaxed evening together, feeling as if we were on holiday. The tranquillity and peace of Bardiya was therapeutic, but it also got me thinking about our strange, isolated, nomadic lifestyle, and I raised what I thought was a new idea with Simon. 'I know we decided we'd have only two children, but David will never be much of a playmate for Alexander. Should we have another baby? A third would be more stimulating for David, too; he so loves company.'

Simon was ahead of me, as usual. His undemonstrativeness meant it was often difficult to know what he was thinking, but he surprised me when he answered, for he had already thought deeply about this. He was scared of the risk of another child with problems like David's, but he'd thought — even as early as the day David was born — that we would have another child, company for Alexander. Only now, though, did he tell me that he'd dreamed of our third child a couple of days after David's birth. I had thought I had protected Simon from my anxieties, but although he was slow to admit it to himself, he knew even then that David would be handicapped.

'You are funny, Simon. Why does it take so long for you to mention such important things?'

'Oh, I don't know. It took me a long time to decide, and I didn't want to pressurise you.'

'You wouldn't — not like that anyway.'

'I thought you'd tell me when you were ready,' he said, folding me into his arms.

'You know me so well ... I was thinking I might try weaning David onto a bottle. I won't conceive again while I'm breast-feeding. If he can manage a bottle, we could see whether our *karma* is good enough to make another babe. And if David can't manage a bottle, I'll continue to feed him. Okay?' We liked the idea of *karma* deciding. David, though, managed a bottle easily, and my monthly cycle returned exactly two weeks after his last breast-feed.

Next morning, we sauntered through the parched forest to an inflatable boat pulled up on a little pebbled beach. We scrambled aboard, Alexander sitting with a leg dangling over one side as if he was riding a horse, and David lying luxuriously on the floor of the boat, on a changing mat and shaded by a large Chinese umbrella with dragons on the handle. We pushed off and were immediately snatched up by the river and swept surprisingly swiftly downstream. Looking north, we could see where the Karnali River bursts out of the gorge at Chisapaani. This is one relatively easy route over the Himalayas for birds that spend the summer in China, as well as a traditional trading route for people. Alexander shouted, 'Look at all the colours of the stones!' The cobbles visible just under the water in the rapids were a blur of coral red, slate blue, ochre, leaf green, bone white and lemon yellow.

David liked the rough bits best; the louder the water slopped against the boat, the louder he laughed. Sand martins whizzed by low, banking to avoid the boat. Osprey sat motionless in treetops, then plummeted into a deep green stretch of river and emerged with fish in their claws. There were sentinel lines of huge cormorants digesting breakfast and looking as if their wings were pegged out to dry. Orange, black and white mergansers, streamlined diving ducks, skimmed over the water. Terns screamed at us. A cascade of a dozen otters came pouring down the bank, then popped their heads up all around us to see what we were. They whistled to each other, lost their nerve, disappeared, surfaced again and again, until we hit another pebbled shoal and rushing rapids.

On the Rajapur bank of the river, there was a huddle of women. I turned to Simon, pointed to them and asked, 'What are they doing?'

Simon shaded his eyes to see. 'Panning for gold! They must be Sonaha. Basistha was talking about them in the office. It is relatively lucrative: pays seventy-five rupees a day, which by local standards is a good wage,' he said, 'but it's more labour-intensive than it sounds.'

'Seventy-five rupees doesn't sound like much money.'

'A kilo of rice costs eighteen rupees, which'll feed a hungry labourer for two days ... well above survival level. Seventy-five rupees is good money.'

'We live in another world, don't we, yet so close physically.' Everything seemed so idyllic that it was hard to imagine our neighbours being locked into iniquitous feudalism.

Simon continued, as if reading my thoughts, 'At least the Sonaha are free, and our project should make agriculture more reliable locally, so that their men will find it easier to get labouring work. Here, people starve if the rains fail or if floods or animals destroy crops. And it is the very poor — not the landowners — who suffer if the rice crop fails.'

'No wonder the locals don't smile much!' I said.

'Oh, they do. They find plenty of excuses to celebrate.'

CHAPTER FOURTEEN

business as usual

AS THE WEEKS AND MONTHS WENT BY, THE ILL-KEMPT sons of the unshaven traders in Rajapur bazaar became used to us and they hassled us less. Shopping trips became more enjoyable, and I began to join in with some of the local gossip. High-caste girls from the 'boarding school' liked to practise their English: '*Namasté,* auntie!' and 'What ees your country, auntie?' or 'How old you are, madam?'; 'Your native place is London. No?'; 'What ees your babyname?'

'He's David — my brother,' Alexander proudly told them. Simon was a big man locally, but although locals had trouble pronouncing his name, Alexander was a greater celebrity in the bazaar. There were choruses of, 'Hello, Alison!', 'How are you Alexandra!' or 'Where you going Ali Sand?' Maybe they thought we were Muslims. In response, Alexander offered a solemn '*Namasté*' or a cheery 'good mauling!' David was too small to be worthy of a name, but all agreed he was a handsome baby. They didn't make us feel like the outcastes that we were.

From our house on the edge of the village, we usually walked into the bazaar along a dirt road lined with hibiscus bushes. African marigolds grew everywhere. Hedgerows were covered in cobalt-blue trumpet-shaped convolvulus that transformed into royal purple through the course of the day. Gorgeous green parakeets squawked. Magnificent mango trees and giant bamboo groves gave shade and shelter for iridescent sunbirds. Then we passed Stork's home:

Sri Ganesh Babu English Residential School
(established in the year 2040)
Temple of Wisdom

Chanted, rote-learned English drifted out from one glassless classroom window. I felt David chuckle; he was amused by the unfamiliar sound. From another classroom, younger voices shouted,

'Ba ba blake seep,
Hab you ainy oool,
Yais sor, yais sor, tree bugs fool ...'

Alexander asked, 'What language are the children speaking?'

Opposite the school was an ancient *peepal* tree and one of Rajapur's two cinemas, an odd, bulging building with mud walls, the roof a patchwork of second-hand, bright-blue, ex-UN plastic sheeting. Here we plunged into a dark alleyway of stalls roofed with corrugated tin sheets and bits of tattered sacking. The air was heavy with human musk, pungent local cigarettes and dust. There was hardly any room to walk, but people rode motorbikes or pushed bicycles through. This is where women mostly came to buy thread and cheap feminine trinkets. I called it the bangle bazaar.

Indian women in saris squatted with knees higher than their shoulders; they, the only female traders always in the bazaar, massaged Tharu villagers' wrists to squeeze on the smallest possible glass bangles without shattering the fragile glass. The wide-eyed, impassive purchasers submitted to this kneading in silence. Men in other stalls sold hookah pipe parts, gaudy hair slides, red tikkas to stick on women's foreheads, false extensions for ponytails (in black or scarlet), exercise books, footballs, balls of string; there were jars full of bright, shiny buttons, cotton reels and needles.

Women carried their money tucked into the sari waistband or close to a breast so that the banknotes came out creased, warm and moist. 'What's that little animal there? Look, it's washing its face.' Alexander pointed underneath one of the stalls. A grubby, skeletal cat shot out from nowhere and the well-fed rat fled. We'd paused at a stall that sold an array of posters of Hindu gods, Hulk Hogan and open-shirted Hindi film stars. These were the idols of the adolescents; Nepalis young and old were astonished that I knew none of their names. 'Please give me this one, grandfather. I would like the man with the cigarette.'

'Two rupees.' He raised two fingers as if telling me to go forth. He had a wonderfully lined face and he peered out through lenses as thick as Coke bottle bottoms.

'Who is this?' I asked, wanting to make contact.

'Two rupees!' he said, shaking two fingers at me more insistently. He assumed we had no language in common; he was probably deaf, too. I so wanted to chat. As I wandered on, a small boy at my side answered for him, 'Sangay Dutta — *burra hero, memsahib*.' At least someone understood me. 'You have nice baby, *memsahib*.' The boy's grin revealed rotten teeth.

Further on was a crumpled old woman. Smiling broadly, she beckoned me over. Her meagre wares — cigarettes, matches, soap powder, chewing tobacco and battered packets of Glucose biscuits — were unenticingly laid out under a disintegrating umbrella on a piece of frayed sack. I could hardly make out a word she said, hindered as she was by an unmanageable set of tandoori-red buck-teeth. I bought matches that I didn't really need, and walked on, nervous of losing an eye to one of the many protruding pieces of corrugated iron. We ran a gauntlet of quips and jibes from insolent small boys. There were shouts of 'twoice-the-proice', mimicking how English sounds to them. Others would shriek, 'Waat-ees-yoourr-name-moi-name-ees-Chhoiayn' (without a breath), mimicking the diphthongs they heard in my impure vowels. Then, realising I was carrying the baby, they'd cluster around to admire him. 'So small. So cute!' How I revelled even in the approval of the bazaar louts.

The bangle bazaar was dark, lively and loud, with music blasting out from stalls that hired out loudspeakers for wedding parties. I was always slightly relieved to emerge into daylight and fresh air again in the main street. The delicious smell of fresh roasted peanuts called us over to one salesman; on the opposite corner, under the aerial roots of a *banyan* tree, others traded in an intriguing selection of relics: the insides of well-used, rusty old umbrellas (or even just an odd spoke), beaten up and scratched second-hand torches, rusty padlocks and single replacement thongs for flip-flops. Emaciated mutts fought for scraps; the teats of the bitches swung as they trotted between rubbish heaps. Bony cats, their matted coats almost a uniform dust grey, skulked under stalls to avoid kicks, or squabbled over scant pickings. An elderly stallion with an unset broken leg hobbled about, nibbling soiled plastic bags; his rheumy, inflamed eyes attracted legions of flies. Goats were down on their knees eating onion skins. There were chickens everywhere. A few ducks — daubed pink or orange to indicate ownership — dabbled around in those drains that were sufficiently blocked with rubbish to contain some stinking black water.

I stooped to enter a quilt, mattress and cloth shop-shack. The proprietors, father and son, were two adipose heaps that seemed to have been poured into opposite corners. The greasy, unshaven father was heaped over the cash box; his broken, gappy teeth were stained chicken tikka red. Son was slumped, limp as a rotten fish, on another mat. Sweat made their skin gleam as if they had been dipped in oil. '*Namasté*, shopkeeper-*ji,*' I respectfully greeted Father, with a cheery grin. He responded with an expressionless chin jerk, indicating that I should be addressing his son. Son looked blank. 'I need a mattress for my small baby, shopkeeper-*ji*.'

'For that?' he asked, stabbing a disapproving index finger at Alexander.

'No, no, for this small baby,' I said, pointing to David in my papoose. 'It must be 102 by 42 centimetres.'

He selected some rhino-grey cloth. 'I will make the mattress one hundred centimetres long and fifty-two centimetres wide.' I had to concentrate hard to communicate at all in broken Nepali, but now I was distracted by Father torturing a ragged, uncombed grandchild. He squeezed her until she howled, then let her go only to grab her matted hair just as she thought she'd escaped. When he grinned at the sport, his blood-red teeth looked like fangs. As she cried, Father asked if he should give her to me so that I could eat her; she then became really terrified. Alexander looked on, horrified, while I thought to myself, 'God! I thought these people loved children!' I tried to distract Father from this merciless teasing with a forceful, 'No, the mattress must be 102 by 42 centimetres.'

'*Tik*,' he agreed, in Hindi.

'When will it be made?' I wondered about suggesting a date to come back, but knew I'd get into a muddle about whether the date was according to the Nepali or the Gregorian calendar. 'Shall I come back tomorrow? Next week?'

'*Ahilé* (now). Sit. Wait.' I was delighted to get such instant service.

'I'll go to the post office and return in a few minutes.' (No response.)

I picked my way down the back street to the post office, stepping over piles of goat droppings, buffalo pancakes and brown puddles left by children with diarrhoea. Alexander skilfully hopscotched between them, and then stopped to observe with coy interest a group of small children playing in the filth with stones and bottle-tops. The post office was open, but deserted except for a couple of lost-looking pink ducks that shat with fright as we entered. Portraits of the king and queen garlanded with now-desiccated marigolds looked down disapprovingly; the queen always looked as if she had just smelled something unpleasant. She probably had. I wondered how often I wore a disgusted look: I often cursed my oversensitive nose.

There wasn't even anyone to ask when it might be possible to buy stamps and post my letters. We returned to the mattress shop, and sat down. They did not seem to notice. The torturee had escaped and her grandfather looked bored again. 'When will the mattress be ready?' I smiled sweetly at him.

'*Ahilé* (now)'. Father and Son remained inert, unblinking; there was no evidence of any work being done, or much cerebral activity either. 'Where is the mattress, then?' I persisted.

Another unhelpful jerk of the chin. These unattractive, slightly wobbly piles of humanity seemed so rude, but this was because I didn't yet understand local manners. I asked, 'Where? The next shop?'

'No.'

'Where then?'

'Close to the hotel.'

'Hotel? Which hotel? The Bageswari, or the tea shop nearby?'

No answer.

'Where? Can I take it? Please show me, shopkeeper-*ji*.'

'There's no need; the mattress is coming now,' he said, wearied by my fussing.

Heading back towards the post office, I noted that fresh diarrhoeal offerings had been deposited in the meantime. I thought about my parents and others who had written saying they might visit us. Everyone at home imagined us living within view of the virgin snows of the great *himals,* and I was quite sure that my mother — for one — wouldn't enjoy stepping between assorted species of faeces. I was getting used to it, though, and Alexander had already developed a sixth sense for avoiding filth.

I became hopeful as I climbed the three steps into the post office. A few people were now hanging about behind the counter, but 'No-one is here,' I was told. '*Hakim-sahib* is drinking tea and will be back soon. Please sit down here and wait, madam. Come sit — here behind the counter … Your son is very handsome. The baby also.' A wrinkly Nepali, wearing an old bush jacket and a loincloth, brought me a chair. His *dhoti* revealed spectacular varicose veins. He seemed to be the guard, a post invariably reserved for the frailest, unhealthiest old men. He was too lowly to sit with the others.

'That's kind, but I need to meet a tailor. I'll come back again in a few minutes.'

The guard stood to attention and spoke. 'The office closes at 4 pm, *huzoor*.'

Back at the mattress shop, we sat until David grew restless and I said, 'I'll come back tomorrow.'

'Sit, sit.' Son's expression asked why I was giving him so much hassle. I waited a few more minutes, idly wondering if these inert shopkeepers ever contract bedsores while at work. More in an attempt to make conversation than out of any real desire to give these men more work, I said, pointing to Alexander, 'This child needs trousers. Can you make some?'

'Trouser banana?'

'Yes,' I said, wondering what I was agreeing to in this odd language, Hindi.

'Not possible.' Nothing was happening here, so I returned to the post office. It was closed.

The following day, I returned, purposefully clutching my measuring tape, hoping that a prop might help me communicate better. The new mattress was lying there, but it was too short and too wide for the cot. Father could not deal with my complaint and said Son was eating and would come soon. I tried the post office again. It was open, but no-one could open the safe containing the stamps. Back to the shop. This time, Son was busy at his treadle sewing machine inserting a piece of cloth on the end of the mattress to make it longer. 'Look. This is too wide.'

'Fifty-two centimetres is correct!' he said.

'It will not fit in the cot; please make it ten centimetres narrower. I will come back tomorrow.' Son looked immensely weary and in need of a snooze to digest his lunch. I returned to the post office, where the wizened old *chaukidar* with spectacular varicose veins told me that it closed for the weekend.

Just around the corner from the post office, beside one of the foetid drains most popular with the pink- and orange-painted ducks, was

Rajapur's biggest private dispensary. *Docter* Bhandari who owned and ran it had been the paramedic at the government health post locally. When the government transferred him to work in the hills, he ignored the directive, and has never taken up his new posting; he continues to be the busiest *docter* in Rajapur. He provides twenty-four-hour, seven-day-a-week health care, while the new government paramedic kicks his heels. *Docter* Bhandari had three month's medical training, but ran a casualty service, stitching wounds and plastering fractured limbs in one shed while his clinic went on in a *pukka* building next to his well-stocked dispensary.

From *docter* Bhandari's house (where Josi, Himalaya and some of the others lodged) the route home was through the square, which was littered with straw for buffaloes and oxen. The Muslim butcher squatted amongst the cow dung selling fly-ridden goat meat. Our second cinema blasted out endless distorted unintelligibilia. There was a barber, too, with a splendid, waxed handlebar moustache. I stopped to watch him at work; he preened, enjoying being the centre of attention. He finished cutting a man's hair, shaved the hairline around his ears with a fearsome cut-throat razor, then set to with a violent head massage, pummelling the scalp with fists, noisily slapping the forehead, vigorously kneading the back of the neck, wrenching the head left and right to make the neck crack; finally, with the fingers of both hands interlocked, he rained blows onto the victim's head with such force that the head recoiled and the barber's knuckles made an odd, bony, rattling sound. The man paid ten rupees, and another — passing the time while waiting to leave town in a *tanga* — took his place in the victim's chair.

'Fancy a haircut, Alexander?' He looked horrified.

'That would hurt!' I would have to learn to cut his hair myself.

Strolling back, we passed one of the other popular *docters*. Balding *docter* Badrinath Jha sauntered along a line of six patients on a bench, listening to their chests in turn with his stethoscope. Someone lay out on a *charpoy* in the street, receiving intravenous fluids from a glass bottle carelessly slung from the corner of the front door of his one-room clinic.

A little further down the main road north out of town, I trod in a cowpat and disturbed a battalion of flies. Shit oozed around my shoe and onto my foot, and the smell wafted up to nose-level. Before I had time to think what to do about it, I found myself dodging bicycles, motorbikes and larger traffic, while clutching onto Alexander to keep him safe. We'd arrived amongst the usual traffic jam of buffalo carts all jostling to get into the rice mills. Thence, the way home was across a large fallow field, luxuriant with cannabis plants that gave off a pungent aromatic smell and made our legs itch. Beyond the itchy field, three fierce dogs tried to stop us passing through their territory. I hesitated, knowing I was foolish to let them see they'd intimidated me; next time I should carry a stick.

'Hello, auntie! This way come!' And one of the smarmy, high-caste girls scored a surprisingly accurate hit when she chucked a stone at the dogs. She beckoned us, palm downwards. As she was showing us a short cut through her compound, she pointed at my foot, and their hand pump and ordered, 'You must wash here, auntie!' She pumped for me while I washed my leg and my sandal.

Then I heard the telephone bird calling from the top of a bush, and at last managed to get a good look at it. It was a self-confident bird, with the same dark line through the eye, hooked bill and long tail as European shrikes. This innocent-looking little bird had a beautiful brick-red lower back that merged into a fine grey head. Mr Gautam, the landlord, emerged from someone's house to see what I was looking at.

'Ah, the *bhanera*! This what-do-you-call-it … mouth,' he said, pouting his lips.

'Beak.'

'This beak is used by Kathmandu Newars for feeding rice to a baby for the first time; it assures wisdom.' It was the rufous-backed shrike, which catches insects, small reptiles and young birds and impales them on thorns where they struggle and squirm until they die or the shrike rips them apart and eats them. After that day, I saw *bhanera* advertising their presence all over the place.

When Alexander and I returned to the bazaar two days later, I managed to post my letters, an achievement that gave me enormous satisfaction. The mattress was lying in the shop: it now wore an extra appendage that had been ineptly sewn onto the end to make it the right length but it was still fifty-two centimetres wide. I repeated my requirements and headed back home again. En route, I noticed a tremulous old fellow in a Muslim skull-cap; a white beard fringed his toothless mouth; he had shaved his top lip. He was squatting amidst heaps of unlabelled seeds on his rattly old barrow made from two old bicycle wheels and planks. '*Assalaamu alaikum!*'

'You're speaking a different language, Mummy,' Alexander said. 'Is it Australian?'

'That's "hello" in Arabic, but I'm not sure that the stallholder is listening.' His face still wore a blank, uninterested stare. I persisted, 'What vegetable seeds have you got, grandfather?' No response.

'What do you want, madam?' a Good Samaritan asked me.

'What has he got?'

'What do you want?' (This could go on forever.)

'Carrots?'

'No carrots.'

'What *has* he got then?'

'What do you want?' (I cursed at not being able to speak better Nepali … or Urdu.)

'What's this?' I said pointing at one heap.

'Lady's fingers.' (Revolting, snot-slimy okra: we had eaten far too many last hot season in Pakistan.)

'And this?'

'*Pharsi.*' (Pumpkin — boring, woody and too sweet.)

'And this?'

'*Baanta* (aubergine).' This sounds dangerously close to *bhaanta* (vomit). We had also eaten this ad nauseam the previous year; Simon had never been keen on them, anyway.

'Hasn't he got any green vegetables?'

'Spinach!'

'Ah! Excellent, *dai*. I love spinach! Which is the spinach?'

The stallholder still would not speak, but he was responding now. Pointing a gnarled, arthritic finger, he indicated five heaps including fenugreek and cumin; baffled by the choice, I appealed to the crowd that had gathered. 'Which is the most tasty kind of spinach?'

'It depends what you like! All are tasty ... if you like them.'

Moments later, a man appeared with three young spinach plants and casually tossed one on each of three piles of seeds to help me sort out which was which. He then wandered away without even glancing over his shoulder. I bought two kinds of spinach, cauliflower, cumin and maize seeds. The Muslim had trouble adding up the cost of the five items, so the crowd helped: he called out the prices, and they shouted back the totals, then dispersed.

I wandered on the thirty metres to the vegetable stall. But there was nothing much on offer: a few wrinkly potatoes, flaccid horseradishes, some tired, red, Bombay onions and some yellowing peas. There never was much. Feeling dismal, and wondering what I could give David to eat, I wandered as far as the *chowk*, the noisy, dusty and fly-ridden crossroads at the centre of the village. It was an unattractive corner where buses revved and honked three-tone horns, soliciting for passengers. Agrawal's shop often stocked food luxuries, but that day all that I could find of interest were 'World Famous' Stud and Mandalay cream remedies for premature ejaculators and white and blue boxes, purporting to have been made in Mayfair, England but looking like museum pieces from the forties. They contained Feminine Cream — for frigidity. We didn't need either remedy.

Another two days later, I was back at the mattress shop. 'The mattress is finished?' I pulled out my measuring tape, trying to look assertive. The extra piece of cloth that Son had ineptly inserted gave the mattress an unconventional shape; it was now about the right length, but it was still fifty-two centimetres wide.

'This will not fit into the baby's cot. It is too wide!' I complained.

'Sit. Sit. I will make it again now.'

'I will come again tomorrow, shopkeeper-*ji*!'

On the next of my now daily visits to the shop, Father snarled silently in response to my '*Namasté*', flashing his gappy, terracotta-coloured fangs. An object reminiscent of a stranded river dolphin lay in the corner of the shop: the mattress now had a waist and shoulders. I took it home, appalled that it had taken a week to achieve a task that should have taken an hour or two. Pummelling made it more or less fit the rosewood cot that the *mysteris* had made for David, and having installed it I laughed at myself for getting so peeved about it all. It did not matter that it had taken a week. I had time, and so did everyone else: this was the one resource everyone seemed rich in and generous with. How maladjusted of me not to recognise this.

I was yet to discover, though, how this relaxed attitude would wreck my chances of achieving anything, and how it would almost scupper Simon's project. Back at the house, I told Sita about the humourless shopkeepers.

'*Mussalmans* never laugh, *memsahib!*' she said, giggling, delighted to jibe at her exploitative neighbours.

CHAPTER FIFTEEN

dust devil

EVERY DAY GULIYA WASHED OUR CLOTHES, HUNG them out to dry, then mopped the floors. It was part of life in Rajapur to wage war against dust, but I told her, 'It is not necessary to clean the whole house daily, *didi*.'

'*Bahini* is unhappy with me?'

'*Melai cushy lagyo — eḳdum.* You are an excellent worker. But you do not need to do so much.'

'It is necessary to clean everything every day.'

Employing most of Guliya's family seemed like shameful decadence, but we giggled a lot and they seemed to find my snipes at men outrageously funny. They were easy, pleasant company; I liked them and only wished I felt more confident about leaving the children in their care. They never seemed to be able to predict problems and never planned their work; I even wondered whether they would notice if the house caught fire.

I was keen to be free to work a little, though, and I thought I might be able to recruit someone to help David with his exercises. On one of our short trips to Kathmandu, we took on a delightful Tamang woman called Shanti. Having previously been employed by an intense Scottish educationalist, Shanti understood and accommodated the strange ideas Europeans have about bringing up children. She knew that we see raising children as more than just fending them off and stopping them crying; she even knew about educational games. Before Shanti came to join us, I warned, 'Conditions in Rajapur are not good. We have no electricity, you will live in a mud hut, and there are snakes.'

'No problem, *didi*. I come from village — this is my life.'

She was in her early thirties, intelligent, self-confident; she spoke good English, Nepali, Tamang and Hindi. It was such a relief to find someone to whom I could chat, and who understood our needs, and she soon took over the organisation of the kitchen and the house. 'Maybe you'll correct all my mistakes when I speak Nepali?'

'No problem, *memsahib*. I can do.'

'Look, I've been writing the names of the spices, flour and sugar. Perhaps you can check these too, and write some new ones? I'm sure your writing must be neater than mine.' She picked up the sugar tin and sounded out 'ch-i-n-ee' even more hesitantly than I would have done. 'Your Nepali writing is very beautiful, *memsahib*.'

'I'm sorry, didn't you go to school?'

'No, I did not have this chance, but I have learned a little bit at adult literacy classes.'

I shouldn't have been surprised. More than three-quarters of Nepali women are illiterate.

Shanti quickly made friends with Guliya, whom she respectfully called *bauju*, sister-in-law, but was angry seeing what a hard time she got from our high-caste neighbours. One evening, I gave Guliya a stash of empty beer bottles that she could sell for a rupee each. Then Guliya left for the day and high-caste children surrounded her, wanting to know what she was carrying; when they discovered valuable loot, they each ran off with two or three until she was left with none. She stood there, smiling blandly. 'Why doesn't she stop them, Shanti- *didi*?'

'She can't; not those Brahmin children. They will cause too much of sorrow for her family.'

'That's awful!' I said.

'Life's like that, *didi*!' I watched, fuming, wanting to intervene. Why was Guliya so passive?

I changed the subject. 'Why's Arjun wrapped his head up like that?' He'd tied his scarf as a splendid turban.

'He has body pain and fever,' Shanti explained.

'Arjun. Are you ill? Should I give you a *checkup?*' He never looked strong, and had an asthmatic wheeze. Probably it was illness that had got his family into debt.

'It is not necessary, sir,' he said to me.

'Don't go wasting your money on consulting *docter* Jha!' I said. 'I can give you medicines if you need them. Please let me help you.'

'Sir.' He was still standing to attention. I so wished I could get him to loosen up a bit. I tried a change of subject. 'Arjun, tell me: is it hard living as a *kamaiya* ... bonded to a landlord?'

'Hard, sir?'

'With a landlord making decisions for you?'

'It is good for us, sir. Secure. We get a place to build a house.'

'But you are not paid for the work you do?'

'It is enough ... We get rice, and sometimes meat.' And he wandered back to his weeding.

Shanti said, giggling, 'He is shy to let you treat him, yaa? They say you are lady-doctor, isn't it!'

I smiled, too. 'Poor Arjun. He is so serious. I wish he'd talk to me. But maybe you know about the system that ties Tharus to a landlord? I ask Arjun and Sita, but I never get honest answers. They must know it is unjust.'

'Life is hard, but that is normal for them. They are treated more like cattles than people. The head of the household gets one *bigha* of irrigated land to grow rice. He keeps one-quarter of the rice he has grown, and the landlord keeps three-quarters. He also gets little bit land for building one small, small house, grow little bit maize and chillies … it is enough to live only. The whole family have to work for that one landlord so that the family have small house until next January.

'When a *kamaiya* needs money for house construction, marriage, medicine, anything, they take loan from landlord. After the contract with that landlord expires, any *kamaiya* wanting to change to another landlord must first pay back the loan. If he can't, he has to carry on working with the same landlord or change to a new landlord who will pay the debt. It is not usually possible for *kamaiya* to pay back the loan — ever. Their debts continue from one generation to the next.'

'Life is so hard for these people.'

'Yes, sometimes the landlord cheats and increases the debt, and these uneducated Tharus don't know. They can't count. Life isn't easy in the hills, but here it is too hard and unfair for the Tharu peoples. I think it is most worst, isn't it.'

With Shanti's help, I pieced together the story of Arjun's arrival in Rajapur. He'd come from the Dang Valley with his parents when he was about three. The family had been forced off their land and were struggling to survive. Relatives though had already settled in Rajapur and sent word that there was enough work. It was a big risk moving, but it was a bigger risk to stay. Lots of Arjun's relatives died in those early days in Rajapur — of fever and of the evil eye. But now he thought that life was good. I'd thought of myself as a bit of a pioneer, but I'd not taken any risks; these people had gambled with their lives when they'd resettled here. Tharus represent seventy per cent of Rajapur's population, but few have any influence: most are *kamaiyas* and seem absolutely owned by their landlord. One landlord, in hospital in Lucknow with kidney failure, even commanded a *kamaiya* to donate a kidney for the transplant operation. The kidney was provided, but the landlord died anyway.

Later, an old neighbour came into the garden. Shanti said something that made the woman turn and leave. 'What did she want?' I asked.

'She came to take vegetables.'

'What — to help herself to vegetables from our garden!' I said indignantly.

'Yes, it is normal; vegetables belong to everyone; but I told her that foreigners live here now so she could not take vegetables any more.'

I felt a pang of embarrassment. 'If vegetables are common property, I should share, Shanti-*didi*.'

'No, you don't need do that. The garden will be stripped in a day!'

'What should we do, then?'

'They know foreigners have different ideas; landlords are mean, too. It's no problem, *didi*.'

I didn't want to be thought of as mean. 'Is rice common, too?' I asked.

'No, no-one takes another's rice; that would be stealing ... And shall I change the bed sheets?'

'Why? Guliya only washed them yesterday!'

'David has vomited; didn't you know?'

'Oh no, not again!'

'He is really sick, isn't he?' she said, looking concerned.

'Yes, he is really sick, and I don't know why he vomits so much.'

'But you are a doctor, isn't it?'

At first the Clever Doctors in Cambridge had thought that David's vomiting was because the salts in his blood were out of balance, and then it seemed to be because of the awful calorie supplements they said he needed. But now, without these, he still vomited several times a week, although it didn't upset him and he did not seem particularly unwell in between times. He did have a recurring problem of constipation: relieving himself hurt so much sometimes. Fortunately, though, medicines helped. Most of the time he seemed happy, burbling away to himself—'dad-dad-dad' — or tunefully gargling on his spittle; he chuckled so much that his good humour was infectious. He was still doing little for himself; I knew now that I must allot plenty of time to stimulate him to develop. I also started patching his good eye as the Cambridge eye experts had half-heartedly suggested

I should. If we didn't do that, the retina of his lazy eye would never develop and he'd only ever have vision in one eye.

Meanwhile, I was delighted to be able to gossip with Shanti in English, and it was wonderful knowing she would sensibly, reliably help care for David — and three-year-old Alexander, too. We tried to think of ways of keeping David close to people to keep him involved. I'd often lie David outside in one of the two small, covered porches of our house, where he was protected from the glare of the sun, but could still enjoy listening to the amazing variety of birdcalls. But this was only comfortable at the beginning of the day, before the flies got really busy. I left him one morning, asking Shanti to bring him indoors after a while, and walked into the bazaar with Alexander to buy some cloth to make curtains. We wandered out into the glare, and soon I pointed across to a whirling spiral of dust. 'Look Alexander!'

'What is it? It looks like a ghost gone bonkers.'

'It's a dust devil.' Then suddenly, as if it had heard me, it changed direction and came charging drunkenly towards us. I just had time to hold the edge of my full skirt over Alexander's nose and mouth. It swept through, leaving us sneezing, sore-eyed, with grit between our teeth.

Each cloth shop in the bazaar had a black, treadle-operated Singer sewing machine outside. Some tailors sat whirring swathes of bright fabric between their dextrous fingers, their frenetic peddling eating up shapeless cloth and miraculously turning it into figure-hugging blouses or full skirts. The noise of their industry mingled with the din of competing, badly tuned radios; each radio was neatly clad in its own gingham or floral outfit. I thought it would be easy to find a willing tailor. It wasn't. I couldn't get the first to understand what I wanted, despite showing him a sample curtain. I tried another; he was adamant that I wanted a different design. What I needed — he said — was a proper curtain: a rectangle of cloth held up by two nails. A third tailor took my new cloth and started cutting it. 'Wait, wait! You don't know what I want yet!'

'Yes, I do — you want a curtain!'

'How many? What size?'

'I don't know. You haven't told me.'

'So why are you cutting the cloth?'

'To make the curtains,' he said, without sarcasm.

'Look, I'll come back with my friend who can explain better.'

Shanti dismissed the third tailor, and we talked to others. Eventually, we found a young man who said he could start right away. He seemed twitchy and hyperactive, and his eyebrows met in the centre like a werewolf's (or maybe I was beginning to have paranoid delusions), but Shanti said he was the best we'd find. Then, as we walked back home, she said, 'These local tailors cannot make curtains.'

'Surely it's not so difficult?'

'They have not seen these items and they do not listen when I explain them.'

Curtain quality wasn't something I was going to get emotional about, but I did want to start doing something useful in this community. Floating my idea with Shanti, I said, 'I'd really like to talk to some of the Badi families. They seem quite poor and isolated, and I might be able to help them. Will you translate for me?'

'You cannot do this, *memsahib*. These are terrible womens. You know what they do?'

'Yes, I know they are prostitutes.'

'Please don't say this word …'

'But I thought that the local people didn't mind them.'

'Not mind? Who told you this?' So many of her friends had been sold to Bombay brothels, never to return. I had touched a raw nerve. Before I came to Rajapur, I'd read academic papers published by respected anthropologists stating that the Badi were part of the caste system; that the long history and traditions of the Badi made them unique amongst prostitutes. They were accepted and integrated in their communities.

Shanti didn't think so. 'No-one talks to them. There are maybe one hundred childrens in these families. Last year, one boy tried go school. Other childrens threw stones and chased him out. Now none of them go school.' So much for anthropologists.

'Will you help me meet them, though?' I asked. 'I'm sure they need help.'

'It is not possible, *memsahib.*'

Shanti brought companionship and conversation, but she also brought her own problems. Her life story unfolded — often tearfully — as we pottered around the house together. 'I miss my daughters so much, especially my baby, the four-year-old. But I had to leave them and run away and hide from my husband. He beat me, usually when he was drunk. Once he found me and beat me all the more for running away. He kept me locked up for a couple of weeks. There was no point complaining; he has friends in the police … Then I got away again and stayed in one women's refuge; it was all right there, but I couldn't see the children. Now they're in boarding school.' Over my years in Nepal I found that her sad story was not so unusual for a Nepali woman. From time to time, I'd see a young woman lying out in the sun recovering from a beating — black eyes, bruised arms, swollen jaw. Drunken husbands were usually to blame.

It was late March, still early in the year, but Shanti complained of the heat: she was making the climate her excuse to leave. After just over a week with us, she took a *tanga* to the ferry at Kothiyaghat and the overnight bus back to Kathmandu. She said, 'I must go Kathmandu to see my daughters. It is visiting day at the boarding school, and I can see my daughter for one day a month only.'

'Phone us if you decide not to come back,' I said.

She didn't phone, and she didn't come back.

I was sorry to lose such a warm companion, but I rationalised her going, knowing that her grief could easily have begun to dominate my life, and that might have been too much for me just then. I had no emotional energy for other people's crises. Shanti's story ended happily, though. We met her again by chance more than a year later, by which time her husband was ensconced with a younger wife, had a child by her and had lost interest in Shanti. She was happily working in Kathmandu, living with a kind Western family, but close to her daughters.

डे डे डे

Thus far, we'd only been living in Rajapur for a couple of months. The generator arrived; we put it in the cowshed and got the *mysteris* back to wire it up and install neon lights, sockets and ceiling fans. I hovered as the *mysteris* worked, still hoping to improve the standard of their work, but they took no notice of me except to demand tea. One *mysteri* asked where the wires should go through the wall, and then went off to get a sledgehammer. This specialist tool was considerably larger than the carpenters' sledgehammer. He used it to smash a substantial crater in the concrete wall. The huge fuse box he'd installed was left dangling from its wires.

'You will attach it to the wall later, perhaps?'

'It is not necessary.'

'Please attach it to the wall.'

'Later, perhaps.' This was as good as saying no. The work never looked finished, but Mr Gautam, the house-owner, was delighted. Clearly my standards were too high.

The house was in chaos for months as the succession of *mysteris* came and went, and came and went again. Each smashed holes — sometimes for no obvious reason — and all left heaps of concrete on the floor. The mosquitoes started getting inside again, but the carpenters were long gone. After the electricians had turned the place upside-down, Mr Gautam sent one of his Tharu bonded labourers to whitewash the inside of the house; this *kamaiya* usually worked in the rice fields further north. It was still cold when he turned up for work early, shivering in a holey T-shirt and threadbare shorts. I offered him some empty bottles. 'These will be good for my *rakshi*,' he announced with a huge grin, revealing that all his front teeth were missing. The painter was hard-working; he seemed happy-go-lucky. Yet he was a bonded labourer, so carefree he was not.

'Do you like *rakshi*?'

He giggled infectiously, just at the thought of getting legless.

'Is that how you lost your teeth? From falling over when you were drunk?'

'*Memsahib* speaks truly,' he chuckled, his gummy grin widening even further. His joviality was infectious, but I suspected that *rakshi* was the reason he was in debt. Perhaps my tip would go on booze too. But who was I to judge? I had never needed total anaesthesia.

Himalaya came around again to check on the workmen, and I offered tea as usual.

'Actually, I prefer coffee.' (Why didn't he tell me before?)

'Ah, that's easy, Mr Thapa; we even have some fresh-ground Nepali coffee already made.'

'Nescafé is better, *hoina*? You, of course, have Nescafé!'

'Yes. That's easy, too; but don't you like Nepali coffee?'

'No, it is not good quality; Nescafé is most best.'

I prattled on about the amusing antics of the whitewashman, but I was yet to learn the Nepali art of interesting stream-of-consciousness conversation. Himalaya butted in with, 'I must take your generator. The office machine is broken and I need send one fax.' And with that, four men appeared, struggled out with our generator and took it away in a Land Cruiser. 'Will we get it back?' I asked tentatively.

'Yes, after five minutes,' Himalaya said. Even phoning from Rajapur was challenging. If no-one had driven over the cable in the bazaar, someone was bound to have tripped over the wires in the office itself. The four men struggled back five hours later, having installed the generator, sent the fax, then disconnected it to return it to our house.

After the carpenters and smiley whitewashman, painters arrived. Again, there was mess everywhere. Whenever they ran out of paint, needed sandpaper or a couple of nails, they would disappear for days, leaving paintbrushes dripping dark blue paint on the freshly white-washed windowsills. By the end of March, the *mysteris* had all gone, and we unpacked.

The day after, the first dust-storm hit. When David slept and Alexander was happily playing, I'd sit up on our roof writing poetic letters home about the superb trees and birds in our garden. My most faithful and prolific correspondent was my father, and I so looked forward to hearing from him. Sometimes, astonishingly, his letters would take just four days to reach us. I'd gaze towards the mountains: for inspiration, thoughts of coldness and to see whether the snow of the *himals* might be visible. Snow or not, the view north was lovely. In clear weather, the mountains looked like cardboard cut-outs lined up one behind the other; three ranges were almost always visible.

On this day, the view was suddenly different. The mountains on each side were starkly visible, but a great black cloud down to ground level obscured the gorge. It looked evil. Contemplating the amazing changes in the landscape with changing lights and weather, I went inside. Ten minutes later, the black cloud arrived. The sun was blotted out, the temperature climbed and dust poured in. 'Oh, this is exciting, Alexander! See how many of the shutters you can close!' I rushed around the house, cursing my stupidity for not predicting the storm and cursing the *mysteris* because the shutters still didn't fit. The storm must have been gobbling up dust for all of the thirty kilometres between the gorge and us, and the malign beast was now determined to deposit parts of Nepal that didn't belong there inside our house.

I could see clearly now why locals regard storms as living things. Dust and grit filled our mouths and made us sneeze. 'Sita says that eagles bring the big, black clouds. Eagles must be very angry with people!' Alexander remarked. I held a cloth over David's mouth and nose. With the sudden, claustrophobic darkness, noise and choking dust, I could have believed Josi and Basistha's chat about the deadly *loo*. I told Alexander stories for half an hour or so, to stave off his boredom; there wasn't much else we could do with this suffocatingly hot wind whistling around us. Then, as suddenly as it had started, a delicious downpour chased away the heat and we peeked out. Our magnificent flame of the forest tree lay deflowered, roots in the air. We dashed outside and stood in the garden in the rain. David laughed as it dribbled off the end of his nose.

CHAPTER SIXTEEN

prostitutes and outcastes

YOU CAN BOIL FROGS ALIVE WITHOUT UPSETTING them: you warm them ever so gently, until they are lulled into a stupor and cooked. I'd expected the heat to build up gradually in the same way, so that our brains would slowly stew and we would acclimatise, but the Rajapur heat increased uncomfortably, in steps. The first was in early March, and had worried Shanti. Each step knocked the breath out of me, sapped yet more energy; Alexander, though, continued to play outside through the worst of the midday heat. It wouldn't get much hotter, I kept saying to myself. But it did. By April, it was getting too hot to walk on any sun-exposed surfaces in bare feet in the middle of the day, and my diary expired in a puddle of sweat. Clothes and sheets felt and smelt as if they'd just come out of a tumble drier. This was Josi's season of 'too much of foot powder'. The mutts from the bazaar spent hours lying in the river, trying to lose heat. They instinctively knew that when the air was hotter than blood temperature, you needed to do something different to cool down.

One afternoon in the middle of April, our third month on Rajapur, there was a knock at the door. An emaciated little man thrust an envelope into my hand and scurried away without uttering a syllable. The carefully handwritten letter read:

> *Amar Shaheed Shree Dashrath Chand Higher Secondary School, Rajapur (Bardiya) Nepal*
>
> *Dear Dr (Mrs) Jane,*
> *The Science Society of Rajapur Higher Secondary School is going to organise an awareness program on AIDS on 24th April. We would like to invite you Madam in that Function. It would be our grateness if you share your ideas and experiences, provide language is not problem. Program is given in next paper attached long with this paper.*
>
> *Yours Sincerely*
> Mr Sudnakar Mishra
> *Prisident Science Society*

The program was also written on a scrap torn from a larger sheet of paper:

> *24TH APRIL '94*
> *GATHERING IN SCHOOL COMPOUND AT 12AM PROCESSION FROM SCHOOL DISPLAYING VARIOUS PLAYCARDS, POSTERS, TAKING A ROUND OF RED LIGHT AREA.*
> *AFTER THAT AGAIN BACK TO SCHOOL AND SHARING OF IDEAS AND EXPERIENCES.*

How could I resist? It was time that I got more involved in the Rajapur community.

The procession passed our house on the way to the Badi community; schoolgirls chanted with passion, 'Down with AIDS!'

They carried large *playcards* announcing AIDS IS EVIL, SMASH AIDS, and daubed anti-AIDS slogans in English and Nepali on any white wall they passed. I arrived at the High School at the tail end of the procession, and tried to shuffle into an inconspicuous place. Pot-bellied Mr Gautam approached, smiling, to tell me that I had been made Guest of Honour; he showed me to a prime seat. I wasn't going to be able to skulk away after a token appearance.

Trying to tune into the proceedings, I leaned across to Mr Gautam. 'Who is speaking now?'

'Gawn Bikas Samitee ka adhyakshe jyu.' I slowly untangled the title: the Rajapur Village Development Committee chairman. He was thanking us for giving our time to attend the meeting, and individually welcoming all the celebrities, not by name but by title: *Inspector-sahib* (police), *Docter-sahib* (the government health assistant), the president of the Geruwa Rural Awareness Association … the interminable list continued. Over a hundred people were here. The women teachers were a gorgeous line-up of colour, with polished toenails peeking out like rows of shiny beetles from under immaculate saris. The children wore smart, pressed, royal-blue uniforms. How did they manage to look so impeccable in all the dust, and with no iron? I was shabby, sweaty and unkempt.

I thought about health education. Fresh in my mind was Himalaya's sickening tale of two men dying of rabies in the north of the island. Was there any hope of preventing further agonising deaths from rabies? Maybe I could persuade villagers to destroy these half-wild dogs. Avoidable rabies was surely a better cause than trying to tackle AIDS, which even specialists in health education and community development found a tough problem.

Balding *docter* Badrinath Jha began a long and impassioned speech in difficult, flowery, formal Nepali. He was being emotional about the AIDS *evilness* — he used the English word a great deal. 'We must uphold Rajapur's honour by evicting the Badi women …' Now, this bigotry — which had everyone nodding in agreement — really interested me; I had wanted to check whether what Shanti had said about the Badi was correct. These *randi* women were clearly absolutely despised; I could believe that Badi children had given up trying to go to school because of prejudice and bullying. It seemed that anthropologists' accounts of them being integrated and tolerated really were complete claptrap. *Docter* Jha ranted on as I felt more and more uncomfortable about being associated with this meeting. The Badi, who were already shunned outcastes, were being made scapegoats.

People kept on leaning across to comment to me and keep me involved, but Alexander was seriously bored. This was clearly a big, all-day event: a social high-spot in Rajapur. After the *docter* came a spotty boy talking about the AIDS virus. He spouted statistics, but said nothing about how people *get* AIDS.

'How many more people are due to speak, Mr Gautam? I am sorry I can't stay long, because of the children.' I was shy of feeding David on stage. 'Do you want me to speak?'

'Indeed. Most certainly.' He was so attentive: a real gentleman. 'It was me only who said you, madam, must be guest of honour. Of course, you must speak. As the only MBBS doctor in our community, it is necessary. Someone will translate for you.'

A running translation would at least give me time to think of something to say, though I was uncertain whether it would be improper to talk about sex and drug abuse. Some cynic had told me that in Nepal there were more non-government organisations 'solving the AIDS problem' than sufferers. I could hardly tell them that, now, could I?

'Okay, I'll say a few words, but can I speak now?' (Better to get it over with.)

'It is possible, perhaps. We had scheduled your Most Important speech last, at the end of the day.'

'I'm really sorry, Mr Gautam, we must go soon.'

'All right, Mrs Simon; you speak now, madam, if you please.'

I handed David to Mrs Gautam — the Vulture — and stood up, still wondering what I should say. I started with some patronising blather about being flattered to be their guest of honour, and then thought that it would be safest to talk about work I had done in other countries. Nepalis love speeches and speech-making, so I tried to make it a bit of an oration. It is not in my nature to bullshit, though, and I was struggling. I told them how *never before* had I encountered such an *unforgettable* procession; unforgettable and impressive. Elsewhere I had been involved in health education work where *children* understood the issues better than adults, and the program had worked because children had become the health educators of their parents and elders. *Here and now* this same process was going on: well-educated, highly motivated and energetic *students* were becoming the *gurus* of health education and were showing adults the right way to go.

All the while, I was thinking guiltily that I should really be giving them a lecture on avoiding drugs, and on safe sex. I retrieved David and sat down, relieved to have Done the Needful, but hardening my resolve to get some real work going with the Geruwa Rural Awareness Association; I wanted to start something more achievable than the eradication of AIDS. I wanted to tell people how to avoid diarrhoea and dysentery, and what can be done after a dog bite to prevent rabies. Now, though, I wondered how quickly I could decently disappear. I managed to slip away a few minutes later.

डे डे डे

Most Saturdays, we took a long stroll as the day was beginning to cool. When David was well, we took him, but sometimes outings distressed and exhausted him, so we'd leave him with Sita. Lately, she'd seemed more confident, and her eyes sparkled like she was in love.

The pleasantest direction was west down to the river. One afternoon, we set out across fallow rice fields, passed a herd of unkempt boys playing football behind the Japanese rice mill, and came to one of the biggest silk-cotton trees I had seen. The fleshy red flowers were long gone, but its leaves hid a squawking microcosm of birds, and ostentatious golden-backed woodpeckers poked about in the bark. I turned to Simon. 'Did you know that woodpeckers have reinforced skulls to prevent brain damage when they use their heads as chisels?'

'Glad to know you've been reading improving literature.'

A pied hornbill flew out, with its mate; their style of flight recalled someone learning to water-ski: wobble, wobble, ski, wobble, glide.

As we left the fallow fields, a flight of black ibises swept in to pick over the soil. We walked down along the rosewood plantation, snaffled mulberries, and wandered on to the river and the tiny Kumale community. Their kiln-pits still smouldered. A skeletal old man coughed as he listlessly hand-turned a potter's wheel and effortlessly formed an elegant, almost spherical, narrow-necked, water container.

'We should buy some — to cool our drinking water. I'm tired of drinking warm boiled water.'

'So am I!' said Alexander.

'I'll pick some up next time we come by on a field trip,' Simon offered. 'They're too heavy and awkward to carry just now — unless you want to balance one on your head.'

'I wish I could.' We walked south, back along the riverbank. The sun was setting and cattle were being driven home with their accompanying cloud of dust. We then turned east again, to join the main track into Rajapur, where the dust was so fine that each step made a small phutting noise, created a crater and raised a little cloud. We hurried back before a home-bound truck could engulf us in dust.

CHAPTER SEVENTEEN

dying for a glimpse of the cool himalayas

IT WAS TIME AT LAST. I DABBED THE SWEAT ONCE again from my eyebrows with my shirt, unstuck my clothes from my skin, stood, stretched. I took David inside, away from the gathering mosquitoes, and then tottered round the outside of the house. I pulled open the door of the cubicle that we called our bathroom. It was not empty. The occupant looked over her shoulder at me. She was angry at my intrusion. We stared at each other; her hateful unblinking gaze disturbed me. She shuffled around to get a better look. The stranger was braced, ready to attack.

I took one step inside, determined to intimidate her, but those cruel, lidless eyes and hard, triangular face unnerved me. She edged away, but her malicious expression said she was not retreating; she wasn't leaving just yet. A leg hung out of her mouth; it still twitched a bit. It'd belonged to the last of the giant crab spiders that had made this room their home. I had been rather fond of them.

She could not bite me while she had her mouth full, but her menacing gaze never wavered, and as I edged further into the bathroom, she shuffled around again, as if getting ready to spring. How could a mere insect make me feel so small? I stripped hurriedly, lunged to turn on the water and retreated to one corner to wait for the scaldingly hot water in the sun-baked pipe to run cool. She, meanwhile, scuttled higher up the wall to avoid the hot water. Then she turned her face to the wall as if disgusted by the sight of a naked, white human; finally, I was safe to enjoy my cold shower.

डे डे डे

Inside the house, Simon was just back from a field trip. 'You were a long time. Were you *very* dirty?' he teased.

'No. I was held up because someone else was in the bathroom.' Then, bewildered by my husband's appearance, I added, 'You should go and have a look in the mirror.'

'Is the bathroom free now, or has Arjun taken to hygiene all of a sudden?'

'The visitor is still there: a female, with six legs.'

'Ooh, was it a tiger?' Alexander asked excitedly.

'No, just a mantis, but I thought she might bite me somewhere sensitive.'

'Were you really scared of a playing mantis, Mummy?'

'It was rather large, and they've got good jaws.'

Alexander went outside to see, while I turned to Simon. 'What's put you in such a good mood! Do you know what you look like? Where have you *been?*'

'Up north, to see Tharu labour gangs digging out silt from the canals.'

'In *this* heat?'

'Yes, they turn it into quite a party.'

Alexander returned. 'Come and see, Daddy. It's not very big at all!' He was holding the mantis in his cupped hands. 'Can I keep it as a pet?' She thought not, and flew back into our bathroom.

'Fancy driving to the main intake on Saturday?' Simon asked. 'We could picnic under the trees.'

'Yes, please. A picnic — goodie!' said Alexander.

Simon smiled, and dust cracked off his face. 'Would you like it? Are you okay … or …?'

'I'm fine,' I said, but I could see Simon had tuned into my hesitancy. 'I'd love to go, it's just that I'm feeling a bit sick today.'

It wasn't the right moment to tell him that I knew I was pregnant.

'You'd better have a shower!' I told him.

'Will you chase out the mantises for me first, Alexander?'

'Okay — *I'm* not scared!'

Thinking back to the time when we'd been trying to conceive David, it seemed so odd, and so different. Then, although I'd been working, I'd become quite obsessed, and did pregnancy tests every couple of weeks or so. The last time we'd been in England, though, the idea of another pregnancy wasn't in my mind at all, and I hadn't thought to pack any testing kits.

Now, back in Rajapur, I just had to listen to my body. I had only just told Simon my news, over a beer on the roof, when Alexander bounded up and interrupted. Distracted, we talked of the trip north, while I wondered what Simon was thinking. 'Driving today,' he said, 'we churned up so much dust that we had to stop to wait for it to clear — often — just to be able to see to drive. I wonder about the dust and David's weak chest.'

'David will be fine; his cough's better now.'

Simon smiled and leaned over to kiss me. 'How do you think David will like it?'

'A trip or a new baby?' I'd lost track of the conversation, and was perplexed that Simon said so little. I was worried that he was worried.

'I was thinking short-term. But longer term, and a burgeoning family … mmm, scary,' he said, with a teasing, pleased chuckle.

'You're happy, then. Good! A picnic will be fun. I'd like that — we all will, I reckon.'

'Yes, I *do* like picnics,' Alexander confirmed.

It was only later — over supper — that we had a chance to talk properly.

'This is excellent news,' Simon said, 'but are you okay to stay here, in the heat? What about scans and things?'

'No, I'll be fine, and we can get a scan done when we go home in the summer. Now tell me what you were up to today!'

'We had another meeting with the farmers, in an attempt to get them involved in the planning. Someone said there was no point in asking opinions, because no matter what is suggested, someone will disagree. Another farmer immediately said there would never be such disagreements. A heated discussion ensued about whether there would be arguments.'

'So you are resigning?'

'Not today … Actually, I don't wholly regret taking on this project. It's interesting. These people have kept the scheme working for a hundred years, but they'd argue about whether water flows uphill.'

I could see that Simon was starting to feel that he was doing something useful locally; he was in his element, stimulated by the challenges, not depressed by them.

डे डे डे

Rajapur in May was hellish: well above blood heat. Everything was hot to the touch. Alexander's colouring crayons melted into a blob of psychedelic wax. The humidity made it like living in a sauna. If you took a deep breath, the air scorched your lungs — or so it felt.

I tried to build in a routine of spending several intensive periods with David each day, exercising him, trying to connect with him, singing songs, but as it got hotter, both of us found it a struggle. My inspiration to achieve anything went. It was disheartening that he never made eye contact with me. He just didn't seem interested. Although he was growing longer, his weight had plateaued. He'd been taking very little solid food lately; this was something else that I wondered whether I should worry about.

Then one morning while I was lounging on the bed, waffling to David about nothing in particular, he uncharacteristically turned to look into my face, made eye contact and then began to laugh. It was as if he'd just noticed I had a baked bean stuck to my nose. He looked and laughed, and seemed elated with what he'd seen. He was nearly eleven months old, and this was the first time he'd convincingly taken any interest in my face — anybody's face. I'd only recently started patching his good eye and getting him to exercise his squinting lazy eye, and perhaps this extra work had encouraged David to look and respond. It was so wonderful to see some progress. This was one huge leap towards his becoming sociable. I felt so happy; David seemed content mostly — delighted, even — with life.

The miserable selection of vegetables in the bazaar dwindled to a few wrinkly relics. There was no cool, refreshing glimpse of the Himalayas from the roof of our house. Even the foothills were invisible now behind a thick miasma of dust suspended in treacly air. The only things that looked fresh were the 'AIDS IS EVIL' and 'SMASH AIDS' slogans daubed all over the bazaar. When I did venture out, I often bumped into Mr Gopal. 'Come and visit the GRAA office so that we can discuss your clinics for the poor, Dr Jane.'

Alexander was increasingly reluctant to go shopping and I enjoyed my trips to the bazaar less and less. I had morning sickness, and David was off colour, so I was loath to leave him for long. Everything was bleached to the colourlessness of Rajapur silt. Each insipid day dragged by. Always the same: heat, glare, flies. I wore my hair in a ponytail to stop it sticking to the back of my neck. If I tried to write anything, my hands stuck to the paper and sweat dripped off my face and smudged it. I sipped lukewarm water. Brain grinding to a halt.

Sponging David cool. Whisking flies off his face. Waiting. Savouring the delicious prospect of a cold shower when evening brought a little respite and I began to feel as if I could breathe again.

I spent the afternoons in the shade of the front porch gazing out from my torpor. Sweat stung my eyes. I was mesmerised by the way convection currents moved the treacly air so that it rippled. Otherwise it was deadly still. Sapping. Hardly a sound except the buzzing of flies. I hate flies. They walk on your lips. They rub their hands together greedily and slurp from your eyes without wiping their filthy feet first. Hardly seems worth the effort to whisk them away, though. And the crows, with their evil, beetle-black eyes, seemed to be waiting for us to melt and die.

But at least the searing heat finished the mosquitoes: itching mosquito bites on top of prickly heat would be a recipe for insanity. The common hawk cuckoo, the brain-fever bird, taunted us with increasingly manic series of *go cra-zee, brain fee-ver, go crazy, brain fever, go-crazy, brain-fever, gocrazy, brainfever, gocrazy gocrazygocrazy* … the call was convincingly ravingly lunatic. The concrete box we lived in was hot enough to bake your brain. I tried — once — to cool the house in the evening by pouring buckets of water all over the flat roof. The water sizzled and turned to steam as it hit the concrete, but it made no perceptible difference to the temperature inside the house. I thought of comfortable Tharu longhouses, and pined for their coolness.

Saturday arrived and we headed north towards the intake of the Budhi Kulo. I now associated field trips with an unslakeable thirst, and so was grateful when, halfway up the island, we stopped by a tiny tea shop. We waited until our private dust cloud caught up and overtook the car, and then we climbed stiffly out. 'Any tea?'

'Tea is not available,' the skinny old man inside said. 'The wind is too strong!' Tea shops often run out of milk and/or sugar, or even tea, but why was wind a problem? He explained that the shop and his house would catch fire. We continued, beyond even the buffalo tracks, the Land Cruiser skidding on the fine river silt like it was wet clay.

We could smell dust, our hot bodies, the hot engine. A panicking peacock appeared trotting — Road-Runner-like — along the track just in front of the car. As we gained on him, he ran faster, with many an anxious glance over his shoulder, until he thought of veering off the road. Alexander giggled at the peacock's stupidity, and David laughed with him.

I thought that it couldn't get any hotter — but it did. The boys began to suffer. Alexander's heat rash thickened into an evil, excoriated mess. Yet he still loved playing outside in the middle of the day, romping in dusty fields with the other lads and coming inside occasionally to gulp down some warm boiled water from the water filter. He ran around, got even hotter and then the itching drove him to distraction. He also continued to insist on wearing his flannelette pyjamas and sleeping under a thick quilt. David grew quieter, a sure sign that he wasn't enjoying it either, though it was difficult to know how uncomfortable he was. Maybe we should flee to Kathmandu. Most sane mothers would. One afternoon I even thought how attractive the cold, grey, penetrating drizzle of an English November might feel, though the aberration never happened again.

Others were more excited with life. Houseflies copulated wherever you looked, even while grazing on your sweat. Male garden lizards celebrated the breeding season by turning flame orange or crimson about the head and shoulders, and so became the most colourful blossoms in our garden. They looked top-heavy, with a large head, and a body that tapered to a long, slender tail. Their big, wide mouths made them look smug, and no wonder: their testicles had increased in size by seven times, to one eighth of the animal's body length. They did self-satisfied press-ups and solemn head noddings on prominent vantage points, suggesting, 'Look. My balls are so huge. I'm irresistible. Which lucky lady lizards will be mine?' And Alexander loved to cheer our local hero on whenever other males came into our garden to challenge him to a sumo-wrestling bout.

A likable engineer came out from Swindon for six weeks, to help Simon with some of the design work. 'How are things there?' I asked.

'Swindon's one big traffic jam, and it's either raining or windy enough to blow your hair off.'

'You won't miss it, then?' His look said he hated it here, too. I tried to cheer him up by talking of the things I found interesting locally, and how the wildlife was constantly changing, often surprising. I enthused about what an interesting place Rajapur is: a crossroads. How, in winter, herdsmen come down from the high mountains through the Karnali Gorge to graze their flocks or buy Indian goods. How I'd almost got run down by three pigtailed horse-riders from Humla who were celebrating arriving in town with a gallop, hanging onto their cowboy hats, like extras from a wild west film. Their ponies were so small that the riders' legs nearly touched the ground.

'You like it here, then, do you?' he said, puzzled.

I said, 'You've come at *the* worst time of the year'.

He was tired of working in remote places, away from his family. He caught none of my delight in the place. 'I prefer Swindon; the climate's nicer.'

'Are you sleeping all right?' I asked.

'No, not really. Mr Adhikari's taken to praying loudly before dawn — weird, reverberating chanting. Anyway, it's too hot to sleep. And I was going to ask … is there much crime locally? Don't we need a night watchman?'

While he was talking, I absently rolled up a newspaper and obliterated a fly. Steve leapt several inches off his seat at the unexpected violence.

'Rajapur's safe enough,' I said.

Hoping, perhaps, to cheer our nervous, gloomy visitor, Alexander asked, 'Do you know any drokes?'

'Jokes,' I translated. He didn't. Alexander's three-and-three-quarter-year-old mind turned to other diversions and he asked, 'Would you like some *kimbu?* There are lots in the garden; they're called mulberries in Nepali.' And he went out to pick some.

A few evenings later, while Steve was dining with us, we had another dust storm. The fruitbats left their roost-tree unusually early.

They knew. I watched, dismayed, as the storm gathered; one of my big back fillings had just disintegrated and we had planned a trip to a dentist in Kathmandu the next day. The weather might put the river into flood, and maroon me on Rajapur Island with toothache. This storm-beast was different, higher than the first. We watched huge, ferocious black clouds spit lightning, right down to the ground. The display was exciting, invigorating. Loofahs growing from vines on the trees danced, and looked so like a string of pantomime sausages that they seemed hilariously funny. Maybe my manic euphoria unnerved Steve as much as the storm. He paced about nervously. 'The wind seems rather strong. And Josi told me about that wind that bakes and suffocates people.'

'You don't believe it, do you?

'Well … he lives here. But you don't seem worried. Does *anything* worry you?'

'I have to see a dentist in Kathmandu tomorrow — that makes me nervous — and I don't like scorpions.'

'Oh, God; are there scorpions here, too?' (I wished I hadn't mentioned them.)

'They're not a dangerous species; the sting just hurts for a day or two.'

'Only pain for days; that's fine, then.' Now he knew I was mad. 'Will this storm go on for long?'

'No, maybe half an hour; we'd best go inside and close the shutters.' He continued to pace about until the rain stilled the storm. Only then did Alexander dare approach Steve. A small something rested in Alexander's palm, and he held it out to him. 'Have some,' he offered, shyly.

'Thank you,' Steve said, as he took it.

'Welk you,' Alexander replied.

'Welk you?'

'Short for "you're welcome",' I translated.

'Okay, but what is it?' Steve asked.

'Wack,' Alexander said.

'It's candle wack,' I explained, '"wack" being the singular of "wax", apparently.'

'Ah, I understand — a droke, at the expense of the ignorant visitor,' Steve said, witheringly.

'Perhaps; or maybe he wasn't offering it as a snack. Alexander likes playing with it, so maybe he thought you would too,' I said, in my son's defence. When Steve finally left at the end of the evening, he had to walk around a sizeable branch that the storm had ripped off a tree growing fifty metres away.

The river was swollen by the storm, so that getting off the island the following day was not easy; Moti knew that if he drove through the river, the diesel engine might take in water, so he borrowed Mr Vaidiya's tractor to tow us across to the beach at Suttee. And that wasn't the only problem. There was Rajapur grit in the diesel, and the engine kept spluttering to a stop. Poor Moti had to disconnect the fuel hose several times and suck it clean. We ground to a halt at the familiar tea shop where Binu and Laxmi welcomed us rapturously again. 'Look how the baby's hair has grown! Such beautiful golden curls! He is now how old, *didi*?'

'*Ah mai*! Ten months and *still* he cannot sit … but so, so handsome.'

Soon after we set off again, Moti slammed on the brakes, leapt out, seized a large stick and went after the kids who'd most recently been riding on the back. Flocks of terrified children scattered, but not before he had whacked several. He returned, sweating, breathing hard, mumbling '*badmas bachha haru*' while they taunted him from a safe distance. I was heartened to see that Moti couldn't get the better of such scamps, either.

We drove on fast now, tyres slapping the melting tarmac of the East–West Highway. As we crossed the Babai River, Moti put his hand to his forehead, down to his chest and up to his forehead again, and I asked Simon, 'Is this river particularly special?'

'All rivers are holy.' The prayer did not help Moti, for the engine next spluttered and died on the Babai weir. David's bottled milk had already cooked, curdled and turned to cheese. While Moti sucked out more grit, I scanned the river. I never tired of watching kingfishers hover then drop vertically at astonishing speed to seize a fish. Then I registered a different shape on the shoreline: the S-shaped forms of two large mugger crocodiles had squirmed out to bask on warm new concrete. Moti cleared the blockage, uncomplainingly spat petrol, and drove on.

The power was off at the airport. The ceiling fans were idle. It was incinerator hot. It stank; flies came to snack at David's mouth and eyes. A man approached, offering to help us check in. 'He's *lato*, madam,' Moti explained. 'Can't hear; can't speak.'

'No wonder he doesn't seem to understand me.' Over several visits, I learned to interpret some of his grunts and gesticulations. The deaf mute managed two others: a burly but retarded youth and a wizened old chap who could carry very little, peered ineffectually through scratched bottle-bottom glasses and couldn't speak Nepali (I never did work out whether this was because he didn't know the language or because he was deaf). This seemingly unemployable trio was making a living: Nepal was looking after its own disabled citizens. Handicapped people are not put away in institutions, but contribute where they can. Even people with very low IQs find useful roles minding goats or fetching water. And because they are part of the community, they are familiar, not frightening. No-one stares; no-one is embarrassed by their difference.

After Rajapur, Nepalgunj airport was pleasantly cosmopolitan. Townies pristine in their going-out clothes tripped over heaps of luggage as they came in from the glaring sun, half-blind inside with their sunglasses on. Men wore new jeans or track suits, women gorgeous saris, little boys were decked in suits with bow-ties and the girls in layered frilly, pink party frocks with jeans under their skirts. Orange-robed *lamas* and wild mountain men looked as uncomfortable in the heat as we were. 'The country is opening up,' Simon remarked. 'When the Soviet Union collapsed, Nepal was able to buy a fleet of large, cheap helicopters and, ever since, people fly here from remote hill districts rather than walk; then they get buses to

Kathmandu or into India. I love the way these hills people always keep their hands busy; if they are not fingering a rosary, they're swinging a prayer wheel. Look, there's even one man spinning wool!'

A skinny dog tottered towards us; it was shaking so much that it could hardly walk. There was something horribly wrong with it — dumb rabies perhaps. I pretended to kick at it to make it go away. I was scared of rabies. It whined and looked even more pathetic. The dog and people looked accusingly at me. 'You must not kick these dogs, *memsahib!*' Moti said, like he was reprimanding a naughty child. 'People will think you are *badmas*.'

'But I didn't!' His accusation stood. I was heartless.

The same evening, I was sitting in the waiting room of *docter* K K Pradhan, the dentist who treats the king, and whose British qualifications were displayed prominently. A patient appeared from the consulting room; he was greenish, clammy and shaking; he staggered slightly, and had to hold onto the reception desk to keep steady enough to pay his bill. I recalled a friend in Oxford who'd had his lip perforated by a dentist's drill. My palms began to get sweaty as I walked into the dentist's treatment room. He wore a north-of-England-style flat cap and a surgical mask. He chatted amiably about life in Peterborough while competently replacing my filling.

CHAPTER EIGHTEEN

the hot season

THESE SHORT TRIPS TO THE CAPITAL WERE ALWAYS refreshing. Kathmandu was beautiful, interesting and familiar. There were avenues of purple jacaranda, heavy-scented jasmine hedges and the wonderful mountains all around, but the air was polluted and drains festered. Piles of stinking domestic rubbish strewn around at street corners made the capital seem uncivilised compared to flat, friendly Rajapur. After a quick check around our pied-à-terre, the flat in Naxal that he'd half forgotten, Alexander came bursting out of a bathroom saying, 'This is the best house in the world! There's a proper toilet. A toilet I can sit on! And there are lights! Look!' He flicked on a switch to demonstrate the miracle. '*And* there are taps — and water comes out of them! I *do* like this house.' Alexander soon made friends again with the landlord's children upstairs. They watched forty-year-old TV episodes of *Batman* through a snowstorm.

While Simon was wrestling for a few days with the bureaucracy in the Department of Irrigation headquarters, I reconnected with expat friends, and went to a couple of playgroups. I was desperately in need of people to talk to, and even hoped that these expatriate mothers might know a physiotherapist. I wanted help to refine the exercises I was doing with David, to make sure that his limbs remained comfortable and ready if ever he could use them. At the first few mother-and-toddler groups, I noticed people glaze over as I babbled on. I was boring, and some of my acquaintances were embarrassed by David. They couldn't see beyond his slow development to his cheering, carefree personality. Although his happiness and laughter were a daily tonic to me, being in Kathmandu was the break that I didn't realise I needed from our isolated life. I grew less manic, less self-centred, as the days passed pleasantly.

Jan Salter dropped around. Native to Southampton, she'd lived in Kathmandu since the late sixties. She first worked as a hairdresser in the Royal Hotel when pigs would sometimes wander into her salon; these days, though, she made a fair living from her art. She had been a surrogate auntie to Simon when he was first in Nepal as an impoverished volunteer in the seventies. Jan came up the stairs muttering and distressed. She left her flip-flops on the doormat and — as always — greeted David first with a tickle and a loud, 'Hello David! How are you today?' He recognised the people who were comfortable with him, and smiled his cheekiest — almost flirtatious — smile for her.

'Have you seen the child worker that those Brahmins downstairs keep, Jane? The poor little bugger sleeps in that tiny alcove under the stairs on a pile of cardboard and rags. He can't be more than seven, and so thin and frightened. He's obviously been brought from the village.' She swept her long, greying hair out of her face so that her jangling bracelets caught David's attention, and he cooed at her. She continued, 'My landlord, Mr Pant, he also has a skinny slave. Last week the boy had a rare moment with no work, and he climbed a wall and jumped off. When he landed, he got a big piece of glass in his knee. It went right in deep. Blood was spewing out everywhere. The kid was almost fainting. Thank God I was home, 'cos the women of the household did sod all except hold him over the drain.'

'Poor wretch,' I said. 'What happened to him?'

'Nothing! Even when Mr Pant arrived, all he did was shout at the kid for playing when he should have been working, so *I* had to take him to Patan Hospital — and pay for the treatment. The doctors said that the wound was so deep, he could have died. I get so hacked off when I see things like this — but what to do? These kids have to work to survive ... and if they're no good, people like Mr Pant can easily find others.'

It struck me, then, how sometimes Hinduism seems so right for Nepal, and sometimes so supportive of those who exploit others.

'But are you painting these days?' I asked her.

'I have a new project — to raise money for a hostel for ex-prostitutes. I'm painting girls with AIDS. You know, those poor girls who were trafficked to India? When they get sick and everyone can see they have AIDS, they are sent right back to Nepal. Do you know, some were seven years old when they went, and are only fifteen now.'

'Sold at seven? That's incredible,' I stuttered. The thought of what these scared little girls must go through sickened me.

'Yes. They're just kids, and I don't have to tell you their lives are finished. It's hard for me to paint such suffering and to hear their sad stories, but the girls enjoy telling me about their lives. They're still very beautiful, and I paint their beauty.' Jan wasn't embarrassed by David's problems either. She saw beyond any handicap: his cute, curly, blond hair, his infectious laughter and the saucy smile that lit up his whole cherubic face. She was straightforward enough to remark on David's family likenesses, something no other Western friend dared do.

'Have you heard the latest rumour?' she asked, clearly dying to tell me. 'It's in the *Rising Nepal* too.'

'No, tell me — I hope it's juicy!' I said, looking forward to a good tale.

'A bit too juicy, I'd say. Apparently a man — a sweeper, I suppose — was working in a dairy one night and there was a power cut.

Maybe he'd been drinking a little *rakshi* … well, anyway, he fell into the milk and drowned. Wasn't discovered for several days, and by that time the milk tasted bad. So there are announcements on the radio telling people to boil their milk before drinking!'

'How foul! Do you believe it?' I asked.

'Not at all,' she laughed. 'It's probably been put about by that new rival dairy.' She slurped her tea. 'Mmm, Jane, David's looking really well. You've done the right thing bringing him out here.'

'Why do you say that, Jan?' I was surprised by her confident judgement.

'Don't you get the papers from home? I've been following a story that made me realise how lucky David is. A tiny baby is in terrible pain and the parents have pleaded with the doctors to stop treatment, but they won't. It's been going on for weeks. They've been watching their baby suffer day after day. It's torture for them. They're almost at the point of nervous breakdown, poor things.'

Jan is an amazing champion of the underdog, and her passions were stirred again.

'Sounds typical!' I said bitterly. 'Why can't doctors learn to listen?'

'It's gone to court, and a humdinger of a legal battle is going on full-swing — while the treatment and the pain goes on. David's avoided all that by coming here; he's a lucky boy!' she said, back to her usual chirpy self and with a huge smile. 'A success!'

I was in a less celebratory mood. 'Ye-es, I suppose so. David's comfortable, and we have no more decisions to make for him — just yet.'

'Well, Jane, we can all see that David is happy here,' she said, reaching down to tickle him again.

'We were so lucky to have been able to run away,' I said. 'A normal family life only seems possible while we're in exile — though it's hard to think of a finer place to be exiled.'

'Surely, if you'd stayed, you'd've been able to stand up to the doctors — being one yourself? It was because you're a doctor that you knew what was best for David, I reckon.'

'No, it would have been a terrific battle,' I said, wearied by the very thought of it. 'David's doctors put tremendous pressure on us to stay in England.'

'Silly whatsits!' Then she turned to a noise and started to giggle. 'Aggh! It must be a ghost! Look!' A cardboard box was sliding into the room. Muffled laughter came from inside it. Alexander then burst out like a jack-in-the-box — 'Surprise!' — and we all laughed.

'Have a biscuit prize for that surprise, Alexander!' Jan said.

She talked about another newspaper story: a child with leukaemia refused to accept treatment, even though without it she knew she would surely die. The parents argued that the treatment was so awful, and the chance of survival so small, that they wanted to leave hospital and enjoy their last months with their child. The courts ruled she should be treated. 'That child suffered horribly and died anyway.'

'What a nightmare,' I said, feeling sucked into a conversation I wasn't ready to have. 'These treatments *are* horrendous, yet if there's chance of complete cure and normal life afterwards, surely doctors have to try? It's too depressing to think about. I'm still so angry with David's doctors. They were so awful; they could have helped so much more. They never understood that we needed to talk through all David's options.'

'Talking is important, I know that. And doctors aren't always wrong, you know. They were truly marvellous when my mother was so ill.' She suddenly looked sad. 'I do miss Mum.'

'Sorry to stir up those memories … You're right, Jan. I'm still too bitter to see things clearly. At the moment, the few failures I've seen overshadow all the successes. There's an endless stream of blue, skinny, breathless children who come into hospital in England, have the holes in their hearts repaired, and then fatten up and live long normal lives. Most of the time, doctors make rational, dispassionate judgements when we parents are too close to make difficult decisions.'

'It's hard for everyone, really, isn't it?' she said.

'Yeah. I worked for a consultant who wouldn't let a suffering brain-damaged child die, but she did the right thing with another family whose first child had been born with an irreparable heart problem. The main pump-chamber was so small that the heart couldn't cope. Intensive treatment would have prolonged life for months at most, but the parents pushed for more tests, more intervention … and got less. Maybe they thought the doctors inhumane as well.'

'What happened?' she asked.

'The child went home and died peacefully. It was that little boy who came to mind when I was pregnant with David. I knew that he would have something wrong with his heart, and I thought about the problems he might have because of it. I rationalised that heart defects are either fixable or lethal, and I could cope with either. It seems incredible now that I thought that way; David's such a joy.'

'I think he's adorable, too.' And she gave him another tickle. This conversation was suddenly too much for me and, changing the subject, I asked her, 'Do you still have lots of dogs?'

'Three now, and the two cats. People bring them to me, and I can't turn them out. My latest had a broken back when he was found. He's getting better at not peeing and messing everywhere now, though, and he's even growing some fur.'

'The dogs must keep you busy, Jan?'

'Yes, but I make time for my painting. I'm going to be presented to the King soon, and my adopted son — you've met him, haven't you? — he thinks it'll help my case to get Nepali citizenship.'

'But only a handful of foreigners have achieved that, surely?'

'Yes, but I have a chance. I'm going to try … and I'm drawing lots too now. I've decided to draw children. Perhaps it's time I did a picture of Alexander and his wonderful blue eyes. And maybe David, too, later. Would you like that?'

'Very much, although you'd have to be quick to draw Alexander. Could you finish a portrait in thirty seconds?'

Alexander, David and I went out daily to feast our eyes in well-stocked shops and supermarkets, indulging ourselves. In Rajapur, all that was available was cloth, flip-flops, bangles, rice (three grades), lentils (six kinds), onions (white or red), garlic and spices. After months away, it seemed almost wicked to be able to buy so many luxuries at a whim: there were breakfast cereals, sardines, baked beans, cheese, chocolate, books, English language newspapers and toilet paper. We could choose between Cadburys, Nestlé, Hershey's or Lindt chocolate; there was French wine, Danish mussels, Japanese seaweed and sake, Branston pickle, slimming foods, tinned cat food, non-sting dog shampoo and even dried potato flakes from Iowa. New Road seemed the height of chic: there was 'Human Fit shirting and suiting' (tailors), camera shops and the unbelievably decadent jewellery shops. I was gazing at lapis lazuli and tiger's eye in one glitzy shop when a consumptive beggar stepped up to Alexander and thrust a plate of money at him. Alexander took a few coins and politely thanked the man.

'Um, Alexander, he was hoping for some money from you. Give him a rupee.' A large, black cow who was thoughtfully chewing a cardboard box looked on dispassionately.

Expat friends gave me hot tips on which of the Fresh Houses had the best range of luxuries. 'There's a new Cold Store on Lazimpat,' Mary said. 'It has frozen prawns flown in from Bangkok, and also beefburgers, sausages and excellent beef steaks.'

'Isn't beef an illegal substance in Nepal?'

'Theoretically. They truck it up from India — that other devout Hindu country — and call it fillet or deer meat.'

David was two months older than Mary's son, Michael. Michael was a bundle of energy, determination and ambition, while David lay back and burbled. Each time the boys were together, the gap between their development had widened further. It was harsh to be confronted by this reality. But life was harsh. Mary talked of her maid and cook, an ageing couple who'd pinned all their hopes on their newly graduated, elder son. He had climbed into a well to rescue a cousin, and both had suffocated in bad air. 'Rakmani and Shiva are devastated,' Mary said. 'They want to borrow a large sum of money from me, Jane. I wouldn't mind, normally, but it is to buy gold and cloth to pay the Brahmins to conduct the funeral. How these priests exploit people! I've tried to explain, but Shiva says that the boy must be properly honoured.'

Rakmani was excluded from the rites because she was a woman. She became an old woman in the year following her son's death; she never really recovered, and the ceremonial expenses impoverished the couple too.

डे डे डे

Sometimes the garrulous office driver Basant took us out, and he relished his role as tour guide. 'Where are we now,' I asked him, 'with all these huge trees and heroic statues of warriors on horseback?'

'This, *memsahib*, is Ratna Park where my King, he make speeches, and he take cannon salute.'

We drove by a scrap of sun-scorched grass surrounded by a battered concrete fence, wrapped in filigree barbed wire and painted puke green. 'These constructions were made to welcome this Her Royal Highness your Queen Elizabeth on her esteemed visit of 1960 by your Common Era calendar. A most smiling and royal lady.'

'Tell me about your King, Basant. Is he a good man?'

'I love my King, *memsahib*, but he different now. Since democracy come, he driving car. How can God drive car? I think this government is no good. Everything is too costly since democracy. I think we must give King back his power.' Unexpectedly Basant put his hand to his forehead, down to his heart, and back up to his forehead. 'Now we coming to most holy place. This is Mahankalsthan.' He pointed to a book shop in the middle of the road, shaded by a huge *peepal* tree.

Some outings were in auto-rickshaws: smelly three-wheeler *tempos* in which it was an enormous strain on the voice to hold any kind of conversation. We'd wriggle inside, and the driver would start the engine with several sharp, noisy, upward tugs on something that looked like a handbrake. David would begin to chuckle, and his elation increased with every graunching gear-change, until he was convulsed with a whole-body belly-laugh. Then he'd happily fall asleep, oblivious as we swerved between potholes or hit a bump too hard. Our drivers — however trendy, however expensive-looking their sunglasses were — each made their quiet prayer, hand to forehead, chest and up to forehead again whenever we passed the holy bookshop.

Now that David was growing longer, I could no longer feed him by holding him or propping him in the crook of a bent knee. I bought a little cane chair that, when packed with four cushions, supported him beautifully. I was pleased with my find, although it seemed crazy to have to travel to Kathmandu to buy furniture: cane grows in abundance in the jungles on Rajapur, and we'd often seen people cutting the rattan-like creeper to sell to chair-makers.

The last of our Kathmandu chores was haircuts, and we presented ourselves at the plush salon in the Shangri-La Hotel, patronised by expatriates and moneyed Nepalis. Here we met a British family who'd recently returned to Nepal. Lorna and John had first met in Nepal while both were volunteers: Lorna was teaching in Beergunj and John worked on stabilising mountainsides. They'd gone home to Britain, married, and had now returned to Nepal with son Andrew, the same age as Alexander, and daughter Katharine, a year younger. Alexander and Andrew struck up a friendship immediately, that continues still.

'We had a few weeks living here at the Shangorilla when we first came to Nepal,' I said to Lorna. 'Gets a bit wearing keeping the children quiet, doesn't it?'

'Yes, we'll be pleased to move out. We've found a house just north of the ring road. Where is it that you are based?' she asked.

'Rajapur, Bardiya District.'

'Ah … now, Jan Salter mentioned you — your husband was a volunteer here, too?'

'Yes, in the seventies; Jan must have befriended most of the VSOs who've worked in Nepal!'

'And the dogs!' Lorna laughed.

'Mmm. She's such a generous soul; now, though, it's time for our haircuts. See you next month!'

Our hairdresser spoke excellent English but she was dour and — like many Kathmanduites — hadn't heard of Rajapur. She was rude about Alexander's cradle cap, too.

'You wash his hair not enough!' she accused.

I squirmed. 'It is difficult under a pump. Things aren't easy in the *tarai*.'

'I once spent one week in *tarai*. It was too difficult and there was so much of dirt and dust everywhere.' I was thankful that she hadn't noticed my cracked, dirt-blackened feet. Anxious that David not be forgotten, Alexander said, 'My brother also needs a haircut!'

She didn't smile at the boys. 'You must cut the hair of the baby by yourself,' she said, unhelpfully.

Haircuts accomplished and shopping piled in a heap in the corner of the flat, our week in Kathmandu had been good, especially for my mental health. But now, even though blaring horns and traffic noise amused David, I was beginning to find the city oppressive. The air stung our eyes, clogged our noses and made David cough. Rajapur beckoned. We were happy to head out to the airport again.

We took a Royal Nepal Twin Otter from Kathmandu back to Nepalgunj. A prominent sign said: 'Please put all your weapons, edged particulars, firearms, etc., onto check-in-baggage'. On board, twenty-two people struggled to pack themselves into the eighteen deckchair seats. Several twelve-year-old 'infants' travelled on parental laps. 'Hmm,' Simon mumbled, 'There haven't been many RNAC crashes, but they have mostly been because of overloading. I remember one flight in 1980 leaving Biratnagar for Taplejung. Flights then were infrequent, and very dependent on the weather; the Chief District Officer was travelling home with all his relatives for Desai, and then he put several sacks of rice in the aisle. The pilot didn't want to fly, but the CDO was determined to travel — and save his family a ten-day walk. Three times the pilot taxied out, but changed his mind at the last minute and went back to the terminal. Finally the CDO insisted, the pilot reluctantly tried again; they took off, but almost immediately crashed and everyone was killed.'

'I suppose you told me that story to cheer me up, then, did you?' I said, not for the first time contemplating how living abroad puts you in touch with your mortality. Expats have double the death rate of stay-at-homes. Accidents are more frequent, illnesses worse, and death not such an unusual event. Whenever there are road or air crashes, the evidence isn't tidied away as it is in Britain. Several local airports had years-old plane carcasses rusting by the runways.

A few days earlier, I'd wandered into the British cemetery, a little plot of Nepal given to Britain in the days when its influence was worth something. It was announced by a splendid masonry arch inscribed: 'British Embassy, *founded 1816*'.

The oldest memorial was a huge engraved obelisk: 'Robert Stuart third son of Sir John Stuart BT of Allanbank in Northern Britain and Afsistant to the first British Resident At the court of the RAJA of NIPAUL died on 14TH March 1820'.

There was another mighty edifice to 'Hastings Young of the 63 Regiment Bengal Native Infantry, Assistant Resident at Nipal died 1840 aged 20'. And a large, walled construction to 'Sacred Memory of Cecilia Anne Broughton the beloved wife of Surgeon D Wright MD Residency Surgeon at KATMANDOO 17 February 1873 and Alexander Bryan only child of Dr D Wright died 17 June 1873'. It was a dangerous time to live in Kathmandu, with smallpox outbreaks still raging through the community.

It seemed strange that there were so few foreign or Nepali names there, but a friend in the Embassy had explained that to be buried there, you had to be British, or on very good terms with the Ambassador. Nepal doesn't allow foreigners to own land in Nepal, or even to be buried on Nepali soil, and so lots of expatriates who have spent their lives here ask to be buried in the British cemetery; not many manage it. Even cremation is a problem, because the holy *ghats* at Pashupati are only for Hindus. The Embassy had negotiated a spot for those whose relatives want their loved ones' ashes sent home — it's behind the maternity hospital, near the place where Simon once saw a kite flying off with a human placenta in its beak. The relatives are told, though, that the deceased was cremated beside the snow-fed waters of the Bagmati.

There were recent burials and memorials to mountaineers, and there was the chilling grave of an entire family who had died in the PIA air crash in 1992. Alexander was with me, and had been hiding behind magnificent old pines and gravestones. He burst in on my thoughts: 'This is a nice place! Come up here!' And he led me to the top of the mound at the centre of the cemetery.

'Mmm, peaceful and shady, and we can see all around.' And I gazed up to the Queen's Forest and across to the green hill of Swayambhu, the holy site where people in crisis go. The sunlight reflected in the golden *stupa* made it look like a comforting fairytale castle.

'When people die,' he asked cheerily, 'when they're planted here, do they grow again?'

'Nepalis think they do. They believe that people are reborn, and come back.'

'Can we find your Nanna, then? She was nice.'

I was amazed that he recalled my grandmother's funeral. She'd died when Alexander was just two. He'd come to her cremation, and when we arrived at the chapel, the priest immediately came over to me and said, 'It is all right that you've brought the child to the service.' Until that moment, it hadn't occurred to me that it might not be. I should have allowed for the English discomfort around death.

'People look very different when they are reborn. Usually you can't recognise them. She could even be reborn as a boy — and boys can be reborn as girls.'

'Boys turning into girls? That's a horrible idea!'

'Nanna might come back as a tailorbird or an elegant langur, then.'

'That would be better … or an ant. I like ants too.'

We often heard of untimely deaths of Simon's colleagues and friends. Most people in the expatriate community knew someone who had died either on the Thai or the PIA crash, two air disasters that happened just before we'd arrived in Nepal.

The little propeller-driven plane droned along the line of the great Himalaya. The middle hills beneath us looked like a frozen, fathomless, choppy sea. Tossed as we were by turbulence and updrafts, we seemed as helpless and insignificant as a lost housefly buzzing over a threatening, deep green ocean. There was no sign of any place to land even a light aircraft if anything went wrong.

I looked out for my favourite mountain, Machhapuchharé, the fishtail. At nearly 7,000 metres, it is as high as the highest Andean giants, yet it looked tiny, overshadowed as it was by the Annapurna horseshoe, the first 8,000-metre peak ever climbed, and the seventh highest mountain in the world. Further west, the Himalaya is dramatically cut down to an altitude of less than 1,000 metres; then the mountains rear up again to another 8,000-metre peak: great, humpbacked Dhaulagiri, the fifth highest in the world. We'd walked up the Kali Gandaki Gorge between those two mighty mountains the previous October, on David's first trek, and already it seemed a decade ago.

Our tiny Twin Otter was playfully buffeted over an enticingly wild area of rusty sandstone outcrops and patches of thick, deep green forest. I fantasised about going there, until I started to feel queasy. Alexander turned pale, too, but the turbulence set ten-month-old David chuckling again. He just loved travelling, and although he vomited a great deal when at home, he never got travel sick. Soon we were over the mighty Rapti River, and descending to a safe, if bumpy, touchdown.

CHAPTER NINETEEN

ड that's life

THE *LATO* MAN IN THE NEPALGUNJ AIRPORT SEEMED delighted to see us again. He helped us carry our shopping to the car, where Moti was waiting, mopping sweat from his face with a towel. Alexander's solemn '*Namasté*' revived Moti's grin. Alexander, blushing slightly, whispered in my ear as we scrambled into the Land Cruiser, 'Can I be a driver like Moti when I grow up?'

'Did I tell you,' Simon asked, 'Moti's retiring when he finishes here — on medical grounds?'

'What's wrong with him?'

'High blood pressure,' Simon said.

'Really? He always seems so calm.'

'I think he worries a lot — about the vehicles he's charged with. He's so conscientious …'

Josi was in the car, too, returning from a meeting in Nepalgunj. He talked endlessly, monotonously, for the five hours it took to drive back. 'While you were away, Mr Simon, there was another big meeting about the project. That *docter* Badrinath Jha had a lot to say. He got too hot under his collar and made a long speech about the *evilness* of irrigation. He is clever and he is troublemaker.'

We got as far as the branch of the Karnali River that sweeps closest to Rajapur bazaar. The water level had dropped considerably since we'd been towed over only a week before, but Moti was still worried that the engine would get flooded on the crossing. He turned off to wait for the tractor.

Josi talked on. 'You know, Mrs Simon, I've been trying to persuade Mr Simon to requisition the Department of Irrigation's elephant for our Rajapur fieldworks.'

'They're dreadfully uncomfortable, Dr Josi. That's why the Rajapur landlords sold their elephants and bought cars instead.'

'You soon learn to move with the elephant, no problem, Mrs Simon.' Then, as I put David into the papoose and wandered towards the river, 'Are you really going to walk there with the baby?'

'Yes, why not? It's not deep,' I said.

'What if you fall?' Josi looked at me. Then a brain-fever bird sounded off, as if to confirm his suspicions about my sanity. I was sweaty, covered in dust, dying to get home and shower.

'If I fall, we'll have a nice refreshing bath!' Upstream, the river looked cool and inviting, but the water I stepped into was a limpid, brown puddle and the river bed was slimy between my toes. I caught a movement out of the corner of my eye, and saw mud-creatures slipping into the river. I'd spooked flap-shelled turtles that looked as if they were carved out of the grey-green mud; they can niftily shut up their rear-ends, hiding legs and tail under a closable car-bonnet extension of the soft shell. As the tepid, brown water swirled around my thighs, I said, quietly, 'Aggh, this isn't at *all* nice, David. Dr Josi was right, but don't tell him!' David burbled to say *he* was enjoying himself.

As we approached our house, we passed the Vulture. 'How are you, Mrs Gautam?' I asked, immediately regretting the question: she looked grey and ill.

'Not well. The heat is terrible!'

'It's not good. Will you go to Kathmandu to see your children? It will be cooler there.'

'Maybe. My husband is there now. He is very ill with fever.'

Simon took David and wandered on into the house while Mrs Gautam continued, 'We think it is malaria.'

'*Ah mai*! Malaria? Is malaria much of a problem here?'

'Oh yes, we have all kinds of diseases: malaria, encephalitis, meningitis, typhoid, dysentery, pneumonia … everything is available here.'

I found Simon on the roof, supping warm Iceberg lager as he rocked David on his lap and read Alexander a story; he'd also been watching me. 'Another consultation?'

'No. Just an opportunity for Mrs Gautam to complain about Rajapur again. She said that Mr Gautam was ill — I'm amazed I didn't hear about it. Maybe I'm only seen as the "ladies' doctor".'

Over the next few days, the atmosphere turned thick, claustrophobic, mud-coloured. There was a beige ceiling to our world, and visibility dropped to a few hundred yards. Alexander asked, 'Why is the sky all covered up?' There were even more flies. Each time an ox cart or truck passed, and whenever there was the slightest breeze, dust flowed into the house like malign protoplasm. By this time, I had a regular trickle of patients: mostly women and a few children. Then a woman came, complaining that someone had looked at her while she was eating her rice and now she had *akhaa lagyo*. *Akhaa* means eye and *lagyo* was used like we'd use 'lurgy', but there was nothing obviously wrong with her eyes.

'What kind of eye disease is *akhaa lagyo*?' I asked Simon later.

'It's nothing to do with eye disease,' he laughed. 'It's the evil eye … a curse. People with conjunctivitis say that their eyeballs are cooked — *akhaa pakyo*!'

A week later, a healthy Mr Gautam cornered me. 'I have one friend; he is needing check-up. Can you do?'

'I'm pleased to see you looking so well, Mr Gautam. Was your malaria quickly cured?'

'I was not having malaria. My problem was kidney infection only, but my friend …?'

'Okay, I'll see him … if you translate for me.'

By now I could get the gist of most conversations, but sometimes I needed to ask for clarification when I was consulting. I strolled across the road to find my patient stretched out on a bed in a room packed with people. Mr Gopal was amongst them. 'Um … maybe your friend would, er … like some privacy?'

'Some what?'

'Maybe he is shy about talking about his problems in front of so many people?'

'He doesn't mind. They all know what's wrong with him.'

'Please ask him, anyway.' He wasn't asked. They were expecting me to perform a laying-on-of-hands or something, but I needed to gather information in order to make a diagnosis.

'What's the problem?'

'Headache.'

'A bad headache?'

'Bad.'

'Where exactly?'

'My head.'

'How long for?'

'Weeks.'

'It is always the same — day and night?'

'Always the same.' I did not have a very loquacious patient. He seemed drugged.

'Do you drink alcohol?'

'A little,' he said, in a way that implied 'a lot'.

'How did it all start?'

'What?'

'Your headache.'

'Just … with a headache. And whenever I get out of bed, I feel dizzy.'

No point in trying to find out about the illness from his symptoms. 'What medicines have you taken?'

He waved limply at the bedside cabinet stacked with tablets, capsules and bottles. 'These, and also some injections: three from *docter* Jha and two from *docter* Bhandari.'

'What kind of injections did you have?'

'Strong injections.'

My audience was growing restless and started talking amongst themselves again. I looked at the heap of medicines. There was valium (a tranquilliser), phenobarbitone (a stronger tranquilliser), codeine (an excellent painkiller that also sedates); there were antibiotics, blood pressure pills, vitamins, antacids, two tonics, aspirin and paracetamol. I was astonished that he was conscious at all.

I needed to think, so I unfurled the sphygmomanometer. There were approving *ahs* and *mmms* from my audience. When I pulled out my stethoscope and ophthalmoscope, there were more appreciative mumblings. Then I got into my performance. 'Look straight ahead. No, not at the light: straight ahead. Open wide! Say "ah"! Breathe deeply! Stop breathing! Say "ninety-nine"! Lie back! Loosen your trousers.' Several women got up to see what I was doing, and seemed disappointed that I was only feeling my patient's abdomen.

Then, finally, I said, 'Everything seems fine. Heart and lungs and blood pressure are all normal. The view of the back of the eye looks fine, so I don't think that there is anything wrong with your brain. I think that the reason that you feel dizzy when you stand up is because you are taking a lot of very strong medicines that are fighting with each other.' People tittered at the idea of medicines fighting. 'The cause of the headache is a problem that is painful, but harmless, and will go away soon on its own. You need to stop taking all these medicines, and avoid alcohol for six months.' Women in the audience nodded with enthusiastic agreement. 'Just take paracetamol and rest for the headache. Then, if the headache and dizziness is still there in three days' time, I will see you again, and decide if any further treatment is necessary.'

'So when should he go for his CT scan, Doctor?' Mr Gautam asked.

'He does not need a brain scan. He needs rest, and to let the powerful medicines wash out of his body.'

'Some special lotion then? What new medicines should he take, Dr Jane?' Gopal asked.

'He has taken too many medicines already, and the medicines are disagreeing with each other and making him feel dizzy. He needs less — not more — medicines.'

Mr Gopal caught me outside. 'Dr Mrs Jane, you are exactly correct about this booze problem. But I am also thinking he needs one CT scan.'

'He does not need a CT scan — if you want to throw money away, please give it to me!'

He started reaching into his pocket.

'No, no,' I restrained him. 'That was a joke. I do not need your money. I'm trying to stop you people from wasting any more money.' Gopal's eyebrows knitted as he said 'Yes, yes, Dr madam. Very good. I see. Why not!' I walked home wondering if I'd ever learn to communicate with my patients; they all spent so much money on useless tests and medicines. Later Simon said, 'CT scans must be the in thing; Josi went off to Kathmandu for one yesterday.'

'Crikey, is he so ill?'

'He said he was feeling dizzy, and that it was necessary.'

'Maybe the poor guy just wants time with his family … and to stock up on foot powder, no doubt.'

A family consulted me one Saturday morning: worried parents and their eighteen-month-old daughter. 'She's been ill with fever for ten days. We've taken her to all the *docters* on the island. She's had injections, creams, tonics and medicines but still the fever is there.' Now, she looked really awful. I unpeeled her clammy clothes and the damp cloth that was wrapped around her bottom as a nappy. She was limp, pale, thin and ill. She did not even have the energy to cry when I examined her. 'I am glad you brought her to see me — I can help her. She has a nasty ear infection. Has she already taken some antibiotics?'

'It is not known. She ate some syrup for three days — some tonic, maybe.'

'She needs a course of antibiotics for a week.'

'A whole week, *doctor-sahib*?' they queried.

'Correct: a complete course; and also lots to drink.'

Simon joined me in our lounge-consulting room. 'They left abruptly. Did I do all right?'

'Yes, fine; he certainly did not help you by making his Nepali clear. He used so many filler words.'

'I just latched onto the fifty per cent I *did* recognise. I was really worried about that poor skinny little thing. Do you think my instructions were comprehensible?'

'Yup. And you told them to come back enough times! I think you should nail up your brass plate and start charging.'

'Get lost!' I spat back. 'I like being useful, but —'

'Exactly! You'd make a very nice living; we could settle down here, and I'll retire.'

'Don't start pretending you've fallen in love with this place now.'

'Oh, it's not so bad here,' he teased.

I was — I knew — seeing people who really needed help, and that made me feel useful. I never did discover whether the little girl recovered, but anonymous gifts kept arriving, so presumably I cured some of my patients.

My pregnancy had again heightened my sense of smell, as well as causing a lot of morning sickness, which (with the heat) sapped my energy. Sometimes in the hush of the middle of the day I'd find myself taken by a profound lethargy. I'd sit in the stifling heat, listening to the brain-fever bird and to flies buzzing. It seemed that they and the garden lizards were the only living things that were awake.

Some days seemed interminable. Both Alexander and David had bad heat rash and David, especially, seemed to suffer. Half a lifetime ago, back in Cambridge, the Clever Doctors had suspected that he had a problem in the sodium balance in his skinny body; this would make him more susceptible to heat stroke. Was I wrong in keeping him away from blood tests and paediatricians? Maybe I should have let them investigate a little more?

Strangely, perhaps, I had no concerns whatever about the next baby. We were convinced we'd have another boy, and I knew he'd be all right. All my anxieties were about David. I felt uneasy until I found a way to stop him overheating. I put wet nappies on him, including one on his forehead. Once he was cooler, he cheered up noticeably. As I got his skin cool, his heat rash looked less angry and bothered him less, too.

डे डे डे

David was often constipated, so when the diarrhoea started, I rather welcomed it — and so did he, it seemed.

At first, he was comfortable and cheery, but then slowly, over the course of a couple of days, he became distant and silent. He'd have periods of several hours together when he was unusually drowsy, too, and it was clear that he was becoming quite ill. He had no fever, but he did not want to drink, and he seemed to have completely withdrawn from life.

When Simon came home at lunchtime, I said, 'David's ill.' Simon looked at me, immediately attentive, ready to absorb difficult news, though he said nothing. We stood in our cell-like dining room. I could hear Alexander talking nonsense to Siru outside the window. 'He's lost interest in drinking. He's drowsy. If he doesn't get thirsty, his dehydration will make him drowsier still, and he may never wake up. What shall we do?' I wanted to absolve myself of clinical responsibility.

Simon took me tenderly by the shoulders and looked into my eyes. 'Is he really ill?' He was checking that he understood.

'Yes, I think he is. Should I give him intravenous fluids? Should I try? Should we evacuate to Kathmandu? What do you think?' I was churning inside, not confident that I could find a child-sized intravenous-giving set in Rajapur, and then not confident that I could succeed in setting up a drip when my hands would be shaking. I wanted to cut and run — hand over to another clinician.

'You really think he's that ill?'

'I don't really know; he's fooled everyone before. Oh, it's so difficult and complicated! To wait, or …? The dehydration could take him, or

— longer term — it could destroy his only kidney. He needs that to survive. Should I try to intervene?'

'Is he comfortable?'

'Oh, yes, he's totally content. So content it seems awful to contemplate attacking him with a hypodermic. Remember the neurologist in Cambridge saying we should de-medicalise David?' I said, though thinking back to those times made me feel even more agitated.

'Yes, but it was easy for him to say that,' Simon said, with a bitter edge to his voice.

'Yes, it was, then — for him.'

Whenever I thought about what David's life was, I felt so, so sad. It seemed that he probably felt ill for about one third of the time. He complained so seldom that it was hard to tell, but he'd go quiet for a few days, and then when he *did* suddenly start burbling and laughing at rude noises again, I'd realise that he must have been feeling bad. Yet I was powerless to help him. I hadn't a clue what caused his quiet, unhappy times. He vomited a lot then; I guessed he felt queasy. 'If one third of David's life is solitary suffering, and another third sleeping, what sort of a life is that?'

'A miserable one. Do you think he's comfortable now?' Simon asked again.

'Yes, he is.' I was pacing about now, feeling sick. 'I'm sure he is.' I was not succeeding in keeping calm.

'Maybe we should just wait and see?' Simon said. 'It might not come to making a real decision. I'm still not sure but … we never will be … and nothing has really changed. Has it?' We were both close to tears.

'No. Though it still seems unreal talking about him like this. He's part of us …'

'I know.'

We sat for a long time, looking at each other, then Simon broke the silence, gently. 'David still doesn't look as if he is ever going to have much of a life. Does he?'

'Yes. No. Not really. And I'm sure that as he gets older, this kind of decision won't get any easier, even if he always remains a baby.

Intellectually, I feel David should decide, but emotionally, it is hard; he's so lovely!' I walked over to him and stroked his cheek. He didn't stir.

'Yes,' I said, 'it's one thing talking about letting nature take its course when there is no threat to David's life, especially when he has seemed so robust; but now it comes to it, I'm not sure ...'

'Let's leave him for a while, anyway.'

'Yes — he looks so content and at peace.' We gazed at him as he slumbered blissfully, a small smile on his face.

By evening, he was still not really conscious, and I began to wonder if he might even drift away in the night. We went to bed and I lay awake for a long time listening to David's untroubled breathing. He had so little. He needed so little. He was so content, yet he was so often ill. What should I do? What was best for him? Was it right to preserve the life of a child who had become ill and miserable and had no prospect of a future? The doctors back in Cambridge might just be able to get him to rally this time, but they couldn't give him a new brain or a future. What *was* best for him? One expert had declared that David's future would be perpetual babyhood and invalidism, yet David's time in Nepal had been charmed, enriched by escaping from England. Alexander, too, was spared his early childhood being dominated by hospital appointments: siblings of children with health problems often suffer dire consequences too. Most importantly for David, there was sunshine, admiration, and all those lovely noises to keep him chuckling. And we'd stopped him becoming a medical object, a pincushion, an Interesting Case.

Then an unearthly howling started; it was a lonely, desolate sound. It moved around, down by the river, like a lost soul searching for a drowned loved one. He was a sad, restless spirit calling to someone he couldn't let go; or that would have been a believable explanation if I hadn't realised that this was a jackal. No wonder locals thought jackal body parts had magical properties. I loved allowing myself to absorb these beliefs; scientific me argued that they were daft, but how uplifting believing in a little magic could be. I'm not religious, but here, rebirth and renewal seemed possible, and that gave me the gift of hope.

I must have fallen asleep, for some time in the middle of the night David woke me with the 'ergh … ergh … ergh' sound he made when he asked for a drink. I found a candle. David's 'ergh … erghs' became more insistent when he could see me. He raised his hands to ask for a drink. I handed him his bottle, full of rehydration solution. He emptied it thirstily and smiled, then belched and chuckled. He looked as if he'd just woken from a long, refreshing sleep. 'Welcome back, David!' I was so, so happy he'd decided to return. I held him for a long time, and he burbled contentedly to me … my happy, unpredictable, beautiful son.

We stopped going out much in the middle of the day, but often took a gentle stroll when Simon returned from work and the day had cooled a touch. Sometimes we took David, and found a patch of soft sand to lie him on. Or we left him with Sita, because some days going out — even for half an hour — totally exhausted him. One dusk, we wandered west towards the river, a route we'd followed many times before. 'I keep noticing that chunk of stone propped under that *peepal* tree. What is it?' I queried.

'It is very worn, but there are carvings. I think they're dancers … an ancient offering to Shiva. People often leave religious carvings or phallus-shaped rocks under *banyan* trees,' Simon said; then added, half to himself, 'Interesting … Rajapur must have been important once.'

A ghostly form caught my eye. I watched this pallid thing hovering, diving down, disappearing, reappearing. In the half-light I could have believed it was a lost spirit — some of Nepal's sounds and sights made the imagination soar — but this was only a barn owl hunting.

The sun and the heat sucked the colour out of the landscape, just as it faded my once-vivid clothes: everything was colourless as bleached sand. I'd spend some of the stifling afternoons in the shade of the porch, whisking flies off David's face or sponging him cool, sitting, brain barely functioning, gazing at flies grazing on my arm, wondering at the vultures. I'd read somewhere that much of the skull is taken up with the eyes, that the brain weighs less than each eyeball; hence they can spot carrion from 3,000 metres. Listless drongos gasped to keep cool. I'd get through most days by bug-watching and planning when I'd take the first tepid shower. Sometimes I'd hold out on having a shower until evening, the most satisfying time. Too early, and I was instantly bathed in sweat again. Too late, and mosquito storm-troopers had massed for their dusk assault on our 'bathroom'.

Simon would come home at sunset and, showered and refreshed, we'd sit up on the roof, high enough to fool the mosquitoes for perhaps an hour. David would lie tracking insectivorous bats as they tut-tutted overhead; Alexander would shoot imaginary enemies who lurked below in the garden, while we sipped warm Iceberg beer. 'I think I'll never tire of watching those egrets flying home to roost … and look how the evening light makes the fruit bats look ochre-red. If only these idyllic evenings could go on forever,' I sighed.

At just the same degree of gathering dusk each evening, our flying foxes would start to fidget and yawn, then quarrels would break out in their giant mango tree; individuals poked neighbours with long clawed thumbs on the leading edge of each wing. They looked like pterodactyls, with their 1.2-metre wingspans. Some would drop off their branches and do a few circuits, returning to bait a tree-mate, making some take to the air before they were ready to stir, squawking indignantly. Then finally the whole colony would follow the leaders and fly off like malign spirits to forage for fruit. While the flying foxes were noisily rousing themselves, the softening colours of evening, lengthening shadows, the orange glow to the landscape and the setting sun were tear-jerkingly beautiful. I don't know whether the emotion came from my half-boiled brain, relief from the searing heat, the brief return of colour, or seeing Simon after what could be long, lonely days, but this was an intensely moving, peaceful hour. It was a time that I savoured.

We had electricity when we ran the generator, but since a tankful of kerosene lasted less than twelve hours, I only ran it for light in the evening, and occasionally — when the heat was too, too unbearable — to power the ceiling fans. Starting it was a struggle, and sometimes, when Rajapur grit clogged everything, I couldn't get it going at all.

I asked Guliya, 'How does the weather make you feel?'

'This is our life. The hot weather makes the rice grow and it brings the rains.' Guliya, with never a bead of sweat, looked strong. I felt like a limp, mouldering, lettuce leaf.

By mid-June, the temperature had reached forty-seven degrees Celcius, and poor David spent most of his days sleeping under wet nappies. Then, as the day started to cool, he'd wake and drink all night. He almost completely gave up eating solids, but consumed pints of milk instead. I got little sleep, and after ten days I was finished. I took the boys up to Kathmandu. The capital seemed cool, and David started sleeping at night again. When Kathmanduites heard where we'd been they'd say, 'How can you live there?'

On Rajapur, pre-monsoon rains quickly turned the few motorable tracks into bogs. Canals and drains overflowed. Moti and the other drivers spent most of their time extricating project vehicles from ditches. Rather than become marooned on Rajapur as the river rose, the engineering team left Rajapur at its most difficult but most interesting time: the time, Basistha had said, that adolescent cobras come into houses.

Simon and Steve-the-Swindonian soon joined us in Kathmandu, where there was a spring-like feel in the Valley: cuckoos called; hill mynahs and other birds frantically stuffed food into their huge youngsters. The first rainstorms started with big blood-warm spots and built to exciting thunderstorms. David guffawed through every one. I loved them, too, and I enjoyed the local idea that thunderstorms are the gods fighting; I could imagine Lord Shiva, god of destruction, throwing thunderbolts at his enemies from his celestial chariot. These June downpours cleared the air, damping down air pollution so that the mountains reappeared. This was a time of lovely light-effects, spectacular cloud formations and fresh new colours. Egrets, parakeets and children's kites flying in front of black storm clouds were startlingly vivid. Alexander spent lots of time on the flat roof with our landlord's children; they taught him how to impregnate kite strings with ground glass so that he could saw through neighbours' strings and capture them.

There were rainbows most days. Sunlight picked out the contours of the low, green mountains of the Valley rim. Even Steve saw the beauty of the views and the medieval city. He became more relaxed but, like any proper Englishman, still pointedly ignored David. Not that I cared much. David was putting on weight again, albeit slowly.

The monsoon was a good time for Simon to take a much-needed break, and we had six weeks to enjoy summer in England. I looked forward to long, warm evenings, blackbird song and bacon, but I wondered how my happy child would be received back home this time, with his disability showing more and more. We'd be celebrating his first birthday in England, but what would that be like?

CHAPTER TWENTY

the gods hear better from here

WE FLEW HOME TO ENGLAND TOGETHER FOR WHAT were to become annual summer holidays to escape some of the monsoon. I looked forward to a relaxing summer break, but we were summoned to another endless succession of pointless hospital appointments: although David's doctors had moved on from the enthusiasm of finding him an Interesting Case, they still managed to disrupt our lives. Alexander soon tired of hospital toys, waiting while David had hip X-rays, while he saw the ophthalmologist, orthoptists again and a vision scientist. The eye experts asked, 'How is the patching going? Have you noticed any change in his squint?'

'Not really, but I've only been putting a patch on for half an hour each day. Is that enough? Should we continue?'

'If you like, but we are not sure what he can see.'

'He sees when it suits him. If I catch his attention, he tracks things for 180 degrees.'

'He probably hasn't got much useful vision. He's turning to your voice.'

'Even when I don't speak or make a sound?' They dismissed his abilities so easily, made so many demoralising, throwaway remarks — yet I knew that they were wrong.

The plastic surgeon who had operated on David's harelip said, 'We've got a very nice cosmetic result. It was difficult, meticulous surgery, but it looks good, I might even say excellent. We'll take photographs … And I think I explained that David will need other operations on his face: one before starting school, another when he's about eight. We should plan to excise those ear pits too.'

'They're not causing any problems,' I challenged.

'They will,' he said, closing any discussion. 'So we need to see David regularly. When are you next back in England?'

'Next summer. But why so many appointments? What are you looking for?'

'Oh, we just like to keep an eye on things,' he said patronisingly. He gave the impression that he hadn't noticed David's other problems.

David was treated by a physiotherapist a few times. The experts said that he was effectively blind, but even from across a large room he recognised Janet, and bawled whenever he spotted her. Yet she was good for him, and showed us how to encourage him in new skills, like starting to sit unsupported. During one session she roly-polied him down a soft ramp to get him to roll over, and he put his arms out to save himself. 'He's showing a fair amount of intelligence saving himself like that!' Janet said.

'Do you think his immobility is just because he is too content? Maybe he is not as handicapped as the doctors think.' The physiotherapist's look said that I was talking rubbish. I broke an awkward silence. 'How should I continue the exercises when we're back in Nepal?'

'There's a book …'

An occupational therapist talked about seating, but her suggestions were no better than what I'd already improvised, and contradicted the physiotherapist's advice. The neurologist said nothing new; he saw little progress, and was very pessimistic about David achieving anything.

We saw a speech therapist, an expert in mouth function, and I said, 'I'm worried. He's so skinny.'

'David's a year old now, isn't he? What does he eat?'

'He can only manage the smooth slop that three-month-olds take. Lumpy food makes him gag. And he's not chewing yet. He gets terribly constipated too.'

'Offer him thicker, more textured food, like Weetbix and baby foods for seven-month-olds.'

'There aren't many baby foods in Nepal. I make his food with a sieve or a blender, but I should be able to give him food with more texture. What can we do about all the vomiting?'

'I'm not sure; I'll think about it.' She never did give us an answer.

There were more trips to London. The cardiologist said that the holes in his heart were pinholes now, and surgery to close them would never be necessary. Then, as we were leaving, I tentatively ventured, 'Um … I'm pregnant, and I wondered whether a scan of the baby might be possible?'

'I'm sorry …' My heart sank. My mind raced. He's going to say no. Then what will we do?

He looked concerned, apologetic. 'I can't do it now. Do you want to wait two hours, or come back tomorrow?'

'For a moment I thought that you were going to say that it couldn't be done. We'll come tomorrow. Thanks. Thanks very much.'

The scan showed — as I unquestioningly knew it would — that the new baby's heart was normal. Simon didn't comment, but I knew that this was a relief to him. I submitted to an amniocentesis too; instinctively I didn't think it necessary, but rational me thought it for the best. I knew it would help further reassure Simon, although as it turned out he was never really easy in his mind until the babe was born. These were all the antenatal care we'd have, except for my DIY urine checks, and the blood pressure measurements that Simon and I did together.

I hunted for someone who could advise me on games to stimulate David and help him develop, but all the experts implied that we could not expect much more progress. Each time I heard this, my frustration at having wasted so much time increased. This was time we could have spent enjoyably with our families, or in the four of us having fun: Alexander was certainly itching for more rough-and-tumbles and pillow-fights with Simon. We wanted to get back to normality, rather than queue to see experts who only disheartened us. All anyone said was 'He's doing fine (… considering). Carry on.'

Yet this ritual of submitting to the system did at least reassure me that, by living in Nepal, David wasn't being deprived of special care. We also avoided the fate of so many families whose lives are dominated by clinical consultations, at great cost to brothers or sisters. Time ran out before we got the only appointment that might matter. David had developed a hernia that could kill him agonisingly if it strangulated. I wanted to see a surgeon to be sure that the risk was as small as I thought it was. But after all those pointless appointments, we couldn't get one with a surgeon; the waiting time was several months for all but emergencies.

We got hold of David's medical notes around this time, because I had so many unanswered questions about his first month of life. During those awful early weeks in hospital, I had begun to wonder whether in my wound-up state I'd got it wrong and imagined or exaggerated the disapproval of David's doctors. Amongst the frantic scribbles of the junior paediatricians, though, there were judgements about Simon — his undemonstrativeness read as lack of caring by doctors who'd never talked to him. In the consultant's careful hand there was, 'Parents are clearly unenthusiastic about doing anything for this baby.' Another doctor whom Simon never met wrote, 'The father returned from Khatmandu and found the presence of many abnormalities in his baby difficult to accept, and they were not keen to pursue treatment.' By the time we read this, though, our animosity towards the doctors had faded to a mild, smouldering resentment, because our decision to flee had been vindicated. I now had enough distance to realise that the doctors were protecting themselves from possible criticism: from colleagues, and from us if we changed our minds, as parents often do.

I quickly tired of the English discomfiture with David's handicap. I found hurtful the way people avoided saying anything about him, or especially to him. I wanted to introduce him to people, but was unsure how to. Several friends, who made no attempt to connect with David, were horrified at Alexander's antics: a favourite trick was to sprint the full length of the living room and take a flying leap over David. It made David guffaw, and Alexander never once made a mistake. Yet although they twitched at each of Alexander's leaps, they dared not comment. It felt like time to return to straightforward, baby-loving Nepal, so we flew east again, my conscience clear.

The plane was buffeted by late monsoon storm clouds as we descended into the Kathmandu Valley, but I was excited to be coming home, and was full of plans and resolutions. Expatriates tend to leave Kathmandu for the monsoon, but I loved it. The thunderstorms were thrilling, even if power cuts followed most downpours. If you looked up, not down into the mud, there was beauty everywhere. The rains invigorated butterflies, bulbuls, fantails and lurid, squawking parakeets. Standing water attracted a white-breasted kingfisher, which dive-bombed frogs under our window. The kingfisher's plaintive calling for his mate, the mooing cows and the barking dogs made David chuckle, which made us more appreciative of the sounds of Kathmandu.

Alexander so loved making his baby brother laugh; he did handstands, passed wind extravagantly and invented other ways of making new noises. Even when Alexander wasn't making him laugh, David was cheering company. He was most animated when there was plenty going on and he was surrounded by people who were comfortable with him. Other children, in particular, took him for what he was: another little person.

David charmed those visitors who could see beyond his abnormalities. His head was large and he hardly used the lower part of his body at all: most of the time he lay with his legs bent frog-like, flopped inert; when he did move his legs, he moved them together, symmetrically. The physiotherapist said that I should do exercises with him to separate his leg movements, because this would help him crawl, then walk. I'd try propping him up on the sofa to strengthen his back and work towards getting him to sit unaided, but he'd wriggle flat as soon as he could. Then he realised that I'd sit him up, so he started to wait until I was engaged on some other task before he slid back into a more comfortable position. When he rolled from his back over onto his front, he was marooned flat on his face, unable or unwilling even to push up on his arms. Once or twice I left him unhappily on his front, and he started to complain. 'Come on, David — roll over. You can do it!' I said, encouragingly, and gave him a clue by positioning his hands correctly. He stayed flat on his front and started to cry. 'Come on, David. Try!' The kingfisher let out his heartbreakingly lonely cry for help, and I couldn't be cruel to David any longer. I rolled him over and blew a raspberry on his tummy to make him laugh.

He was completely free of ambition, and utterly content just lying on his back watching the world go by. I'd often find myself gazing at my beautiful baby in his private paradise, wondering what would become of him. Would he ever walk? Would he end up in some awful institution somewhere, where he would be fed and watered like a zoo animal? Would he be a huge burden to Alexander when we were old and decrepit?

The most troubling question for me was how much forcing him to exercise was torture and how much it would improve his quality of life. The physical exercises seemed such a trial for him. And his eye got irritated under the sticky patch, so I had to work hard on games that kept his attention, made him look and distracted him from rubbing the patch off. He loved being tickled and I could tease him with a tickly hand that swooped in from different unpredictable angles. The experts said that he hadn't any useful vision, but I watched him scan the room to see where the next tickle was coming from — it was obvious that he could anticipate and see reasonably well, when he wanted to; when it was fun.

डे डे डे

Simon wanted to see how Rajapur and the river changed during the monsoon. Our Nepali friends thought it odd, but Simon took Alexander on this exploratory trip, while David and I stayed in Kathmandu. My excuse for not going was that I wanted to finish work on a travel health guide. I also looked forward to enjoying some time alone with David. While I worked, he contentedly batted one or other of the dangling toys on the A-framed device that we called his multigym. If I got absorbed in writing for too long, though, he'd tease me for attention, saying 'ergh, ergh,' asking for a drink. I'd stop work and squat down by him and say, 'This is milk, David. Milk. Say "milk".'

'Ergh, ergh,' he'd say again, with a cheeky sparkle in his eyes, as if he *could* say it, but wouldn't. Then, when I gave him his bottle, he'd lob it skilfully half the length of the room, then laugh. So I'd retaliate with a tickle game.

The adventurers returned singed and sun-frazzled, but invigorated. David welcomed Simon and Alexander with a happy 'dugdugdug,' waggling his head from side to side like a Nepali.

'Was it fun, Alexander?' I asked.

'I fried!' he announced, with four-year-old pride. Simon was unusually effusive and told of the freshness of the *tarai,* with the rice fields looking almost luminously green and the *sal* forest all freshly washed; he talked of the fearful heat, blinding glare off the silt and the unslakeable thirst on their thirteen-kilometre walk, slither and wade from the ferry to Rajapur village. 'And I had to drink Fanta! It wasn't nice,' Alexander chipped in. 'The best bit was when I skidded into

Mr Rajaram's house! Like this!' And he took a terrific run-up, skied on his bottom the full length of the marble hallway of our flat and crashed into the front door. David rolled over to look and chuckled at his clown of a brother. So Alexander did it again. 'That was fun! It was fun in Rajapur!'

'You cried at the time, and you frightened the ducks!' Simon teased.

'No, I didn't.' David's hilarity increased as Alexander began a did-didn't argument. Then he continued, 'I didn't like those dug-out *dinghies*. They wobbled and it felt like we'd fall out! *And* they were full of water with only rocks for seats!'

The trip was four days of slipping, waist-deep wading and sweating their way around the island, initially with Alexander on Simon's shoulders, and then in buffalo and bullock carts.

'It took us six hours to reach the river at the northern tip of the island, up near that expanse of dry, sterile cobbles where we picnicked in June. Remember? There was water north, west and east of us, and we were still three kilometres from where the river had been in June. It was a struggle getting there, and it took even longer to get back in the dark, but it was great to understand why the farmers have such problems controlling the river.'

'Why do they need to control the river?' I asked, realising how ignorant I was of Simon's work.

'When flood defences start to fail, it can end in whole villages being washed away, or the opposite extreme — no water, no crop; starvation.'

'Gosh, our neighbours live in such a hostile environment.' My idyllic vision of Rajapur was fading fast.

'Yup, that's why I'm here. This was a light monsoon, and it's useful to know that any repairs would still have been impossible. Access is just too difficult. We spent sixteen hours on the road and slumbered into Rajapur at 10 pm, where I transferred Alexander — still asleep and still muddy — into bed. The cart driver just turned round and went back the three hours to his village. The bullocks knew the way even in the dark, so the driver could sleep all the way home. And the next day we continued our explorations, and then took a buffalo cart sedately back into the twentieth century the day after.'

'Quite a trip!' I said. 'I'm sorry — almost — I missed it. But tell me … surely not many expatriate engineers would have made a trip like that?'

'It wasn't such a great expedition. We were only away four nights,' he said, self-effacing as ever.

'Yes, but most wouldn't have gone. What if you hadn't?' I felt proud of him.

'Nothing, but maybe that's why Nepali engineers get so pissed off with foreign "experts" pontificating about Nepal when they only have a fraction of the picture. And it was fascinating to hear Arun, the hydrologist, thinking out loud about what he thought the water could do; it's all so complex. I've seen the river at its most uncontrollable. This is a dangerous project. It might be risky to interfere too much. It was an interesting trip, but poor *docter* Bhandari was having a hard time.'

'Yes, I know. Rajapur even got a mention in the *Kathmandu Post* — because of all the deaths from Japanese encephalitis.' I felt a pang of guilt not to be there to help, especially knowing that this was the season when *docter* Bhandari struggles to save snakebite victims as well as the usual dysentery and typhoid.

'Oh,' Simon interjected, 'and while we were in Nepalgunj, Bishnu came to say hello; he's landed a nice job as a DoI clerk and is doing well.'

'Great. I thought he deserved better than working as a cook in Rajapur.'

डे डे डे

Late September brought our first glimpse for months of the snows of the Himalayas. After the rains, the lower mountains of the Valley brim looked particularly lovely: clean and a rich, deep green. Villages clinging onto the Valley sides looked attractive and amazingly remote. The rains painted the landscape in sharp, saturated colours and made everything wonderfully lush and new. Yet Kathmandu was growing fast with people moving in from the villages: there were building sites everywhere. My nose registered the smells of jasmine, mouth-watering wafts of spicy cooking, pungent old goat and blood, diesel and urine. Piles of fermenting refuse at most street corners made me gag, but Kathmanduites seemed not to notice the squalor, except that they'd clear their throats noisily and fruitily whenever they passed anything polluting.

When the devout take their ritual pre-dawn bath there is a lot of loud throat-clearing as part of the purification before prayer. That was protection enough, until early in October when bubonic plague struck in Surat, India. Doctors had been the first to run away, and they led a veritable stampede of at least 200,000 people; if the doctors were scared, no wonder the public panicked. Meanwhile, in Nepal, we saw people walking the streets wearing surgical masks. Schools and movie halls were shut, and the border with India closed in the East. Newspapers announced, 'Keep cool there is enough tetracycline', which precipitated panic-buying of the antibiotic. In the *Rising Nepal,* between an ad assuring us that 'Nepal Sausage is Quality and Integrity' and one suggesting 'Life is not simple, like Waiwai noodles', there was a report of a man with a cough who'd turned up at the hospital at Biratnagar, near the Indian border; he had been refused admission and was placed under armed guard in a field.

We were over 1,500 kilometres from the outbreak, yet tourists fled Kathmandu and expatriate friends asked me if they should leave too. 'Surely *you're* not staying here — not with the children? Surely little David is not strong enough, if …?' I couldn't convince them that there was no real risk — not for us. Plague is a disease of extreme poverty, unlikely to strike us in our marble palaces.

I mounted my own public health campaign: every few days I set fire to the heap of stinking rubbish on the street corner nearest to our flat. My high-caste landlady came out to commend my action, while I hinted that she, too, could help. 'This work cannot be done by us!' Finally, the Municipality started trucking it away and for a few months Kathmandu was relatively clean underfoot. There were never any confirmed cases of plague in Nepal, and after all the hysteria subsided, the death toll totalled fifty-two, while Japanese encephalitis killed a couple of hundred in Nepal alone, including dozens on Rajapur that year.

Soon after that the Municipality put up signs announcing: CLEAN GREEN HEALTHY KATHMANDU. Who were they trying to kid? The air, too, was far from pure, and I had a lingering worry that the pollution might give David one of those nasty chest infections that the cardiologist had predicted.

In our flat in Kathmandu, the boys slept side by side in two single beds pushed together. One night I woke to an uncharacteristic, urgent and unhappy sound from David. I went into the bedroom to see David with his feet on the floor, but his body propped upright against the bed. Astonishingly, he appeared to be standing, supported only by his shoulder blades; a few seconds later and he would have completed his tumble out of bed onto a thinly carpeted concrete floor. But why had he not fallen? How did he recognise the danger when he'd never fallen from anywhere, and was supposed to be so handicapped? He always seemed floppy, weak and incapable, yet this time he'd saved himself. Was his incapability simply lack of motivation?

It was easy to be unambitious for David while he was content, and while he looked and acted like a small baby. Perhaps he needed to be pushed; with the right stimulation, he might become more independent. David was slowly clocking up his developmental milestones, but I kept thinking that with more specialised advice, we could help him to achieve more.

I continued to look, although I suspected that no-one in Kathmandu had much to offer. Perhaps that was what made me even more interested in finding out what locals did. I asked driver Basant, font of misinformation, but always good for a story, 'Why do people wrap string around *peepal* trees?'

'They are trees of Ganesh, *memsahib*,' he replied, 'You can see the shape of his elephant's nose in the tree. These strings are from vests of sick children; parents take cottons from vest of sick baby, they wrap it around Ganesh-tree and child gets better. It is very best medicine.' He'd stopped the car close to a big old *bo* tree: a fig with multiple trunks and beautiful leaves with long, long drip-tips. 'Look, this tree has cured many children. Maybe we should do special *pujaa* for poor David?' Basant had gone back to calling him 'poor David'. He wasn't so chubby any more; he did not look well. I didn't know why and I had started to wonder about getting another doctor to look at him again.

'Do you worship Ganesh, Basant?'

'Of course, *memsahib*.'

'But I thought you are Buddhist, Basant-*dai*?'

'You are very true, *memsahib*. I Buddhist-man, and I also liking Ganesh. He help me, *memsahib*.'

'He certainly seems popular. I think he may be the most popular god in the Valley?'

'I think also, *memsahib*.'

'So, tell me, Basant, what do you do when someone in your family is ill?'

'First I go to temple or see the *jhankri*. Then if we not better after one or two weeks time, then we go hospital and get some injection.' For him, conventional medicine was only worth a try when all else had failed, but he added, 'I cannot go temple these days.'

'You can't?'

He asked me, 'You know why I wear these white dresses, *memsahib*?' Basant now wore white trousers, shirt, plimsolls and a white woolly hat to cover his shaved head. 'My Daddy, he did die.'

'I am sorry …' I'd half forgotten that white is the colour of mourning in Asia.

'It no problem, *memsahib*. He got very old and he had big drinking problem.' Basant's bereavement was a difficult time, not because of grief — he seemed relieved to be rid of the old inebriate — but because during his year-long mourning he was not allowed to go to the temple. Being isolated from the gods was no holiday. If anyone in the family was taken ill, he would be forced to take them to the hospital.

Not all families are so traditional, though. A five-month-old Chhetri child, the firstborn, suffered a bout of diarrhoea which two different doctors failed to cure. The infant got thinner, and the diarrhoea continued, so the mother then tried the *jhankri.* This holy man told her to keep away from doctors and take the child to Swayambhu on the forested hill that overlooks Kathmandu. The site has been hallowed for over 2,000 years. Tradition holds that the valley was once a lake where lotuses grew and pilgrims came to meditate and commune with snake deities. A bodhisatva called Manjushri was so taken with the spot that he smote the retaining hill with his sword, allowing the lake to drain and the snakes to be purged. As the clear waters receded, a flaming sacred lotus in the centre of the lake changed into Swayambhu hill. There now, watched by four pairs of enormous all-seeing eyes set in a gilded tower above the huge white dome of the *stupa*, pilgrims may circumambulate, turning 211 prayer wheels that bear the holy mantra *Om mani padme hum*.

Swayambhu is a place to find peace, and it is also an auspicious place to die. That was where the emaciated little Chhetri child's four grandparents took her. They prayed at the ornate pagoda to Hariti, a demoness who protects against infectious diseases — and also helps with exams and law suits. I took a stroll around the temple complex at Swayambhu, continuing, I suppose, my quest for help for David. It is one of innumerable holy high places in the land that seem to say that the gods will hear us better from up here. It was bustling, but strangely tranquil, and the view out over the city was magnificent. Finally, I stopped outside a small pagoda with intricate silver doors; inside there was just enough space for the ragged jodhpur-clad priest and a couple of devotees. There was a queue outside. I said to a young monk, 'I seek the shrine to Hariti.'

'It is there,' he said, pouting towards it with his lips, 'but you cannot go inside, *didi*. Non-believers are not allowed.' A thud behind me, rapidly followed by another, made me turn. Something, moving fast, brushed against my leg. The monk's face distorted into a grimace of disgust, and the second rhesus monkey felt a worthy foot up his holy bum. The dominant rhesus male, incarnation of Lord Hanuman, was now looking down from the roof. He stood victorious; his testicles, which were the size of oranges, swung gently between his legs.

The Chhetri family prayed, pleaded and left many offerings for Hariti, but the infant died. Yet it was a satisfactory end in an auspicious place: it is dangerous for children to die at home. That would bring bad luck long-term to the surviving family. The body of the little Chhetri girl was taken from Swayambhu down to Pashupati by the holy Bagmati River for the last rites. There the Hindu priests said that a lot of long, complicated, expensive prayers must be said to pacify the child's spirit; since the first child had died the others would all turn out bad unless the right *pujaa* was performed. So during a time when Western parents would be grieving for their lost daughter, this mother's main emotion was fear. Fear of what further disaster the dead child might bring down upon the family and her unborn children, and concern about raising the money to pay the priests; fees are paid in gold and in saris, for the priests' wives.

CHAPTER TWENTY-ONE

blood sacrifice

EVERYTHING STOPS FOR THE FESTIVAL OF *DESAI* IN late October, and we took a week away in the mountains. We'd even allow David a holiday from eye-patching and physiotherapy. It would be our last adventurous trip before the new baby grounded us and I would, for a while, feel fulfilled and contented as a full-time mother again. We knew instinctively we were having another boy, but I was impatient to know who he'd resemble at first, impatient to fill our home with more carefree baby-babble. I also knew that the birth would be a relief for Simon — it would prove correct my intuitions that this baby would be healthy.

We piled into a clapped-out Land Rover and rattled and wound north for most of the day until, as the sun was setting, the driver stopped at the landslide that had removed the dirt road. We tumbled out, and Dhan Bahaadur organised us with amiable bossiness. He'd been recommended by his agent because he was strong and didn't smell. He would carry David in an oblong basket used normally to transport few-month-olds. The way ahead was a scary scramble across a mess of slippery micaceous sand, boulders, roots, streams and smashed trees — all above a 500-metre drop. Locals danced and hopped all around me, giggling while I struggled, unbalanced by a six-months-plus pregnant belly and an overlong drawstring skirt. I was clumsy, but I was a proper woman who'd proved her fertility. It felt the most natural thing in the world to be heading off into the hills when so very pregnant. They patted my belly in a congratulatory way, giggling cheekily about the baby and the baby's father. They laughed as they lifted Alexander across the most difficult patches, or pulled me across. The evening air smelt fresh as we sauntered the final ten kilometres to the stark hotel at Dhunche and four hard beds.

Next morning, we were quickly in amongst sinuous red tree trunks festooned with trailing lichens. There were orchids, maidenhair, and staghorn ferns hopping with tiny birds. Rhododendrons gave way to small-leafed oak, and we blundered into a troop of cream-coloured langurs. I stopped to watch them banqueting on wild custard apples. White-eyes twittered around me and Dhan Bahaadur's flute-playing was transporting; it reminded me of the absence of birdsong in Nepal — one of the country's few deficiencies.

Then Alexander broke the spell by coming 'brrmm, brrmming' back along the path. He'd reverted to his motorbike game: speeding along, steering with a stick. The atmosphere was intoxicating, but the effort of walking made my womb start to contract. I started to think about what might happen if I went into premature labour. I felt worried; I felt pathetic. If Alison Hargreaves managed to climb the north face of the Eiger when six months pregnant, then I should be able to manage this relatively gentle walk. Surely.

The lovely countryside enticed me on, but next morning the contractions seemed ever stronger and my womb felt cannonball hard. I suddenly started to lose faith in my intuitions. Until that moment, I'd been sure that there would be no problems with this pregnancy, that this baby would be all right; but then what would happen if I went into labour now, and what if this baby got stuck in my pelvis as David had? I didn't want to worry Simon, but I was losing confidence fast. The way on would take us down a rough path that tacked over an awesome landslide: it would be a 1,000-metre scramble or scree-run to get into the densely forested Langtang Gorge.

I sat on a bench in the sun outside a shack-shop just above the landslide. I ordered tea. Up ahead, now tantalisingly close, were snowy mountains of the next great Himalayan ridge — in Tibet. 'Look, Simon,' I said, pointing, 'up and across the valley, amongst the pines ... yes, it is — Himalayan blue sheep. Can you see them?' How I wanted to continue and see more wildlife! I vacillated still. If I'd been my patient, I'd have pronounced me mad. It seems strange, now, that the experience of David's problems hadn't made me expect more disasters. Some sense about the baby I was carrying told me that everything would be all right. Simon was more worried, but to him walking in the hills was such a normal thing to do that it didn't occur to him that it was daft to be such a long way from a decent maternity hospital.

Two young trekkers came gasping into the tea shop. 'Shit — what a climb that was! Let's have some Coke.' A Nepali walked through, breathing hard from the ascent, then a very fit-looking Australian slumped down on the bench beside me. 'Hey, man. I'm glad I'm on the way back.' Just looking at the sweat trickling from him convinced me that I shouldn't go on. I finished my tea, stiffly got to my feet, turned my back on the landslide and walked back the way we'd come.

Everywhere we paused, and even sometimes when we didn't, laughing people gathered round, pushing to peer into David's basket. How he loved being a celebrity! His big smiles displayed his first, very late, very new teeth. A mother said, 'Take him out of the basket. He is unhappy alone in there!'

'He's *cushy*; he's comfortable. He likes travelling this way.' He lay there: serenity surrounded by chaos. I wonder what went on inside his young head. Noticing his limp legs tucked immobile in the basket, one woman uncovered him, '*Cheek, nees, soom, jee* ...': she counted his toes, checking whether he was normal, while he chuckled. 'He isn't comfortable. Take him out!' she commanded. I needed guidance if I couldn't carry my own baby. Another woman took him from the basket and plonked him on my lap. He started to complain. 'There!' Proof of my neglect. I produced a bottle. 'You have no milk, *didi*?' a woman with a baby tied to her back asked.

'I'm pregnant; that's why I'm not feeding the baby,' I said, patting my huge belly. My baby moved reassuringly as if in response. This was no excuse, though. 'Are you ill, *didi*? Do you eat good foods in your country? Why aren't you giving the baby your milk?' (What's wrong with this woman?) 'And why has this baby no teeth?'

'He's got three!' I countered.

'And you are pregnant again too soon, *didi*! Having the next baby will be hard for you!' These weren't the only Nepalis who thought that we needed family planning advice. One of Simon's middle-class Kathmandu friends had already recommended a good vasectomy clinic.

We spent a night in a basic little lodge at Bharku, and emerged from the smoky gloom into the sharp morning sun. A ram stood on the dusty path; he had African marigolds between his horns and there was a smouldering heap of juniper leaves beside him. A group of men sauntered up, and one of them, dressed in a grubby skiing jacket and woolly hat, began droning in Tibetan. While the others watched, he smeared butter and scattered uncooked rice here and there, and sprinkled the sheep with *rakshi* from an old Fanta bottle. The ram looked rather overwhelmed and knelt down. The *lama*'s chanting stopped and all eyes were on the sheep. He nudged it to its feet with his foot. It stood motionless. Then, after a long time, it shook itself like a wet dog and everyone relaxed, smiled and dispersed; the *pujaa* was over and the sheep settled down to nibbling marigolds and even the smouldering juniper incense.

Later, someone else unceremoniously and with considerable skill lopped off the sheep's head with a single swipe of his *khukuri*. I was so surprised that I did not have time to distract Alexander. The dispatch was so clean and painless that Alexander was puzzled rather than upset by it, and after some time peering at the carcass he asked, 'Which end does the head fit on?'

The bloody neck was daubed on door lintels, people's foreheads and other auspicious places and the blood from the carcass dripped into a saucepan of millet flour to make an unpleasant variant of black pudding. Nepal is an amazing cultural mish-mash, but I had not expected blood sacrifice in a Buddhist community, though a fresh goat leg nailed to a prayer flagpost in the previous village should have forewarned me.

डे डे डे

Invigorated by even this short time in the mountains, we returned to Kathmandu, and it was soon time for the boys and me to return to England: the baby was due in a matter of weeks. It would also be an opportunity to reconnect with the medical experts who could help David, perhaps.

I called in at Simon's head office in Cambridge to give some documents to William. 'Gosh, you look well, Jane! Nepal must be suiting you. I've heard that the Wilson-Howarths have been putting our visiting advisors and consultants through their paces. They say you like Rajapur!'

'Remember that time when you'd just come back from your reconnaissance of Rajapur? I think you described it then as interesting rather than nice. It's not an easy place.'

'That I could tell, even on my two-day visit, but you've stuck it out. I don't think that Jim and Sally are enjoying it at the moment, though.'

'Oh, dear. They're such a pleasant couple that I thought Simon would enjoy their company. He's so isolated — and I thought it would be stimulating for him to learn from Jim's experience of river training. Simon hasn't mentioned that they're struggling; but when we're apart, he always tries to sound positive. He only unburdens himself when we're back together again.'

'Simon never looks stressed …'

'No, but you all are — aren't you? And it must be difficult, because Sally and Jim do seem to worry about things rather a lot, and Jim has been ill. Sally put him on a cleansing diet, but they can't get any of the foods he's supposed to have … but, hey! Did you hear about Simon's epic adventure with Alexander during the monsoon? They walked and bullock-carted right up to the canal intake in the north of the island, boldly going beyond the reach of four-wheel-drive …'

He laughed. 'Must have been hot.'

'Yup — when they got back to Rajapur bazaar, Alexander was so thirsty, he drank a whole bottle of Fanta for the first time in his life. He usually loathes it! They went to the so-called *hotel* — that nasty shack in the centre of the bazaar — that has the only fridge on the island. Being served from that fridge must be a prestige thing: the drinks are all lukewarm.'

'Hmm, warm Fanta. Unenticing, I'd say. But you love a bit of a challenge, don't you!'

'Yes, maybe we do, but it is also good to be doing something useful, and it *is* a fascinating place. We've had some amazing encounters with tigers and rhino, crocs and river dolphins, and it's a great place for bird-life. I used to be a rampant conservationist, but I'm beginning to understand how difficult it is to protect a reserve properly when people are starving just outside.'

'And you've another baby on the way. Congratulations.'

'We've had to entertain ourselves somehow!'

'Great to see you looking so well.'

He laughed again, looking around, wanting to change the subject. I'd been too lewd. Maybe he thought I'd gone native. Maybe I had. Western music jarred horribly lately, but the sitar was transporting, and I'd even find myself humming along to Nepali pop songs on occasion. I changed the subject for him. 'How's life amongst the Ivory Towers then?'

'Oh, pressurised as ever. The firm needs more work.' The company was going through a lean patch, with lots of redundancies. While Simon was working on Rajapur, he would avoid that fate.

My first priority back in Cambridge was to try to find advice or books on how to stimulate David. I had a couple of months, and maniacally I started phoning around, pleading for appointments for David to see the full range of medical experts. I also needed advice on his vomiting.

Although, nominally, the neurologist was the paediatrician coordinating David's care, I had become his medical advocate. The neurologist had no useful ideas about the vomiting, but he did suggest we consult researchers in London with a special interest in assessing how babies see. I'd asked the ophthalmology consultant about David's vision. 'He has severe cortical blindness.'

'But he can see.'

'To a limited extent.'

'I think he can see quite well. Can you give me some tips or literature to help me help David develop his vision and use his eyes more?'

'There isn't much written. Maybe *you* could write a book about bringing up a blind baby.'

'It's me that needs the advice. And, anyway, he doesn't seem blind. But have you noticed his appealing mannerism of cocking his head to one side when he looks, especially if he is teasing.'

'Odd head movements often go along with visual field deficits.' Here we go again. I talk of a cute mannerism; doctors talk of oddness, abnormality and defects.

We took the train down to London where David spent half a day looking at flashing lights, but the battery of sophisticated neuro-developmental tests still didn't clarify whether David didn't look or couldn't see. The academics said, 'He's fascinating. We'd like to do more tests and another scan.'

'Have the results come up with anything that will help him, and me?'

'Um ... His squint is quite pronounced, so he still needs to exercise his lazy eye. Patching is a good idea. We'll look at him again next time you are back in England — after the scan.'

'I'm not sure that there is any point in a scan. Do you think he can see?'

'It is difficult to say, but he is such an interesting case. We'd very much like to test him again.'

They knew less than I did.

The Cambridge doctors advised that I could continue to patch David's good eye 'if I liked'. I didn't like, and — more to the point — neither did David. When I asked directly if patching would help or not, I was told 'Maybe. It is difficult to say.'

I didn't know how to react to the experts' lukewarm advice, but then no-one had ever seemed to know what David needed. Janet, the physiotherapist, saw him again, and my half-blind son, with his limited intelligence, recognised her instantly and howled at the prospect of another workout. Whenever he could, he'd blot her from his view — make her disappear — by rolling away and presenting his back to her.

He went back into hospital for his hernia repair. This was a nightmare return to the ward where we had suffered so much turmoil, and where we had grieved for the normal baby we had expected. Several of the nurses who had helped us through that difficult time remembered us and were amazed at how well David had got on. 'He's so bonny, Jane. You have done well for him! Look at his lovely rosy cheeks. What a beautiful healthy baby he is now!'

'How's the murmur?' I asked the spotty house physician who was doing David's pre-op checks.

'Murmur? He has no murmur.'

'Are you sure?' In my determination to act like an ordinary mother, to de-medicalise David, I'd stopped listening to his heart. I snatched up the houseman's stethoscope and listened. 'His heart sounds normal!' David had repaired the holes in his heart himself; now there was no question of him needing that heart operation. And the blood tests they did before the operation were all normal too. He'd been neglected medically for so long, yet he was thriving! David was doing well, but I was still anxious when I went down with him to the operating theatre. He woke up promptly after the anaesthetic this time, and only later the anaesthetist breezed up and said, 'Your son is difficult!'

'I know that — what now?'

'He has a very narrow airway and I had to call an ENT consultant to put down a very fine tube. If ever he has another anaesthetic, you must warn the doctors … and croup would be very dangerous for him.' I thought we'd completed the catalogue of David's abnormalities, but still they found more problems. David himself seemed fine, though, content as ever.

डे डे डे

Simon's maiden aunt, a stalwart of the Pony Club in Sussex, helped take children from Ingfield Manor School horse riding. Seeing how the Ingfield staff cared for children afflicted with cerebral palsy made her wonder whether David could get some help from them. It seemed a long shot to me, but after we had been at the School for Parents for only a couple of hours, they had a feel for David's problems. 'We'll be able to help you get him more mobile, more independent.'

What was different about the school was that the staff treated David like a person. They talked to him, reasoned with him, looked at what he as an individual could and couldn't do, and they tried things to see what worked best for him. They laughed with him, tickled and teased, quickly recognised his love of weird noises and produced a range of new sounds to interest him and make him laugh. Up until this moment it hadn't occurred to me just how inadequate all other 'expert' attempts had been to connect with him.

The Ingfield staff suggested ways to encourage David to get mobile, and they had lots of information to help me make contact with him.

'Songs work really well; they are attractive and a good way of helping children learn basic language structure. Sing to him all the time! And then you can use colour and movement and mirrors to get his attention.' Ideas came pouring out like manna from heaven.

We made a plan for David and me to attend a School for Parents course the following summer. Just to think of David as being a pre-school child was a change. I hadn't even considered that he would ever go to school.

Then they asked, 'Hasn't he got any shoes?'

'Er, no … he's not walking, so I hadn't thought of buying any.'

'He needs shoes. He's seventeen months old. And you should stop dressing him like a baby.'

'Yes, you're right; he is growing up.' It was not easy to buy shoes for David, though: he'd never used his feet, so they hadn't grown. Finally, I found some dinky pram shoes for a three-month-old. These shopping trips taught me that David was now obviously abnormal. People looked at him and then looked away, too embarrassed to look and see his charms.

Simon, back for my planned caesarean section, looked tanned and handsome, but thinner and — in a short-sleeved shirt — under-dressed for the English winter. His month without us in Rajapur had been difficult, and he'd been relieved to get away.

'Sally came down to Rajapur to cheer Jim up and cook amazing dishes for us all, but the generator wasn't powerful enough for the new oven we'd bought, so she was a bit stuck with the wrong recipe books. Sally's frustration made Jim more miserable than he'd been before. She was still trying to make him stick to this complicated diet — something to do with only acid foods one day and alkali the next. Then there was a great drama about needing an egg-timer. Sally assumed that since Guliya couldn't read, she couldn't use a watch or cook soft-boiled eggs. Poor Mr Rai and Basant were sent chasing around Kathmandu trying to find this device that they'd never heard of. We were all cooped up in this small house, going around in circles trying to sort out the project and getting on each other's nerves. I ended up sending them off to Tigertops, which was therapeutic. Should have thought of it earlier.'

'We're lucky to have Tigertops to escape to, aren't we? I wonder what it would be like stuck in the middle of a desert with days to travel for a change of scenery or company.'

'You'd just take longer breaks less frequently,' said my ever-pragmatic husband.

Simon was in the operating theatre for Sebastian's nice, uncomplicated delivery by caesarean section on the twentieth, and I fought to be allowed home on Christmas Day. I left hospital with instructions that for six weeks I must lift nothing heavier than the new baby. I wasn't supposed to pick David up. And hoovering, of course, was another dangerous activity.

When they were fed and clean, I'd leave the babies lying together on a Nepali quilt on the living room floor. I put a blanket over them while I pottered in the kitchen or helped Alexander with various projects: he was always so full of ideas and constantly brimming with new enthusiasms. The first time I was surprised to find, on checking the babies, that the blanket was completely off Sebastian and all on David. It must have happened by mistake: David surely was not sufficiently aware or calculating to pull a blanket deliberately off his little brother. But he did it again and again. And David would often roll on his side, presenting his back to Sebastian so that this supposedly blind child couldn't see this new, unwelcome arrival. David clearly disapproved of my absence in hospital — and now I'd had the audacity to reappear with this unnecessarily noisy and demanding object that took so much of my attention. David was responding with normal sibling rivalry! I wondered whom he loathed more — his new brother or his physiotherapist. He was jealous, and I was delighted. Perhaps the new baby would drive David to great things.

We borrowed a special supporting chair on wheels with lots of straps, which allowed David to sit and do more with his hands. Soon he began to enjoy short sessions in it. He composed a special number on a percussion instrument, managing a range of notes punctuated with thumps on the wall behind him. It also meant that he could sit up and join in with us at mealtimes.

In the few days before we went back to Nepal, we shopped frenetically. We dusted off an old suitcase and fired into it all manner of things for David: leg splints to help him stand, rattles, percussion instruments and other toys that made noises, shiny attractive things to encourage him to look, an inflatable sausage for him to roll on or over, plus packets of instant foods that he could eat easily. We also bought a home-school package for Alexander. Then, when Sebastian was three weeks old, we flew back to Kathmandu.

David, at eighteen months old, still looked like an infant, and people assumed I'd had twins. Soon after take-off, the maternal Royal Nepal chief stewardess bustled over, '*Two* small babies! This is difficult for you.' She disappeared into the cockpit with Sebastian for two hours.

CHAPTER TWENTY-TWO

poor *pooss* baby

IT WASN'T LONG AFTER TOUCHING DOWN THAT I WAS itching to get back to Rajapur: pining for clean air again. We escaped the filth trapped in the Kathmandu Valley, but the pollution overflowed at the Thankot pass and oozed downwards, like a malign organism, seemingly chasing the car. We left that behind only to meet the next problem. Teams of men still worked on damage from floods that occurred around the time David was born, eighteen months before. They shovelled spadesful into baskets to clear innumerable huge landslides, keeping Kathmandu's supply line open. Bailey bridges were in place at all the river crossings; cars and lorries queued to cross them. 'Nepal hasn't a hope,' Simon mumbled, suffering to see his beloved Nepal struggling so.

'What?'

'There's a vast program of new road-building, but Nepal can't maintain what she already has. They hadn't finished repairing the damage of the bad 1987 monsoon before the '93 flood arrived.'

'How long was it before vehicles could get through last time?' I asked.

'Six weeks. There was no petrol, diesel, bottled gas; nothing from the lowlands … the valley's pollution problem was solved overnight!'

'There are *so* many crashed trucks,' I said in Nepali, trying to involve Kumar, who was driving.

'Now, it is not bad, *memsahib*.' Frighteningly, Kumar turned right around to reply. 'Before, truck drivers took strong drink to keep awake and there were twenty new crashes each time I drove this way.'

I turned to Simon. 'Doesn't anyone here worry about dying on the roads?'

'No, I guess everyone is pretty fatalistic. While you were away, I heard a story from someone working on the roads project. He saw a bus driver staggering about on the road, covered in blood, and offered to give him a lift to hospital. But the driver insisted on being taken to the nearest police station. He wanted to be arrested to avoid a lynching.'

'What do you mean, "lynching"?'

'That's the only way people feel they can get justice, with the police being so corrupt. He was a new driver, and complained that he didn't realise he was approaching a dangerous bend because there were no warning skid marks. The bus went over the edge, but some rocks stopped it plunging all the way down. There were about a hundred people on board; four died immediately and twenty more were dead before reaching hospital. The injured were evacuated in flagged-down buses, but there was no doctor at the nearest hospital. I don't know what happened to the casualties.'

'That's appalling!'

'It's not as bad as the latest trend of drivers running over injured people. If you kill someone on the road, it costs 1,750 rupees in compensation, but hospital fees run into many thousands so drivers ensure that their victims are dead.'

'Drivers plural? Surely there's only been one case?'

'No, apparently it happens ...' Simon spoke with the fatalism of a defeated Nepali.

'Doesn't this kind of thing ever get to you?'

'Yes, of course it does, but these are acts of desperation. Someone who is only just managing to support a burgeoning extended family can't afford to get into debt, or he and all his relatives would starve.'

'And the tourists talk of happy, smiling, friendly Nepali people. Don't the police stop these murders?'

'Not usually. The police sometimes arrest a relative of the accused. There are plenty of murderer's fathers incarcerated in jail. Untouchables have an especially bad time; some die inside.'

'Die? How?'

'The warders incite violence amongst the prisoners — using inmates to control each other. And there's torture and malnutrition ... Nepali prisons aren't nice places.' I didn't want to hear any more.

I gazed out at the stream of vehicles strung out ahead. The one in front had 'Hron Please' on the back; the next, 'Horan Pileese'. The children were content for a while, but the winding road was beginning to make us all feel queasy. Kumar, who had the figure of someone who enjoyed his food, announced it was time to eat, and pulled in at a favourite shack in Mugling. He demolished a huge pile of rice, while we sipped tea. We already felt we'd been travelling for long enough, and we hadn't even reached the plains. Yet I was enthusiastic about getting back. Our second year on Rajapur promised to be full and busy. I looked forward to seeing the changes.

Much later, Simon said, 'The East–West Highway, at last.'

'What a relief. Where's this then?'

'Narayanghat. The *tarai* has been totally transformed since I first came here in the seventies. The drive between Narayanghat and Hetauda took two days then — with buses running to and fro between ferries across the great rivers. Now it takes less than two hours. The countryside has changed, too, with so many hill people resettling where there was just forest before.'

The road, recently repaired with an Asian Development Bank loan, was straight and smooth now, with tarmac wide enough for a vehicle in each direction, plus a gravel hard shoulder, then the rice fields a metre below. I no longer needed to brace myself or worry about protecting the babies from jolts. I could see David's attention caught by animal and vehicle sounds and also the changing scenery outside: a cinema bill-board, yellow mustard fields, colourful elegant women who walked with water pots balanced effortlessly on their heads. Water buffalo peered into the middle distance. A man was trying to sell something at the roadside; he held up what looked like the tyre of a small motorbike but it was covered in bronze scales. Then I realised: 'It's a pangolin! Why would anyone buy a live pangolin?'

'Hmm? I dunno, and I don't suppose the seller cares, as long as he makes a little money.'

Kumar drove fast, weaving between radishes drying on the roadside, people wobbling along on bicycles, cows, goats, pigs, chickens, toddlers and drunks, all blissfully unaware of how close they had come to death. Best not to look.

I came around from a drowsing half-sleep as Kumar swerved to avoid two oncoming buses in an overtaking race. One, with vomit streaks on the outside, had 'NICE BUS' across its windscreen; the other said 'LUCK'. Then the road unexpectedly left the newly harvested rice fields. We zigzagged up over a sparsely forested spur of 1,000-metre-high Himalayan foothills. After 200 straight, flat kilometres, the contours came as a relief. Dusty, spiky forest growing out of folded and smashed primeval sandstone merged into lusher woodlands as the road made a breathtaking descent to the startling green fields of winter wheat flanking a languid, rippling Rapti River. Dusk gathered. The road took us through increasingly wild country. Black-naped hare fled into the forest; a jungle cat was briefly caught in the headlights. Above, scrub was burning on the hillsides in huge straggly rings of fire.

After eleven-and-a-half hours on the road, the atmosphere in the car was disgusting. Both David and Sebastian had vomited on me, and our sweating bodies stank. Walking into the seedy Hotel Sneha seemed like entering paradise. We were greeted by an obsequious man with slicked-back hair and a forced *betel*-red grin. He showed us into a huge, high-ceilinged room. On the back of the door of our room, a big notice announced, 'Rooms are Swept and Swabbed Daily', but under the beds lurked an array of stuff including the week-old remains of someone's lunch. The greasy, downtrodden youth who came to sweep up looked puzzled when I asked whether anything could be done about the leaking plumbing. 'It is normal,' he said, 'for pipes to leak when they have water in them.' Then, in English, 'This hotel has *full runningwatersystem* hot-cold also twenty-four hour daily thankyou madam yesplease.'

It was so good to wash and change, and we slept deeply despite drips and baying dogs. Early the next morning, we headed on through farmland and then the rich *sal* forest of the Royal Bardiya National Park. Simon said, 'The river moved a lot last monsoon and it's really difficult to drive anywhere on the island these days. Buses and trucks can't get to the bazaar any more. We'll approach from the east this time, and cross on the Kothiyaghat ferry.'

'Good; that's a more direct route than last year.'

'Yes, but it takes two hours longer.'

Only a couple of hours before we were due to leave for Rajapur, driver Basant introduced us to a woman who was willing to work for us in Rajapur. Doubting she'd come, I said. 'Can you be ready to go to Rajapur tonight, *bahini*?'

'I am ready, *memsahib*. I have nothing more to lose,' Ganga said cheerfully.

I looked into her beautiful face, expecting her to say more, but got nothing. 'The journey takes two days; it is a long way from Kathmandu.'

'That is very good for me, *memsahib*,' she said, with an excited smile; she didn't avert her eyes like most young Kathmanduites would. Gurung women are used to speaking up for themselves but, even so, I didn't really expect her to return. She did come back — with a very small bag — and happily climbed into the cab of a small truck we'd hired to get David's chair, some solar panels, a whole yak's cheese and other essentials to Rajapur.

We set off later and when we reached Gularia were surprised to recognise our truck at a roadblock. A policeman flagged us down and, alarmingly, marched Simon away into the police station. I couldn't catch what the policeman said to Simon, but he looked unperturbed, and seemed to be joking with him. With his sun-bleached hair, lean, fit build and his six feet of height, Simon couldn't have looked more different to the squat Nepali police with their well-cultivated paunches. He soon reappeared, climbed into the car and we drove on, in convoy with the truck. 'Well?' I asked.

'There was no problem,' he said, back to minimalist communication mode.

'What was it all about then?' I pressed, dying to know.

'The police thought that the truck driver and his mate were abducting Ganga.'

'What?'

'We're close to the Indian border here, and there is a lot of trafficking of young girls — going to Indian brothels. They like beautiful hills girls,' Simon said.

'Oh, so Ganga's beautiful is she?' Simon didn't rise to my bait. 'Didn't Ganga explain?'

'No — you know that Nepali women usually go quiet in situations like this. And the truck driver — the twit — said that Ganga was his cousin. He's Chhetri, and very clearly not related to Ganga, with her high cheek bones and almond eyes. So the police were suspicious, and waited for us to corroborate the story. Been waiting since 5 am.'

Another couple of hours of rattling and bumping got us to the river at Kothiyaghat, and we tumbled out for a glass of sweet tea to wash the dust down. Simon was now in an unusually talkative mood. 'I'm in awe of this river since Alexander and I came here during the monsoon. You know, it runs so fast there's a special monsoon *dinghy:*

it was a decaying, ten-metre wooden tub fitted with an old lorry engine that took up a quarter of the boat. It's tremendously dangerous, but marvellously unique, like a lot of Nepali innovations. The truck engine had been modified so that a long prop-shaft drove a tiny propeller sticking out at the back, and the whole arrangement turned between the passengers, so that anyone going too close would be minced. Instead of a starting handle, six men wrapped a thick piece of rope around a flywheel and ran like hell with it up the bank. When the engine finally started, it was graunched into gear and — belching thick, black smoke — chugged out across a kilometre of water. With all the sediment and turbulence, the water looked like boiling soup.'

'The Karnali really spreads that much in the monsoon? It's not much more than a hundred metres wide now.'

'Yes; all the flood plain, including where the tea shop is on the other side there,' he said pointing, 'is an expanse of fast-moving water.'

'So what happens to the tea shop?'

'They move it twice a year!' he said, chuckling at me as if it was obvious, and the kind of thing that any shopkeeper in Cambridge might do.

'Didn't you say that the monsoon was light this year?'

'Yup — whatever that means.' Once again, I felt thankful that I'd never been marooned here for long by the awesome powers of nature.

डे डे डे

Arjun and Sita welcomed us, and Guliya smiled her sunniest smile when she saw Sebastian. 'Another son! The *sahib* must be very happy that *memsahib* has made him so many sons, but next there must be a daughter, to look after *memsahib* in old age.'

'I have had the family planning operation, so there will be no more children. Three is a good number.'

'Ah mai! Memsahib has had her womb turned upside-down after only three children?' Guliya tutted. 'And there is no daughter?'

'Three children is enough,' I repeated.

'*Kanchha* was born when, *memsahib*?'

'Nearly a month ago.'

'*Ah mai*, a *Pooss* baby. A poor *Pooss* baby! *Pooss* is the hardest month, when cold gets inside our bodies. We get fever. It is the season when calves — and human babies — die. But Dabid is fat and smiling also.' She was uncharacteristically garrulous in her delight and scooped the new baby out of my arms. 'Handsome *kanchha*. But he has no hair!'

'He'll grow some. He'll have beautiful blond curls like David and Alexander, and he's called Sebastian.'

'Ah, handsome *Sabass*!' *Sabass,* meaning 'well done' in Nepali, was a good name; she approved.

Ganga settled in a thatched hut in the garden and Sita joined her — for company. Nepalis don't like sleeping alone. We heard them giggling through the wattle and daub walls, but we were chased to bed early by the evening chill and by fatigue. Ganga emerged next morning looking bright and cheerful, and gave every appearance of being perfectly content in her new home. She puzzled me. I guessed she was in her teens, yet she seemed more confident and mature than her years.

I found the cold more penetrating that winter. It was a struggle getting out of bed for Sebastian's middle-of-the-night feeds, though being awake in the small hours let me listen to weird night sounds. Owls shouted at each other like bad-tempered neighbours, and on several successive nights there was the lonely, otherworldly howling of a jackal down by the river again. Locals say that jackals grow horns at the time they howl like this, and that these horns (which you can buy — dried) give their owner magical powers — to see in the dark, and to seduce women.

The weather was nowhere near as cold as an English winter — it never freezes in the plains — but the nights and mornings felt perishing because of the damp, and because our house was bare: a paraffin stove was our only heater. The stove was smelly, and sometimes rained black smuts on the babies. Penetratingly chilling mists lurked for hours after dawn. It took days for washing to dry. The sun seemed too distant to drive away this malign presence that locals knew took life. People loomed like ghosts out of the morning miasma. They wore thin cottons; few possessed any warm clothes. Goats wore coats of old sacking.

The previous year this weather had seemed beautifully mysterious, but this year I saw the cold, muffled villagers, heard the relentless coughing and the dawn chorus of phlegm clearing. My neighbours' talk of illness unnerved me so that when David started coughing again, I wondered — not for the first time — just how unhealthy this dank, dusty climate was for him.

David's coughs and wheezes didn't faze him; in fact, such new noises amused him and were more stimuli to make him laugh. That reassured me and allowed me to get on with life. I'd decided to institute a ruthless new home routine: it would include school, a proper program of physiotherapy for David, plus games to exercise his squinting lazy eye, and I'd produce more varied foods.

Our house, whitewashed less than a year before, already looked shabby and grey-streaked. The speed of decay surprised me, but the garden was colourful with pansies, canna lilies, carnations, marigolds, bougainvillaea, jasmine, papayas, mango and banana. Beyond, the fields, which were fringed with blue weeds, were green with winter wheat or bright yellow with mustard. The sun enticed us outside so that it was pleasant washing by hand pump in the garden. Friends in England couldn't imagine us sitting out to do our lessons in January.

That first morning, I set up Alexander's home-school on our flat roof at nine. There was always plenty to watch from up there, and the winter colours in the early morning sun never ceased to warm my heart. Endless processions of buffalo carts each laden with thirty sixty-kilogram sacks of rice (1.8 tonnes in all) passed from the largest rice mill in the country on their way to the nearest road-head across the river. I'd put a blanket over Sebastian and David against the chill, but David continued to disapprove of his new brother and kept exposing him. I tried to focus on Alexander's lesson, but then realised that the sun, while it drove away the chill, rapidly became too bright and hurt David's eyes. I rigged up sunshades for the babies. Then, when we finally did settle to the first lesson, I realised that we couldn't do the first part with what was available in Rajapur. It focussed on a teddy bears' picnic, and required access to a photocopier, macaroni, paperclips and split pins. We moved rapidly on to part two: the birthday party. 'We can't do this either, Mummy,' Alexander announced.

'Why not?'

'We can't have a birthday party without any friends. I'm going to play with my real friends. Look! Siru is here!' And Alexander left to join the games in the garden. Sebastian was beginning to demand a feed anyway.

It wasn't only David who was put out by Sebastian's arrival: Alexander, too, was dissatisfied with him. 'Mummy, can't you put him back in your tummy and bring out a bigger brother — I'd like a brother I can play with.' Home-school was never easy, and I began to accept that if I'd got Alexander to sit down and do anything for ten minutes, I should count that as a success.

The warming winter sunshine cheered me and made me a more contented housewife. I resolved to make more effort in the kitchen. I picked David up so that we could tour my domain.

'Sita, I can't find the cheese grater.'

'The other *memsahib* threw it away.'

'Why?'

'It is not known, *memsahib*. She became very angry with the grater and threw it over the wall.'

'Sally was angry with the grater?' We both started to laugh, and David joined in. 'How can you be angry with a grater?'

'It is not known, *memsahib*.' And Sita ran off, trying to conceal her hilarity. That was only the second time I'd heard her laugh since we'd returned.

Sita had aged. She no longer wore her cheerful, traditional Tharu skirt, but a matronly black sack-of-a-garment. 'Why the change?'

Her reply was an inscrutable smile. Guliya told me that she'd got married, but there was no joy in her announcement. 'So she's found a handsome Tharu boy?'

'Not handsome: an old Brahmin; there is another wife.'

Slowly, I pieced the story together. She must have been pregnant when I'd left Rajapur in June, hence the sparkle in her eyes. The baby allowed her to move into the Brahmin's house and become an official wife. The senior wife, though, and all the other women in the household thoroughly disapproved of this lower-caste woman's intrusion. When only a daughter was born, mother and baby were so victimised that life was utterly miserable, and finally the child died — from neglect, Himalaya said. Sita left the Brahmin, or rather was forced out by the senior wife and mother-in-law, and was back living with her parents again.

Nothing of her anguish showed on Sita's face. She still maintained her inscrutable smile: Nepalis — particularly lower-caste Nepalis — are so very good at hiding their feelings; or were they just better than us at accepting the hurt and then moving on, living from day to day once again, and taking pleasure from life's highs? Fatalism can be liberating. Maybe it is that in the West we suffer from having too long-term a view; we are too analytical, too used to blaming someone or something.

Even now, after so long living in Asia, I realised how little I understood, how much of an outsider I was still. Language, culture and Simon's important role kept us apart, but I wondered what Guliya's family really thought of me. I don't suppose they considered whether they liked me or not. In Rajapur, everyone's lineage was known; no-one knew our grandparents, parents, uncles, cousins.

It wasn't just that we were foreigners. Simon's Nepali colleagues were outsiders, too, and they lived like expatriates, aloof from their uneducated compatriots. None of us could ever be part of this tight-knit community of interconnected and interdependent dynasties. We were transients, a source of income, and incomprehensible most of the time.

Maybe Guliya had written me off as a dreadful miscreant: the arrival of a handicapped baby is often interpreted as a woman reaping the wages of sin: bad *karma* because I deserved it. Yet she did not seem to have judged me.

डे डे डे

February and March are glorious months in the plains. The evening and dawn light makes everything look particularly beautiful, and I'd half forgotten just how diverse and changeable the garden bird life was in Rajapur.

As spring arrived, nest building started in earnest, and bulbuls took over the hibiscus bush close to where we sometimes did home-school. A pair of tree sparrows started building a nest in the window of our kitchen, and I looked forward to watching the nestlings grow, and using them as a teaching aid for Alexander. No sooner was the nest built, though, than I discovered Arjun sweeping it away. Surprised that this Hindu didn't have more respect for his fellow creatures, I asked, 'What happened?'

'I have cleaned it, sir!'

'Why? I like to see the birds making babies.'

'They don't make babies — they lay eggs. They are also dirty, sir. They must be cleaned away.'

'I'd like you to leave these birds in peace.'

He didn't disobey me, but Guliya demolished the next nesting attempt by the sparrows, while Arjun started on the lawn. 'What are you doing?'

'Cleaning away the grass, sir.'

'Why?'

'The garden looks beautiful when it is clean. I am making a path to the front door.' He also 'cleaned away' the clump of catmint that I used to make mint sauce. He regarded nature as useless, unless it could be eaten, burned for fuel or made into something. The Nepali word *jungle* describes useless waste ground: it is not the exciting home of Tarzan. *Jungle* is full of venomous snakes, man-eating tigers and spirits, demons, headless ghosts …

डे डे डे

Winter rains had left parts of the bazaar very muddy, making it even more of a struggle to take David out. Children played in the filth, making toys from discarded cigarette packets. Two tortured a puppy, swinging it around by its hind leg while it screamed. Everyone fights to survive here — even the pets.

The garrulous woman with the *betel*-stained buck-teeth seemed pleased to see that we were back; she beckoned to Alexander and gave him sweets. When I paid for them, she gave us more.

I wandered into a cloth shack-shop in the bazaar, on a mission to find cheesecloth to cover our whole yak cheese. The shopkeeper, a surly old *mussalman,* was sitting beside a small but sturdy metal safe; he touched it affectionately from time to time. '*Namasté*,' I greeted him. No response. I continued. 'I would like some muslin cloth, shopkeeper-*ji*.'

He stared at me blankly. He shouted for his son, who understood my Nepali–Hindi. His bare-bottomed toddler lurched up to me with venom in her eyes and hit me as hard as she could. She was too small to hurt me, but the malevolence of the unprovoked attack upset me. '*Badmas bachha*!' I complained. The father smiled indulgently, as if he'd been cultivating the child's behaviour.

Changes in the river had made access onto the island much more difficult, so I expected there to be less in the bazaar, but the two vegetable stalls were still there.

'How much are the potatoes?' I asked in Nepali. Then not understanding his answer, I said politely, 'What was said, brother?'

'He says they are ten rupees a kilo.' Astonishingly, someone was addressing me in good, clear English. 'My shop is close by, so I know all the prices!' I turned to a man fifteen years my junior, dressed in crisp white.

'Surely he did not say ten just now!?' I queried, nonplussed by being able to talk in English.

'He was speaking in code!' That, I didn't believe. Later Simon explained how easy it is to mistake *das* (ten) for *asi* (eighty). Then the man announced with a regal wave, 'I will translate for you whenever you come to the bazaar!'

'That is kind, but I'd like to learn to speak Nepali. I need practice.'

'You English are so polite!' he said, bitingly. 'But you must learn Hindi. Nepali is too quaint. In your spare time, you can teach me English also.' He fondled Alexander's hair, and tried to grab his cheek; Alexander darted behind my skirts, snarling.

'Your son is very naughty,' he accused.

'No; he gets fed up with strangers touching him before they've even said hello. I sympathise.'

'He should be more friendly. I will tell you one thing: I met your husband. He came to buy sandpaper, and I gave him some, a little used but still good. He didn't have to pay a penny piece for it. He does not speak good Nepali. Anyone can tell he is not Nepali!' What a strange thing to say. Who would mistake tall, blond, white Simon for a Nepali, however well he spoke the language? I loathed this guy already. 'Look, I've come to buy vegetables,' I said.

'Give *memsahib* potatoes!' he commanded, and I was soon able to get away.

Nepali-run shops were more of a giggle, and there were so many impertinent questions: 'Why are you so old and your children so young?', 'How much does your husband earn?', 'How many other wives?' Meanwhile, others rummaged in my bag and asked about what I'd bought, at what price and for what purpose. I loved these exchanges. I was also pleased to discover a new enterprise: a stall selling freshly cooked, spicy samosas. The accompanying chilli-laced fresh pickle evolved through an astonishing range of colours, from puce to radioactive green, but it always tasted good. These became our junk food treat, and Alexander and I often returned home clutching samosas in a hot, greasy bag made out of recycled newspapers.

The teachers soon visited us again. Stork looked even more gaunt and grey. She desperately wanted children. She was idle, bored and unhappy. Poor, grey, solitary thing. Although my Nepali was now quite fluent, I still struggled to think of anything to say to these women. For want of inspiration, I offered them Sebastian to cuddle. Stork coughed wetly over him. She didn't know about microbes. She roughly grabbed the bundle covering David's nether regions and asked what it was. He laughed, enjoying the rough attention. I explained nappies. Their expressions suggested that they thought nappies unhygienic. Toddlers in rural Nepal are left bare-bottomed; dogs eat what the children produce, and sometimes even lick their bums clean. Another long, awkward silence. Alexander decided that this was a good time to climb around the windowsills; he found a flat, desiccated gecko behind one of the shutters. Delighted, he unstuck it, took it to show the teachers and asked what it was called in Nepali. They shrank back.

Knowing I'd regret it, I asked about Stork's symptoms. There were still plenty. She had stopped taking the ulcer medicine that I told her she must take long-term, so her abdominal pain was back. She interrupted my enquiries about her stomach with complaints of painful breasts. She had all her old symptoms, and she was coughing. 'So are all of us,' I hastily interrupted. David coughed on cue, and Stork's sister-in-law understood that I could not help. 'Perhaps this is normal during this cold season? Many people are ill during *Pooss, hoina?* Have you fever, *didi*?' Stork knotted her brows, crumpled up her face, and moved her hands up to her head as people do when about to launch into an intricate diatribe about their symptoms. 'No,' her sister-in-law interrupted, and rapidly changed the subject to meaningful things. We talked of the cost of my paraffin heater and my continuing need for a proper *carpet*. Then they gulped down their tea and left.

CHAPTER TWENTY-THREE

anniversary party

'I THOUGHT WE'D HAVE A PARTY,' SIMON ANNOUNCED unexpectedly. 'The first anniversary of moving to Rajapur seems as good an excuse as any. Himalaya can organise it. He hasn't got much to do, and he'll get the etiquette right.'

'A party — great. Glad you feel like celebrating!' I said, quite excited by the idea and slightly surprised that Simon had suggested it. He wasn't really a party animal.

'The team deserve it. They'll seize any excuse to swallow large quantities of cheap whisky.'

'And we should have a housewarming, celebrating the arrival of all our mod cons,' I said, pleased that we now had room lights run by the generator.

'One mod con … Anyway, I must ask the village plumber to install the second mod con. I'm looking forward to our first solar-heated shower.'

We'd brought solar panels from Kathmandu (fifteen hours' drive away) and pipe from Gularia (two hours' drive). When the plumber arrived, he started shoving it all together. He stuffed in short lengths of string to seal the joints, and when we complained of leaks he explained — in all Brahmin seriousness — that pipes always leak. I was an educated woman; had no-one explained this to me? The trick was to wait a bit, then rust slows the flow. 'How long must I wait *dai*?' I asked.

'Maybe one year only,' he said sagely.

Alexander studied his impressive girth and asked, 'Has the plumber got a baby in his tummy?'

I was keen for other improvements, too. Doing anything out in our bathroom after dark meant carefully balancing a torch on end, or searching out matches and candle-stumps, so we called the electricians back to install lights in the bathroom. We also asked them to rewire the socket in the kitchen to power a different — but still small — oven. The electrician's 'boy' was summoned so that his teeth could be used to strip off the plastic insulation, and then bare wires were stuffed into an existing socket. They then ran the wire around the outside of the house, fixing it in a couple of places with bent nails; it entered the shower room and loo through glassless windows. The new light bulbs were held in place by a nail through a half hitch in the wire.

Foolishly, I suggested that the wires might come through connecting walls, but I soon wanted to eat my words when I heard the familiar sound of a large sledgehammer striking the fabric of the house: the hole for the wire to go through was a new crater twenty centimetres across. It was a mess, but even so I was quite excited at getting light just from the flick of a switch. Guliya, Sita and Ganga were impressed too. Whenever Ganga switched on a light, she'd touch her hand to her forehead, her chest and her forehead again, giving thanks in the Hindu equivalent of crossing herself. I inaugurated the new oven — one that was compatible with the generator — by cooking a quiche for lunch. My first attempt at making pastry from the strong, local chapatti flour using a beer bottle for a rolling pin was not good. Biting into the pastry, I said, 'Ooh, this is hard!'

'Mmm, I like this hard,' said Alexander. 'Can you make hard every day, Mummy?'

Just before seven on the morning of our party, Alexander announced, 'A goat has come on a bicycle!' Panty, cook in one of the other project houses, had parked his bike in the garden; tied onto the luggage rack was a cute harlequin kid with large, perplexed eyes. Panty was less attractive, a hoary, stubbled forty-year-old.

Himalaya arrived next — with a pick-up full of chairs, cauldrons, beer, glasses, vegetables, plates, firewood and Bhakta Bahaadur, another cook. 'Where did you find all this stuff?' I asked Himalaya, most impressed.

'I have been to one marriage hall and have arranged forty glasses, forty plates; everything!'

'A marriage hall in Rajapur? Excellent!' said I. 'You are a star!' He looked bewildered at being so described. Despite all the conversations we'd had, I still had trouble speaking to him in the right way, and he often misunderstood my weak attempts at humour; best stick to safer ground. 'Tell me, Mr Thapa, is it really bad luck to be born in the month of *Pooss*?'

'Who told you so?'

'Guliya. It does seem like a hard month.'

'No, it is not bad luck. Guliya is ignorant, *hoina?* King was born in *Pooss.*'

'So Sebastian is in good company!' Himalaya gave me a look of disapproval, or maybe it was just confusion. 'I think we'll need some mosquito coils for this party,' I continued.

'I will arrange,' said Himalaya.

Jim and Steve came punctually. We climbed onto our roof where we could get some cool air and also hear if the children called out. 'How are things?' I asked the newcomers.

'This place is really growing on me,' Jim said, 'It's a really very attractive season: so fresh, almost autumnal. I love the crisp mornings, and the winter sunshine. We have the cheekiest little bulbuls in our garden ... and the staff in the office are a great bunch. Dinesh, who replaced Dr Josi, is excellent, and so keen. You know he's that nice hydrologist Arun Amatiya's cousin?'

'Oh, yes, Alexander likes him. I heard that Dinesh is popular in the office too, because he loses at cards so often! Everyone apparently sees it as fair redistribution of wealth — of his huge consultant fees! So tell me, Steve, how are you enjoying Rajapur this time?' I said. 'It is at least cooler than on your last trip. You must be sleeping better?'

'I might, if the dogs didn't keep me awake. I was up on the roof at 3 am throwing stones at them — it was very satisfying to score a couple of direct hits. That stopped them.'

'How are you getting along with Ram Kumar?'

'He's quite decorative — he smiles a lot.'

'But does he do any work? I wasn't sure about employing him as your cook, but he was homeless, destitute and desperate for work. He was a *kamaiya* — a slave, effectively — who has just been released from his bond. I don't suppose he's good at organising himself. I can tell him what to cook if you like?'

'No, he's okay. I thought I'd try supervising him myself, yesterday, but it was painful watching him shuck peas onto the floor, then spend a long time chasing them around the kitchen — with a spoon. Maybe I'll cook for myself. I'm a dab hand at baked beans on toast topped with sardines.'

'Not that easy. None of the ingredients are available in Rajapur — not even bread.'

The Nepalis started to arrive an hour later, Himalaya with them. 'Mosquito coils?' I enquired.

'I will arrange!' (Why do Nepalis say 'no' so seldom?) Good Hindus should be teetotallers and, anxious not to offend, I offered, 'Fanta? Coke? Sprite?'

'We need hard liquor!' And they started downing tumblersful of Mirnov Nepali vodka. The men got more excitable with each glass, and I began to wonder whether any of them might fall off our flat roof. I was pleased to see that at least I was not required to make polite conversation.

Four ladies arrived: Devi, the secretary who couldn't type; Himalaya's new teenage wife; a woman I didn't know; and Sarmista, the draftsperson, who had a terribly pox-marked face. She looked too young to be scarred by an extinct disease, but public health teams had still been systematically searching for smallpox cases when I'd first visited Nepal in the mid-seventies.

The women sat in a silent row, sipping Fanta, looking poised and beautiful in their silk saris. I spoke to the unknown woman sitting closest to me. 'Are you working here?'

'I am not working. I am accompanying my husband; he is the new Deputy Project Manager.'

'Ah, Mrs Lama. How do you find Rajapur?'

'Quite boring really!' Her English was excellent; she must be a graduate at least. 'No, I never graduated — I have no profession.' Help. Now what can I ask her? I sipped the disgusting Fanta that I'd dared not lace with vodka for fear of shocking the ladies. No decent Asian woman would drink spirits. 'How do you pass your time? Cooking? Sewing?'

Himalaya sidled up. 'We must serve snacks now, *hoina*? I searched everywhere in the bazaar, and could not find paper napkins anywhere. Give me newspapers,' he commanded.

'You know we can't get English language papers in Rajapur, and Arjun can't read.'

Then I hit on the idea of doling out handfuls of nappy-liners, but wondered whether they might offend anyone's religious sensitivities. I watched while guests examined them and discussed what they could be. 'It is not paper and certainly not made in Nepal. Perhaps it is geotextile?' Then I saw the rate at which the vodka was disappearing, poured myself a beer and returned to sit with the ladies. I turned to Mrs Lama. 'What is your accommodation like?'

'We are living in the new project compound at Murkatta; it is a long way from the bazaar. It is all right,' she said pulling a face that said it wasn't.

'Have you any idea why that place is called Murkatta?'

'I expect that someone saw a ghost,' she said, as if ghosts were a normal part of life. '*Murkatta* means a ghost that carries its head under its arm. This kind cause so much of trouble because they get inside houses easily, because they are not too tall.' She clearly believed what she was telling me.

'If you are scared, why don't you move into Rajapur; we like it here.'

'No, I am not scared, and anyway we must utilise project accommodation,' she said. 'When we first heard about Rajapur, we came to know that wild boar was available; we imagined we would be living in *jungle* and got quite excited about it' — I was warming to her, now — 'but the compound is in a bleak place: no trees; quite boring really. Water is a problem; the hand pump is a long way from my house. It takes the boy all day to cook one meal!'

'Yes, life is quite isolated here, but it is interesting,' I said, 'Have you ever been into a Tharu longhouse?' I told her about my outings, wondering whether she might translate for me if I went to chat to our Badi ladies. Might she be interested in learning about the local communities? 'Not really.' She had the appearances of her position to keep up. She told me about her adventures, too. 'You know I have also visited England. I lived for one year in Bedford while my husband studied. I worked in Sainsbury's. It was fun and interesting also, working on supermarket check-out.'

I caught a snatch of conversation interspersed with giggling. Gauri, a sociologist, was talking to Steve. 'Now Mr Ee-steeb-sir, have you met our Badi community yet? I am thinking that this Rajapur project had brought very good business for our Badi women. One Japanese, he came to see our project and Project Manager-sir told us to arrange *every* kind hospitality for this gentleman. We thought he might like Badi lady. You like I arrange for you also? Only fifty rupees — they not too costly!'

'Thank you — you are very kind but no ... *no* ... NO.' Steve was backing away.

'I estimate that more than twenty-five per cent of project staff salaries has ended up in Badi coffers. They provide very nice services!'

More giggles. 'This Japanese gentleman, he bit nervous and he got very upset in Rajapur. He worry too much about his stomach and he eat only bananas and Scotch. Then he find snake in bathroom and he rans away.' Schoolgirl giggles turned to guffaws. I wandered over and drained a bottle of Mirnov into Gauri's glass. 'Now I will have daughter, Mrs Semen!'

'Why do you say that? Are you married?'

'No!' More giggles. 'But he who get this last bit from bottle will get the bad lucks of a daughter.'

'But *I'd* like a daughter. Shall I drink it?'

'Many Nepali womens also say this — to help in the old age. But too many womens is bad luck.' He was inebriated, so I didn't bother to counter this. It was midnight. Most of the spirits and 'heavy snacks' were gone, and Himalaya indicated that we could now serve the rice and curried goat. I was relieved, since serving food signals the end of a party. When Nepalis start eating, the priority is speed, not elegance, and the cooks were frantically dishing out rice, meat and then fruit salad, only just managing to keep up with demand. As soon as the food had been eaten, everyone left with bewildering abruptness. Even the drunks departed on cue.

The following evening, Dr Josi invited us to his farewell party, and to sample Newar *momos*. I sat again with Mrs Lama. 'Lovely evening. I do like watching these house geckoes hunting insects.'

'They are very poisonous!' said Mrs Lama. 'Many times, whole families have perished when a gecko has fallen into milk heating on the fire. The family has drunk the milk and all died!' I turned to get Basistha's take on them. He sat gazing into the gloom beyond the generator-powered lights of the verandah, and unexpectedly a gecko landed — splat! — on his bald head. He leapt up, looking distinctly unnerved. 'They are harmless!' I reassured him.

'No! Very poisonous.' Maybe it is their weird eyes with vertical pupils that unnerve people.

Josi appeared with more Mirnov and some Bagpiper whisky, and turning to Steve asked, 'How is your good-for-nothing *kamaiya* cook?'

'Oh, Ram Kumar? He's still smiling.'

'You are being too soft with him. Each time you say "*Namasté*" or "thank you", he gets a little closer to heaven. Useless fellow! He will not work nicely if you are so soft!'

'I'll start kicking him, then, shall I?' the mild-mannered Steve said.

'Yes, with him I think that it is necessary.' Josi had missed the sarcasm. Steve looked bewildered.

I left the men to their strong drink, and walked out into the peace of slumbering Rajapur; it was late, around 10 pm. The moon was yet to rise. Gentle chanting floated from the temple: the devout celebrating the eleventh night after the new moon.

How easy it was to love Rajapur on cool, still evenings like this. At home, the now inseparable Ganga and Sita were singing to a wide-awake David, who was loving the attention. Ganga said, 'Dabid laughs a lot when Sita sings; her voice is not nice!' And the women giggled with him. Then, when David realised that I was back, he burbled a delighted greeting: he was clearly pleased to see me, and that lifted my heart.

डे डे डे

People often wandered in through our garden gate; some came to stand and stare, some to beg, some to help themselves to fruit and occasionally even to talk. The first time people came to take flowers, I asked them what they were doing. 'Picking flowers,' they said, without sarcasm. 'They are beautiful!' — as if I didn't know. I had lots, and they had no gardens.

One visitor was a thin man of fiftyish with the marks of smallpox on his face. He squatted down, unpacked a box-shaped harmonium and began to sing to his own accompaniment. The long, complicated verses were punctuated by melodic interludes when he yawned widely, but I was transported and when I brought David out to listen, an appreciative smile spread across his face.

The glum harmonium player returned quite often to half-heartedly play while frisky boys cavorted around him. I'd give him a few rupees and a little rice. Each time he came back, Ganga scolded me for giving him too much. 'That's why he keeps coming back.' Saying that I enjoyed his visits was no excuse.

Then, in the middle of March, a lad with lovely grey-blue eyes came to play a boat-shaped violin with a bow that had bells on the end. Judging by Ganga and Sita's giggles, the song was lewd.

For us, this marked the beginning of Holi, the Hindu celebration of sexuality. The story goes that Lord Krishna happened upon some lusty maidens who were bathing naked in the holy Jumuna River. He thought that he should teach them a lesson in modesty and absconded with their clothes. The red powder that people throw at each other symbolises the maidens' blushes, and youths tease young women by singing suggestive songs. Schoolchildren and groups of young men armed with squeezy bottles or buckets of coloured water form daubing and squirting hit squads. Bright powders appeared for sale in the bangle bazaar. Even the ostracised Badi women padlocked their homes to join in.

The pox-marked harmonium player returned again, but with a colour-splattered percussionist and two male dancers. One of the dancers was dressed in a sari and ankle bells, and the other, in his pyjamas, wore women's jewellery and a painted moustache. We brought David and Sebastian out to enjoy the promised spectacle. David reclined in Ganga's lap, smiling contentedly. Sebastian stared goggle-eyed, fascinated.

Their dancing was hilarious, and as we laughed the babies chuckled too. The visitors sang Hindi love songs, but between refrains the fellow in the pyjamas went into a routine that made him look like a constipated duck, and the sari-wearer did seductive hip-wiggles, made all the funnier because of the cross-dressing. The *tabla*'s wonderful vocabulary of reverberating sounds made it seem to talk to the harmonium. I gave the performers a roll of small notes and they moved on to repeat the performance next door, where we all watched again.

I'd seen bawdy eunuchs in Pakistan. They were the only unveiled 'women' out on the streets, and how they revelled in the stares they attracted. The men in our Rajapur garden had stubbly beard growth, so they had not been castrated: they were part-time transvestites. I told Alexander that the person dressed in a sari with a false ponytail was a man. 'Why does he want to dress like that?' Alexander asked, bemused.

Returning home, two thoroughly daubed Badi women approached; they wanted to put yet more colour on Alexander. He ran away, saying, 'Are they men, too?', and hid. They turned on me. I stood smiling, and they respectfully put another smear of red on my forehead. When I thanked rather than abused them, they went off giggling. I felt a camaraderie with these fellow outcastes. Ganga was mortified, though, and whispered, 'These are no-good women!'

'I know that they are *randi,* but I still like to talk to them.' I wanted to show off the fact that I knew the Nepali for prostitute.

'*Randi* is a bad word; *memsahib* must not say this word. These are bad women,' she scolded.

When Alexander came out of hiding, Sita said to him, 'Come — you and Siru must go play Holi.' Alexander smiled, not needing a translation.

Holi was relief from Alexander's home-schooling. We were both keen to find distractions: almost anything seemed more attractive than 'making a teddy bears' picnic.'

Consultations also provided welcome breaks. I tried to avoid practising in Rajapur, but each week there were always a few curious enough or desperate enough to see me. Vulture was a regular, and she called around just after seeing a doctor in Nepalgunj. She refused tea as usual. 'It makes my gastric problem worse.' Today, her dowager hump made her look crushed; she was suffering. She clutched a fistful of little notes documenting her consultation, investigations and prescriptions. 'Are the prescribed treatments good?' she asked. Despite the fact that it was all written in English, I could not fathom what was being treated. A small crowd had already gathered to listen; people hung over the wall and others filtered into the garden to hear more easily. David, sitting strapped into his high chair, looked like he was giving an audience.

Mrs Gautam began to tell me unabashed about her heavy painful periods. Then, 'I've had an ultrasound.' (Normal.) 'The blood test said that I'm anaemic. Is this treatment good for this anaemia?' The quantity of iron tablets that she'd been given was insufficient. She'd been given unnecessary antibiotics and treatment for giardia that she didn't have, albenazole for the worms, anti-emetic tablets (she was not nauseated), and she had Ayurvedic powders for kidney stones that she also didn't have. 'These iron tablets are very good for anaemia. Take them.'

'And the other medicines — these are also good? Since starting this treatment, I have not been feeling well.' She hadn't even been given a painkiller for her heavy periods. I floundered, struggling to say something that wouldn't undermine her confidence in the other doctor.

Himalaya brought his wife 'for check-up.' He'd married a cousin from Mahendranagar a few months before. Now she was being sick in the mornings.

I haltingly asked a few questions and she burst into tears. The more I tried to comfort her, the louder her sobs grew. 'Are you feeling very ill?' She looked up at me, a thin scared child, tears spilling from her eyes, and nodded. 'This awful feeling will go away when you get to the fourth month.' Her sobbing increased. 'I'll take your blood pressure, and explain everything.'

Then David developed a puffy red eye, and my medical mind immediately leapt to the most frightening possible diagnosis: a rampant infection, which can track up into the brain. It is rare, but I wanted to be ready with antibiotics and went to *docter* Bhandari's medical shop. 'I'd like some injectable Augmentin.'

'There is none,' he said, unapologetically.

'Is there flucloxacillin or cloxacillin perhaps?'

'We have amoxycillin and cloxacillin combined,' he said, turning to get a box.

'I don't like combinations. Do you have any cephalosporins?'

'What are they?'

'Antibiotics. What injectable antibiotics do you have?' I asked.

'This: oxytetracycline and lidocaine.' What was that combination for? 'Or chloramphenicol?' Too dangerous. 'Or amoxycillin and bromhexine?' I began to wonder how many of these weird medical concoctions had been dumped in unsuspecting Nepal.

'I'll take the amoxycillin and cloxacillin.' I felt very insecure again, realising that few essential medicines were available in Rajapur. It was a small comfort to know that we could get out to the hospital in Nepalgunj in a few hours if David became ill. I had an uneasy day before I realised that the red eye had probably been from a mosquito bite. I'd overreacted.

CHAPTER TWENTY-FOUR

the wild west

ONE OF THE THINGS THAT WE WANTED TO DO WHEN we returned to the Royal Bardiya National Park at the beginning of February was to speak to the naturalists. The farmers on Rajapur had built new lookout platforms, and told Simon incredible tales of elephants coming on nightly raids across the river, but could these rumours have been contrived to get compensation? Ganga came with us on this trip to help mind the babies, so that the three of us could take it in turns to stay with David or Sebastian, or ride with them. Alexander looked forward to more lemon pudding, and we would find out whether there really had been a population explosion of big game.

The misty air was surprisingly chilly in the early mornings. Inside the forest, though, sunlight sparkled on droplets caught on spiders' webs and shone through orchids and ferns so that even shrivelled brown leaves looked like works of art. Melodious, bubbly golden orioles and coucals called against the background rhythm of surprisingly quiet elephant footfall — a sound that recalls someone slopping around in rather-too-large fleecy bedroom slippers.

Arjun and Mrs Gautam had been so dismissive of the jungle that I wondered how Ganga would react, but she effused infectious delight in all she saw: hog deer, a jungle cat, a pair of cavorting mongooses. She said, 'How lovely … peacocks.' And looking towards russet-brown spotted deer as they cascaded between the trees, 'the *chital* are *so* beautiful.' Our *phanit* pointed out fresh pug marks — of a tigress leading two kittens. There were sloth bear prints at the first river. A large, gawky, white-necked stork picked around in the shallow water, making ripples. I thought of Stork and wondered how her symptoms were progressing. Into the thick forest again, and an intoxicating fragrance from a kind of honeysuckle; another bush smelt deliciously of toasting sesame seeds. It was peaceful, but in many places the forest had been smashed to bits: the now large elephant population was putting pressure on the reserve.

When we'd first arrived in the district, there had been just two elephants in the park; then five more bulls walked in. They'd followed a traditional migration route that now crossed agricultural lands, acquiring a taste for rice and wheat on the way. The five walked right through the boardwalk-lined main street of the small town of Mahendranagar — they must have looked like gunmen intent on a showdown. The following year, more elephants arrived, and yet more, so there were now forty in the Park. Experts said that they would move on again. But the elephants stayed, and we'd often see trees that had been pushed over or gored by disgruntled elephants. We'd be treated to views of groups of cow-elephants and calves and would watch delightedly, until angry tuskers saw us off. The jungle was always full of surprises and I'd lost track of the number of times we'd gone from revelling in blissful tranquillity to sheer terror in the space of seconds. These wild elephants had become increasingly unpredictable. They were getting hassled too much when they crossed the river to snack on Rajapur rice.

Pressure for space was huge, and not only for elephants. A spot in the elephant grass smelt of death, and we peered down on bones that were still red with blood. 'Is this a tiger kill?'

'Yes, a tiger killed another tiger; it's never happened before,' the naturalist with us said.

The elephants shuffled languidly on, down and across a small river and into forest with a broken canopy, luxuriant with tree-sized shrubs. The thick vegetation in this next part of the reserve gave off a delicious scent of curry leaves. Several of the largest trees wore honeycombs: like giant scrota, but covered in a seething mass of wild bees.

We broke out into the warming rays of the sun. Seed heads protruded from the yellowing elephant grass all around us; each tuft was decorated with baubles of dew that caught the dawn light. The farmers were right: there were good reasons for wildlife to roam outside the Park and to raid crops on Rajapur Island. There wasn't much to eat in the reserve at this time of the year, so those with big appetites crossed the river.

There, on Rajapur Island, poachers especially target rhino. Rhino habitually defecate in certain places and reportedly always reverse into their favoured toilet area. Poachers excavate steep-sided pits at sites of communal rhino-lavatories so that when a rhino reverses in to relieve itself without so much as a glance behind, it tumbles into the trap. Then the single horn is sold to become a component of a fever remedy and the rest of the carcass is left to rot.

There was an unexpected sound of a very large animal, close by. It was pushing through the tall, scrubby undergrowth. The *phanit* became tense. Our elephant's ears went out. She looked towards the sound and a deep rumble came from within her. David started to laugh at the weird reverberating sound that you sense with your intestines, not your ears. Elephants can communicate with these rumbles over ten kilometres. Through this infrasonic chit-chat, our elephant knew long before we saw the approaching animal that it wasn't an unpredictable, randy wild bull, but a friend. Alexander and Simon were on board.

Simon said in a stage whisper, 'Just seen a jackal!'

The *phanit* laughed with relief, yet it showed how very difficult it was to identify anything in this *jungle* — even something as large as an elephant. Our elephant let out a long luxurious fart that started David laughing again.

A snapping sapling cracked like a gunshot. '*Jungle ko haathi!*' the *phanit* said. David, too, became alert as we sped off towards the sound. Elephants always have to keep three feet on the ground, otherwise the strain of their enormous weight on their joints would be too much; they do not really run, but they achieve an exceedingly fast, uncomfortable shamble. As we got close to where we guessed the wild elephant must be, my elephant's ears went out and she refused to go on, despite much kicking. A resounding whack on the skull made her push on through five-metre-high scrub and thorns.

Then we saw him, twenty metres from us: a big bull with a highly domed skull. This seemed too close, especially with Alexander prattling on about Shere Khan, Colonel Haathi and Mowgli; he was frighteningly audible, thirty metres away on the other elephant. The wild bull elephant was unruffled, though, and sauntered away, quickly disappearing into thicker forest and the company of some friends and relations. The sun chased away the mist and dew and warmed us through, but hurt David's eyes, so it felt good to stop for breakfast.

Simon and Alexander got back late. Alexander was breathless with excitement. 'We saw three tigers. And an angry elephant. And a rhino having a bath. He looked cross and snorted at us!'

'Is that true?' I asked, incredulous.

'Yes,' said Simon, and filled in the details. 'After we all saw that bull elephant, we plunged into a patch of thick forest. Then, as casually as you like, the *phanit* said, "There's a tiger!" He was pointing back into the underbrush. We saw one tiger, then another, and another. We watched them for a while, hardly daring to breathe; even Alexander stayed quiet! After a few minutes, the female and year-old cub wandered away further into the scrub, but the male stayed behind.

'He strolled around a bit, but mostly just sat, relaxing. Our elephant knocked down a few trees to get closer, and the tiger yawned and looked uneasy. But it turned out not to be us who'd unsettled him. All of a sudden, he glanced behind him, leapt up and charged towards us. A split second later, an enormous and very angry tusker burst out of the undergrowth, clearly determined to see the tiger off. The tiger fled without a backward glance. Which left us face to face with a furious bull elephant.'

'Didn't you hear the elephant coming?' I asked.

'Astonishingly, no. Both the *phanit* and our elephant were anxious to leave, but there was no room to turn, because we were in a tunnel of forest. The tusker stood blowing and flapping, looking as if he was about to charge again. That was enough for our elephant, and she suddenly retreated backwards at speed — while I marvelled at how fast an elephant can move in reverse when motivated. We soon lost sight of the tusker, and there were no sounds of pursuit. I think he was content to have seen us off, too.'

'Blimey! I hope you were hanging on to Alexander!' I said.

'Of course, but I did drop the lens cap.'

I turned to Bhim, the new manager of the Tigertops lodge, and asked, 'How dangerous are these elephants? Have there been any accidents?'

'A few — but no deaths yet!' he grinned. 'Sometimes the elephant will get upset, and run off. That happened once, and the *howdah* got smashed and the tourists fell off, but no-one was hurt much. I do wonder what would happen, though, if one of the wild bulls tried to mate with one of our females!' Everyone laughed and, encouraged, he went on. 'There are four or five naughty bull elephants in the park; sometimes they try to visit our elephants at night, but they are not interested. Any of these bulls might charge without provocation. They've just had too many battles with villagers. But tell me, Simon, did you notice anything about the elephant who charged you?'

'Yes — he had a very strange, dome-shaped skull.' Simon replied.

Bhim walked over to a photograph on the wall of the restaurant. 'Like this?'

'Yes, exactly like that!'

'Ah, now, you have just met the notorious Raja Gaj,' Bhim beamed.

There was a pause before Simon asked me, 'Well? Did *you* see anything?'

'Mmm, some superb scarlet-breasted sunbirds.' No-one seemed impressed at my sighting.

Ganga joined us, bringing Sebastian over to me for some milk. She'd identified Bhim as of her Gurung caste, and unselfconsciously addressed him as 'brother'. He visibly bristled at such familiarity from a mere servant, and moved away. This gave the other foreigners in the restaurant a chance to chat to us. They were a British couple. He leant across. 'Do you live in Nepal? It must be wonderful staying here long term.'

'Yes, we love it, but it is quite an isolated existence, and I wonder how long it'll be before we start turning a little strange!'

'We'll let you know,' he said, laughing.

Next morning, I went out with seven-week-old Sebastian, while Simon stayed with David. Over breakfast, I asked Simon, 'How did you enjoy your lie-in?'

'Great — a rare treat. I sat out on the verandah with David. I could see him listening intently to birdcalls that we don't hear in Rajapur. A pigmy woodpecker that makes a sound like a billiard ball bouncing on marble really made him chuckle. I wonder how much he understands.'

David gave Simon a knowing look, and smiled.

डे डे डे

Back on Rajapur Island, we often joined Simon on work trips or on his one-day weekends drove out for a picnic. Distances were small, yet the thirty-kilometre drive from the bazaar in the south-west of the island to the northernmost point took two-and-a-half hours. There were so few motorable tracks that getting anywhere took us teetering along the edges of rice fields or the embankments containing irrigation channels. It was difficult to retain any sense of direction.

Our best trips were when we managed to set out early, when villagers were busy. Tharu women were washing up in the canals, using the fine silt to scour away the stuck food; others carried water in huge globular clay pots or great piles of firewood on their heads, or home-made conical baskets containing chillies, vegetables, seeds or cow dung fuel. Small babies wearing colourful cloth tea-cosy hats were tied to their mothers' backs while they worked. Men and young boys, many carrying skeins of grass that they were plaiting into ropes, drove cattle out to graze; a few were fishing.

That day, two engineers were with us: Kedar and the new man, the deferential Dinesh. They were talking animatedly in the big front seat about politics and old friends, then Kedar burst out, 'The Tharus are so stupid. If they didn't waste so much of time trying to catch these tiny fish they could get a proper job and buy some good-sized fish.'

I didn't know how to respond to their prejudice, so I changed the subject. 'What do all those symbols painted on the houses mean? There are lots of bicycles and ploughs — everywhere I look.'

'Elections are coming soon. There may be riots in Kathmandu. These signs denote political parties and they can be understood even by the illiterate villagers,' he explained.

There hadn't been much rain for months, but gaudy Tharu clothes were a tonic against the bleaching sun. Winter wheat grew in some fields, but half of the land was fallow: until Simon's irrigation work was completed, there would continue to be water scarcities. A stationary buffalo cart blocked a ford beside a broken bridge. One of the buffaloes had decided to sit down to cool off. Two men pulled at his horns and one guy picked him up by the tail, but all that did was roll the buffalo over so that he could bathe more comfortably. I welcomed the chance to stretch my legs. Weird squawks drew my attention upwards to the topmost branches of a vast mango tree.

Simon followed my gaze. 'Those birds look precarious perched so high,' he said.

'C'mon, can't you tell a flying fox from a chicken?' I taunted. 'They're the largest species of fruit bat in the world. See them squabbling and screeching — they're as bad-tempered and uncouth as monkeys … to which, apparently, they are related.'

Simon smiled. 'Fascinating' he said, 'but I was looking at the peacocks, silly!'

The shape of the northern tip of the island had completely changed during the last monsoon. When the Karnali River floods, it does so spectacularly. It rips away large trees and huge boulders as well as villages, if it has a mind to. It leaves just vast beaches of polished pebbles. It seemed bleak, remote and inhospitable. Yet now it was deceptively peaceful. I loaded David into his backpack and Alexander led me off to have a paddle in the river. While he wallowed, I watched glistening particles of mica as they tumbled by in the water. Then some Tharu men who were firing sods into the mouth of an irrigation ditch to divert water further down said, 'Hey, don't sit there!'

'But I want to sit in the shade,' I said, ignoring the warning.

'Don't!'

I got up again quickly to pick three-pointed acacia thorns from my bum, while they laughed at me. A boy with a catapult around his neck asked Alexander in English, 'What is your name?' But he wasn't interested in the reply, and he wandered off taking casual pot-shots at chestnut-headed bee-eaters, gorgeous gymnasts of the air.

I sat awhile, watching fast-moving mergansers fishing, and then, within the sparkling water, a line of rocks caught my attention. Then I realised that the rocks were moving. It was a troop of monkeys swimming across the river. Wandering out between the acacias, I found the prints of spotted deer, porcupine and monkey, and there were dozens of three-stone fireplaces. Villagers had camped up here while they cut thatch grass.

I envied the simple, natural life that the islanders seemed to live. They got almost everything they needed from the island, and could live off the land: an idyllic, untroubled existence. I wandered further, and noticed amongst the cinders of another little fireplace a discarded medicine blister-pack. I stooped and picked it up, curious to see what these people might need to take. It was an empty Valium packet!

These people had real stresses. Illness frequently killed here, and a failed crop spelt starvation. This was no idyll.

The heat was fading as we turned south. At Guptipur, on the eastern shore of the island, criss-cross tripwires set three metres above the ground rang a bell that woke the villagers so they could light fires to frighten the thieving elephants away. But they'd come back; big bull elephants need to eat 350 kilograms of forage a day, so they're determined to pillage the stacks of newly harvested rice. Simon said, 'Some farmers have stopped growing wheat because it attracts elephants; whole areas that are close to easy fording places are left fallow, where last year they were brimming with winter wheat. Wheat prices are already depressed by overproduction in Europe and the US — there's no margin for feeding wild animals.'

'Does international price-fixing really affect the Rajapur farmers?'

''Fraid so. They tried growing linseed here instead, in the hope that the elephants, rhino and wild boar will leave it alone, and that the market will justify the effort of growing it. The farmers can only make a marginal profit on winter crops anyway, because of all the transport costs, including using the ferry to get them off the island. And that's not even considering losses from plundering wildlife and plagues of grasshoppers. Living next to a National Park makes things even harder. You know, the penalty for killing a wild elephant is life imprisonment; the compensation if an elephant kills someone is only 3,000 rupees, perhaps three months' wages — but the figure's irrelevant, anyway, since no-one can recall any compensation ever being paid. Three-quarters of the park budget pays the army to police the park, protecting the animals from poachers, but not farmers or their crops and livestock.'

The river was biting into red silk-cotton trees, so that only sad skeletons remained, their horizontal branches and eight-metre buttresses making them strange-looking monuments. The whole island was marching west, and it seemed incredible that Simon's project could halt the power of the river. A convoy of nine buffalo carts arrived, carrying stones for the protection work. Other buffaloes chewing the cud stared at us. The men of Guptipur — looking almost as disinterested as the animals — roused themselves to come and talk; women, too, came to stare. Mothers carried babies slung on hips; the children were naked except for the mandatory red bonnet with a tassel on top.

An old woman hobbled up to admire our children. 'You've come from the Irrigation Department? Look!' She pointed twenty metres out into the river. 'My house used to be out there! But ... what to do?' she said, helplessly. The present flood protection works had come too late for her, but maybe all the gabions that were being put in place would stop her needing to move again.

I looked in admiration at the ingenuity of these villagers: they could make so much from their scanty local resources. They used hollow silk-cotton tree trunks for troughs and dug-out canoes. Stumps with holes carved in them were planted vertically and received horizontal bamboo poles to form a simple but effective gate. There were conical cane fish traps on roofs. Tables and benches were made out of rough planks or slatted cane, and the sealed wattle and daub grain bins were works of art.

I was distracted by a couple of boys chasing a slow-moving child with a stick. I realised she suffered from cretinism — from insufficient iodine before birth. 'Look how those children are treating that poor little girl, Mr Kedar!' I said, feeling shocked and upset. 'Can we stop them?'

'No. It is not necessary. It is normal to beat these stupid children if they don't do their work. Everyone must work in the village. She needs to eat — so she has to work.'

Alexander reappeared from his explorations proudly carrying an enormous buffalo skull in one hand and a pelvis and some ribs in the other. Travelling in a car with a dead thing upset Dinesh, though. He expectorated theatrically all the way back, and was off sick the next day.

CHAPTER TWENTY-FIVE

last-ditch doctor

ON TRIPS TO KATHMANDU, I'D CATCH UP WITH Joanna, Anna, Mary and other expatriate friends. Gossiping freely in English was therapy to mitigate my isolation and my feeling like a pariah in Rajapur.

A common complaint amongst the Kathmandu expat women was how their husbands' six-day working week limited their explorations of Nepal. So when Lorna vaguely suggested a husband-free trek, I responded enthusiastically, and a plan slowly took shape. We'd go around the time that Simon's office moved up to Kathmandu for the monsoon.

Leaving Rajapur in the first week of May would mean that the children would also avoid the very worst of the prickly heat and the sleeplessness that we'd suffered in last year's pre-monsoon sauna. The plan seemed more and more enticing as the heat increased. Already David and Sebastian stayed naked except for nappies. I'd gaze longingly towards the mountains trying to make out any snow, but it was unusual now to be able to see that far. The air — and everything — was thick with dust. I even had to wash flowers before arranging them in a vase.

This year, though, the children seemed happy. We'd often now set up school under a mango tree in the garden, David apparently supervising from his special chair, where he chatted and followed the movement of birds that were busy all around us. I'd be aware of sweat dribbling down my back, between my breasts and into my eyes, and I'd look forward to the end of the day when I'd run the scaldingly hot water from the tap before having a long tepid shower. Then, freshened up, and in the cool of evening when it was possible to breathe again, I could see once again the beauty of the plains. Simon would return from work and we'd all move up onto the roof and sip warm Nepali-made Star or Cheers beer. It was a good time for David to be out unshaded — the sun didn't hurt his eyes.

I yearned for rain, but the occasional light showers soon evaporated, and a miasma of dust three metres high hung over every road and track for several hours after a bullock cart had passed. I'd shop much earlier now. Even so, everything was becoming a struggle again — especially taking David out. Heat sapped my motivation to do anything. Guliya — who, despite my remonstrations, was still lifting the rice straw mats and dhurries to sweep and mop the whole house every day — showed me the seven small scorpions that she'd killed one morning. 'Seven! That's terrible!' I said, rather shocked.

'It is normal in this season,' Guliya said, without emotion.

'What if a scorpion stings David?'

'Great pain will be felt. Death is also possible.'

With the heat came flies, and with the flies David got conjunctivitis, though some of *docter* Bhandari's chloramphenicol eye-drops cured it in twelve hours. There was a plague of itchy, hairy caterpillars: in the house, in the loo, everywhere. I was standing contemplating all these new hazards when I realised that Ganga was at my elbow. '*Memsahib*? Come see ...' She led me to a place in the mulberry hedge from which small squeaks emanated. There was a nest, and inside, gasping to keep cool, were three bulbul chicks. 'So, so small and weak, *memsahib*.' She smiled at the treasure she'd discovered.

The heat set everyone thinking about sex: sparrows, bulbuls, hornbills, and inside the house the jumping spiders were at it. It was the wedding season, too. Processions came past our house playing hectic, invigorating numbers with lots of squeaky clarinet solos. A saxophonist, a clarinettist, a trumpeter and drummers led one procession, and close on their heels was Mr Vaidiya's large red tractor, slowly towing a trailer containing the principal women guests in richly coloured saris, a settee, a wardrobe and other necessities for the happy couple, who would leave the wedding party with all their new furniture to set up their new home. After the tractor and trailer paraded the menfolk, mostly in ill-fitting Western-style suits, Nepali hats and foreheads lavishly adorned with red tikka.

If ever home-school got started at all, the wildlife and village life was a lovely distraction for me while Alexander was colouring something or thinking up yet another excuse to avoid work. We both found the lessons inane and getting to a natural history lesson that focussed on woodlice seemed the last straw. Now, I am fond of woodlice, but there weren't any in Rajapur. It was improvisation time again. 'Alexander, have you seen any interesting creepy-crawlies lately?'

'Yes, playing mantises are my favourite. They eat their friends. And there is a great big moth too ... *ekdum* huge ... and some beautiful flies outside the toilet. They've got mirrors on their bottoms.' He showed me midges maniacally zooming in pointless circuits; their backsides sparkled with iridescent, reflected sunlight. A seven-centimetre-long hawk-moth was tucked up sleeping in the corner. It startled us by squeaking when I prodded it awake. It was a clumsy great animal, with an abdomen as long and as fat as my middle finger.

I hassled it out onto my hand, where its wings started frantically quivering to warm up its body enough to fly away. After a minute or so of wing-quivering, it managed to take off, flew around in a small circle, crashed, took off again and flew back into the bathroom.

'Let's make it do it again!'

'We'll leave it in peace. See if you can find three kinds of beetles.'

David started coughing again. His appetite was diminished, but he could be tempted by his favourite spinach soup, and eating still cheered him up. On the second day of this illness, when I asked Ganga to make him more soup, she said firmly. 'He must not eat this.'

'What? Why not?'

'Dabid has cough and fever; he must not eat spinach.'

'Why not?'

'It will make him ill.'

'How?'

'Spinach is cold food.'

'We'll heat it.'

'When hot it is also cold. Dabid must not eat it.'

'These foods are good for him — especially while he is ill. Spinach contains lots of vitamin A, which is healing.' But I couldn't convince Ganga with science.

Simon came home with his shirt stuck to his back and headed straight for the water filter. While he was rehydrating, I asked him, 'Could you explain this hot–cold food stuff? Ganga refused to feed David today — she's never been so determined about anything before, so I ended up feeding him while she watched me in absolute horror — as if I was deliberately poisoning him.'

'No, I don't understand it. I don't know how many times I've asked, but apparently it is so obvious to Nepalis that they can't believe that you don't know about it. It does seem to parallel the medieval idea of humours of the body, and the important thing is that if you have a hot disease, you must avoid hot food or the illness will get worse. I'd love to be able to follow it, but to me there is no logic to it, and the best I've ever got is what appears to be a completely random list of foods that are hot and cold. And confusingly, there are foods that are classified as hot when raw and become cold when cooked! My landlady in Dhankuta always tried to stop me eating oranges when I had a cold. Dinesh had a dry, tickly cough recently, and was eating Rara noodles — the ones that say "Most Hygienic One" on the packet. The *peon* rounded on him — he's someone no-one would listen to otherwise — and said, "How can you eat that? Take these crackers instead." I can't think of anything worse for a tickly cough than dry biscuits, but that was the correct food, it seemed.

'By the way, may I send Dinesh to see you?' Simon continued. 'I really need him to be at work with all these deadlines looming, but he's in a real state.'

'Of course I'll see him. Dr Last-Ditch — that's me. I expect he's already taken a load of inappropriate medicines and I'll have all the usual problems working out what are side-effects and drug interactions. *Please* tell him to bring all his medicines with him. What's wrong with him?'

'I don't know. He keeps going on about shingles, and yesterday he even asked me if it could kill you! It just looks like he has an infected spot on his face.'

'Shingles? Why shingles?'

'That's the diagnosis the skin doctor he saw in Kathmandu last month gave him. The specialist thought it was bad enough to prescribe acyclovir, and also said Dinesh should have a lion painted on his stomach!'

'Did he get it done?'

'Yes, he commissioned an artist to do it. It looked really splendid.'

'Not sure I can match that sort of advice, but I should be able to reassure him,' I replied.

Twenty-four hours later, and after considerable pressure from Simon, I saw Dinesh open our ridiculously huge gate. I was sitting on our odd little foam sofa, doing marching exercises with David while he chuckled at me. Dinesh walked unsteadily through our luxuriant garden, up the three concrete steps and rapped on the warped mosquito screen. He wore a huge dressing on what was obviously a very thick upper lip. 'Come in, come in.' His stiff new jeans buckled audibly as he sat.

'Oh, madam Dr Jane, I am so very worried about myself. Yesterday I felt so ill and depressed, I decided to leave for Kathmandu; I thought I surely needed some blood test, but then *docter* Bhandari shaved my moustache and all the pus came out and that was a great relief to me. Now I am seventy per cent better!'

Dinesh was usually so cheerful and dynamic, it upset me to see him so distressed. I needed to reassure him. 'Simon mentioned that you were worried about shingles. This is not shingles. Bhandari's treatment has been good. You are recovering already!'

'Ah, yes, Bhandari said it was not shingles, and Simon-sir said it was not shingles, and now you, madam Jane, also say it is not shingles, and so I do not think that bad, bad pain is coming back. It was so terrible. My whole body pained me.'

Later, Simon asked 'What did you make of Dinesh's diseases, then?'

'You don't sound very sympathetic,' I said. 'He was worried sick.'

'I could see that, but what was wrong with him?'

'You'll be pleased to know that I was able to confirm your diagnosis, although I reckon he had more confidence in your clinical skills than mine! It must have been a nasty abscess, but he'll be fine. I convinced him, I think, that he didn't have a deadly disease — or smallpox. You know, I continue to be surprised at what worries even educated people like Dinesh. He talked about his fear of curses and ghosts — that seemed a bit wimpish. Don't worriers get teased?'

'No, not much; although Himalaya thinks Dinesh is neurotic. Usually it seems all right to admit to being scared. The other day one of the landlords told us that he fell from a first floor window during the night. A ghost had come in to steal his chickens and he fell out trying to chase it away!'

'Did the others believe him?'

'Yes, absolutely. They were impressed that he could fall so far and not get hurt. It showed how strong he was!'

'He was probably drunk,' I said scathingly. 'Drunks survive nasty falls because they are relaxed when they hit the ground!'

'Is that your prescription?'

'Mmm, good thinking. Shall we have a beer?'

'Excellent idea. Actually, I wondered whether Dinesh thought that some spirit of the dead came out of that buffalo skull. The one that Alexander brought home when we were all out on that field trip the other day?' Simon reminded me.

'So *that* was what all his obsessive throat-clearing was about on the drive back from Guptipur — he was trying to stop that badness entering. Poor Dinesh.'

डे डे डे

Simon hadn't had a day off in weeks, and he looked exhausted. His relationships with Nepali counterparts were constrained and sometimes strained by the political games and power struggles that were going on in Kathmandu. He had to be so careful. He would often be very distracted when he came home in the evening; he seemed unwilling to talk about his concerns, yet found it difficult to leave them at work. I said, 'Let's stroll down to the river — you coming, Alexander?'

'No, I'm going to stay with David and Sebastian and Sita. We're doing work. But it's seclet work.'

'Okay.' I never worried now about leaving the children. Ganga, Guliya and Sita were lovely with them, and the whole community seemed to keep an eye on them. If ever I went out looking for Alexander, someone always knew where he was and where he'd been. I said to Simon, 'Let's walk by the potters' settlement. We need another jar to cool our water in.' As we headed towards the river we were greeted often, and a Brahmin woman approached and said, 'Your big son was at the top of this mango tree today. With that Tharu boy,' she added, rather disapprovingly. So far, such caste prejudices passed over

Alexander's head. Then there was a shout from behind us, and Alexander was running to catch us up.

We walked west along hedges of hibiscus and jasmine covered with lapis-blue convolvulus, passed the largest houses where the high-caste people lived and through a Tharu quarter where the huts all had attractive relief animal designs around the doorways. Beyond, near the Karnali River, a footpath lined with African marigolds and yellow-flowered, blue-leafed prickly poppies guided us past a sky-blue Shiva swathed in cobras. We took off our shoes and approached the fine Shiva *lingam*, embraced by a delicate silver cobra and sitting in its representation of female genitals. Lovely alabaster figures and a huge black bull looked on, worshipping the phallic *lingam*: symbol of Shiva's power to create and renew. 'Can we meet Shiva, Mummy?'

'Well, yes, I suppose you can. People say that thunderstorms are the gods fighting and throwing thunderbolts at each other, so next time there is a storm, maybe you should look!' The orange-robed *sadhu* who was sweeping away the morning offerings gave Alexander fruit. Someone was playing religious music on a harmonium, and when we turned towards the musician, Alexander said, 'That's the plumber!'

From the temple, we headed upstream. At first I thought that we'd mistaken the place, but then found the pits that had been their kilns, their ingenious mud cattle troughs and holes where the stakes supporting their houses had been. The Kumale had left not many days before. A recent burial — an untidy pile of turf, bamboo and saffron cloth — explained their departure.

A little further on, we passed a shack where a middle-aged woman lived. She had a goitre that was so huge it was pressing on her windpipe, and her breathing was laboured. She needed specialised surgery that she'd never get.

Then the smell of wood smoke and boiled milk reached my nostrils. While Alexander built another sandcastle, we sat on *charpoys* outside the riverside tea shack and ordered glasses of sweet tea to wash down the dust. A young man was in the river up to his knees, his back towards us. He'd secured pieces of old flip-flop to act as floats on his diminutive net. I watched, admiring the local ability to improvise, then began to wonder who would fish in such shallow water so close to a busy ferry. The fisher turned around grinning, *'Namasté, memsahib!'* It was Ram Kumar. Having failed as a cook, he was trying to make a little money from fishing. You'd never guess that he was struggling to make a living.

Simon's gaze was focussed somewhere in the middle distance: he was miles away. 'Are you okay?' I asked him.

'Mmm.'

'Whatcha thinking about?'

'Nothing … peaceful here, isn't it? So how's the *memsahib* and her staff today?'

'Okay. Guliya went to *docter* Jha's today. She was feeling dizzy, so he gave her a saline infusion. Fat lot of good that'll do her; I wish they wouldn't waste their money on *docter's* fees. Arjun's been there, too, because his belly was "blossoming". I don't understand why they won't save money and consult me.'

'Maybe Arjun thinks you're only a "lady doctor" — and there's your dubious interest in the Badi …'

'Oh, dear, another cultural cock-up? No matter — I expect it's Guliya's belly that's blossoming; she's probably pregnant again. Arjun needs a vasectomy!'

'No wonder he won't consult you!' Simon said, grinning.

I asked the child who brought the tea, 'Little brother, you are how old?'

The tea-stall owner, squatting by the cooking fire, replied for him. 'He's three-and-a-half.'

'He looks so very grown up, washing up the tea glasses,' I replied in Nepali. Then to Simon, 'He's going to be old before he's twelve. These kids never have a childhood, do they?'

The river was quiet and still apart from the occasional ring of ripples when a big fish broke the surface. After panting through the heat of the day, the birds were becoming active again. A green barbet let out his echoey *krrow-krrow-krrow*, and a peacock on the little island opposite shrieked a loud *pea-ow, pea-ow*.

'Are you going to tell me now what's going on at the office?'

'Mmm? Oh, several things,' Simon replied. 'There's not much progress, and what has been started is going wrong. The contractor for the east–west road is kicking up a fuss saying he's been misled. I can sort that out, but I've realised that there are other problems and we need to do some more design work. And, as ever, there isn't enough time; the construction season is so short … Mr Lama saw what a mess some of the designs were, and was being very supportive, but he couldn't pressure them to redo the work. And, anyway, he's been transferred now.'

'Won't word get around if these local consultants produce shabby work?'

'Reputations can be bought and sold here … except for foreign consultants like me. It's a minor nightmare working with four different consultants, and the contractors and the government engineers, and then there's the Minister with his bright ideas and — of course — the Bank.'

'"Minor nightmare" sounds like an understatement. And I suppose that you are held responsible for absolutely everything.'

'Yup. If anything goes wrong, the first response is to get me to sign some kind of let-out letter, rather than try to sort it out. But it's all right. I think we'll solve this current mess. One of the Department of Irrigation engineers has a cousin who sounds as if he might be good. Hungarian-trained.' But Simon wasn't as confident as he tried to sound. 'The problem is also that the new senior engineer is unpopular. He doesn't gamble and he doesn't drink either — not even tea!'

'Gosh — does nearly everyone gamble, then?'

'Nepali staff say that there isn't much else to do here except work, drink and gamble.'

'I wish they didn't expect you to work non-stop, too. Can't you stop them dropping by at 6 am to discuss things that could easily wait a day or three?'

'Not really — look, there's a government holiday coming up: New Year's Day, the first of the month of *Baisakh* 2052. Office clerks all do a *katha pujaa* — they burn incense over their ledger books. Let's get away to Bardiya and catch up on the latest elephant gossip. We both need a break.'

CHAPTER TWENTY-SIX

clinics for the poor

DAVID'S PHYSIOTHERAPY, ALEXANDER'S HOME-SCHOOL and the chores left little time, but now that Ganga could mind the children I felt more relaxed about occasional short outings without the boys. I'd drop in on the Geruwa Rural Awareness Association every so often, hoping still that I could motivate them, but the office was always locked.

Then, a full year after I had first talked of working with the GRAA, I bumped into the general secretary again. 'What about our health project, Mr Gopal?' It was time to be more pushy.

'But Dr Jane must know … we cannot start anything until wife of our committee chairman is out of hospital in Lucknow.'

'Have I met the chairman?' I asked, thinking this was surely an irrelevant excuse.

'You, madam, have not met, but he is very king pin.'

'Umm … Perhaps this is not a good time for you to start this work?' I was beginning to suspect that they weren't really interested.

'Ah. Yes, yes, but you are very right, Dr Jane. We must start. Why not! We thought that you had no leisure time. Let us have meeting!'

A couple of days later, I was ushered between too many people crammed into the tiny, bare office. The same baby-milk tin full of dusty plastic flowers was on the windowsill, and the room was still crawling with weevils. Nothing seemed to have changed, except that there were a few more files.

'I think that you are not knowing our vice-president, Mr Dig Vijay Tharu?' Gopal then interrupted his own introductions, greetings and ritual opening platitudes to say, 'This *gastric* problem, you know, madam Dr Jane, my missus has same also. What to do?' His mouth was stained brick-red.

'I think that you have forgotten the advice I gave you last year! You are still chewing *paan,* and if you won't pay attention to me, what hope is there of illiterate villagers listening?'

'They are different!' he said frowning. 'Yes, yes, of course I am still smoking and it is not possible to live without chillies and *paan*. Should I go to Kathmandu for endoscopy?'

'You — do — not — need — endoscopy. Are we all here? Shall we start?' I plunged in, ignoring local protocol, tiring now of all this stalling. 'Thank you for inviting me again. I am delighted to learn from Mr Gopal that you are still interested in adding a health component to your work. Whatever we plan now will be your work, not mine, but I am sure that it could be a really useful and sustainable project. I will only provide technical expertise to help you start, because — after all — I am a newcomer and cannot understand all the problems that you have to live with.' They all smiled, slightly puzzled. They were used to being told what to do, but I wanted them to own this work. 'I will only be in Rajapur for two more months, so we must work quickly too.' There were whispered discussions; people looked confused.

An outsider turned up. She wore voluminous culottes and a luminous yellow baseball cap saying *STAR* in big letters on it. 'I am T P Pratibha,' she said. This seemed a strangely formal introduction from an educated young woman. What was I supposed to call her? T P? She was the United Nations volunteer from south India that I'd heard about. She was fast-talking and enthusiastic about the health program and would help me with translations.

I continued by telling the meeting about a successful project I had run that reduced diarrhoea outbreaks by eighty-nine per cent in an illiterate community in Indonesia. The essence of that program was simplicity: no lecturing, lots of tea-drinking and relaxed chatting, lots of time getting to know the villagers and offering them only simple basic information. 'This is the secret!' Everyone was nodding and smiling approvingly. I was elated.

'We will make a program for you to run one trainings here, Dr Jane, and we will approach the international funding agencies for money to do this work. How many weeks will your trainings run for?' My euphoria evaporated. The aid industry has made 'trainings' very popular in Nepal by paying a generous allowance, serving good food and vodka, and distributing briefcases and pens. This was not at all what I had in mind.

'What I want to share with the villagers is so simple that it will only take five minutes to pass on; any training I run will take very little time— a maximum of one day.'

The participants, even Pratibha, who had seemed in tune with my thoughts, now looked troubled. Gopal had talked of empowerment and community participation, but then wanted to be told what to do. They wanted to start from scratch, instead of building on existing community skills. Their lack of pride in themselves and their indigenous wisdom was depressing. 'Yes, you are expert, Dr Jane, and you must give us trainings.'

'Why don't we go to a village and chat to the villagers about their problems and what we might be able to do to help?' Slightly to my surprise, everyone agreed that this was a good idea and we resolved to visit Ghumna village a couple of days later. They seemed keen again, and perhaps finally I had stimulated them to start something useful.

Pratibha chipped in. 'We must walk to the village. That way we attract less attention. Can you walk?' Her question made me smile. Maybe, after all, the GRAA was going to surprise me with their commitment, and wear me out by walking for hours in the heat of the day. Suddenly our business was concluded. 'Shall I go then?'

'Yes, yes. Why not?'

डे डे डे

I approached the Geruwa Rural Awareness Association office at nine o'clock, as arranged, feeling suddenly insecure. I was carrying Sebastian, but this was the first time I had left Alexander and David for more than an hour or so. The office was locked, and I cursed. 'Typical. No-one here. They've forgotten ... or they will be an hour late!' Then, as I turned to look for somewhere to sit, I heard a loud, '*Namasté,* madam!' Mr Gopal appeared behind me; Pratibha (still wearing her bright-yellow baseball cap, but now in a *kurta pyjama* outfit and bum-bag) emerged from a shop and Dig Vijay also materialised. 'Do you need rest or shall we go straight?' the considerate Gopal asked me.

'Let's go!' I said, with some enthusiasm. Gopal and Dig Vijay led the way through the bazaar, but soon got entangled in greetings and exchanges. Important people. Pratibha and I ambled ahead and past the Bageswari Hotel, which was looking as squalid as ever. It proudly advertised 'Lodging and Futing'.

'What *is* futing?' I asked her.

'Fooding: bad *daal bhat*,' she explained.

We passed the customs post, the police station and the hundred-metre-high telephone transmitter mast (to service the seven telephones in Rajapur), and tacked between waiting *tangas* and the horses that pull them. We ambled on to where the dirt road strikes east to the ferry at Kothiyaghat, and then turned south. Suddenly, only a few hundred metres from the bustle and noise, it was delightfully rural, and quiet enough to enjoy the birdcalls. The brain-fever bird was in particularly good voice. How easy it is to forget that the countryside and unspoilt villages are so close: the cinemas, blaring Hindi film songs, the muezzin calling from the mosque and the general bustle made Rajapur bazaar seem like an oppressively big town sometimes.

It was late March, and there had been no rain for months. With each step, we disturbed fine, fine silt, so that our feet and legs each seemed to carry their own diminutive dust-clouds; yet it was still cool. Pratibha said, 'I love walking. I walk everywhere! It gives me time to think and often I will meet someone along the way and we talk to pass the time.' She was a zoology graduate, but when I delightedly pointed out tiger butterflies and mantids, she hardly glanced at them. Disappointingly, she didn't share my passion for small wildlife.

'Here we are at Ganesh-*tan*,' Gopal announced. 'This is most holy place and people have come here to worship for maybe four hundred year. Then, one very terrible day eight years before, the old *peepal* tree here itself burned down and every Hindu man contributed and we built one new temple.' Gopal took off his shoes and bowed down low to the amorphous, red-daubed rock inside the little temple. Dig Vijay did a quick bow from the gate.

I said, 'I expect Ganesh protects people from rampaging elephants?'

'No,' Gopal replied, as if I was daft to link the elephant-headed god of literature and jollity to the unworthy, untameable *jungle*.

We walked a leisurely half an hour, our feet — amusingly — making soft *phut, phut* sounds as dust was fired sideways with each step. When we arrived at an unimpressive collection of huts, Gopal unexpectedly said, 'This is Ghumna.' A middle-aged man received us while women brought *charpoys* for us to sit on and people gathered to stare. Gopal launched into a wordy introduction: Nepalis love making grand speeches. But partway through, a thin, wrinkly old chap with authority arrived, and Gopal started again. It was only then that I realised how politically ambitious Gopal was. Finally I managed to restrain his oratory and turn the discussion to health and the villagers' needs. The villagers' response was embarrassed, puzzled silence. And they stared at Sebastian, my strange, bald, pale, hatless baby. Slowly, we coaxed them into talking, but Gopal's political agenda and the villagers' reluctance to chat made the discussions flounder before they'd begun. Perhaps, also, they were tired of visits from outsiders with grand ideas who either did nothing or swindled them.

Then, to my dismay, Gopal launched into questions about the villagers' toilet habits. He then turned to me, pulled a face and said (in English, fortunately), 'These people are very dirty!'

I could have kicked him. Instead, I said, 'Think how life must be for these people. Imagine if you lived here.'

'That is impossible,' he responded.

'But, Mr Gopal, if you had no water, you too might not wash as much as you would like!'

'It is their ignorance only.' He clearly couldn't imagine himself ever being so deprived.

'Let's ask about their health problems,' I said. We heard about fevers, pneumonia, diarrhoea, skin infections, rabies and then the treatment of snakebite. Villagers worried about being bitten, and we heard that treatment involved sucking out the poison and then rinsing the mouth with *rakshi*. Others applied the anus of a chicken to the bite site, which — they said — sucked out the poison and, in doing so, killed the chicken. It was more or less as Basistha had described. 'Do you go to Rajapur for treatment?' I asked.

'We do not go.'

'But it is close by?'

'It is close by. We go to buy cloth and salt and kerosene and steel for ploughshares; that is all we need from these outsiders. And we like to go to the cinema. That is also good.' Films were their only escape — a way to forget for a while.

'Could I see inside a house?' A giggling gaggle of women took me into the enormous, thatched longhouse that dominated the village. I stopped to admire the geometric animal designs around the doorway. There were cheerful-looking elephants and strange beasts that might have been chickens or antelope. 'Which is your part?' I asked.

'We don't live here!' They giggled all the more at my mistaking them for the important family.

'Oh, should we come another time?' I felt embarrassed that they were showing me around someone else's home, but I should have known that my ideas of privacy were foreign to them.

'It is no problem, sister. Come look,' they beckoned, tittering at my discomfiture. It was very dark inside, for the few windows were fifteen-centimetre-long ovals criss-crossed with sticks. Once I'd become accustomed to the gloom, I saw the two-metre-high grain storage bins that split the longhouse into units for each of the five families who lived here. At one end was the kitchen: it was clean and neat, having been freshly swept and replastered with a solution of cow dung and mud, as it was every morning. There were a few cooking utensils, but no personal possessions at all. A dung fire still gently smouldered in a mud-plastered pit in the middle of the kitchen area, making that end of the longhouse smoky enough to sting my eyes, and I suppressed a cough. When the women were cooking the evening meal, the air must be intolerably thick, but smoke-filled traditional longhouses are unattractive to mosquitoes, so this practice would give them some protection from malaria and Japanese encephalitis. I often heard the story that Tharu people have a special genetic resistance to malaria — that they are especially adapted to the inhospitable plains environment — but this is nonsense. Any special 'resistance' is at the price of a large proportion of children dying before their first birthday, but this harsh reality didn't make as nice a story as the idea of special malaria-resistant genes.

My eyes were drawn to a decorated corner with an altar with clay animals on it, and white handprints on the mud-plastered wall above them. Just inside the doorway — which had no door — was a mural. Pratibha explained, 'This is Lord Krishna; he was a womaniser, and therefore popular with Tharu women; he is often featured in their art.'

Her body language said that she considered Tharu women little better than whores. There was also a very recognisable representation of King Birendra and, next to him, a figure resembling Elvis Presley beside a pale-skinned woman wearing skimpy, tight, Western clothes, posing provocatively. Beneath these incongruous figures was some lovely abstract artwork suggesting women dancing. I said, 'It's beautiful. The house, too, is lovely and so cool.'

'This is not a good house,' my Tharu tour guide said. Nepalis often criticise their country in a destructive way, and now even here there were aspirations for modernity. This woman's dream home was a stark, strong, low-maintenance reinforced concrete box, like ours in Rajapur.

A woman gestured to take Sebastian, and he delighted her by smiling and cooing in her arms. 'I am childless,' she said, in halting Nepali. 'If you have three boys, you can give me this one?'

'My husband will be angry if I give away his sons!' I replied. She knitted her brows, knowing that I must obey my husband, though reluctant to give my baby back.

Outside again, we collected Gopal and headed back to Rajapur via the new *kamaiya* settlement. The previous year, the government had given these slaves some uncultivatable land close to the river. The Landless People's Problem Resolution Committee had issued 53,050 certificates of land ownership that year — the *Rising Nepal* reported — but these impressive figures belied worthless gifts. Later, during the year 2000, His Majesty's Government finally yielded to international pressure, liberated all *kamaiya* in Nepal and wrote off all their debts. This didn't solve their problems, though. Landlords, forbidden from employing their former slaves, bought tractors instead. The *kamaiya* are free now, but there is little work; many risk starvation.

The fifteen *kamaiya* houses here at Ghumna were shabby shacks, and it looked like the river would soon take back the land. 'These people are so poor, Mr Gopal.' Despite the drought at this time of the year, ponds of stinking black waste water had accumulated close to the community's hand pump. 'The water doesn't drain away here.

When the rains start, they will be knee-deep in water and hunted by mosquitoes! Can you help them?'

'Of course. It is all arranged! We have asked WaterAid to come.' I was so impressed! What a pleasure working with these people was going to be. It had been worth the wait: finally they were taking ownership of this project, and something useful and sustainable would come out of it.

Ambling back into Rajapur, the hot sand rose in small explosions — *phut, phut* — with every footfall; silt spilled around my sandals and scorched my feet. The men loitered. As I walked on with Pratibha, I encouraged her to talk; I wanted to know more. 'You must know these people well?'

'Yes, I have spent so much of time in this village. I know each and every one of these people. I have even befriended the untouchable goldsmiths. These Tharus, they don't care so much about caste issues, but they also refuse to drink water from a well that these Sunars have used. But we can work with them, no problem. I can help them with these caste problems.'

'You can? Excellent. But what do these Tharus think about their high-caste neighbours?'

'They don't trust these Brahmins: they always outsmart the Tharus; they pay small, small sums for labour only, or cheat them in other ways. So the Tharus try to keep away from them now, unless they are desperate for a little Brahmin money. Tharus used to own all the land here, but it is mostly lost now. And these outsiders behave strangely and are rude, even though they are all Hindus. My villagers don't understand them. Brahmins don't even know how to offer greeting in Tharu language — they speak Hindi or Nepali only.'

'But things must be better now for the Tharus — now that they can travel by bus, and buy medicines?'

'The Tharus have very little money. Everything is too expensive: Brahmin medicines; their clever things.

Not for the first time, I realised just how distant I was from my Tharu neighbours.

Pratibha continued her impassioned eulogy. 'I like these Tharus, but my problem is with these GRAA people. I have been here for eighteen months and I have achieved nothing. No thing. I have tried my level best, but they don't listen to me.'

I wasn't surprised. Mature, politically-ambitious Nepali men would never accept advice from a young Indian woman, however intelligent she was. Pratibha was too idealistic to talk them around gently and empower them to run their own projects.

I told her about projects in other countries that had been destroyed by impatient outsiders bulldozing through local sensibilities, and then told her one of the success stories. 'I visited an impressive self-help project in a Karachi slum a couple of years ago. The slum dwellers had to organise a small committee and write a note — on any old scrap of paper — asking for technical advice from the Project. The secret of success and sustainability, they told me, was not to rush the community into starting work before they were ready. Most groups took six months to organise themselves sufficiently even to write that note. Things happen slowly here, too, and if you try to rush things the GRAA committee will dig their heels in.'

'No, no. It is not like that. They just want a servant to do all the work for them. If I wait and wait to motivate them, nothing will happen at all!'

I felt for her, but didn't know how to help. Perhaps her impatience was making the GRAA committee deliberately slow up.

Back in Rajapur bazaar, I said, 'I'm going to Kathmandu for a few days, but I'll draft a detailed plan for the health education program before I leave.' Gopal looked delighted. 'Yes, yes, and you can meet your friends in the international agencies and raise funds for our works also.'

'We won't need big finance. We can work with the resources you already have. In that way it will be sustainable.'

Gopal didn't look keen. Was it money that was really motivating him?

'We will arrange one meeting … soon, madam.'

'Do we need another meeting? You know that I am leaving Rajapur forever in a matter of weeks?' He waggled his head to tell me he knew. I left, dispirited.

When, a couple of days later, I delivered my plan to Gopal, he asked, 'When will we receive our first cheque? Which agency will support us in this work?'

Finding it difficult to hide my frustration, I replied, 'We're not ready to ask for funding yet.' The atmosphere went very cold, and I left wondering whether I had pushed too hard. Perhaps they were finally beginning to realise that I was not going to raise the capital for them to build a hospital, that what I was proposing was going to involve work and commitment. It might make them local heroes, and even help them politically, but it wouldn't make them rich.

Vulture came around again shortly afterwards to add to my despondency. Maybe she read my mood for, unusually, she leapt in without any preliminaries. 'You are leaving Rajapur! I love you and do not want you to go. And I need your furniture.'

'I'm so sorry. Most of it will go to another project, but I will do what I can,' I said, intending that Guliya's family would get anything that there was to give away. Mrs Gautam sighed deeply and shambled off. I'd never liked her.

डे डे डे

We'd lived on Rajapur though two hot seasons, yet there were many places I hadn't seen. I'd often wondered what lay behind the heavily padlocked gate of the central temple to Rama. The gaudily painted, bile-green, squared-off dome towered over the shacks of the bazaar, but I was uncertain whether non-Hindus would be welcome inside.

One afternoon Alexander and I ventured in through a waist-high gate within a gate — which it turned out had always been open. Inside, so close to the noise and smells and flies of the bazaar, was a surprising corner of tranquillity. Even now in the April drought, the lawn was green, and shrubs and trees were in flower. There was an open well in the corner of the garden. We ambled towards the main temple and found two slumbering male bodies; the head of one was shrouded in orange — the priest, then. The other was less obviously religiously affiliated, and scowled at me, but beckoned; he seemed to be suffering tremendously in the heat. Maybe he was ill, or hung-over. We approached. He stared blankly at us. 'May I stroll here? Is it all right?' I was worried that I might give offence somehow. He smiled a welcoming smile that told me I should relax: Hindus have a pragmatic approach to religion, and local children ride on carved temple bulls as if temple courtyards are playgrounds. Temples are places to sleep, chat, and relax as well as to pray and seek practical help from the gods.

There was a subsidiary shrine housing a cross-legged Lord Shiva, immaculately fashioned from glistening marble. He wore a cobra for a scarf, which adorned the god's neck and curled over him to shade his head from the sun with its hood; to me, this image made him look more of a recreator than a destroyer. Devotees had smeared vermilion powder on his forehead and someone had placed fresh hibiscus flowers in his lap. He was flanked by smaller effigies of his consort Parbati and his son Ganesh; they had also been decorated with red powder and flowers. Before the holy family was the frying-pan shaped *yoni* symbolising the vagina and womb.

A woman asked in smooth, high-caste Nepali, 'What does your son want to do?'

'Just look,' I said. She beckoned with a friendly smile and opened the door of the central temple; inside were more superb alabaster figures. A friendly-looking, bespectacled attendant appeared; he was wrinkled and naked except for a loincloth. He pointed out a group of magnificent standing marble statues dressed in red robes with gold trimmings. Two figures, one with the face of a monkey, knelt in adoration on each side of the group.

We sat enjoying the cool tranquillity of the place for a while. 'Come any time,' the priest called after us as we ducked back through the gate and into the hubbub of the bazaar.

I was delighted to discover, for once, that bananas were on sale. The arrogant Muslim supervised again as I bought the market's entire stock of thirteen. Then I caught a waft from the samosa stall and couldn't resist buying some. We passed an ascetic in a loincloth and waist-length dreadlocks; he was sucking on an ice-block. An ice-block — I couldn't believe my eyes. We next encountered salesmen selling them from grubby wooden boxes on the backs of their bicycles. They'd managed to freeze these delicacies without electricity by evaporating a solution of ammonia. I forbade Alexander to eat them for fear of gastroenteritis. 'Oh, Mum! That's boring!'

डे डे डे

Three weeks after our visit to Ghumna village, Pratibha dropped by. There were no preliminaries. She launched in with, 'Gopal sent me. We need one meeting with the GRAA committee to plan the health program, but I am going away to Kathmandu for ten days. I am tired of working with them. I do everything: each and every thing. I am their secretary, their servant. You know they missed the deadline for submitting the proposal to WaterAid for the Ghumna *kamaiya*! I typed the letter; all they had to do was sign and post it. I had done everything for them. Every thing. I tried my level best. And now these poor *kamaiya* will not get their water supply and latrines.'

'Just let me know when they're ready to start work. I'll be here.'

'They will never be ready …'

Pratibha took a month to reappear. She was still tense. I reminded her, 'I *am* leaving in four days, you know!'

'We must have one meeting to discuss the health program!' she said.

'We can meet this afternoon or first thing tomorrow, but what can we do in four days?'

'I will contact the committee and let you know!'

'Okay, but I should run a health education training session for the women already trained in income generation skills, and I could do this tomorrow or the day after, in a couple of hours. I could also run a training session for the GRAA committee so that they could become trainers. The health messages are so simple that anyone can learn them. And if the committee understands, they can build health education into all their work.'

Two days later, before 7 am, Pratibha and Dig Vijay turned up. They seemed surprised that I was leaving forty-eight hours later. We did some more talking in circles. 'Shall I run a demonstration health education session for the committee? At three tomorrow?'

'It is as you wish, Dr Mrs Jane,' Dig Vijay replied.

The following day was my last in Rajapur. It was hot — very hot. Everything felt hot to the touch. David looked hot and unhappy. He had also developed heat rash again. I wanted to sit with him to sponge him cool. I didn't feel good either. I was feverish and just wanted to get out of Rajapur. I had diarrhoea with spasms of colicky pain, provoking numerous urgent trips to squit on our squat-plate. It interrupted packing. The breeze that got up in the middle of the morning seemed to give some relief from the heat at first, but it whipped up great drifts of dust that made me sneeze or cough depending upon its density. Everything was covered in dust. The heat — and diarrhoea — sapped my ability to think. Yet I needed to perform passionately to convince the GRAA committee of the value of health education. I needed to be impressive, to motivate them to take on a task that could prevent unnecessary misery. We could do nothing about the poverty, but we could stop some people dying.

Most of the committee turned up late, and just as we were about to begin someone came to talk to Gopal. That delayed our start for another twenty minutes. 'I want to convince you that health education is effective in reducing disease and suffering; it is sustainable and does not rely upon outsiders.' People yawned. 'It is not costly and it is easy to do. Merely teaching villagers to wash their hands breaks the cycle of disease transmission in diarrhoea.' More yawns.

I moved on to what I thought would be the rivettingly horrible details of slow death by rabies: the fear, the pain, the convulsions, drowning in tenacious, rope-like saliva. They seemed unmoved. I began to despair. Suddenly Gopal woke up. 'When someone is bitten by a dog,' he said, 'he will rub the bite with a bit of chapatti and then throw it to other dogs. If the dogs eat the chapatti, then there is no rabies. If there is rabies, then other dogs will see the chapatti and avoid. Is this true, Dr Jane?'

'You could try the trick, but you must also clean the wound properly by scrubbing under running water for five minutes, then dousing with *rakshi*. That's a good health education message.'

Dig Vijay offered another local treatment. 'Take the mud from a field wasp nest. Grind it up, make a paste out of it by adding water and roll it into balls. When these balls are rubbed into a dog bite wound, the hair of the dog that bit you appears in the balls if the dog was rabid.' I could not imagine the point of this ritual, but at least they were showing some interest and even becoming quite animated.

I asked Dig Vijay to summarise the diarrhoea and rabies health education messages in two minutes. He talked for ten minutes, before I interrupted: 'Can anyone summarise in thirty seconds?' Suddenly it turned into a game and there was a competition amongst the committee members to summarise, as everyone timed them strictly. With so much repetition, they learned the key points, and they leapt in to correct those who missed out anything.

We were running out of time. 'Now, how would you now start your health promotion campaign?' I asked. That silenced the committee again. 'Look — I am an ignorant foreigner!' They laughed, puzzled. 'I know nothing about Nepal; I know even less about Rajapur. How can I tell you how to work? You are the experts!' They looked at each other, baffled and embarrassed. High-status people like me just didn't say things like this. 'How — would — you — start?' I repeated.

Silence.

'You would go into the village …? Who would you talk to first? Might you meet the village headman?' Silence. 'I am going to Kathmandu tomorrow. I cannot do this work for you. You must come up with ideas. The first stages will be slow …'

Pratibha (whom I had forbidden from participating) could not keep quiet any longer. 'Perhaps we could work through those we have already trained in the villages — the people who know you?'

'Ah, yes. This is a good way to begin,' said Gopal.

'Look, I gave you an outline of two ways that you could run health education locally. These are not necessarily the best ways to work, but criticising them might help you to get started. Have you read them?' They had not. 'I have another copy, which you might like to circulate around the committee?' A minion took it from me, punched holes in it, dusted off a few weevils and — once again — inserted it into a file without anyone having read it. 'I will wait to hear when you get started,' I said, knowing there was no hope now that they'd achieve anything. Rajesh had warned us that Rajapur was a difficult place. Pratibha was right, too. I had failed.

Gopal said, 'We also are coming to Kathmandu after some weeks. We will contact you and you will introduce us to your friends in the international agencies. Then we can arrange funding.'

'It is easy to raise money for worthwhile health programs, but first you must show that you can start something. It will be good for you politically, too. Think what local heroes you will become if you can — at minimal cost — reduce disease in the entire population of Rajapur Island!'

'Not heroes; not film stars,' Gopal said with knitted brows. 'We will call you, madam, when we come … after some time.'

And so I left Rajapur.

CHAPTER TWENTY-SEVEN

school for david

THE POWER WAS OFF AGAIN AT STINKING NEPALGUNJ airport. The ceiling fans were still. Sweat dribbled into my eyes and down the small of my back. Amidst the throng, Simon spotted an influential landlord and supporter of the GRAA, and he presented me to Mr Krishna Prasad Sigdel. 'Gopal has told me about you only, madam.' A pair of copulating flies landed on my moist forearm and another on my lower lip. 'We were *most* disappointed that you did nothing — not one thing — while you were living in Rajapur. Most disappointing, *hoina?*' He didn't allow me to articulate a defence but in turn introduced me to a man of about forty with slicked-back hair and expensive dark glasses. 'Come!' he quickly continued, 'You doctors must get together.'

Doctor S S Achariya didn't greet us, didn't smile. He was too busy clinically assessing David, who was burbling happily on my lap. He said, 'This is a case of …'

'Where do you work in Kathmandu?' I interrupted.

'Yes, I have one paediatric clinic in Baagh bazaar, isn't it; and I think this is a case …'

'Ah, a paediatrician! I'm also trained in paediatrics. You must be very busy!'

'Yes, busy. This,' he persisted, now pointing at David, 'is case of mental retardation!'

'It is very astute of you to notice that my son has problems.' I wanted to give him a lecture about the hurtful way that doctors talk about patients. I wanted to kick him where it hurt. I knew that Alexander was listening, even although he did not appear to be. 'How old is this child? … and he can't sit up? Can he talk? *Achha*, definitely this is a case of mental retardation.'

Ye gods, how I hated doctors sometimes! How was I going to shut this fellow up?

'Yes, he has problems,' I said, 'but he is a very happy baby and he keeps *us* cheerful too. We love him. He also understands quite a lot, so it is unkind to speak about him like he is a specimen.'

'With mental retardation, he will understand nothing.' I couldn't identify the stronger emotion: was it anger, incredulity or distress at the way he regarded my adorable baby? He was no better than the doctors in England!

Then my distress deepened and turned to fury when I noticed that the deaf mute had been beaten up. Both eyes were black and he had yet more teeth missing. The burly retarded youth and the half-blind old man whom he usually organised sat looking sad, unoccupied, lost. I turned to Simon. 'Most Nepalis see the person before the disability — unless they are doctors — so why has the harmless *lato* been picked on like this?'

'Oh, it'll be some family dispute or drunken argument. There's a lot of violence here.'

'I've wanted to believe that handicapped people are accepted here. They aren't, are they?'

'No; they're tolerated, but they're also a source of embarrassment because they're seen as a divine punishment. Maybe being ignored in the West is better than being beaten up in Nepal.'

I wanted to believe that the disabled could have a good life in Nepal, but my dream was being undermined. I heard my plane landing. I pulled back the grubby curtain of the security booth mumbling to Simon, 'I hate this place. I need some mountain therapy. See you next week.'

It wasn't until after take-off that a strange feeling of loss struck me. It was so odd to have left David with Ganga and Simon. This was my first separation from him, and I didn't like it. Yet we'd only be away for a week, and I was determined to enjoy this taste of cool freedom with my friends.

Alexander, Sebastian and I stayed overnight with Lorna in her marble palace with *Gone-with-the-Wind* staircase and chandeliers. Alexander thought this was unbelievable luxury and said, 'Lorna's water is *so* delicious!' The climate felt wonderfully fresh, but our biggest treat was drinking flat, boiled, cooled water from the fridge.

Next morning we assembled at Sundarijal, at the edge of the Kathmandu Valley. Calm, organised, fluent Nepali-speaking Lorna mustered the team. We'd employed a porter for each of the children, and the four older kids fired endless volleys of questions or demanded songs or stories as they were carried up. Like most treks, this started with a hard, steep ascent. Lorna was in fine Scottish voice, while I gasped the odd monosyllabic reply and was grateful whenever we stopped to rest. Four-year-old Andrew always brought water to me first, or a few tiny wild strawberries. 'Jane needs to drink to make milk for the baby,' he explained. Even he could see how very unfit I was. It was four months since my caesarean section, but it seemed less.

After the sun-bleached colourlessness of Rajapur and the grey dustiness of Kathmandu, though, we were quickly into beautiful

Nepal again, in rhododendron forest carpeted in crimson petals. I knew how to pace myself and was enticed on by views of terraced ridges and misty hints of snowy peaks shyly peeping out. Finding succulent orange-yellow raspberries to snack on made it feel like we were in paradise, though I did keep wondering about David. We'd soon be going back to England for a month's leave, but just at that moment I was content to stay in Nepal.

A helicopter flew over. Dangling beneath was a compressor for running a jackhammer.

'Where's *that* going?' I said.

Lorna said, 'D'you think it's something to do with that United Mission project? They're diverting the Melamchi River to bring drinking water to Kathmandu. I hope we'll get a swim in the Melamchi later — if there's any water left in it. It's so hot today.'

'*This* is a pleasant temperature — it was a full ten degrees Celcius hotter in the *tarai*!' I teased. It was so good to be up in the mountains. Lying now on dry grass in the shade of a pine tree, catching my breath, I asked Lorna. 'Will you go home soon?'

'Yes. Doesn't everyone desert Nepal during the monsoon?' she replied.

'Almost everyone I suppose — except impoverished volunteers and missionaries.'

By the middle of the afternoon we'd reached a low pass that looked down on the hamlet of Chisapaani — another place called Chisapaani, or cold water. We paused to look back. There was a refreshing breeze, and voices drifted up to us from far away. Tsering Sherpa, our guide and minder, pointed out the route we'd taken along a series of ridges, now muted by evening mists. We seemed to have covered an astonishing distance: although it amounted to only about eight kilometres, we'd climbed about 1,000 metres.

It had been a good first day. The children were in high spirits, and Sebastian was content. It was time to go down into the world again. Alexander was running ahead and I joined him. We charged along hand in hand, while he jumped and slithered until he slipped and dangled from my arm. Then, 'Let's do it again, Mummy!' Away from the sweltering plains, I was as exuberant as Tigger on speed.

The Chisapaani lodge advertised 'Hot Shower', which sounded delicious, especially now as the sun dipped behind the mountain ridges, the temperature plummeted and my knees started to stiffen up. The facilities, though, turned out to be still in the planning stage: there wasn't even a dry tap or a door on the proposed shower room. The lodge-owner offered a bucket of cold water and a mug. I resisted and returned to the children, who were busy drawing scenes from the day. Andrew added castles and Alexander dinosaurs to the scenery. Elegant, fashionable Joanna produced a bottle of malt whisky and, as I sipped from a tin mug, Andrew asked earnestly, 'Will this make milk for the baby too?'

Eighteen-year-old Ambur was marvellous with little Sebastian, even though the other porters teased him about doing women's work. On the rare occasions when Sebastian cried, Ambur sang high-pitched Nepali lullabies. There were horrified gasps from passers-by when they saw an all-but-naked, hatless infant, though. 'Surely he will get cold and become ill! And what is that around his bottom?' Alexander was delighted to be in Andrew's company, and they strolled the mountain paths in deep meaningful exchanges on Lego or gabions: they must have been rare four-year-olds who had even heard of gabions. Alexander's exuberance continued and when Andrew tired or he bored of chit-chat, he charged on, the cooler climate having released boundless energy. Every so often he'd come running past, or would appear up a roadside tree high above us. He was in paradise, and so was the child-porter assigned to him, who passed the days whittling and snacking on wild fruit.

By the third day we'd reached a patch of fine rhododendron forest: within a few metres there were white, red and pink blossoms; higher still there were lilac-coloured flowers; and the waxy leaves were a sumptuous, shiny deep green. Chandra, a huge bear of a man, picked flowers for all the children. When we arrived at the lodge at Mangengot at 3,285 metres above sea level, Tsering said, 'We'll have garlic soup tonight. It will protect you from altitude.' It wasn't the altitude that disturbed our sleep, though, but the cold. For most of the last month, Sebastian had been naked except for a nappy; now I dressed him in a vest, two sleep suits, a thick romper suit, woolly hat and knitted boots, and wrapped him in three shawls. He still did not feel particularly warm when he woke during the night for a feed. Dawn didn't come quickly enough, but the morning was lovely; we could see snow-caps and — unbelievably — there was frost. The children played skidding games.

Having achieved a high point, we began a long, steep, hard-on-the-knees descent. The first part of the day took us through rhododendron forest — all red trunks and peeling bark, bird calls, and purple primroses — and down to an ill-maintained suspension bridge across a thundering torrent. Sun streaming through the river spray created rainbows. We crossed gingerly, one by one. Planks were missing and others were clearly very rotten. There were odd twanging sounds as the bridge bounced under us. Even the porters edged over cautiously and Joanna, who was on her first trek, only managed to cross by focussing on the far bank and feeling for where she needed to plant her feet.

Beyond the bridge, we got into a gruesome discussion about plane crashes and the Thai air disaster in Kathmandu a couple of years before. The conversation then meandered on to jungle survival tactics, and Tsering showed us how to light a fire without matches using daphne wood. While he rolled the sticks one on another and smoke began to rise, Lorna mused, 'I so love the mountains. I've always found them solid and reliable. But do you know when I was teaching in Beergunj, I took a group of students up to Kathmandu on the bus. The girls were all from the *tarai*, and as the bus snaked up the Trisuli Valley they screamed in terror thinking that the mountains would fall down on them! I guess if you've been brought up under the big skies of the plains, sheer valleys seem claustrophobic.'

'Sorry,' I said, interrupting as I struggled to my feet. 'I need to walk on before I seize up completely.'

We'd been walking down forever, it seemed, but finally we reached another decaying suspension bridge. It was as far down as we could go, at about 1,500 metres below Mangengot. Above, at the head of the valley, there was still a little snow on the smooth U of the 4,380-metre Gosankund pass. Shadows were lengthening as we bathed our feet in a cool, clear steam. I suckled Sebastian, and Andrew appeared with the water bottle again. Lorna disappeared behind a large rock to wash. I hadn't the energy to freshen up. For the first time, I cursed having to breast-feed; it saps energy and provokes an unslakable thirst.

As Sebastian fed, I looked around and realised with horror that, having come down, we had to climb again. I chugged up on automatic pilot. The final ascent back up to Tarke Ghyang at 2,740 metres meant we'd completed 2,500 metres of climbing (up and down) that day. Why did I put myself through this? The trek I'd done just after David's birth had been painful, too. Silly, really. I didn't have anything to prove. Finally, I stumbled into the lodge and slumped, knowing that the pain would be worse after I'd rested. Alexander came bounding in. 'Look what I found! Tsering-*dai* says that this snake has changed its clothes, and I can keep its skin.'

Our stay in the village of Karkani stands out in my memory. I asked the one-legged owner of the lodge where I'd find water to wash. 'There is none.'

'How many months of the year do you have water problems here?'

'Twelve,' he answered flatly. In the chat that followed, he told us how he'd lost his leg. He'd been a politician, opposing and exposing local prostitution rackets. The Helambu Valley is well known as a centre for exporting prostitutes, although it is a problem in most regions of Nepal. About 5,000 minors are sold to Indian brothels every year so that the rest of the family can survive. It was big business, and this guy had to be silenced. The racketeers' paid thugs came in the night with an axe; it was a messy attack, but the politico survived. I said to Lorna, 'So much for the happy, smiling, carefree Nepali people.' Then, thinking out loud, 'Perhaps Ganga's story was true after all. It sounded exaggerated when I heard it from Basant. Did I ever tell you?'

'No, do. Basant's gossip is always entertaining.'

'When Basant recruited Ganga to work for us, he passed on various stories. Ganga's own mother had — he said — tried to sell her into prostitution, and that's why she'd fled from Darjeeling to Kathmandu. That's why she had been willing to work for us and — unusually — was willing to travel with us. When she first joined us, she had said that she had nothing more to lose, but wouldn't elaborate. Basant, as ever, had all sorts of theories that mostly seemed crazy, but maybe the whole thing was true. She's never spoken about it.'

By the time we were nearly down to the road again, Joanna and I were hobbling, clumsily holding hands like two little old ladies, while Tsering gently taunted us with offers of porter rides. The children soon stripped off to frolic naked in the Melamchi River while glistening turquoise damselflies dipped daintily in the water around them.

When it was time to leave, Chandra waded in and gently scooped up an armful of giggling children. Lorna, who was clearly invigorated by the trek, then entertained us with songs on the hot, dusty, bumpy, three-hour drive back into Kathmandu; she also awarded each child a medal improvised from shiny two-rupee coins.

It was great to get back. Simon and David were there in our flat. David broke off playing with his multigym to greet me with a huge grin, a head-waggle and a friendly 'dugdugdug'. Alexander did a special dance to make David laugh and was rewarded with a chuckle that degenerated into huge belly-laughs in response to another tickle-game. David's family *was* important to him! But then when David set eyes on Sebastian, a black look clouded his face, as if to say, 'Oh, you've brought *that* back too!' And he turned his back to block Sebastian from his view.

I emerged from our loo mumbling gratefully about Western toilet designs that avoided the need to crouch. My knees were so sore. It was a full two months before I could squat painlessly over a hole in the ground. 'Right, who's going to shower first? I bet we stink!' I challenged Alexander.

'Ah, you expect to wash, do you?' Simon said. 'There's no water — hasn't been for weeks apparently. Buddhi has put in a hand pump downstairs, so you can splash some groundwater over yourselves, but it smells a bit, it's a bit oily, and it turns clothes brown.'

'So that explains the odour that greeted us!' It was good to freshen up and exchange the smell of stale armpit and crutch for stagnant groundwater. While I was bathing Alexander, I discovered a tick feeding behind his left ear. It had been there some days for it had swollen from sesame-seed size to the size of a kidney bean. 'Hold still,' I said. Then as I removed the beast, Alexander said, 'What was *that*?' But I'd fired it into the toilet before it could freak him out.

A few weeks after the trek, the phone rang. 'Hello, madam, I am Gopal, general secretary of Geruwa Rural Awareness Association. I am pleased to talk to your goodself only.'

'It is nice to hear from you too, Mr Gopal.'

'Thank you, madam. I am here in Kathmandu these days. How is madam Dr Jane getting along raising funds for our clinics for the poor?'

'I haven't started. I've been waiting to hear from you — with your plans.' There was a pregnant pause. I broke the silence with, 'Actually, I'll soon be working for WaterAid, helping them design a health education package. How is *your* work going?'

'Ah, yes. We will begin soon. Yes, yes; why not?'

डे डे डे

For a month that summer we were in England again and celebrated David's second birthday there. We also attended a two-week course at Ingfield Manor's school for parents. It was run by Scope, the charity for children with cerebral palsy that used to be called the Spastics Society. This was the first time I'd had much contact — as a parent — with other families with children who had problems, and there were so many. The other children seemed unattractive, and I found the levels of disability appalling, shocking. Most children with cerebral palsy are incredibly stiff, and it is their increased muscle tone that immobilises them. They needed to be immersed in warm water before they could get their bodies working at all. One mother took two hours to feed her son at every meal. Her patience was astonishing, yet still he was painfully lean. How did she cope? What frustration these children must experience in getting anything done. What must it be like, battling with your body every minute of the day just to get it to do what you want? David had a happier, easier life; it was floppiness and lack of muscle tone that incapacitated him.

During our days together, I began to get to know these children and saw their beauty, and especially their sense of fun and mischief. I saw what strength both the children and their parents had. Soon any small achievements — by any of the children — were a reason for us all to celebrate and cheer; they gave everyone a lift. At the end of the fortnight, the boy who took two hours to eat each meal walked right across the room. The look of pride and triumph on his thin, taut little face brought tears to my eyes.

The school integrated real education with basic skills, including learning to eat, use the toilet, move and talk. It went on in a small, bright, modern gym full of music and colour, where staff used attention-grabbing tricks and were quick to compliment children on the smallest, seemingly trivial, responses. 'Good listening, David,' they said when they saw him still to speech, or 'Clever boy — you are really trying,' when his lips moved a little to imitate a sound, or 'You *are* looking nicely, David.' Suddenly I could see that he really was responding and thinking about what was going on around him. This realisation was a tremendous boost, and I cried some more happy tears.

At first, we worked only on getting David to sit unsupported, and on positions that would help him to crawl. He found lying on his stomach really difficult, yet he wouldn't try to move onto his back. We taught him to roll over, and even to use a potty. Thus far, he had seldom made any attempt to save himself if he toppled, but he started to put out his hands for balance. We encouraged him to take notice of us and especially to make eye contact, and to make sounds in response to our speech. By repeating on cue, he managed 'ah' and 'mm' sounds for the first time. And when he responded, he was rewarded with praise and flattery, with soap bubbles blown around him or with rude noises from a groan-stick. The staff had quickly caught on to David's enjoyment of weird noises. This was the first time in his life that any health professional had treated him like a person. They teased him, and even accused him of having the stubbornness of a terrible two-year-old. It seemed so strange to compare David in any way with other children of his age. But why shouldn't we? He was two.

David burbled away when we were at home together, but he was mostly silent at Ingfield, or he cried. He cried a lot there, and that gave me a knot in my stomach. This schooling was hard, exercising muscles he'd hardly ever used. Our lessons (for I was learning as much as David) lasted only until lunchtime, but often David was so exhausted by the activities that he fell asleep at his work, over his snacks or even on the potty.

I was pretty much convinced that this was good for him, but often I wondered whether struggling like this was going to help him enough. Should I leave him to his private, self-contained paradise? Could he really achieve much? Most of the time, in my heart, though, I knew that I must work with him. He was no longer a baby; he was becoming difficult to carry. He must learn to help himself. I would implement Ingfield's plans to get him mobile.

He largely ignored his lower body. He had always tended to lie with his legs flopped in a frog-like position, and when he got frustrated he moved his legs together. We worked on this, starting with musical games, imitating marching and the separate leg movements he'd need to start crawling. Slowly we built up to sitting, and then standing from sitting. The first time we got him upright was a huge struggle. He needed help from two adults because it was like trying to get a rag doll to stand; but then, as David began to realise what he could do, and I became practised in supporting him, we managed more and more easily, and for longer periods. And he could hold up his heavy head better than I would have imagined possible. When we demonstrated this marvellous standing trick back at home and it earned him applause from his grandparents, uncle, aunt and the rest of the family, he looked really pleased with himself, if flushed from the effort.

Even so, in the evenings away from the School for Parents and back with Simon, I began to wonder yet again. 'Do you think David will ever walk?'

'I don't know. He is so completely lacking in ambition.'

'I keep wondering whether we are torturing him by making him work so hard. Yet he looks so victorious looking down on Sebastian.'

'Yes — we must try ...'

The school day always ended with a snack, and David tried all sorts of new foods: mashed strawberries, banana, kiwi fruit, soft biscuits. Some were textured like Weetbix; some he was able to put to his mouth himself. He managed to feed himself sponge fingers, and he learned that he could cope with a variety of foods without gagging. He started to learn to drink from a cup, too.

Every day there were innumerable new tips. Staff pointed out, for example, that stiff children love soft textures, but that floppy children like David find hard objects attractive and reassuring; he never had liked soft toys. They showed me so much, and gave me hope, but most of all they taught me that David was a developing person, and I needed to be reminded of that.

Ingfield had equipped me with the resources and motivation to get David moving, and we left there with a program of tasks to work on. Sometimes he was very disconnected from me and from his surroundings, but now I had techniques for attracting his attention, and his sense of humour became all the more obvious. His favourite tease still was to gesture for his bottle of milk, take it, then with a big grin toss it several metres, say, 'Dad, dad,' happily and do a Nepali head-waggle.

It was marvellous to talk to the Scope experts. I happened to mention David's brothers, and how advanced Sebastian seemed. 'Is it just in comparison to David, do you think?'

'Probably not. Younger siblings of children with special needs have to be precocious. They realise early on that they have to get on with life.' That was just what Sebastian was doing. He started by crawling at the age of five months, and rapidly became very self-reliant.

That intense time with other mothers made me look at myself and realise how little care I was taking of my own appearance. The skirts and dresses that I regarded as my smart gear had become shabby, bleached by the sun, and were years behind the fashions. My hair hadn't been cut properly for a couple of years either, so I booked in at a salon in Billingshurst.

'I'd like something that's easy.' The hairdresser couldn't understand anyone not owning a hair drier.

Fortunately our friends and relations were attuned to our lifestyle in Nepal. We even met up with Mahesh and Anna. Mahesh was an old friend of Simon's, now in England with his family. Like us, they divided their time between England and Nepal. Mahesh was researching the causes of poverty. They found themselves renting a house on a former council estate. He saw how poor, stressed mothers with too many small children shout at their kids. 'It's just the same as village life in Nepal!' Then, to Simon, 'Will you never grow any fatter?' And he talked of when they'd first worked together in Dhankuta. 'I couldn't keep up with you — no-one could.'

The rest of our summer with my parents-in-law consisted of long, mellow summer days, good company, walks in Sussex beech and oak forests, strawberries and cream, newspapers, public libraries, and wine: wine that hadn't been boiled on the docks in Calcutta. We were honoured guests wherever we went, although our relatives were puzzled at our loathing of candle-lit dinners: a reminder of power-cuts in Kathmandu. Alexander — now aged five — thought that England was excellent because there was no school, although he couldn't understand why adults fussed so when he handled matches or knives. He was competent, after all.

It was a joy to push David around in a buggy on pot-hole free pavements and footpaths. He could seem in such a world of his own, but he became more animated on outings — or treks. On one farm, I watched him watching an arrogant cock chasing his hens. David was fascinated; a smile spread across his face and he began to titter, until at the next *cock-a-doodle-do* his giggles turned to belly-laughs. He laughed till he cried. His good humour was infectious, but in English strangers' eyes he was becoming increasingly ugly, a freak. They saw his over-large head, would look and then look away, and so miss his wonderful sunshine smile and mischievous sparkling blue eyes. I wondered how much of it David sensed.

CHAPTER TWENTY-EIGHT

A new home in Kathmandu

WE NOW MADE KATHMANDU OUR BASE SO THAT Alexander could start school at five. Simon continued to spend a lot of time in Rajapur, which was hard for us all, but there was plenty to recommend living in the capital. Our new home was in the south of the city, near Patan Gate. It boasted a relatively good water supply and a large garden which hid all kinds of small wildlife that made new, weird sounds to entertain David. A pair of scops owls shrieked at each other each evening. Often the owls seemed to compete with a din that sounded like an out-of-true circular saw and then faded to an extended stereo fart as the cicada ran out of breath. This really appealed to David's faecal sense of humour and made him laugh out loud. There were also squawking magpie robins and mynah birds, twittering tailorbirds, and hoopoes with their mellow *poo-poo-poo* calls. Alexander said, 'I like those birds — they're rude too!'

I loved looking out from our roof garden; the bougainvillea that climbed all the way up here attracted sunbirds. I watched street life, or gazed out to the clouds clinging onto the nearest mountain ridges, and the *himals* beyond. To the west was the deep green ridge of the Queen's Forest: it rises 1,000 metres above the valley, and we'd often go there for weekend picnics. It was so close to the city, yet leopard and wild boar lived there; from the *stupa* at the top you could see Annapurna to the west, Gauri Shankar to the east, and Swayambhu below.

Another favourite spot was the temple of Vajra Yogini. One Saturday we walked there past partying families: children dressed in their frilliest weekend-best, men getting drunk, women cooking vast quantities of *daal bhat* in enormous cauldrons over wood gathered from the forest. The revellers danced to bad Western pop music or screechy Hindi film songs blaring from huge speakers. Above them, nestling in the mature pine forest that leads right up to the rim of the valley, the temple is laid out on several levels under three golden roofs, and decorated with thunderbolts, superb mythical animals, and — incongruously — domestic pots and pans. There are waterspouts where birds, monkeys and resplendent bird-wing and swallow-tailed butterflies drink.

We sat in the top courtyard, David resting on my lap. I pulled out a plastic box and we started lunch. Suddenly there was a scuffling sound. We were surrounded. In a split second, one rhesus monkey had got Alexander's sandwich and a second was climbing over me and David to reach into the box to filch another, while a third was approaching us from behind. I threw the lunch box to one side and tried to kick the nearest thief away, but the monkeys shot back up to their vantage point on the temple roof with their spoils. Locals laughed at us. David, too, chuckled at all the excitement and my shouting, but Alexander sobbed. 'My lunch! I want my lunch back!' David realised that his brother was upset, and his mirth melted into puzzlement and a pout.

'Don't worry, Alexander,' I said. 'Look, David thought that the monkeys were funny, and we've got plenty of food; we'll just have to go straight on to our pudding.'

'Mmm, pudding.' Apple turnovers cheered Alexander, but he kept watch nervously while he ate.

We walked down to the medieval village of Sankhu and, in no rush to get back, we stopped to ask, 'Which is the path to Changu Narayan?'

'If you are going to Kathmandu, you take a bus from here. The road is good now. Why go up there?'

'We like eating the air,' Simon said.

'Why? It is not necessary. Catch a bus!'

On the climb up, a group of Chhetri women carrying baskets of manure slung from headbands stopped to smile at David, who was snugly tucked up in his papoose. One woman wanted to talk; she was breathing harder than the others and looked anaemic. 'Your baby is how old, *didi*?'

'Two.'

'My youngest son is one. Take him. He will be a good friend for your boy.' She'd seen David's problems and was offering us a companion-servant. 'Take my son so that he will not have to spend his life shifting manure, *didi*. Take him to a good life in your country!' How incredibly sad that offer made me feel. She looked really tired. We climbed on up and into the carved courtyard of the medieval retreat that was the temple. Here I admired the meticulously sculpted fifth-century Garuda, the birdlike mount of Vishnu. There was also a superb seventeenth-century relief of a king and his queen on elephant back. Despite the distractions, though, I couldn't get this desperate mother out of my head. She haunted me. I still think of her now.

At home most mornings, I awoke to the sound of a temple bell, and often incense floated in through the mosquito screens of our bedroom window. From there we could watch the dawn worshippers lighting earthenware butter lamps, sprinkling petals and scented water, placing flowers and vermilion powder offerings to the shrine to a wonderfully happy-looking, pot-bellied Ganesh. The bell never seemed to stop ringing. The English couple who'd lived here before us moved out because the temple bell disturbed them. I loved this piece of real Nepal so close and visible, and Ganesh looked particularly magisterial when people lit candles around him after dark. Religion here wasn't yet only for the older generation. Even cool-looking youths in leather jackets, slicked-back hair and designer sunglasses who pedalled expensive mountain bikes would pause to genuflect before the elephant-headed deity.

Our shrine was attended by a neighbour. He walked awkwardly and had a wide-eyed anxious-looking expression, from disobedient muscles drawing his face into tension. He had cerebral palsy and was close to God, hence his role. He was always laughing, friendly and seemed carefree, but I had trouble understanding his jerky, slurred Nepali. Another man who was horribly disfigured by neuro-fibromatosis — the elephant man's affliction — ran a shop locally; everyone was used to the shocking appearance of a face with dangling bits of extra flesh. Our neighbours never even took a second glance. How much better and more normal this seemed than our habit in the West of expecting everyone to be physically and mentally perfect. Why do we tidy imperfect people away out of sight in institutions?

Soon after we moved into our grand city house as Ganesh's neighbour, a strange rumour started circulating — that the universally popular Ganesh wanted to drink milk; suddenly every Ganesh-*tan* had queues of people trying to get him to drink. There were white puddles everywhere and a city-wide shortage of fresh milk. The street dogs thought they'd reached *nirvana*. No-one knew where the rumour had started, but everybody accepted it as the truth: there were articles in the newspapers about it. No-one questioned it.

Another odd event emphasised just how different this community was to the lowlands. I was awoken around midnight by shouting and drum-banging. It sounded urgent, but I couldn't make out what was being said, for the words were Newar. I looked out to see a lunar eclipse. I asked Basant about it in the morning. 'Moon was ill last night. A dragon was eating it and low-caste peoples shout and make noises with drums. Noise is medicine for moon.'

'But surely there is no caste amongst Newar Buddhists, Basant-*dai*?'

'We have twenty-six castes, *memsahib:* three castes of priests, then merchants — Shresthas like me only — craftsmen, farmers, potters, barbers, blacksmiths, mens that help with dead body, gardeners, musicians, tailors, drum-makers and sweepers. Maybe I forget some ...

This new culture was impenetrable, and the Newar language was also impossible. I had been able to get the gist of the Indo–European Tharu and Hindi languages — there was vocabulary in common with Nepali — but there was nothing recognisable in Tibeto–Burman Newar. Newars have kept control of the city (and government bureaucracy) by using their difficult language, and through nepotism.

By now, Sebastian was sitting up and keen to be on the move. Eating as much food as he was offered, he was very content and a very vigorous little thug. He loved tormenting David whenever my back was turned or I was out of the room. David was as smiley as ever in his new home, cheering us up with his unfailing good humour — until Sebastian pulled his hair.

David's three big pleasures in life were his multigym, getting one up on Sebastian and eating. Gourmet-like, he'd minutely examine his hand deciding which particular fingers he should suck: thumb and index finger together were his favourites. He grew chubbier with more choices of foods, and whenever Ganga lifted him into his special chair to eat, he would almost burst with excitement. As she approached with a bowl of thick soup, his exuberance was hilarious. He'd start laughing and would wave his arms with such excitement that only the straps of his chair stopped him doing a head-dive onto the floor. The chair was good for keeping David involved too. Although he still had great difficulty moving food around his mouth and so ate little of the meals we enjoyed, he could at least sit up at the table and join in with the prattle that accompanied supper. He always looked as if he was processing everything that was said.

David seemed so well that I felt confident to leave him and Sebastian with Ganga for a couple of hours when the VSO and the Peace Corps asked me to help with occasional lectures. Debbie, the American nurse, would give an embarrassingly glowing introduction.

'Dr Jane has actually *lived* in the *gaw* for two years with three small children. She *really* knows Nepal and she knows what you all are going to face out there.' She talked of the *gaw* as if Nepal was divided into Kathmandu and 'the village'. Each batch of sixty or so wide-eyed, newly arrived volunteers seemed more anxious than the last. They kept asking about snakes, seemingly not believing me when I said they are rarely seen and seldom cause trouble except amongst agricultural workers. 'You do need to know about mosquitoes and ticks,' I said, as I projected an image of Alexander's tick. I showed them a photograph of a colourful blister beetle too. 'Their secretions cause inflammation and sometimes blistering about twelve hours after contact, but Nepali species cause a mild reaction. I tried crushing one on my forearm and it caused a slightly itchy reddened area.' Then, to a bewildered-looking volunteer sitting in the front row, 'Do you disapprove of scientific investigation? You're looking at me as if you think I'm insane!'

'No, I don't *think* you're crazy. I *know* you're crazy!'

We lived in a quiet neighbourhood, close to the British School and the International Club. I could socialise freely with Western friends now. Ganga, too, seemed happy with the change, and soon made friends locally. Alexander and I would cycle around the winding back-streets avoiding the congested parts of the city, enjoying the sunshine, catching wafts of flower perfumes or mouth-watering spicy smells from kitchens, watching a mother oiling a baby or removing headlice, a carpenter at work, children playing *chungi*. We often got punctures, but there was always a bicycle shop close-by where — for a few rupees — someone would fix it. The way these mechanics worked had exasperated me when I first came to Nepal. They'd undo various nuts and bolts, drop them into the roadside dust, and then a lad would be ordered to pick them up. It had all seemed so inefficient — but now I saw that it provided training and employment for the apprentice.

Living in Kathmandu gave me lots of opportunities to work once more. I helped at a free clinic near the huge *stupa* at Bauddha and this work drew me into contact with the poor and destitute of Kathmandu.

Few of my patients' problems were soluble with medicines. One woman sticks in my memory. She said, 'There is a ball in my stomach. Take it away, *huzoor*.' I examined her and said gently, 'You know that you are pregnant?'

'There is no pregnancy, *huzoor*.'

'Where is your husband?'

'Gone. He left three months ago.'

'And you have four other children?'

'True, *huzoor*.'

'Where will you have the baby?'

'There is no baby, *huzoor*.' This poor woman had no husband, no money and soon there would be five little mouths to feed. She was desperate and just didn't want this baby to be born.

'Where will you give birth?'

'It is not known, *huzoor*.'

We offered to help get the baby adopted, but she never came back. She, more than anyone, also made me realise how badly poor Nepali woman needed access to family planning clinics — to liberate them from the consequences of unlimited fertility.

A Scotsman turned up at the clinic, asking for help for a friend. He was a Buddhist monk, fresh from a two-month retreat; he radiated tranquillity. 'So, why isolate yourself like that?' I asked.

'To learn. I had a lot of anger and it was unhealthy. I got tremendous outbursts of rage during the retreat, against my mother, the girlfriend that dumped me, my brother — but especially my mother. Slowly I realised that the anger was within me: it was pointless being bitter about the way other people had treated me. So I began to understand my anger, accept it and it then stopped being a problem. Now I am peaceful.'

'And it took two months for that realisation?'

'Yes, but retreats can be for even longer; those who will become high *lamas* spend longer in meditation. Two of my friends have been bricked up in a house; food is posted in through a slot and they will stay there alone for two years; they don't even wash.'

Expats working for an American family-planning charity asked me to join them, but I was soon disillusioned because they were such a long way from understanding any of the problems they purported to be solving. They wanted to offer counselling to couples before they consented to being sterilised. On the face of it, this seemed like a worthy goal, but the village wisdom about sterilisation was that it didn't work, it hurt, wound infections were common and sometimes women died after the operation. With that sort of information circulating, no amount of American-style counselling would convince people. I started looking at the clinical facilities and often found congealed month-old blood on operating tables. We needed to improve the quality of medical care before getting obsessed about counselling, but my bosses wouldn't consider a change of focus, even if it would save lives. Perhaps if my worries about David hadn't made me emotional, I could have had the patience to convince them. Perhaps if Simon had been around more, he'd have calmed me down. Maybe I needed a two-month Buddhist retreat.

Later when I got a chance to rant to Simon about the organisation, he said, 'Yes, but good work is being done, too — remember that surgeon you told me about who was so skilled that he could operate painlessly with very little anaesthetic?'

'But his work was exceptional, and it's overshadowed by doctors like that gorilla in Beergunj who slaps patients during their operations! Do you know he said that lower castes don't suffer pain in the same way as we do! He really believed it, too.'

'Hmm, did you know that there is no word for empathy in Nepali?' Simon said.

'That doesn't surprise me. At another clinic, we got onto the subject of litigation. The maximum awarded for negligence is only 500 rupees, so relatives lynch sloppy surgeons. One doctor told me that if an operation is going badly wrong, it is best to run away rather than linger and try to save the patient. Perhaps inbred Hindu fatalism stops doctors preparing for complications. It'd never occurred to me that a culture of litigation could be an influence for good.'

'Yes. In Nepal you are not allowed to learn from mistakes. It is the same in engineering too. But don't only focus on the problems — it's lack of quality control that's upsetting you, and that's a problem in the National Health Service, too. Surely, most Nepali patients are helped by the family-planning services? I hear that even Arjun is considering a vasectomy the next time there's a family-planning camp in Rajapur!'

'If you believe that ... But, anyway, what if one of our friends died because of carelessness? Imagine if Guliya died and left poor disorganised Arjun to raise all his children?'

'There is a lot of good stuff going on. Compare that to William's groundwater project, which — eight years on — hasn't drilled a single tubewell because the World Bank's priorities have changed.'

'I guess you're right; I wish I had your patience. Say, did anyone ever take any notice of that work you did on the Bagmati Basin strategy when we first came to Nepal?'

'No, of course not. Most of our proposed solutions were written off as culturally insensitive.' Recommendations made by Simon's team had actually been quietly implemented, though without reference to their work. One suggestion was a sewage treatment works upstream of Pashupati, the temple complex where Hindu pilgrims from all over India come to bathe and where people are cremated beside the holy, festering Bagmati River. The 'culturally insensitive' sewage works was completed seven years later.

Simon skilfully changed the subject to a less emotional topic. 'Talking of family planning — look at this in the *Kathmandu Post!*' The headline read, 'Man gets son after 11 daughters'. The proud father was quoted: 'It was my fond desire as well as compulsion to beget such a large number of children due to illiteracy and ignorance.'

CHAPTER TWENTY-NINE

over the jalja pass

BY THE TIME THAT THE OCTOBER DESAI FESTIVAL came around again, we had the confidence to try a trek right away from the usual tourist routes. This time I'd take a comprehensive medical kit. Alexander and I peddled through Patan Gate and into the labyrinth of brick-paved alleyways of the medieval city, and propped our bicycles outside a tiny pharmacy with tonics and medicine packets stacked tightly from floor to ceiling. It was good to be reminded of one positive outcome of aid to the country: quality, affordable basic medicines that had been made in Nepal. The plump, cheery Newar shopkeeper pulled out an assortment of drugs while expertly attending to other customers. One bought an Elastoplast for a gashed finger, another came for a single throat lozenge, and another for a strip of ten paracetamol tablets. Between dealing with the immediate needs of his other customers, he put together little paper bags containing a few doses of antihistamines, antibiotics, antiseptic, dressings, injectable emergency drugs and syringes. It cost me the equivalent of $5.

A day's drive west of Kathmandu, Baglung town nestles amongst the forested 'middle hills'. It looks down on the swollen Kali Gandaki 200 metres below.

'Remember walking here before there was a road?' Simon asked.

'Ooh, are we going that way?' Alexander said, and charged down the narrow footpath. He tripped, got up, and continued on down, chasing a swallow-tailed butterfly as big as my hand. He fell over again, got up, but this time he was crying. He'd landed in some nettles.

A stooped old woman was picking nettles using bamboo chopsticks; this was free food that she'd cook as a spinach dish. She saw Alexander fall and approached with a handful of scruffy-looking weeds. 'Rub this *titepati* in; it stops the pain.' He understood and obeyed without comment, and it did help.

It was aromatic and I realised it was artemisia: the basis of a malaria cure discovered in China 3,000 years ago and newly rediscovered by the West. Simon caught up and said, 'This is a useful plant. People also shove it up their noses — as a headache cure. Personally, though, I prefer swallowing a paracetamol.' By this time, Alexander's pain had gone and I thanked the woman. It took a few more moments before she realised that we could communicate, but then she asked me, 'Who is the father of your children?'

'The *bideshi*,' I said, pouting at Simon.

'And the other men?'

'I only need one husband,' I grinned.

'Even one is too many,' she cackled in agreement. I heard David's responsive laugh and turned to see Kanchha Lama approaching; he was carrying David in a specially made *dhaka*, an extra-wide conical bamboo basket slung from a headband.

David was protected from the sun with some tasteless purple flowery dress material, but innumerable village women wanted to remove it to peek inside. He loved the attention and Kanchha Lama also seemed to enjoy the reflected glory, answering all the inevitable questions. How old? When had he had the harelip repaired? Were babies in England always carried like this? Sometimes when we stopped for a rest a whole gaggle of giggling women would crowd round to admire him. David dealt kindly with his fans, chuckling back at them and offering a 'dad, dad, dad — oh, dad, dad, dad'. One admirer came to talk; she looked intellectual because she wore glasses. 'My son brought them from Pokhara.' Only then did it occur to me how unusual it was to see village Nepalis wearing glasses; many of the older people must be half-blind for want of spectacles.

The other porters mercilessly teased Kanchha Lama, not because he was doing women's work by carrying David, but because he wasn't very bright. He was short, solid, as strong as a buffalo, but astonishingly gentle with David. As soon as he was off duty, he'd pick fights with the other porters. They were all obsessed with wrestling, competing to roll over impossibly huge boulders or inventing other trials of strength. And whenever they saw oxen or buffaloes fighting — even in a field 200 metres below us — they would cheer them on to further violence.

Lakpa Sherpa, who carried Sebastian, was — by contrast — mild and charming. He was an 'old' man of forty whom everyone called Grandfather and he sang Sebastian soothing Sherpa love songs. Kipa Sherpa was our *sirdar*, with young Ang Kaji as his sidekick. There was also Kaji the cook (known as 'Real' Kaji), who had a helper called 'Spare' Kaji, and so with the porters who carried the tents and other luggage we were a big party: twenty-one in all. It seemed decadent, but we were providing easy, well-paid employment where employment opportunities were poor. Two of our team were an affectionate young couple; she was disabled by curvature of her spine from TB.

She carried our month's supply of eggs. They spoke of their troubles in finding work: since the footpath had been improved, traders found mules cheaper, more reliable and not likely to go on strike like human porters. I wondered how this couple would manage in future, because she was weak and wouldn't have coped with a normal, twelve-hour portering day.

Our pace was leisurely; we stopped often for Alexander to play or to pick himself up after falling again, to rest, to feed the babies, or to rescue things that David had lobbed out of his basket. The frequent pauses allowed the porters to gamble, fight and sing. The team seemed to treat the trek like one long party. Two of the three Kajis made flutes by whittling bamboo as they walked; they'd meticulously craft an instrument only to chuck it into the path-side undergrowth, mumbling, '*Krap ho.*' Soon they'd start anew on another, until they were satisfied with the sound. Then they made enchanting, fluid music to accompany the singers.

Rajiv, who had brought a *madal*, also played. It was such a contrast to the atmosphere on our first trip with a troubled, bitter untouchable and an inhibited Brahmin for whom music and indeed anything stimulating (alcohol, sex, chillies) was sinful. Brahmins were not even allowed to eat boiled stinging nettles — they might be too exciting. The Sherpas seemed to get more out of life, and it was amazing what they could make. Alexander wanted to use a *khukuri* and so they carved one out of wood, and then a rifle, and a short Roman sword too. David amused himself in his basket with three bells on a bright yellow handle, or a teddy rattle.

Clouds still clung to the higher slopes of the surrounding mountains: the monsoon was slow to dissipate that year. Homes were freshly replastered for the Desai festival. They were whitewashed on the top half, with a coating of rich, sunset-red laterite clay below. Several village shops displayed what looked like dishcloths, except that they were puce and orange and sticky; they were made by mixing flour, water, sugar and colour, and squeezing it through a shaper.

Alexander said, 'They look sigusting!'

Like Christmas at home, this festival is the time when families get together; people working in Kathmandu and Pokhara walked home to their villages. The men carried nothing while women struggled behind, bent under luggage and children. For the festivities, most villages had constructed huge swings, each made from four giant bamboo poles and plaited grass rope. We stopped often to watch older kids in formidable competitions to see who could swing highest. Younger children kept a safe distance for fear of being flattened by the *lingi ping*; instead, toddlers amused themselves in shot-putting contests with huge boulders. Alexander was invited to try, but they laughed at his incompetence and timidity. When we next stopped to rest at a *chautara*, he wanted to practise swinging — on the aerial roots of the *banyan* tree.

Early on the third day, we reached one of many places in Nepal that are called Phedi, and a steep 500-metre climb had me minutely examining flowers again — as an excuse to slow down and catch my breath. It was marvellous to see how little soil the so-called forest killer *Osbeckia* needed to thrive; its dog-rose-shaped, purple-pink flowers peeked out everywhere from brick-hard clay. The steep path took us into fine pine forest with white and purple wood anemones and geraniums carpeting the ground; chunky grey lizards with yellow spots watched us walk by. Outside one hamlet, an emaciated woman lay in the sun. She had a hacking, wracking cough; it was too late for treatment: she was dying of TB.

Fields and terraces were brimming with drooping rice that whispered in the breeze. In Rajapur, the harvest would be well underway, but at this altitude the crop was only just turning golden. All flattish ground was under cultivation, so there were few places to camp.

We pitched on one rare vacant area, by the primary school. We peeked inside the five small, empty classrooms to see puddles in the packed-mud floors. The only facilities were blackboards and bits of timber for children to sit on. Alexander, who now attended the British School in Kathmandu with its computers and huge library, was astonished that this could be a school. Some boys snuck up and shouted, 'You are *queerie*!' and ran off, giggling at their boldness.

One of the few challenges on this trek was finding shade for David when we stopped in the hot, glary middle of the day, because the sun hurt his eyes. In Lumsum village, there was no shade anywhere except beside a large, new building. It was not until we'd settled David on a groundsheet that I realised that this was the clinic. 'When will the health assistant come?' I asked waiting patients.

'*Docter-sahib* is visiting his family in Jhapa.'

'Jhapa — but that's way out east in the *tarai*.'

'It *is* far. He may come after one or two weeks.' Yet still they waited.

I turned to Simon. 'This government health assistant has just deserted these people — what are his patients supposed to do while he's away?'

'Don't be too critical,' Simon reasoned. 'He works without back-up or support and never has a proper break, so why shouldn't he visit his parents at the equivalent of Christmas?'

Vacillating about whether to admit that I was a doctor, I eyed up a man whom I could tell — even from across the courtyard — had pneumonia. Sweat poured off him, and he was breathing hard. I cursed not bringing more antibiotics. I said nothing. Then I realised that our *sirdar*, Kipa, was 'treating' a patient whom I had not even noticed. She lay, a tiny, emaciated, ragged heap, at the feet of the man with pneumonia — her father. She was about five and also had pneumonia. 'Oral rehydration sachets won't help her, Kipa, but I have the right treatment in the medical kit I've brought for my children.'

I dripped antibiotic syrup into her mouth while explaining how the rest must be given. Her father was so ill and listless that he didn't seem to be listening.

Then Father said to me, 'I need medicine also, *huzoor*.'

'There is none,' I said, still feeling uncomfortable at the unapologetic way Nepali is spoken.

'That,' he said pointing with his pouting lips, 'is the wife of *docter-sahib* — she has the key.' The health post was surprisingly well-stocked with an excellent range of basic medicines. Magnanimously, I gave him a course of antibiotics. As I explained how he should take them, I repeated what he needed to do to save his daughter's life, but he was busy ranting about how it needed a *bideshi* to come to help and why wasn't the government man here.

He was angry, yet the longer I spent in the developing world the more I realised that doctors are not as useful as people think. Most medical problems do not really have medical solutions. Medicine merely patches people up, to suffer again. I might have 'saved' the five-year-old that time, but I doubt that the child survived for long. As an outsider passing through, it is easy to convince yourself that you are doing good by handing out medicines, but there is no easy cure for poverty.

Other people hopefully sidled up and, as I hurriedly packed up and tried to leave, I made quick assessments of the rest of the patients: a woman with a few septic spots; a man with an old cut on his leg, which was healing well; a boy with a slight cough; a girl with scabies. None of them were in desperate need. I fled, shouting, 'Give the child lots to drink.'

Now all the porters knew that I was a doctor. Stimulated by this revelation, spotty young Ang Kaji complained to me of a sore leg. Expecting to see a pimple or two, I offered to treat it, but he pulled up his trouser leg to reveal a tense, swollen, infected knee. I was amazed he could walk at all, let alone carry a heavy load. I said he must take the one course of antibiotics in Kipa's medical kit, and suggested that he rest. 'Of course he cannot rest!' Kipa said, but some of Ang Kaji's load was redistributed amongst the others.

By the time we stopped at our fifth campsite, near the village of Moreni at an altitude of 2,590 metres, the air was chilly. Passing a huddle of simple wooden-roofed houses with rocks on top to stop the tiles blowing away in storms, we watched a Pun Magar family ploughing a rare patch of flat ground. An unpleasant array of tweezers and implements for excavating bodily orifices and plucking out nose hairs were tied around the man's neck. The Annapurnas were in view now and, ahead, a forest of sinuous red-barked rhododendrons; looking out between the trees, we caught increasingly spectacular views of the *himals*. Finally, we reached the gently rounded Jalja La, a pass at 3,414 metres where we camped on short grass, seemingly only one ridge away from Dhaulagiri *himal*.

The wind up there upset David. If the breeze blew in his face, it provoked a primitive diving reflex and he acted as if he was drowning. His expression reminded me of the faces he made in those early days in hospital when he vomited so much. I cuddled him close until the tents were up. As soon as he was inside, he was happy again, chuckling at the flapping sounds as the wind tugged at the tent. These sounds were a lullaby for us all.

Next morning, there was frost on the ground and the view of the mountains against clear, blue skies was stunning. The glistening white horseshoe of Annapurna looked far and small now; closer, lower interlocking misty ridges appeared more impressive. Dhaulagiri, that whale of a mountain carved out of ice and black rock, seemed only an hour's walk away, although it would have taken days to reach.

The morning sun was warming, and I was so invigorated by the view that I was inspired to wash my hair. 'Spare' Kaji boiled up some water on the Primus stove, and I knelt over a bowl and poured water over my head with a tin mug. It was delicious getting clean again — from the neck up, anyway. I couldn't understand, though, why the comb wouldn't go through my hair. It wasn't usually a problem. Then I noticed a tinkling sound as I moved, and realised that my hair was frozen. This was the sort of altitude where people say that by lying with your head in the sun and feet in the shade, you could get sunstroke and frostbite simultaneously.

We were in a birders' paradise: rufous-bearded tit, Himalayan goldfinch, white-browed fly-catcher, chestnut-bellied blue rock thrush and beautiful niltava popped in and out of the low rhododendron forest. There were meadows of ground orchids, geraniums, primulae and gentians. The forest on the sheltered, drier side of the pass was a mix of magnificent maples in autumn colours, majestic hemlocks, gigantic juniper, blue pine and silver fir: stately trees, so tall it was hard to see to the tops. Beneath, the air smelt of pine and ancient wood, and it was green, so green. Even boulders and tree trunks were covered with a cosy blanket of moss; ferns and orchids sprouted from every available crevice and Himalayan pied woodpeckers played peek-a-boo.

The eighth day saw us looking down into the wide lake-bed that is the Dhorpatan valley at 3,000 metres. Braided, gravelly streams and rivers flowed through a bleak peat-bog grazed by a few stocky ponies whose manes and tails blew in the cutting wind. Otherwise, the valley was strangely deserted; nearly all the people who cultivate this area flee to lower altitudes as soon as they have dug up their potato crop. Whole families were walking out with most of their possessions in a single conical basket slung from a headband: chickens rode on top, toddlers on shoulders, wooden yoghurt pots dangled from belts and nose-hair tweezers dangled around each man's neck. Some led cows wearing bamboo muzzles to stop them browsing.

To cross the wide, sweeping valley we had to wade through four fast-flowing, painfully cold, thigh-deep rivers. The bed of the biggest was a mass of large, smooth, slippery boulders. I began to cross gingerly. Seeing me hesitate, Pemba plunged in, his feet also slipping off the boulders, but he was so very strong that it did not slow him down one bit. He grabbed my elbow and started dragging me across while I shouted '*Bistarai*!' ('Slowly!') On wet, spongy, dryish land again, I watched in awe as majestic golden eagles played on updraughts high above us.

From Dhorpatan, we took a four-day detour west to the village of Sera. We were soon in the still air and welcome shelter of a deep, steep-sided valley. Forest grew luxuriant and lovely again. There were conkers for Alexander to collect, and the porters stopped often to crack open walnuts. Where there were no trees, grassland was dotted with blue gentians, poppy-red potentilla and lilac-coloured dandelions. Kipa told me that the red-berried cotoneaster made a particularly good pot-scourer. This side-valley was precipitous, so that the path was forced over spurs and tacked back and forth across the river. Suspension bridges had been built by slinging wires as thick as my wrist between masonry bulwarks. Plumbeous redstarts and men worked the cold, clear river; in places it poured through elaborately channelled bamboo fish-traps, but all people seemed to catch were five-centimetre-long tiddlers.

The Kham Magar people of the village of Sera lived in two- and three-storey flat-roofed houses with dark, rank alleyways where pigs snuffled, searching for scraps and worse. Alexander picked up a fifteen-centimetre woven bamboo tray. When someone is ill, the badness is enticed onto the tray with some rice and other goodies, and then the whole thing is thrown out of the house. There were lots lying on the paths. Locals were horrified that he had picked one up; he'd now catch the exorcised disease.

We considered walking down to the East-West Highway near Balubhang, a route that looked short and easy on the map, but would mean climbing several high passes. It would be quicker to return via Dhorpatan, and so, reluctantly, we decided to retrace our steps. The police, too, seemed anxious for us to leave. They were unusually distracted, rather than being amused by meeting foreigners with children. A few months later, helicopter gunships were deployed against Maoists, and the area became a battlefield.

The porters had arrived back in Dhorpatan far ahead of us, and the tents were already up when we arrived. The wind seemed to be doing its best to flatten them again. I asked Kipa, 'What made you choose this place to camp?' wondering if proximity to a tea shop that sold whisky had influenced his decision.

'I thought that you would be interested. This is the source of the holy River Ganga.'

I pointed towards an unscenic soggy patch where water spouts discharged into the peat bog. 'What? Those spouts that are dribbling water over there?'

'Yes: there are eleven.'

'But surely the source is in India?'

'This is the true source of the holy Ganga.' The porters unloaded the babies into tents and David was soon laughing loudly at the sounds of the tents flapping. Local children arrived to stare and a boy shouted, 'There are babies in every tent! Come see!' Another boy peered into our latrine tent to check if it was true.

The next day we strode over a low pass and caught up with many of the Dhorpatan summer residents in the village of Bobang, where they spend the winter. The closer we got to the road, the more Nepali travellers we saw, too. Now that the Diwali festivities were over, people were leaving their villages and returning to the cities again. Foreheads were covered with puce or vermilion yoghurt and raw rice *tikka* to ensure a fortuitous journey. One particular family, with lurid rice dripping off their foreheads, stopped on the path to share a snack. Alexander approached, interested. 'Would you like some *churpi*, *babu*?' they offered.

'Dinus didi,' he politely accepted; he popped a tiny piece into his mouth, pulled a face and said, 'Aggh! *Jiskaune mansi*!'

'Why do you think they are teasing you, Alexander?' I smiled.

'They've given me a stone to eat ... and look, they're laughing now!'

'*Churpi* is smoked cheese,' Simon explained. 'You put it into your cheek to soften it. It's good travelling food because it lasts so long!' Alexander spat it out and the family laughed even louder.

By the time we'd walked as far as Gulmi, I could have continued forever, except that we were running out of luxuries and Simon was pining for coffee. He was optimistic about buying more, though, since this was Nepal's main coffee-growing region. He kept disappearing into village shops. 'Any luck?' I asked him.

'Nope, but I gave my *salaams* to Queen Elizabeth and Prince Philip — or rather, their portraits inside that shop. Seems funny to see the British royal family here and not King Birendra and Queen Aishwarya. The shop belongs to the family of a Gurkha soldier.'

We came to a grubby office with a straggly coffee tree growing outside and a rusting sign announcing the Coffee Development

Board. Simon asked where he could buy coffee locally. They said, 'We don't drink *that* stuff here! Local farmers can't sell it for much, so it all goes down to Bhairahawa and then to India.'

The last few campsites were idyllic, grassy terraces within a few metres of various fast-flowing rivers that — now we were low enough — were warm enough to swim in. Finally, on the nineteenth day, we caught the night bus from Ridi bazaar and reached Kathmandu at nine the next morning.

It was excellent to get home to fresh bread, butter and marmalade and good Nepali coffee. We'd all been invigorated by the trek. David was tanned and chubby. His chit-chat and chuckles said that he felt good too. As soon as we got into the house, I reinstalled him on the quilt under his favourite toy, the A-framed multigym, and he returned immediately to his beloved game of batting the dangling toys above him. As I bathed Alexander, I lost count at forty-two grazes and scars on his legs — but his enthusiasm was unscathed.

'When will we go trekking again?' he asked.

CHAPTER THIRTY

expats and fireworks

A GURKHA SOLDIER SALUTED AS WE DROVE THROUGH the huge steel gates and into the British Embassy compound for the Guy Fawkes celebrations on November the fifth; we'd left Sebastian at home asleep with Ganga. We sauntered into the garden to join a surprising number of the British community, along with a few Anglophiles. Many of the non-British seemed bemused as they watched the guys being piled onto a three-metre-high bonfire. I suppose that incinerating life-sized effigies of a man who tried to kill a bad king *was* odd. It seemed even stranger so far from home. As it was ignited, an American voice said, 'Now, this is *real* weird!' Even Brits were unnerved when one of the guys — a teacher at the British School who was now feeling a little too warm — leapt off the pyre and ran into the bar.

Two Gurkha officers announced the start of the fireworks display by setting off dozens of firecrackers. It sounded like machine-gun fire. Most of the children screamed and ran inside. David, though, sitting close to the action and fascinated by the flames, started laughing at the first bang and guffawed at every explosion or outburst of shrieking from the other children. He loved it. And when a very large firework came powering through the crowd, narrowly missing his pushchair, he almost exploded with exuberance. He was the only child who enjoyed the fireworks.

Bonfire night coincides with the festivals of Tihar and Laxmi *pujaa* when people light candles all around the outside of their houses to entice in the goddess of wealth. Like the tooth fairy, Laxmi leaves coins under children's pillows. In a country where the legal tender is a range of exceedingly grubby notes that are rumoured to give people typhoid, the appearance of a stash of shiny coins *is* miraculous. On the first day of the festival, good Hindus leave food out for crows. Then, on the second day, dogs are honoured: mangy mutts wander the streets, wearing marigold garlands, wondering why they're being fed rather than kicked. On the third day, Alexander nearly fell off his bicycle when he saw people painting a cow red; others were garlanding her and feeding her rice and sweets.

All through the celebrations, Kathmandu is loud and beautiful; brass bands roam the streets and, with firecrackers and rockets firing everywhere, the atmosphere can seem more like a battle zone than a religious festival, but it was all much to David's continuing glee. Supervised by David in his little cane chair, we lit some fireworks up on our roof garden. Randomly exploding rockets were by far the most exciting. One fired backwards into the bottom of the flower vase we were using as a launching pad, and another changed course immediately after launching, tore through the jasmine and narrowly missed entering a neighbour's window. David was delighted.

Ganga usually stayed with us in our palatial house, but while we'd been away trekking, she'd spent time with the man whom she called her husband. He was probably her senior by thirty years. He'd come to our flat in Naxal a few times saying that he couldn't live without her, but each time he was so drunk that he could hardly stand, and since — at that time — Ganga clearly didn't reciprocate the emotion, Simon sent him away. Whatever had happened before, though, it was clear that she was in love again. She giggled breathlessly when she talked of him, and she now braved the tongue of his first wife and took time off at the weekends to be with her 'husband'. Meanwhile, the other wife phoned frequently to give me bulletins on her latest crises that always centred around the fact that Ganga didn't do any work in *her* house. The woman was excruciating; her high-pitched whining gave me earache, and I began to pretend I couldn't speak Nepali.

As the weeks went by, Ganga's girth started to increase. 'Does your husband know about the baby that is coming?'

'He knows. He is very happy, *memsahib*.'

'Are you happy?'

'I am happy, *memsahib*.' I worried for her. She seemed so streetwise, but then I'd catch a glimpse of a naive little girl and was shocked to remember she was still a teenager. 'Has he ever hit you?'

'He is not like that. He is always kind to me, *memsahib*. Only the senior wife is a problem.'

'If you need any help, or if you want to stay here with the baby, or if you want me to arrange for you to see a doctor, all these are your choices. We will help with money or anything, but be sure that it is your decision: one that will make you happy.' And 'If you stay with him, does he have enough money for two wives and another child?'

'Money he has plenty, *memsahib*.' I sensed that she was planning to leave us.

डे डे डे

Simon had taken another phone call at 6 am, and when I surfaced from my sleep-deprived stupor I asked, 'Another irrigation emergency, then?'

'Not today.' Then, casually as you like, 'Was there an earthquake last night?'

'Ha ha, very funny. I know my desk is a mess, but it's not that bad.'

'No, I'm serious. Wasn't there a tremor? Did you really not feel it?'

'No. One little snuffle from Sebastian or David at the other end of the house and I'm wide awake, but earthquakes … why should I wake up for an earthquake? I'm knackered, don't you know.' I felt ugly and irritable.

Basant arrived to take Simon to work, and he was amazed we were so calm about the tremor. 'In Asan, every bodies ran outside crying. Everyone was thinking this was big earthquake again. My Mummy, she still remember the bad earthquake in the year 1990.'

'Wow — not many years ago …'

'No, not Common Era … this was before I born, maybe sixty years before. My Mummy young girl then. Everything fells down. Lot of peoples die. It was very horrible. Then last night my Mummy think it happening again.'

'Do you think there will be another quake soon?'

'Nobody know, *memsahib*. Nobody know,' said Basant, with a huge, careless grin.

Other slight tremors followed, and there was a lot of talk about the big quake that was overdue. At school, Alexander did earthquake drill. When he and his classmates heard the siren they had to dive under their desks with their hands over their heads — not that it would do much good. It was a tense time: while traditionally designed buildings will withstand quakes, Kathmandu's innumerable new reinforced-concrete high-rises, which were constructed with as little cement as possible, would collapse like houses of cards if there was any significant seismic activity. What could we do, though? I was as fatalistic as a Nepali, although I did boost my medical kit. The quake never came.

I reconnected with Mary. Alexander asked about her son, 'If Michael is two and David is two — why can't he walk and play like Michael?'

'David has been ill, but he's doing well getting up on his feet these days, isn't he?'

'Yes, that's fun. He always laughs when we clap him!' This was the first time that five-year-old Alexander had spoken about David being different. David had developed his own unique technique for moving about. Lying on his back, he'd bend up at the waist, raise his legs above his head and then flick himself around as his legs came down to the floor again, and thus he banana-rolled around the floor at surprising speeds. Sometimes, if I'd been out of the room for a while, he'd have disappeared from his quilt and travelled several metres to a more interesting part of the house. He seemed happy on his explorations, and was untroubled about lying on the hard wooden floor, but then staff at Ingfield School had explained that floppy children feel secure against hard surfaces.

David also developed an amusing technique for dealing with his arch-enemy, Sebastian, who had already achieved a great deal of mobility. At eleven months of age, he was an accomplished climber, summiting two metres of security bars with calm competence. He'd also adopted an endearing upright glide on one knee, so that he looked as if he was cruising around looking for someone to propose to. The technique enabled him to travel fast, get nearly everywhere and carry a large number of plundered toys. When Sebastian came skiing over, David would raise his legs and flatten his pestilential little brother. Sometimes he could keep him pinned down for some minutes. This kind of canniness gave me hope. David's development might seem slow, but there *was* progress, and I was optimistic that he'd achieve much more. That faith kept me sane.

I loved Kathmandu for its lively chaos, even though sounds of hawking, spitting and phlegm-clearing were a constant reminder of the muck that was in the atmosphere. The poor air quality didn't help David, though, and he often suffered chest infections. The pollution was a new phenomenon. Until 1951 there were only five cars in Kathmandu: four owned by the royal family and one by the British Ambassador. They were all carried in — in bits — by porters. When Simon had first come to Nepal in 1971, there were still hardly any vehicles. Now nearly everyone seemed to own a car, or expected to ride in a taxi or a *tempo.*

Away from the biggest streets, though, the air was clearer, and so I limited David's outings to the least polluted parts of the city. Even so, there were days when David was subdued, and his appetite was also poor. He vomited often, too. Whenever this happened, I'd stop his exercises and let him heal himself while I worried. I was haunted by the Cambridge doctors' prognostications that he wouldn't live long. How I yearned to make him better, or at least to make him feel better.

He was also troubled by constipation, yet it was difficult to give him a better diet since he could still rarely manage food with any texture. Puzzlingly, despite his enthusiasm for food, he'd never shown any interest in attempting to feed himself, and he was still unable to sit unsupported. Yet I still wasn't convinced by the experts who'd judged David to be profoundly intellectually handicapped. They'd also said that he was blind, and clearly *that* wasn't true.

David's worrisome interludes of illness were short and infrequent that autumn, though, and life in Kathmandu was mostly pretty relaxed for us. Alexander enjoyed the British School. The teachers — like the rest of the expat community — were a selection of oddballs, but there was an easy atmosphere, and the international community was so enriching. The school followed the British National Curriculum, but Alexander's classmates included Japanese, Dutch, Swiss, Indian, French and Pakistani, and even a few Nepalis. Lessons could bring in all the multicultural resources of the children and their parents, and Alexander's geographical knowledge at age five — based mainly on talking to his friends — was impressive. Especially during our summer visits to England, I recognised just how different Alexander was compared to children raised in Britain. The most obvious difference was his maturity and broadness of view. He hadn't lost his innocence or childish ability to play, but he enjoyed conversations with adults, and he saw no problem in playing with any child of any age; he was wonderfully gentle and patient with little ones. He was never fazed by differences, and cultural diversity was of interest rather than a reason for prejudice, though — like our Nepali friends — he did like to classify people.

डे डे डे

The Nepali New Year was welcomed by the firing of the ancient cannons from Ratna Park. It seemed to start auspiciously, but the beginning of 1996 was not good. David had more bouts of illness, and this was the spring of the terrible storm on Everest that killed eleven foreign climbers, and many Sherpas too. The American clinic was busy with the heroically helicopter-rescued foreign casualties. It was an expensive storm. The climbers had paid $100,000 to climb Everest, and who-knows-how-many tens of thousands to get down again. Sherpas who couldn't walk off the mountain, though, stayed there forever.

Even after Sebastian's first birthday, he continued to wake every night at 3 am for a snack. I resolved to stop breast-feeding him, then wondered how in my sleep-deprived, testy state I'd get him to settle in the middle of the night, because I was used to suckling him back to sleep. I decided to wean him just as soon as he slept through. Ganga thought that weaning a child as early as thirteen months was very strange. She wouldn't accept that breast-feeding is exhausting, that I'd done enough.

We lived close to Alexander's school, so didn't need much time to get all three children up and changed and out in time for the start of his lessons. Sometimes though, one or both little ones would fill a nappy just on the point of departure, or Sebastian would demand a feed, or David would vomit — again — all over a clean set of clothes. Sometimes the two babes had to go out in a disgusting state; they often had to wait for breakfast, and Sebastian would howl all the way to school. I'd load David into the buggy and Sebastian into the papoose and we'd have to jog along the street to the disapproving stares of Nepalis, who clearly thought I was deranged for not stopping to feed the protesting baby. They didn't understand my senseless obsession with getting Alexander to school on time. I ignored them and kept telling myself that soon things would get easier again, when Sebastian started sleeping through the night.

Meanwhile the hardware shop at the bottom of Kupondol High Street had been taken over by house martins. Neither the birds nor the customers seemed to take any notice of each other, despite the way the martins skimmed close to people's faces, and despite the birdlime that was being deposited over the paint tins, cisterns and lavatory bowls. Martins are a welcome sign of spring, and no-one would dare upset them. Falgun, the auspicious month for weddings, came around again and there were brass bands everywhere. Usually the musicians wore slept-in, once-white uniforms, with gold epaulets and peaked caps. They improvised upbeat jazzy tunes that made it hard to resist dancing. The rhythms were fast for a brass band, but even the tubas managed to keep up with the breathless and chaotic pace.

After weeks of uncertainty, Ganga finally left and moved in with her husband. She'd decided to brave the whingeing senior wife as a penance — her *karma* — for living with her lover. I was happy for her, but with Simon still away in Rajapur, I needed to find help.

Eventually I found Maya, who was fiftyish and calm. She was shy at first with me, but as soon as she spotted David, she strode straight over and immediately connected with him. He smiled a welcome as she touched him. He knew at once who was comfortable with him, and ignored those who were embarrassed by his differences. Maya stayed with us six days of the week. I felt confident to leave the babies at home with her while I walked Alexander to and from school. My only problem was convincing her that it was good for David to be made to 'ask' for things and to be made to work a little to get the things he wanted. She was kind and tried always to make life easy for him.

Now that Maya could baby-sit, Alexander and I could enjoy short outings again. Local shops and stalls were full of treasures, and there were always sweets on sale. If I'd refuse to buy him yet another Indian Milky Bite or Chinese White Rabbit, he'd say, 'Oh, be helpful, Mummy. They are one rupees only one piece!' Alexander was sounding more and more like an Anglo–Indian.

CHAPTER THIRTY-ONE

david stands tall

TONY BURST INTO MY HOUSE. I WASN'T EXPECTING him. I hadn't even realised he was back in Nepal. He swept David onto his lap, settled himself on our sofa, and launched straight in to tell me what he had decided about my career. David, who normally hated being cuddled, lay quietly on Tony's lap, smiling up into the face of this exceptional, compassionate doctor. Tony didn't seem to notice David's big head and now obvious disability. I don't think that Tony realised what a rare experience this was for David. Most Westerners hardly acknowledged his presence, and none ever dared to pick him up.

'What I need to start with, Jane, is for you to train some Nepali paediatricians to screen for the effects of birth asphyxia. We're following a cohort of one-year-olds, looking at how they've done after various events during labour.' He talked at me — fast. Years ago, Tony had worked in west Nepal in a Save the Children clinic. These days, he was a consultant based at the Institute of Child Health, London. A dazzling intellectual, he was committed to innovative but basic research to help children in developing countries. It was refreshing to be treated as an academic again, but, 'Blimey,' I blustered, wondering how much my brain had atrophied, 'neurology never was my strong point.'

'No, it's nothing difficult. It's the kind of thing you've done a hundred times on the wards. These Nepali paediatricians are good clinically, and marvellous at salvaging very sick infants, but we need to develop a rigorous double-blind screening regime that will stand up to scientific scrutiny.'

'It sounds high-powered, but I'll give it a go, if you think I'm up to it.'

'Of course you are. Come down to the Prasuti Griha tomorrow and I'll formally reintroduce you to Dr Manandhar. You know how important these pleasantries are …' And so I found myself back in the maternity hospital. Tall, bespectacled, Brylcreemed Dr Manandhar took us on a tour of his small, minimally resourced but impressive neonatal intensive care unit.

'We had one very nasty outbreak of gastroenteritis here,' he told us. 'We traced it to the hands of the doctors becoming cross-infected from towels. We couldn't afford paper towels, so I invented this new system. We collect newspapers, tear them into squares, autoclave them and now we have no problem with gastroenteritis. And look here — this incubator is also my invention. It is simply a wooden box, and the baby is kept warm by this light bulb.'

'Excellent — this is real, appropriate technology. Have they adopted this idea at the Kanti Children's Hospital?' I asked.

'I do not think so. You see, I'm not an easy man. I cannot go there,' he said grinning mischievously. 'They are frightened to let me inside.' He'd clearly made enemies through his outspokenness and passion to do something worthwhile: in Nepal, once you have offended someone there are no apologies, no forgiveness.

'Look, help me here,' he continued, obviously enjoying this discussion amongst equals. 'This child has some syndrome. Can you suggest a diagnosis? He has small brain, microgenitalia and multiple deformities. He will not do well.' My face must have showed the smouldering guilt that surfaced if I was confronted with another child in crisis, because Tony said, 'I expect you've had enough of talking about syndromes.' He switched back into medical mode as I marvelled at his sensitivity.

Tony wanted me to work with a professor of paediatrics. Our brief was to make friends with one-year-old children, and thus assess their level of development. We did no fancy neurological tests. The biggest challenge was getting the Prof. to sit on the floor and play with the kids, rather than — as is the local style of medical practice — towering over them and scaring them. Together we examined a line-up of infants who had been born at the maternity hospital. We didn't know who amongst them had experienced traumatic births, but our assessments established what treatments during labour were helpful and protective and which were dangerous or just a waste of resources. Even at a year old, though, the disability of some of these children was immediately, blindingly obvious — and distressing.

I felt and understood these parents' pain as they struggled to raise their damaged children. One boy suffered frequent epileptic fits. His mother saw this and his handicap as a punishment for the sin of eating meat during her pregnancy: she was not only struggling to raise a child with huge problems, she was also wracked with guilt.

'I take him to the temple often. He is peaceful there. He is close to God.'

In Nepal, there is no-one to teach parents to give physiotherapy, and there are very few places where these children could be left for a few hours to give mothers a little respite. Next, then, I was drawn into running clinics to support children with handicaps. I say 'drawn in', because although I was keen to help with such worthwhile — and, in Nepal, unique — work, I wasn't sure how I'd handle seeing others struggling with problems that I had not come to terms with myself. The scheme was stimulating and inspiring, though, and I was surprised just how much I had to offer to other parents, even if sometimes we'd end up crying together. In private, each of us wept because our children struggled, and because we knew that it was their destiny not to be long with us in this life. We thought of rebirth and renewal, though, so we had hope; and our shared tears gave us solace.

An impressive physiotherapist called Sobha worked with these children; she bustled around at such speed that the fall of her sari streamed out behind her like a blue comet's tail. She organised and chivvied and encouraged and listened, teaching mothers how to care for their children. Meeting her and watching her work gave me a much-needed reminder of the importance of physiotherapy. With this stimulus, I refined David's daily exercises, which I'd learned at Ingfield School for Parents.

At first it had taken both Simon and me to get David standing, but by now I could manage on my own. David's new daily 'work-out' happened at the centre of our home, and whenever we got David upright, everyone cheered and clapped. Even one-year-old Sebastian joined in with the applause. This made David beam with satisfaction. He was so very proud to be taller than his rival, and loved looking down on him. This competition was going to be the best motivation to get David mobile, and maybe he'd even start catching up.

He still showed only an intermittent interest in connecting with us, but he took notice when there was food, or danger. In common with all children, David hated his face being washed, and he visibly baulked whenever I approached with a damp cloth in my hand to wipe his face. He knew what was going on generally, and I could see him looking and responding more than he ever had. His strength and stamina had improved noticeably, too, and with this new interest in his surroundings, his head, which had looked so heavy and hard to hold up, became a proper part of him, and only lolled now when he fell asleep. David's doctors had said that he was profoundly intellectually handicapped. They thought that he would be totally dependent all his life, that he might never walk or talk and that he might need to wear nappies forever. Now, though — at long last — he seemed to have decided to join the real world. He was going to prove them wrong once more. He would get mobile. He would become independent.

By now, Simon had been stuck in Rajapur for months. The project was going through a crisis. He was under huge pressure, working impossibly long hours, seven days a week. He needed the distractions of his family. It was so frustrating to be fifteen hours' drive away. He'd plan escapes, but new problems kept cropping up, making him delay and delay.

Finally in mid-March, with the reluctant approval of Alexander's teacher, I decided to go to Rajapur. Within minutes of hearing of our plan, Maya was already packed. Her tiny bag contained a spare sari and little else. Child-like, she spent most of the journey giggling and pointing things out to Alexander. He, too, was thrilled with this trip. He was going to be on holiday while his classmates were slaving away. Many times each day he asked, 'Are they all working now? Goodie! I'm not!'

It felt great to be home, in the village where David had spent the first two years of his life, but it was a strange return. Everything was familiar, yet we'd lived an odd, isolated existence here. When we'd fled England with David, it had felt like going into exile, and I guess this is truly what it had been, for we'd always been outside this tightknit community. Alexander, though, was soon playing with Siru again, and Sita and Guliya smothered David in affection. Little had changed for their family except that they'd paid off their debt and bought a scrap of land to build a flimsy house on. To have contributed to freeing one family from bonded labour mitigated some of my Presbyterian guilt about keeping servants. Arjun hadn't seen the family-planning doctors, so Guliya had a ninth child who was suckled by both her and her daughter-in-law. Sita, still in her matronly black sack, looked old. Little Atti remained doll-like; Sebastian was already taller and heftier, yet she must by now have been five; he was two.

Electricity had at last come to Rajapur, but soon after we'd unpacked, the sky turned black, there was a single thunderclap, and the power failed. The celestial rumbles caught David's attention and made him smile quietly to himself. It was lovely to see that he'd surfaced from another bout of nausea. Lack of power changed Rajapur into the natural village I'd imagined when — David's whole lifetime ago — we'd first heard that we were to live here. I was feeling in a romantic mood when Simon returned from the office; we climbed up onto our flat roof and opened a big bottle of San Miguel beer. Alexander and Sebastian soon joined us to help eat pistachios and play peek-a-boo around the solar panels. The air was fresh and invigorating; we watched the sky redden into a spectacular sunset; Vs of wedding-white egrets flew home to roost. Alexander kept David involved by jumping over him to make him giggle. I sat listening: to the flip-flop of someone walking below, to mothers shouting, buffaloes and cows lowing for their calves, a baby crying, a mournful conch-call from the central temple, a sad *pea-ow* from a peacock. A boy shouted an invitation to Alexander: 'Ali-sand — come play!'

Simon wasn't hearing any of this. I said to him, 'I've never seen you so tense about work. What's getting to you?'

'Oh, lots of things — deadlines, politics, corruption ... but you'll be pleased to know that the Maoists have become a force for wildlife conservation! If anyone starts shooting wildfowl or anything for the pot, the Maoists arrive the next day to help themselves to the weapon!'

I wasn't convinced by his attempt to seem light-hearted. 'You skilfully changed the subject!' I chastised. 'Tell me what's going on in the office.'

'There's too much to do. I've been relying on the team to work without me checking everything, but someone made a huge error in calculating the volume of gravel needed for the road. It should mean someone losing twenty million rupees. So I wrote to the project manager, pointing out the mistake and apologising for it. He said that I'd done the wrong thing, and that I must never apologise. I should have hidden the mistake and fudged the figures. But I don't work like that ... People aren't allowed to admit mistakes here, and so they can't learn and develop. They rote-learn everything at school, and as adults seem to go through routines without thinking through the consequences. It's so depressing.'

Simon wasn't sleeping well. He hadn't had even half a day off in months. One of the biggest pressures was that he had to be constantly guarded in what he said. He recalled that fortune-teller friend again, in the sleepless small hours, and he dreamed of insanity and living rough under a bridge in London. I'd imagined that through being there with Simon, I'd be able to talk freely about David's increasingly frequent and sapping bouts of illness, but knew that just then I couldn't add to his worries. Anyway, David was looking ever-stronger. He was growing fatter day by day, and our tensions faded as we revelled in being a family together again.

While Simon was busy at the office, Alexander, Sebastian and I explored. Usually we wandered past the Sri Ganesh Babu English Residential School, which had a freshly painted motto to celebrate the arrival of power on the island: 'A smile costs less than electricity, but it gives more light than it!'

We'd walk towards the river, and that first morning, as soon as the boys spotted the water, they stripped naked and were in. I sat on the river-washed cobbles and watched the *dhobi-wallahs* thrashing bed sheets clean. Someone had left a few hibiscus petals and marigold heads close to the water's edge as an offering. Five brown-backed Tharu women, each carrying a small bamboo basket, were collecting stones to build the east–west road that Simon and his team had designed. The women smiled at the children, but when I greeted them they looked scared. They were worried, I suppose, that I'd bewitch them.

Refreshed, the boys charged off, shouting, 'Let's go on the boat!'

I recalled walking across the river here with David in the papoose, but now it was too deep. The only way to a road from this side of the island was by small passenger ferry that could cope with nothing larger than rice sacks and motorbikes. We watched passengers struggle aboard with bicycles and pay their two rupees to be poled across to Suttee bazaar, where buses could take them on the twenty-hour journey to Kathmandu.

Alexander led us to the makeshift tea shop by the ferry and assertively ordered Frooti mango juice, tea and Glucose biscuits. As I sat sipping my glass of tea and the boys graciously accepted tweaks and praise from other customers, I reflected on what a privilege it had been living here and how much we were all enjoying this interlude in the country. Then I thought about the inflexibility of the British School and cursed them because they were driving us to return to Kathmandu too soon. Separations were hard for all of us, but the construction season, when Simon needed to be in Rajapur full-time, was nearly over. Soon — during the forthcoming school Easter holiday — the five of us would make a second attempt to walk up to the Langtang glacier. We wouldn't have to steel ourselves for much longer until the family was next back together.

The renewed admiration and the fresh air in Rajapur gave David back his sparkle. He teased Guliya and Sita as he teased me, and he loved it when they laughed with him. One lunchtime, while I was spooning his favourite banana into his mouth, he paused in his eating and — unusually — his gaze met mine. Then with a sly, provocative look he said, 'Nana!'

He threw his head back and laughed loud and long, clearly delighted at his joke. It was as if he'd always been able to speak, but until that moment had chosen not to. It was as if everything that had gone before had been a bad dream. I was elated: too excited for words. I danced around the room, giggling with delight, while David laughed and laughed. Then I crashed into a little table and his laughter turned to guffaws.

At Ingfield School, when we'd encouraged David to speak by repeating 'mmm' and 'da-da-da' and 'ba-ba', we'd seen him subtly moving his mouth in response. Surely now he'd start talking to us properly. Surely now he wanted to make contact with us. When I'd calmed down, I took him out of his supportive seat and got him standing. He looked so proud and so satisfied, suddenly confident enough in his balance even to reach out and touch my lips in an affectionate gesture. Soon — very soon — I was going to get David walking — and talking. We were leaving Rajapur the next day, but before Simon joined us again in Kathmandu I was determined that David would welcome his father as a two-year-old should.

CHAPTER THIRTY-TWO

renewal

I'D RETURNED TO KATHMANDU INVIGORATED, BUT my optimism didn't last. Soon after we'd left Simon in Rajapur, David became ill; he started losing weight again and I felt I'd lost contact with him. When he slept, he was calm, but he looked troubled when awake, and he no longer teased me or called me to him. I felt so impotent as I struggled hopelessly to identify the source of his distress. How I wished I could bring back the mischievous twinkle in his eyes. Completely at a loss, I contemplated going back to Britain, but knew in my heart of hearts that even the cleverest of doctors couldn't cure him. Partly as a sop to my conscience, I took him to the American clinic, where they just threw up their hands in dismay to be presented with such an obviously abnormal child. Their medicines did control his vomiting, though, and let him sleep more restfully.

He rallied for a while but his sparkle had vanished and he didn't giggle any more. Perhaps I was fooling myself, but it was almost as if he'd decided that it was time to go. Perhaps he'd finally become frustrated with his floppy, disobedient body. Worry turned to guilt — yet again. I lay awake endlessly, arguing with myself. Might some expert somewhere be able to help him? Perhaps we should look again … But I knew that this expertise didn't exist, even in England.

Knowing didn't make it any easier, though. It was torture watching him fade like this.

During those low weeks, I often tried to telephone Simon, but incessant dialling was rarely worthwhile. Even if I did get through, I could hear people repeatedly interrupting or asking him to sign something; it was impossible to talk freely. We couldn't even enjoy the comfort of chatting about the pointless or mundane. Sometimes he could call out from the office, late, when most people had left, but in Rajapur they worked long hours. It broke my heart to hear Simon's exhausted voice echoing from his cheerless concrete office.

I don't really recall the details of David's final deterioration. I was badly sleep-deprived, and I was worried — more worried than I had ever been. Then one night in March, I woke feeling scared. At first, I had no idea what had disturbed me. Then I heard his rapid, laboured breathing. I leapt out of bed and ran to him. He was away somewhere — not really sleeping, but not really conscious, either. David's breathing was fast, but he wasn't struggling or distressed. He'd inhaled vomit into his lungs. Rolling him onto his side didn't help. I sat on his bedside, watching his tranquil face, arguing with myself.

Normally after an inhalation like this, treatment is attempted in an intensive care unit, but the chances of survival are still not good, even in the best hospitals in the world. There would be little hope in the poor facilities that were available in Nepal. Evacuation wasn't a realistic option either. The reduced oxygen in the aircraft would stress his failing breathing further. We'd decided long ago that we wouldn't put David through pointless medical treatment. And — I argued with myself — I didn't think even a good intensive care unit would do any more than extend his life for a few days. He was comfortable and he would die here, without needles and tubes and the pain that came with them.

I rubbed his back and talked soothingly to him; maybe I imagined it, but a hint of a smile showed on his face. I sat chatting with him. I lay with him, whispering. Dawn came, and David remained tranquil. I began to doubt my judgement. Perhaps if I took him to hospital now, they could make him better. Perhaps he would get through this. I started trying to call Simon again. Pacing between David and the phone, I was finding it harder and harder to keep calm. How I prayed for contact with Simon.

Maya took Alexander to school. Then David vomited profusely, and all my courage failed. I suddenly couldn't cope with the responsibility. I scooped David up and told Basant to drive us to the American clinic on the other side of Kathmandu. Sebastian, used to staying with Maya, waved me goodbye happily, as if I was just going off to work. In the car, David's breathing became more erratic, yet he looked more relaxed than he'd been for weeks. It took forever to cross Kathmandu.

My face must have said it all when I walked into the clinic. People were out of their seats before I mumbled, 'I think he's stopped breathing.'

फेरि भेटौला डेभिड

I'd fleetingly regretted taking David to the American clinic that last morning, but his was a good death. His passing was easier than it would have been in England, and our mourning could be upfront and healing.

Nepali friends told us that he had served his short sentence for some mistake in a previous life, and soon, in the next incarnation, he would be reborn with a whole body. He'd avoided his life sentence. He had chosen to pass on early to a better life. His death was a renewal. His next life would be favoured. He would be happy — again. I could almost see him chuckling there and then. We'd made the right decisions for him.

Now, I was looking out from a trance. Simon squatted to arrange an armful of white arum lilies from our garden. I lay my home-made wreath of jasmine on the little wooden coffin. It was a soft, grey afternoon, a perfect summer temperature. Sun streamed through breaks in the light cloud cover. It spotlit the Queen's Forest high on the Valley rim. The golden *stupa* at Swayambhu glinted and beckoned. It was lovely to be surrounded by so many friends. Fifty of us were gathered on the hillock in the little walled patch of Britain in the centre of Kathmandu. Here, beneath ancient pines and mournful bottlebrushes, Gurkha officers sleep with missionaries, diplomats with drug addicts, and mountaineers with surgeons' wives. Britons had been laid to rest here for 190 years.

In the centre of my wreath, Alexander placed David's favourite wind-up purple dinosaur, saying, 'Now David won't get bored after we've planted him.' Friends brought flowers or draped mourning-white *katas*. Dour, white-haired Reverend Brodie was saying something in his soft, lyrical Scottish accent. I felt Simon slip his arm around my waist and I sought Alexander's hand. We walked forward only half aware of what was happening. David's deterioration had been what we'd expected all his life. Even so, it was unreal standing here now in the British cemetery.

A pang of conscience struck me now, though. I felt just a little wicked to have slipped the book into the coffin without asking the Reverend Brodie if he minded. I'd put the extraordinary little book full of minute Tibetan script on David's chest: a Buddhist friend had had it blessed by his *guru* and said it would guide David through the difficult journey to the next life. Our David was supposedly nearly blind and had never talked, so could he, aged two and three-quarters, read a book in Tibetan? The idea made me smile, but I sensed that orthodox Reverend Brodie would have disapproved. At the end of the funeral service, he certainly mumbled a typically British complaint about the weather. I thought it perfect. A fine, caressing mist had descended as

David's coffin was lowered into the ground and I'd wanted to throw up my arms and welcome — in a very un-English way — this gentle blessing. It comforted me to notice others smiling and saying, 'A good passing. He will make the transition into the next incarnation easily.' Rain had welcomed us on our first touchdown in Nepal. There was the disastrous monsoon that coincided with David's stormy arrival. It was there as a benediction when I emerged from the American clinic the day David died; it had seemed to say that his was an untroubled departure. And that's what it felt like now, at his funeral.

The Reverend Brodie was rounding off his short address. He'd talked around some Old Testament verse that asks, 'Is all well with the child?' to which I think it is God that answers, 'All is well with the child.'

We stepped forward and threw white canna lilies onto the coffin, deep now in the shadowy grave. Others threw in handfuls of sand. Then, the formalities completed, we lingered awhile. The sun broke though. Alexander rejoined his classmates, who were romping in piles of pine needles and playing chase amongst the gravestones and ancient memorial obelisks.

A Rabindranath Tagore quotation was rumbling around my head:

Death is not extinguishing the Light
but putting out the light because Dawn has come.

CHAPTER THIRTY-THREE

departures

JUST OVER THREE YEARS AFTER WE'D COME TO Rajapur, we returned there for the last time. Simon's colleagues threw a party for us. We gathered at nine in the morning to drink whisky, vodka, rum and beer. A lavish breakfast of mouth-watering chicken curry, spicy vegetables and biryani rice awaited us. Unusually — no doubt in deference to our funny Western etiquette — the ladies (led by the boys and me) were invited to head the stampede to the food. Sweet rice pudding with cashews and raisins followed — and then there were long, flowery speeches, while gentle, auspicious rain fell. Major Chhetri's pronouncement when we'd first arrived in Nepal came echoing back: 'Things that start in the rain end well.' This was a good ending.

Five-year-old Alexander bounced onto my lap.

'The rain feels warm,' he announced. 'It's just like our David is weeing on us again!' We'd come to associate rain with David. It always made us smile.

Rek Raj spoke eloquently about Simon's contribution to the project and to the professional development of his local colleagues. It was more than just rhetoric. They liked him; they liked his quietness; they liked the fact he spoke Nepali. Rek Raj covered the other elements of the standard Nepali leaving speech. He gave the usual blanket apology for anything that they had done to offend or upset Simon. They all hoped he would forget any bad things and remember only the good parts of his stay in Rajapur. At that moment, I couldn't think of anything bad. Just as Major Chhetri had foretold, our time here — our time with David — had been charmed. They presented Simon with a fine brass water pot, garlanded us with marigolds, and plastered our foreheads extravagantly with vermilion, yoghurt and rice-grain *tikkas*.

By mid-morning, the party was already very drunken, and the men were giggling like schoolgirls, so we drifted away. We stepped aboard a dug-out ferry as Moti threw our marigold garlands into the river and put his hand to his forehead, down to his chest and up to his forehead again in a prayer. I watched the garlands float away — down towards the holy Ganga. I had a lump in my throat, and had to blink tears away.

I'd learned a lot, grown a lot, seen a lot. The boys had incorporated Asia into their bones — its colours and laughter, its smells, its rhythms, its tolerance and patience, its compassion, its lack of ageism. We'd all absorbed something of a Nepali outlook, pace and philosophy, which had prevented us being swamped by David's problems. In Nepal, it was easier to take life day by day, but we could look forward, knowing that David would 'sunder the bonds that caused him suffering', and that he'd be renewed.

The Chinese say that there is no scenery in your home town. They're right. Being in another place heightens the senses, allows you to see more, enjoy more, take delight in small things; it makes life richer. You feel more alive, less cocooned. The family was certainly closer for our intense times here, and our precious memories live on with us. Most importantly, I realised how privileged we'd been to have been able to protect David from his doctors, and from English embarrassment when faced with disability. David was a person in Nepal. That snug thought made me smile again, and it struck me that my years in Nepal had given me some of the very richest and highest of times, as well as the absolute lowest.

The marigold garlands had gone now; only fish broke the surface. A lapwing took to the air, scolding us, *'Did ye d-do it? Did ye d-do it? D-do-do-do-it?'* Moti looked forlorn as we floated away, so Alexander shouted a reassuring, *'Pheri betau la!'* (the wonderfully optimistic 'see you again') and waved madly. Moti's stubbly face broke into his lovely, always-disarming smile, and he waved back. *'Pheri betau la! Bye-bye!'*

फेरि भेटौला

We took a long route back home to Kathmandu, having finally decided to explore the beginning of the old trade route that had made Rajapur important. We ambled north–west through the Chisapaani Gorge, where the largest river in Nepal has cut through the last 1,000-metre-high ridge of the Himalayan foothills and bursts out into the delta of islands of which Rajapur is the biggest. We walked through forest that was busy with birds, langurs and colourful butterflies, and along a ledge high above a still-pristine river that swirled between fluted polished limestone walls seventy-five metres apart. Waterfalls streamed off the ridge-tops into sheer ravines.

Wherever there was a scrap of soil amongst the ravaged crags above us, emaciated trees struggled to cling on: a poignant metaphor for the way so many Nepalis eke out an existence, defiantly surviving on less than nothing. It made me think about the way David had clung onto life, too.

Just beyond the gorge, we found some flat ground and put up the tents. After two years in congested, clamorous Kathmandu and the recent raucousness of Rajapur bazaar, the tranquillity was breath-taking. Even if I strained to hear, there was a wondrous absence of traffic noise.

As if to emphasise the isolation, a serpent eagle let out a tortured, lonely cry. The evening star appeared and the Hale-Bopp comet soon showed itself beautifully framed in the now black V of the Karnali valley. In the darkening sky, the long comet's tail grew longer, transfixed in its celestial motion above the jagged western horizon. In Kathmandu, it had been no more than a smudge above the Queen's Forest, but here its glorious double-spume tail streamed out like spindrift off a mountain top, illuminating its patch of the firmament. Shooting stars scored holes in the night. The comet seemed to celebrate the first anniversary of David's death, and also the end of our time on Rajapur. What a show had been put on for us. It was a good time to be leaving.

For three days, we wandered pleasantly along valley bottoms, pausing to wallow in rivers and build sandcastles. Alexander gathered handfuls of shells, coloured cobbles and the iridescent wings of dead damselflies. 'I'm collecting nice things for David. We'll put them on his grave later, and make it look beautiful,' he explained.

As we crossed the wide, fast-flowing Bheri River, the sound of water slopping against the dug-out ferry brought back a vision of David chuckling to similar sounds when we'd explored the Karnali, searching for river dolphins. Simon turned awkwardly to remark, 'You know we've already seen the upper reaches of this river? On that last trek with David to Sera: that was the same water … way north of here.' I could see him eyeing up the next ridge, 2,000 metres above us. As soon as we stepped out of the boat, he said casually, 'If we climb onto the ridge, we'll get a great view to the north — of *himals,* maybe … and Achham District, certainly.' He knew I'd be tempted by

Himalayan views, so we climbed over the joint-jolting, sun-baked, terracotta-red soil, dotted with ironwood trees that gave no shade.

Finally, hot and steaming, I sat down to rest at the pass in the shade of another huge, old tree-couple: a holy *peepal* tree and a *banyan*. Simon joined me: after the exertions of the day, we sat imbibing cool air. The view north was of wild, broken, ocean-green country, looking like an oil painting of a storm-tossed sea. There were few villages, no roads. It was easy to see, now, why people walked down south from here to shop for Indian goods in Rajapur. 'Do you think if the clouds cleared to the north, Simon, we'd see snow on the *himals*?'

'Maybe on a good day … but the Himalayas are low at this end of the country. Dhaulagiri is the last great mountain, and even that's a long way east of here.'

Looking back the way we'd come, there was cultivated land as far as I could see between the Siwaliks and the Mahabharats on which we sat. I tracked the rivers flowing into the great Bheri and meandering towards the gash of the Chisapaani Gorge, dim and distant on the horizon. Rajapur bazaar was another thirty kilometres still further south.

Then, slowly, I realised … The glimpses of white that I'd seen from our house in Rajapur and had found so refreshing were a mere sprinkle of spring snow on the low, tree-covered ridge on which I was sitting. We never could have seen the *himals* from Rajapur. My early, starry-eyed, cool view of eternal snows had all been a delicious mirage. It made me smile to think how I'd managed to delude myself with this misunderstanding, but it didn't matter. It was inspiring at the time. Rajapur, too, had seemed idyllic: a perfect refuge for David amongst straightforward, accepting people, in a place where death is at the very centre of life and people are upfront about differences and disability. Nepalis can and do react badly to the disabled, yet it doesn't matter. There is a lot of hurt to be borne in raising someone like David.

It is impossible to cosset an abnormal child wherever he might live, but in England even talking about David was taboo. His disabilities made him an uncomfortable subject. I censor myself now to avoid awkwardness, often saying that I only had two children. Yet I want to talk tenderly of how we'd been blessed, both with our chance to know David and his charming personality, and with being able to live a full life with him in Nepal.

One of the most shocking and distressing aspects of my medical practice after I left Nepal and returned to Cambridge revolved around my struggles to support bitter parents — parents whose unresolved outrage and heartbreak makes their lives hell even decades after losing a child, or after some event that harmed a child. The anger and anguish overshadows the good things their lost child had given them. Too easily they have forgotten the joy of loving even an imperfect child.

Following my pensive gaze, Simon broke in on my thoughts. 'Lovely, isn't it!'

Then, smiling, Alexander pointed out a pair of eagles that were circling above us. 'Look!' he said. 'They've brought the thunder.' There was serious weather brewing. Lightning was lashing the mountains far to the west. Sunlight streamed through grumbling storm clouds that played like tiger kittens around the mountain ridges. The wind was howling a fitting lament, but I was invigorated by the way it tugged at my hair.

'Don't worry,' I reassured him. 'David won't let the storm break until we've found shelter.'

'But I like it when David wees on us! It's nice rain.'

Locals say that thunderstorms are the gods fighting, and Alexander knew that this was our David having fun. He had a new body and had assumed the position of crown prince to Shiva, god of destruction and renewal. Somewhere up in the sky, David was leading a heroic celestial battle, throwing thunderbolts from his flying chariot pulled by giant peacocks.

the heart sutra

The Bodhisattva of Compassion,
When he meditated deeply,
Saw the emptiness of all life
And sundered the bonds that caused him suffering.
Here then,
Form is no other than emptiness,
Emptiness no other than form.
Form is only emptiness,
Emptiness only form.
Feeling, thought, and choice,
Consciousness itself,
Are the same as this.
All things are the primal void,
Which is not born or destroyed;
Nor is it stained or pure,
Nor does it wax or wane.
So, in emptiness, no form,
No feeling, thought, or choice,
Nor is there consciousness.
No eye, ear, nose, tongue, body, mind;
No colour, smell, taste, touch,
Or what the mind takes hold of,
Nor even act of sensing.
No ignorance or end of it,
Nor all that comes of ignorance;
No withering, no death,
No end of them.
Nor is there pain or cause of pain,
Or cease in pain, or noble path
To lead from pain;
Nor even wisdom to attain!
Attainment too is emptiness.
So know that the Bodhisattva
Holding to nothing whatever,
But dwelling in wisdom,
Is freed of delusive hindrance,
Rid of the fear bred by it,
And reaches peace.

From *Puja: The FWBO Book of Buddhist Devotional Texts,*
Windhorse Publications, 1999

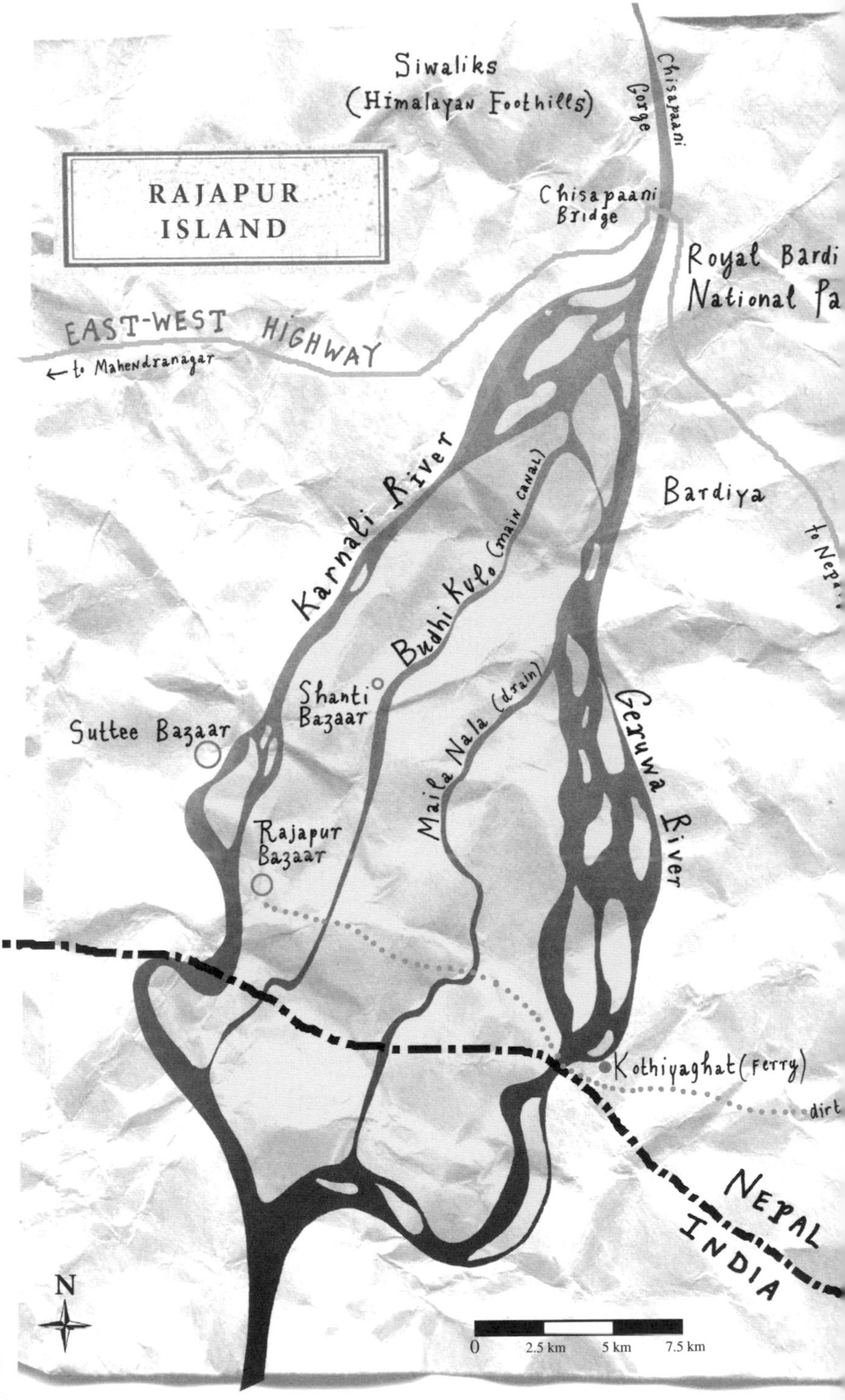

RAJAPUR ISLAND

Siwaliks
(Himalayan Foothills)
Chisapaani Gorge
Chisapaani Bridge
Royal Bardi
National Pa
EAST-WEST HIGHWAY
← to Mahendranagar
Karnali River
Budhi Kulo (main canal)
Bardiya
to Nepa...
Shanti Bazaar
Suttee Bazaar
Maila Nala (drain)
Geruwa River
Rajapur Bazaar
Kothiyaghat (ferry)
dirt
NEPAL
INDIA
N
0 2.5 km 5 km 7.5 km

a note on nepali

The Nepali language is written in the wonderfully phonetic Devanagri script, which comprises forty-six characters, not including the half-letters that are also in common use. It is not easy to transliterate into the astonishingly unphonetic English language. Devanagri vowels are pure, but can be nasalised, and consonants can be retroflex, aspirated or non-aspirated. There are, for example, four different 'd' and four different 't' sounds.

I have tried to keep things simple, but have followed the convention of writing the aspirated 't' of the Tharu people — which also appears in Mr Thapa's name — as 'th'; this is pronounced like the 't' in 'tap', but with a slightly more forced explosion of breath against the teeth. I have written the word for water as *paani,* as this is pronounced with a long 'a', akin to the 'a' sound in 'hard', rather than the short 'a' in 'had'.

Syllables in Nepali tend to be stressed equally, so to an English ear 'Hima*laya*' becomes Hi*mal*aya. And Ne*paul* becomes *Ne*pal. I have also — unconventionally — put accents on the final 'e' sound in *namasté* and Machhapuchharé, to communicate that this final 'e' is sounded. The double 'h's indicate that the 'ch' is aspirated.

A further challenge is the fact that spoken words sometimes differ from written. People generally call the Nepali winter month '*Pooss*', but its literary form is '*Paush*'. Finally, where a Nepali word is close to a recognisable English word (including slang), I have spelt it so that that origin is clear: hence '*ḳhushi*' becomes 'cushy'.

I have referred often to R L Turner's *A Comparative and Etymological Dictionary of the Nepali Language.* This was first published in 1931, but there are Indian reprints, and it is also available online.

Despite the difficulties, Nepali is a reasonably straightforward language, and generally Nepalis are very accommodating of foreigners' clumsy attempts to communicate in their language. Only about half of the nation speaks Nepali as their mother tongue.

glossary of nepali, hindi, wildlife and technical words

A

aak: *Calotropis gigantea,* shrub with dull mauve flowers and thick leathery leaves (Nepali)

achha: Good; also used like 'okay', in agreement (Hindi)

acyclovir (or **aciclovir**)**:** tablets or cream used to treat shingles and cold sores

ah mai: Expression of surprise (Nepali)

ahilé: Literally 'now', but usually implying some time in the next few hours (Nepali)

akhaa: Eye (Nepali)

Apgar: Scoring system developed by Dr Virginia Apgar to assess the health of a newborn

assalaamu alaikum: Arabic greeting used by Muslims — 'Peace be upon you'

ayurveda: Ancient system of traditional herbal medicine used all over the subcontinent

B

baagh: Tiger (Nepali), and loosely used in the hills to describe leopards, too

babu: Nickname for a child (Nepali)

bachha: Child (Nepali)

Badi: Caste of hereditary prostitutes (Nepali)

badmas: Naughty; mischievous (Nepali)

bahaadur: Brave; often the second given name for boys (Nepali)

bahini: Younger sister; used to address a younger female (Nepali)

Baisakh: The month of the Nepali year that runs from mid-April until mid-May

banana: To make (Hindi)

bandar: Monkey; rhesus macaque, *Macaca mulatta,* as opposed to langur (Nepali, Hindi)

banyan: Multi-trunked fig tree with aerial roots, *Ficus bengalensis;* called *bar* in Nepali

barking deer: Muntjac

Basant (also transliterated **Basanta**)**:** Spring; also a given name (Nepali)

bazaar: Market (Arabic, Nepali, Hindi, etc.)

besharma: Shameless; morning glory, *Ipomoea fistulosa*, a straggly flowering shrub (Nepali)

betel: Leaf of the betel pepper plant, *Piper betle*; see **paan**

bhai: Younger brother; used to address a younger male (Nepali)

bhanera: Rufous-backed shrike, *Lanius schach* (Nepali)

bideshi: Western foreigner (Nepali)

Bishnu: Saviour god of the Hindu trinity; a popular given name; also spelt Vishnu

blackbuck: An attractive small antelope, *Antelope cervicapra;* weighs 25–45 kg

Blighty (or, more correctly, **belayat):** England; the origin of the English slang word

blue sheep: Wild sheep with blue-grey wool, *Pseudois nayaur*; weighs up to 70 kg

bo tree: The peepal fig, *Ficus religiosa*

boarding school: A school where all the teaching is done in the medium of the English language; also called English-medium schools. Pupils don't always board

bodhisattva: One who postpones entry to *nirvana* (paradise) in order to help others (Sanskrit)

borborygmi: The onomatopoeic name for gas moving in the small intestine

Brahmin: Highest Hindu caste; the priests. Strict Brahmins are teetotal vegetarians

brain-fever bird: Common hawk cuckoo, *Cuculus varius*

Buddhism: In Nepal, Buddhism is of the Mahayana (or Vajrayana) form, popularly known as Lamaism

bulbul: Crested birds which form affectionate couples and so feature in Oriental love poetry

bundh/bandh/bund: Earth dam to contain water; *bandh* also means a strike (Nepali)

burra: Big (Hindi)

C

caste: The social position of Hindus; low-caste Hindus often convert to Islam or Christianity to improve their lot

charpoy: Literally 'four feet'; string bed used throughout the *tarai* (Nepali, Hindi)

chaukidar: Watchman (Nepali, Hindi)

chautara: Stepped, stone resting place where travellers can take off their loads. Shaded by a *peepal* and a *banyan,* and often dedicated to someone (Nepali)

chha: Is; there is (Nepali)

Chhetri: Warrior caste; the second Hindu caste, and the caste of the kings of Nepal

Chisapaani: Place name meaning 'cold' (*chiso*) 'water' (*paani*) (Nepali)

chital: Spotted deer, *Axis axis* (Nepali, Hindi)

chitthi: A letter; adopted into English slang as 'chit' for an official slip of paper or note (Nepali)

chungi: Child's game: kicking a blob of sliced inner-tubing to keep it in the air (Nepali)

coucal: The crow pheasant; noisy common cuckoo, *Centropus sinensis*

cushy or **khushi:** Happy, pleased, content. Adopted into English slang to mean easy, comfortable (Hindi)

D

daal bhat: Lentils and rice; the main food of everyone in Nepal

dai: Older brother (Nepali)

Desai: The most important Nepali festival in late October, when families reunite

didi: Older sister; form of address to someone who is older and requires respect (Nepali)

dinghy: A small boat (Hindi, Nepali)

dinus: Please give me ... (Nepali)

dacoits: Bands of robbers (Nepali, Hindi)

docter: Invented spelling to distinguish non-medical practitioners from medical doctors

dhobi: Laundryman (Nepali, Hindi)

dhoti: Loin cloth (Nepali, Hindi)

DoI: Department of Irrigation of His Majesty's Government

dolphin: The 2½ metre long Gangetic (freshwater) dolphin, *Platanista gangetica*

dookha or **dukha:** Pain, but also hurt, distress, trouble, misfortune, sorrow, sadness (Nepali)

dzo: Yak-cow cross (Tibetan)

E

eaters of cows: Non-Hindus

ekdum: Very, lots (Nepali)

EM: English-medium (school); see **boarding school**

ENT: Ear, nose and throat surgical specialist/specialty

F

Falgun (or **Phalgun**, but pronounced faagun)**:** Nepali month running from mid-February to mid-March

febrile: Feverish

flying fox: Great Indian fruit bat, *Pteropus giganteus*

G

gabions: Stones and boulders wrapped in wire baskets to stabilise hillsides and riverbanks

Ganga: The river Ganges; a popular given name amongst Hindu men and women

Gangetic: Of or relating to the river Ganges

Ganesh: The elephant-headed Hindu god of wisdom and jollity

Garuda: The bird-like 'vehicle' for the Hindu god Bishnu

gecko: *Hemidactylus flaviviridis,* the common house gecko; about 10 cm long

gharial: Thin-snouted, fish-eating crocodile, *Gavialis gangeticus*; only dangerous to fish (Hindi)

ghat: Paved river bank used for bathing, washing, rituals and boat docking (Nepali, Hindi)

ghora: Horse (Nepali)

gompa: Buddhist monastery or lamasery (Tibetan)

gora: Fair-skinned (Nepali, Hindi, Punjabi, etc.)

GRAA: Geruwa Rural Awareness Association; an NGO located on Rajapur island

guph: Chit-chat; the origin of 'guff' in English, meaning nonsense (Nepali)

Gurkha: Mercenaries in the British army, originally recruited from Gorkha in Nepal

guru: Teacher; in English, used to mean a spiritual teacher or guide (Nepali)

H

haathi: Elephant (Nepali, Hindi)

hakim: Boss (Nepali, Hindi)

hero (or **hiro**)**:** Male film star, but literally a star or diamond (Hindi)

himal: A mountain that always has snow on it (Nepali)

himalaya: Place of eternal snows (Nepali, Hindi)

hoina: A frequently used expression meaning something like 'isn't it?' (Nepali)

Holi: Spring festival of colour that falls on the full moon in the Nepali month of Kartik

hotel: Place to eat, sometimes just a shack. Not always somewhere to stay

huzoor: Sir; your honour (Nepali, Hindi)

I

intake: The start of an irrigation system, where river water enters canals

intubate: Put a tube into the trachea so that breathing can be assisted artificially

J

jelabi: Coils of crisply fried batter covered in syrup (Hindi)

jhankri: Holy man who performs ceremonies of healing and other essential functions (Nepali)

ji: Respectful suffix used by Hindi-speakers; equivalent to sir/madam

jungle: Wild, useless, uncultivated land (Nepali, Hindi)

K

kamaiya: Bonded labourers; effectively, slaves; a system outlawed in Nepal in 2000

kanchha: Last-born male child; kanchhi is the female form (Nepali)

karma: Effect of former deeds; the good or bad luck people have; fate (Nepali, Hindi)

kasto: How (Nepali)

kata: Silk scarf given to honour someone and show respect (Nepali, Tibetan)

kati: How [much] (Nepali)

Koch's disease: Another name for TB; honours the German physician who discovered the cause of the disease

khola: River (Nepali)

khukuri: Short, curved blade, used as a hatchet (Nepali)

krap or **karap** or **kharab:** Broken, worn out or useless; is this the origin of 'crap'?(Nepali)

kulo: Ditch for irrigation or drainage (Nepali)

kurta pyjama: Long shirt and loose baggy trousers (Urdu, Hindi)

L

la: A mountain pass (Tibetan)

lama: Buddhist holy man who has studied and fasted for years (Nepali, Tibetan)

lato: Deaf mute (Nepali)

Limbu: An ethnic group from East Nepal who enjoy drinking alcohol

lingam: Phallic symbol of Lord Shiva in his role of divine creator (Sanskrit)

lizard: The common garden agamid or 'bloodsucker', *Calotes versicolor*

lorry: An ox cart; carries loads over terrain inaccessible to four-wheel-drive vehicles (Nepali)

lungi: Cloth wrapped around like a sarong (Nepali, Hindi)

M

madal: Double-ended drum that is rested on the legs of the player (Nepali)

mish-mash: A mixture of things or ingredients (Nepali)

month: Nepali months are usually 29 to 32 days long, but may differ from year to year

Moti: Pearl; man's given name, or an affectionate nickname for a woman, meaning 'fatty' (Nepali, Hindi)

mugger or **marsh crocodile**: *Crocodylus palustris;* rarely over 4 m in length

murkatta: A ghost that walks around with its head tucked under its arm (Nepali)

mysteri (or **mistri**)**:** Artisan (Nepali)

N

namasté: Very formal greeting with hands placed together as if in prayer (Hindi)

namaskar: Obeisance, salutation; even more polite Hindu greeting (Sanskrit)

Newar: People of the Kathmandu Valley who have their own language

nirvana: Paradise; ultimate absorption into the absolute (Sanskrit)

NGO: Non-government organisation; often charitable and involved in community work

P

paan: A digestive: a folded betel pepper leaf containing betel or areca nut, lime, spices and often chewing tobacco. Useful appetite suppressant for the poor (Nepali, Hindi)

padi or **paddy:** Rice field (Malay)

pangolin: Scaly ant-eater, *Manis crassicaudata*

pariah: Outcaste; dirty and polluting; someone born outside the four Hindu castes (Tamil)

peacock: The mount of Kumar, the god of war and guardians of the gates of paradise. The eyes of the male are said to secrete seminal fluid and the feathers are thought to heal

peepal: *Bo* tree; a kind of fig, *Ficus religiosa*, with long 'drip-tips' at the end of each leaf (Nepali, Hindi)

phanit: Elephant driver who is of higher status than a *mahout* (Nepali)
phedi: The foot of a hill; a common placename in Nepal
pheri betau la: Literally 'Let us meet again' but used in the sense of 'Until next time' or 'See you again' (Nepali)
phul: Egg, flower or testicle (Nepali)
Pooss (also spelt **Pauss** or **Paush**)**:** The month from mid-December to mid-January
pujaa: Hindu or Buddhist prayers or a festival; usually involves an offering or sacrifice (Sanskrit)
pukka: Proper; permanent structure or something made of concrete (Nepali, Hindi)
purdah: A screen used in some strict Hindu or Muslim households to keep the women out of view

Q

queerie (or **kuiré**)**:** White-skinned foreigner (Nepali)

R

rakshi: Distilled, home-made liquor (Nepali)
ramro: Good, beautiful, handsome (Nepali)
randi: Prostitute (Nepali)
ropani: One-twentieth of a hectare; the area that can be transplanted in a day (Nepali)
rupee: There are about 8 Nepali rupees to an Australian dollar

S

sabass (also **shabash**)**:** Well done (Nepali)
sabon: Soap (Nepali)
sadhu: Hindu holy man; ascetic
sahib: Gentleman; respectful title for people of rank, and Europeans; sir or Mr
sal: Ironwood trees, *Shorea robusta,* with wood so dense it sinks in water
samosa: Spicy, savoury puff pastry triangle (Hindi)
sano: Small (Nepali)
Sanskrit: Sacred Indo–European language of Hinduism
shital: Shady and cool (Nepali)
Shiva: Mahadev, the god of destruction and recreation; most powerful of the Hindu trinity
Silk-cotton tree: The Indian red silk-cotton tree or *simal*; *Bombax ceiba*
sirdar: Local leader of a hunting trip or trek (Hindi, Urdu)
Sita: Devoted wife of Rama who entered fire to prove her virtue; the model for **suttee**
stupa: Sanskrit word for a solid, Buddhist, breast-shaped shrine; a microcosmic mound; also called **chorten** in Tibetan
suttee (also spelt **sati**)**:** The practice of burning a widow alive on her husband's funeral pyre

T

tabla: A squat Indian drum, usually played in a set of two
tailorbird: Warbler that 'stitches' its nest with spiders' webs onto large leaves
tarai: Gangetic plains; the lowlands of southern Nepal and the adjacent plains of India
tatri tree: Flowering hardwood, *Dillenia pentagyna,* also known as *tantari* and *ram phul*
tempo: A three-wheeled, motorised taxi
thatch grass: *Kās (Saccharum spontaneum),* which bears attractive white seed-heads
Tharu: Disparate groups of peoples of the Nepali lowlands, with different languages
thug: Worshippers of Kali who strangled their victims with a silver rupee in a silk scarf (Nepali)
tiffin: Luncheon; a north of England provincialism that was adopted into Indian English
Tihar: Hindu festival in November; also called Bhai Tikka, Diwali or the Festival of Lights
tikka: Red mark on the forehead (Hindi, Punjabi)
titepati: Literally, 'bitter leaf'; *Artemisia;* a common weed in the hills
turtle: The Indian mud or flap-shell turtle, *Lissemys punctata,* grows up to 27.5 cm long

V

vajra: Thunderbolt, but also thunder, lightning and great misfortune (Nepali, Sanskrit)
VSD: Ventricular septal defect; a hole in the ventricles of the heart
VSO: Voluntary service overseas

selected bibliography

FOR KIDS

McGough, Roger, *The Kite and Caitlin*, The Bodley Head, London, 1996

And there are many more at www.nspcc.org.uk/Inform/OnlineResources/ReadingLists/Bereavement/

FOR GROWN-UPS

Baum, J D, Sr F Dominica, R N Woodward, *Listen, My Child Has a Lot of Living to Do: The Partnership between Parents and Professionals in Caring for Children with Life-Threatening Conditions,* Oxford Paperbacks, UK, 1990

De Hennezel, Marie, *Intimate Death: How the Dying Teach Us to Live,* Random, US, 1998

Geralis, E ed., *Children with Cerebral Palsy: A Parents' Guide,* Woodbine House Inc, US, 1998

Humphries, Steve and Pamela Gordon, *Out of Sight: The Experience of Disability 1900–1950,* A Channel Four Book/Northcote House Publishing, Bristol, UK, 1992

Kubler-Ross Elisabeth, *On Death and Dying*, Tavistock Publications, London, UK, 1970

Richardson A A, 1983, 'Physical Impairment, Disability and Handicap in Rural Nepal', *Development Medicine and Child Neurology,* vol 25, pp 717–726

Wilkinson, Tessa and Sr Frances Dominica, *The Death of a Child: A Book for Families,* Julia MacRae Books/Random House, 1991

Wilson-Howarth, Jane, *Bugs, Bites and Bowels: The Essential Guide to Travel Health*, Cadogan Guides, London, 2006 (4th edn)

acknowledgements

This book has had an exceedingly long — and at times painful — gestation. It began as a simple travel narrative, and I felt shy of sharing David with my readers. However, my agent at the time, Sarah Leigh, noticed that there was something missing and suggested that rather than gloss over David's troubled existence, he should come centre stage. Once I committed to this becoming David's book, it started to take shape and assume a form that pleased me. It has grown, then, during the ten years I have been working on it, into an unrecognisable being. It is a book that I have often lost confidence in, particularly when several literary agents were rude about it.

Many, many kind souls, though, have encouraged me and renewed my conviction that this was a story worth telling. Hilary Bradt is perhaps the person who has done most to keep me on track, but Rosie Denmark, Jan Salter, Jill Sutcliffe and Sue Holmes made many gentle editorial suggestions in the early stages. More recently I have appreciated encouragement and expert advice from Humphrey Hawksley, Dea Birkett and Nick Austin. Members of Cambridge Writers have helped, including Sally Haiselden, Sheila Bennett, James Carnegie, Jocelyn Glegg, Helen Culnane, Stephen Hammond, Will Tate, Joy Vousden, Carl McCarthy, Yvonne Jerrold, Calvin Dorian, Janet Menell and others. Mahesh Pant answered questions on Nepali culture and language. Information on bird life was largely gleaned from the privately published *Birds of Nepal* by R L Fleming Sr, R L Fleming Jr and L S Bangdel (1976). Much of the description of the funeral was plagiarised from a letter by Dr Bill Piggot. Stories about life in Nepal from Jan Salter, Lorna and John Howell, Dr Matthew Ellis, Matt Freidman, Dr Jeff Smith, Himalaya Thapa and, of course, Simon Howarth have also been incorporated into the book. Simon's exhaustive knowledge of Nepal and Nepali has been my richest resource, and it is impossible to acknowledge adequately his unstinting support and understanding through all the pangs of giving birth to this book.

I also owe a big debt of gratitude to Isobel Dixon of the Blake Friedmann literary agency, who helped with the final shaping of the story and then convinced Murdoch that this was the book for them. It has been a delight to work — even at such distance — with the Murdoch team, especially my editor Tricia Dearborn.

First published in 2007 by Pier 9, an imprint of Murdoch Books Pty Limited

Murdoch Books Australia
Pier 8/9, 23 Hickson Road, Millers Point NSW 2000
Phone: +61 (0) 2 8220 2000 Fax: +61 (0) 2 8220 2558

Chief Executive: Juliet Rogers
Publishing Director: Kay Scarlett

Project Manager and Editor: Tricia Dearborn
Concept and Design: Lauren Camilleri
Production: Adele Troeger

Wilson-Howarth, Jane.
A glimpse of eternal snows.
ISBN 978 1 921259 26 5 (pbk.).
ISBN 1 921259 26 4 (pbk.).
1. Wilson-Howarth, Jane. 2. Women physicians – Nepal – Biography. 3. Children with disabilities – Care – Nepal.
I. Title.

610.695092

Map of Rajapur Island on page 420 by Antonia Pesenti
The Heart Sutra (slightly edited from the original) is reproduced with the permission of Windhorse Publications
Front cover photograph copyright © Getty Images
Back cover/internal photos courtesy of Simon Howarth and Jane Wilson-Howarth

PHOTOS: Opposite title page: Alexander and Arjun in our garden in Rajapur; *p 6*: Shiva temple in Rajapur bazaar, with a horse-drawn tanga 'taxi' on the right; *p 27*: Alexander with David in hospital, just after his harelip repair; *p 60*: Jane and David by the Dhobi Khola, in the Kathmandu Valley; *p 97*: Simon, Alexander and David in our garden overlooking the Dhobi Khola; *p 139*: Thatch grass is cut in Bardiya and brought to Rajapur in dug-outs; *p 200*: Buffalo carts on Rajapur get to places that 4 x 4 vehicles can't reach; *p 229*: Mountains peeking through the monsoon clouds above the Langtang Valley; *p 268*: Passenger ferries on Rajapur were also used to get tangas across (the horse swam); *p 331*: Jane, David and Alexander in the paddling pool, Rajapur; *p 357*: David standing proud and tall, having just learned how at Ingfield School; *p 380*: Footbridges like this are used in the remotest parts of Nepal; *p 413*: The Buddha's all-seeing eyes at Swayambhu, Kathmandu.

Printed by 1010 Printing International Limited. Printed in China.